S0-ABC-693

ADOBE® PHOTOSHOP® CS2
REVEALED

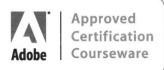

Adobe | Approved Certification Courseware

ADOBE® PHOTOSHOP® CS2
REVEALED

By Elizabeth Eisner Reding

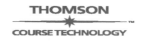

Adobe Photoshop CS2—Revealed

by Elizabeth Eisner Reding

Managing Editor:
Marjorie Hunt

Product Manager:
MT Cozzola

Associate Product Manager:
Emilie Perreault

Editorial Assistant:
Shana Rosenthal

Production Editor:
Catherine G. DiMassa

Development Editor:
Rachel Biheller Bunin

Composition House:
Integra-India

QA Manuscript Reviewers:
Danielle Shaw, Ashlee Welz

Text Designer:
Ann Small

Illustrator:
Philip Brooker

Cover Design:
Steve Deschene

Proofreader:
Wendy Benedetto

Indexer:
Joan Green

COPYRIGHT © 2006 Course Technology, a division of Thomson Learning, Inc. Thomson Learning™ is a trademark used herein under license.

Printed in Canada.

1 2 3 4 5 6 7 8 9 WC 09 08 07 06 05

For more information, contact Course Technology, 25 Thomson Place, Boston, Massachusetts, 02210.

Or find us on the World Wide Web at: www.course.com

ALL RIGHTS RESERVED. No part of this work covered by the copyright hereon may be reproduced or used in any form or by any means—graphic, electronic, or mechanical, including photocopying, recording, taping, Web distribution, or information storage and retrieval systems—without the written permission of the publisher.

For permission to use material from this text or product, submit a request online at www.thomsonrights.com.

Any additional questions about permissions can be submitted by e-mail to thomsonrights@thomson.com.

Trademarks

Some of the product names and company names used in this book have been used for identification purposes only and may be trademarks or registered trademarks of their respective manufacturers and sellers.

Adobe® Photoshop®, the Partnering with Adobe logo, Adobe® InDesign®, and Adobe® Illustrator® are trademarks or registered trademarks of Adobe Systems, Inc. in the United States and/or other countries. Third party products, services, company names, logos, design, titles, words, or phrases within these materials may be trademarks of their respective owners.

The Adobe Approved Certification Courseware logo is a proprietary trademark of Adobe. All rights reserved.

Credits

Some of the images used in this book are royalty-free and the property of Getty

Images, Inc. and Morguefile.com. The Getty images include artwork from the following royalty-free CD-ROM collections: Education Elements, Just Flowers, Portraits of Diversity, Sports and Recreation, Texture and Light, Tools of the Trade, Travel Souvenirs, Travel & Vacation Icons, and Working Bodies. The Morguefile images include artwork from the following categories: Objects, Scenes, Animals, and People.

Figure 16 in Chapter 6 is used with permission from Wacom Technology Corporation. Figure 20 in Chapter 14 is used with permission from www. digitalartmuseum.com. Figure 19 in the online appendix, "Portfolio Projects and Effects," is used with permission from Big Brothers/Big Sisters of America.

Disclaimer

Course Technology reserves the right to revise this publication and make changes from time to time in its content without notice.

ISBN 1-59200-832-1

Library of Congress Catalog Card Number: 2005923048

Thomson Course Technology and *Adobe Photoshop CS2—Revealed* are independent from ProCert Labs, LLC and Adobe Systems Incorporated, and are not affiliated with ProCert Labs and Adobe in any manner. This publication may assist students to prepare for an Adobe Certified Expert exam, however, neither ProCert Labs nor Adobe warrant that use of this material will ensure success in connection with any exam.

Revealed Series Vision

The Revealed Series is your guide to today's hottest multimedia applications. These comprehensive books teach the skills behind the application, showing you how to apply smart design principles to multimedia products, such as dynamic graphics, animation, Web sites, and video.

A team of design professionals including multimedia instructors, students, authors, and editors worked together to create this series. We recognized the unique needs of the multimedia market and created a series that gives you comprehensive step-by-step instructions and offers an in-depth explanation of the "why" behind a skill, all in a clear, visually-based layout.

It was our goal to create books that speak directly to the multimedia and design community—one of the most rapidly growing computer fields today. We feel that the Revealed Series does just that—with sophisticated content and an instructive book design.
—The Revealed Series

Author's Vision

The target audience for this book is a savvy user who wants important information and needs little hand-holding. If you have a sense of adventure, an interest in design, and a healthy dose of creativity, this is the Photoshop book for you. The focus is hands-on, and the style is informal and to the point. My goal is to not only instruct but inspire you to explore the richness of this program and your own design vision.

Special thanks to the following team members:

- MT Cozzola, who took on the formidable task of managing the entire project and made it seem easy. What problems?

- Rachel Bunin, the development editor who knows better than to work with me, but does so anyway. She knows how to make me laugh when I feel like crying.

- Cathie DiMassa, who managed the production end of things, and made everything turn out all right.

- Danielle Shaw and Ashlee Welz Smith, who were able to make short order of a lengthy book by doing a super job of getting the bugs out of these chapters.

- Nicole Pinard, who helped make this vision a reality and who makes assembling the perfect team possible.

- Marjorie Hunt, whom we are delighted to have back at the helm as Managing Editor on this project.

- Christina Kling Garrett, who can answer any question and solve any problem.

I would like to add a special thanks to my husband, Michael, for his emotional and professional support, and to my mother, Mary Eisner, for her support and enthusiasm. Their contributions make this book possible.

Elizabeth Eisner Reding

Introduction to Adobe Photoshop CS2

Welcome to *Adobe Photoshop CS2—Revealed*. This book offers creative projects, concise instructions, and complete coverage of basic to advanced Photoshop skills, helping you create dynamic Photoshop art! Use this book as you learn Photoshop, and then use it later as your own reference guide.

This text is organized into 16 chapters plus additional online bonus content. In these chapters, you will learn many skills including how to work with layers, make selections, adjust color techniques, use paint tools, work with filters, transform type, liquify an image, annotate and automate a Photoshop document, and create Photoshop images for the Web! The online appendices provide additional coverage on Adobe Bridge and offer extra practice in creating eye-catching projects and effects. The online content is available for downloading from www.course.com/Revealed/photoshopcs2.

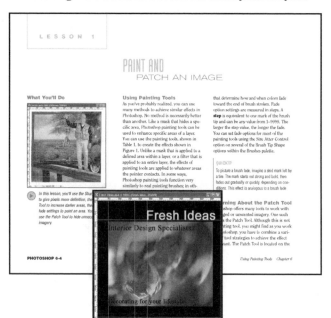

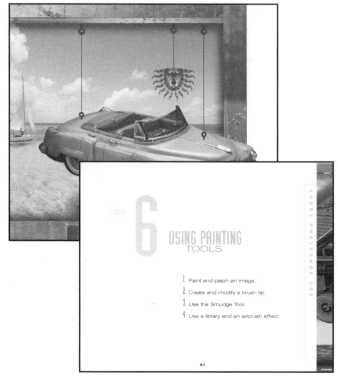

What You'll Do

A What You'll Do figure begins every lesson. This figure gives you an at-a-glance look at the skills covered in the chapter and shows you the completed Data File for the lesson. Before you start the lesson, you will know—both on a technical and artistic level—what you will be creating.

Comprehensive Conceptual Lessons

Before jumping into instructions, in-depth conceptual information tells you "why" skills are applied. This book provides the "how" and "why" through the use of professional examples. Also included in the text are helpful tips and sidebars to help you work more efficiently and creatively, or to teach you a bit about the history behind the skill you are using.

Step-by-Step Instructions

This book combines in-depth conceptual information with concise steps to help you learn Photoshop. Each set of steps guides you through a lesson where you will apply Photoshop tasks to a dynamic and professional project file. References to large colorful images and quick step summaries round out the lessons. You can download the Data Files for the steps at the following URL: www.course.com/Revealed/photoshopcs2.

The figures in this book are provided to help you follow the steps, and the callouts should help you locate icons, buttons, and commands on the screen. When a figure points out a color or color change, you should use it to guide your eye to the relevant location on your monitor screen.

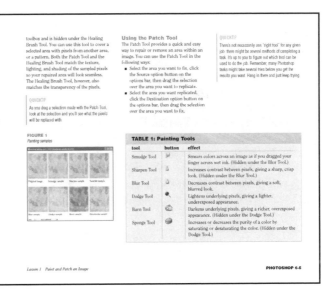

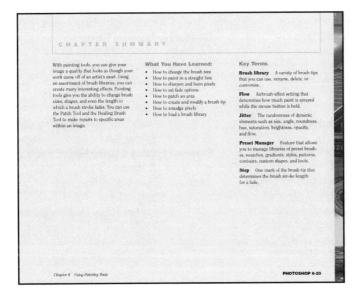

Chapter Summaries

This book contains chapter summaries that highlight the key tasks and terms you learn in each chapter. You can use these summaries as a quick refresher should you find you need to review information you learned earlier in the book.

B R I E F   C O N T E N T S

x

CHAPTER 2　WORKING WITH LAYERS

CHAPTER 3 MAKING SELECTIONS

CHAPTER 5 PLACING TYPE IN AN IMAGE

CHAPTER 6 USING PAINTING TOOLS

CHAPTER 7 WORKING WITH SPECIAL LAYER FUNCTIONS

CHAPTER 8 CREATING SPECIAL EFFECTS WITH FILTERS

CONTENTS

CHAPTER 14   PERFORMING IMAGE SURGERY

CHAPTER 15   ANNOTATING AND AUTOMATING AN IMAGE

Intended Audience

This text is designed for the beginner or intermediate computer user who wants to learn how to use Adobe Photoshop CS2. The book is designed to provide basic and in-depth material that not only educates but encourages you to explore the nuances of this exciting program.

File Identification

Instead of printing a file, the owner of a Photoshop image can be identified by reading the File Info dialog box. Use the following instructions to add your name to an image:

1. Click File on the menu bar, then click File Info.
2. Click the Description, if necessary.
3. Click the Author text box.
4. Type your name, course number, or other identifying information.
5. Click OK.

There are no instructions with this text to use the File Info feature other than when it is introduced in Chapter 1. It is up to each user to use this feature so that his or her work can be identified.

Measurements

When measurements are shown, needed, or discussed, they are given in pixels. Use the following instructions to change the units of measurement to pixels:

1. Click Edit on the menu bar, point to Preferences, then click Units & Rulers.
2. Click the Rulers list arrow, then click pixels.
3. Click OK.

You can display rulers by clicking View on the menu bar, then clicking Rulers, or by pressing [Ctrl][R] (Win) or ⌘[R] (Mac). A check mark to the left of the Rulers command indicates that the Rulers are displayed. You can hide visible rulers by clicking View on the menu bar, then clicking Rulers, or by pressing [Ctrl][R] (Win) or ⌘[R] (Mac).

Icons, Buttons, and Pointers

Symbols for icons, buttons, and pointers are shown each time they are used.

Fonts

Data and Solution Files contain a variety of fonts, and there is no guarantee that all of these fonts will be available on your computer. The fonts are identified in cases where less common fonts are used in the files. Every effort has been made to use commonly available fonts in the lessons. If any of the fonts in use are not available on your computer, please make a substitution.

Menu Commands in Tables

In tables, menu commands are abbreviated using the following format: Edit ➤ Preferences ➤ Units & Rulers. This command translates as follows: Click Edit on the menu bar, point to Preferences, then click Units & Rulers.

Power User Shortcuts

As a bonus, a Power User Shortcuts table is included at the end of every chapter. This table contains the quickest method of completing tasks covered in the chapter. It is meant for the more experienced user, or for the user who wants to become more experienced. Tools are shown, not named.

Certification

If you are interested in becoming an Adobe Certified Expert, you can refer to the ACE grid, available for download, at www.course.com/revealed/photoshopcs2.

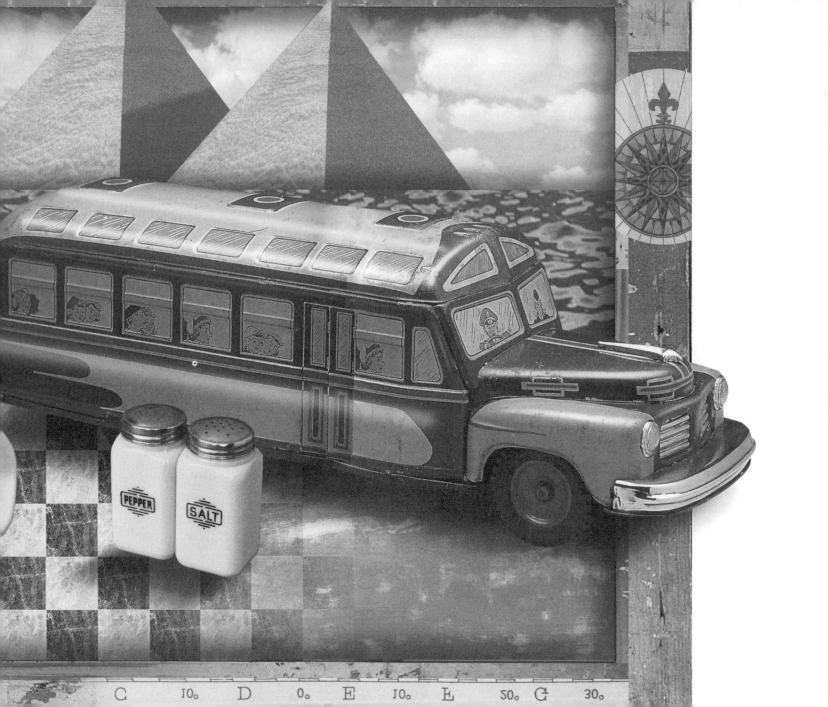

chapter **1**

GETTING STARTED WITH
ADOBE
PHOTOSHOP CS2

1. Start Adobe Photoshop CS2.

2. Learn how to open and save an image.

3. Use organizational and management features.

4. Examine the Photoshop window.

5. Use the Layers and History palettes.

6. Learn about Photoshop by using Help.

7. View and print an image.

8. Close a file and exit Photoshop.

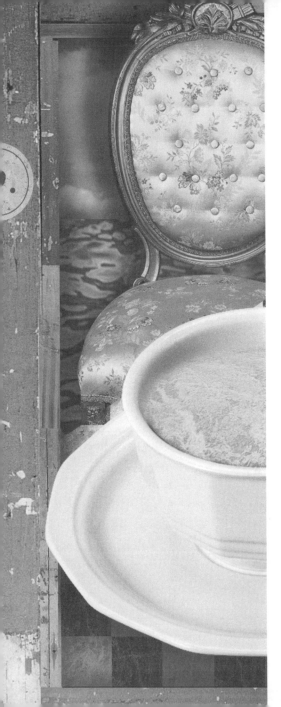

GETTING STARTED WITH
ADOBE
PHOTOSHOP CS2

Using Photoshop

Adobe Photoshop CS2 is an image-editing program that lets you create and modify digital images. 'CS' stands for Creative Suite, a complete design environment. The Adobe® Creative Suite consists of Adobe Photoshop®, Adobe Illustrator®, Adobe InDesign®, Adobe GoLive®, Adobe Distiller®, Adobe Bridge®, Adobe Designer®, and Adobe Acrobat® Professional. A **digital image** is a picture in electronic form. Using Photoshop, you can create original artwork, manipulate color images, and retouch photographs. In addition to being a robust application popular with graphics professionals, Photoshop is practical for anyone who wants to enhance existing artwork or create new masterpieces. For example, you can repair and restore damaged areas within an image, combine images, and create graphics and special effects for the Web.

QUICKTIP

In Photoshop, a digital image may be referred to as a file, document, picture, or image.

Understanding Platform Interfaces

Photoshop is available in both Windows and Macintosh platforms. Regardless of which type of computer you use, the features and commands are very similar. Some of the Windows and Macintosh keyboard commands differ in name, but they have equivalent functions. For example, the [Ctrl] and [Alt] keys are used in Windows, and the ⌘ and [option] keys are used on Macintosh computers. There is a visual difference between the two platforms due to the user interface found in each type of computer.

Understanding Sources

Photoshop allows you to work with images from a variety of sources. You can create your own original artwork in Photoshop, use images downloaded from the Web, or use images that have been scanned or created using a digital camera. Whether you create Photoshop images to print in high resolution or optimize them for multimedia presentations, Web-based functions, or animation projects, Photoshop is a powerful tool for communicating your ideas visually.

Tools You'll Use

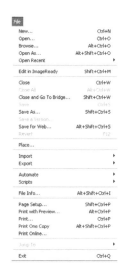

File	
New...	Ctrl+N
Open...	Ctrl+O
Browse...	Alt+Ctrl+O
Open As...	Alt+Shift+Ctrl+O
Open Recent	▶
Edit in ImageReady	Shift+Ctrl+M
Close	Ctrl+W
Close All	Alt+Ctrl+W
Close and Go To Bridge...	Shift+Ctrl+W
Save	Ctrl+S
Save As...	Shift+Ctrl+S
Save a Version...	
Save for Web...	Alt+Shift+Ctrl+S
Revert	F12
Place...	
Import	▶
Export	▶
Automate	▶
Scripts	▶
File Info...	Alt+Shift+Ctrl+I
Page Setup...	Shift+Ctrl+P
Print with Preview...	Alt+Ctrl+P
Print...	Ctrl+P
Print One Copy	Alt+Shift+Ctrl+P
Print Online...	
Jump To	▶
Exit	Ctrl+Q

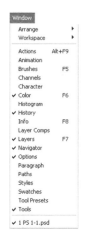

Window	
Arrange	▶
Workspace	▶
Actions	Alt+F9
Animation	
Brushes	F5
Channels	
Character	
✓ Color	F6
Histogram	
✓ History	
Info	F8
Layer Comps	
✓ Layers	F7
✓ Navigator	
✓ Options	
Paragraph	
Paths	
Styles	
Swatches	
Tool Presets	
✓ Tools	
✓ 1 PS 1-1.psd	

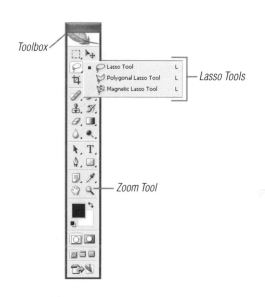

Toolbox

Lasso Tools

Zoom Tool

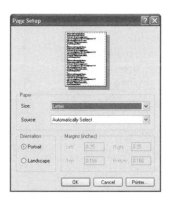

Page Setup

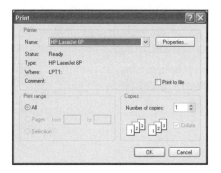

Print

Palette well

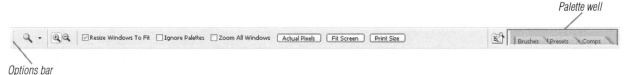

Options bar

START ADOBE
PHOTOSHOP CS2

What You'll Do

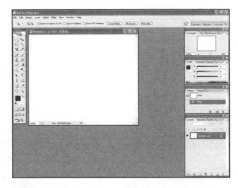

In this lesson, you'll start Photoshop for Windows or Macintosh, then create a file.

Defining Image-Editing Software

Photoshop is an image-editing program. An **image-editing** program allows you to manipulate graphic images so that they can be reproduced by professional printers using full-color processes. Using windows, various tools, menus, and a variety of techniques, you can modify a Photoshop image by rotating it, resizing it, changing its colors, or adding text to it. You can also use Photoshop to create and open different kinds of file formats, which enables you to create your own images, import them from a digital camera or scanner, or use files (in other formats) purchased from outside sources. Table 1 lists some of the graphics file formats that Photoshop can open and create.

Understanding Images

Every image is made up of very small squares, which are called **pixels**, and each pixel represents a color or shade. Pixels within an image can be added, deleted, or modified.

QUICKTIP

Photoshop files can become quite large. After a file is complete, you might want to **flatten** it, an irreversible process that combines all layers and reduces the file size.

Using Photoshop Features

Photoshop includes many tools that you can use to manipulate images and text. Within an image, you can add new items and modify existing elements, change colors, and draw shapes. For example, using the Lasso Tool, you can outline a section of an image and drag the section onto another area of the image. You can also isolate a foreground or background image. You can extract all or part of a complex image from nearly any background and use it elsewhere.

QUICKTIP

You can create a logo in Photoshop. A **logo** is a distinctive image that you can create by combining symbols, shapes, colors, and text. Logos give graphic identity to organizations, such as corporations, universities, and retail stores.

You can also create and format text, called **type**, in Photoshop. You can apply a variety of special effects to type; for example, you can change the appearance of type and increase or decrease the distance between characters. You can also edit type after it has been created and formatted.

QUICKTIP

Photoshop records each change you make to an image on the History palette. You can undo or redo a recorded action as necessary. Photoshop records actions for the current session only; it discards actions when the program closes.

Adobe ImageReady CS2, a Web production software program included with Photoshop, allows you to optimize, preview, and animate images. Because ImageReady is fully integrated with Photoshop, you can jump seamlessly between the two programs.

You can also quickly turn any graphics image into a GIF animation. Photoshop and ImageReady let you compress file size (while optimizing image quality) to ensure that your files download quickly from a Web page. Using optimization features, you can view multiple versions of an image and select the one that best suits your needs.

Starting Photoshop and Creating a File

The way that you start Photoshop depends on the computer platform you are using. However, when you start Photoshop in either platform, the computer displays a **splash screen**, a window that displays information about the software, and then the Photoshop window opens.

After you start Photoshop, you can create a file from scratch. You use the New dialog box to create a file. You can also use the New dialog box to set the size of the image you're about to create by typing dimensions in the Width and Height text boxes.

TABLE 1: Examples of Graphic File Formats Supported in Photoshop

file format	filename extension	file format	filename extension
Photoshop	.PSD	Filmstrip	.VLM
Bitmap	.BMP	Kodak PhotoCD	.PCD
PC Paintbrush	.PCX	Pixar	.PXR
Graphics Interchange Format	.GIF	Scitex CT	.SCT
Photoshop Encapsulated PostScript	.EPS	Photoshop PDF	.PDF
Tagged Image Format	.TIF or .TIFF	Targa	.TGA or .VDA
JPEG Picture Format	.JPG, .JPE, or .JPEG	PICT file	.PCT, .PIC, or .PICT
CorelDraw	.CDR	Raw	.RAW

Start Photoshop (Windows)

1. Click the **Start button** `start` on the taskbar.

2. Point to **All Programs**, then click **Adobe Photoshop CS2**, as shown in Figure 1; if the Scratch volume dialog box opens, click **OK**, then click **No**.

   TIP The Adobe Photoshop CS2 program might be found in the Start menu (the left edge below your name), or in the Adobe folder, which is in the Program Files folder on the hard drive (Win).

3. Click **Close** to close the Welcome Screen.

4. Click **File** on the menu bar, then click **New** to open the New dialog box.

5. Double-click the number in the Width text box, type **500**, click the **Width list arrow**, then click **pixels** (if it is not already selected).

6. Double-click the number in the Height text box, type **400**, click the **Height list arrow**, click **pixels** (if it is not already selected), then specify a resolution of **72** pixels/inch.

7. Click **OK**.

8. Click the **arrow** ▶ at the bottom of the image window, point to **Show**, then click **Document Sizes** (if it is not already displayed).

You started Photoshop for Windows, then created a file with custom dimensions. Setting custom dimensions lets you specify the exact size of the image you are creating. You changed the display at the bottom of the image window so the document size is visible.

FIGURE 1

Starting Photoshop CS2 (Windows)

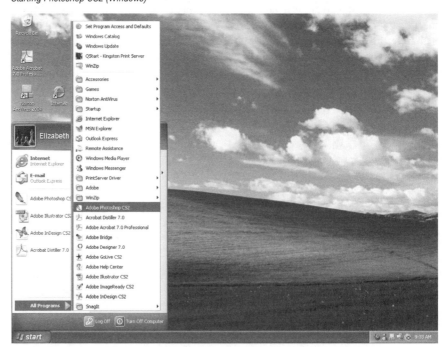

Understanding hardware requirements (Windows)
Adobe Photoshop CS2 has the following minimum system requirements:
- Processor: Intel Xeon, Xeon Dual, Centrino, Pentium class III or 4 processor
- Operating System: Microsoft® Windows 2000 (with Service Pack 4), or Windows XP (SP1 or SP2)
- Memory: 320 MB of RAM (384 MB recommended)
- Storage space: 650 MB of available hard-disk space
- Monitor: 1024 × 768 or greater monitor resolution with 16-bit color or greater video card
- PostScript Printer PostScript Level 2, Adobe PostScript 3 PostScript Level 2, Adobe PostScript 3

FIGURE 2

Starting Photoshop CS2 (Macintosh)

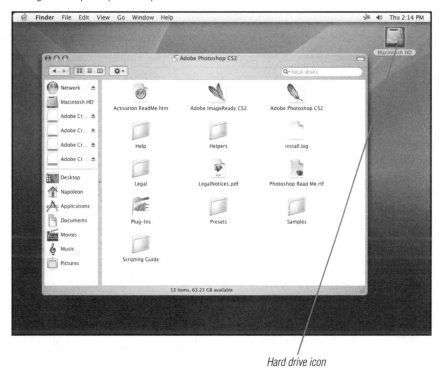

Hard drive icon

Understanding hardware requirements (Macintosh)

Adobe Photoshop CS2 has the following minimum system requirements:

- Processor: PowerPC® processor (G3, G4, or G5)
- Operating System: Mac OS X version 10.2.8 through 10.3.8 (10.3.4 through 10.3.8 recommended)
- Memory: 320 MB of RAM (384 MB recommended)
- Storage space: 750 MB of available hard-disk space
- Monitor: 1024 × 768 or greater monitor resolution with 16-bit color or greater video card
- PostScript Printer PostScript Level 2, Adobe PostScript 3

Start Photoshop (Macintosh)

1. Double-click the **hard drive icon**, double-click the **Applications folder**, then double-click the **Adobe Photoshop CS2 folder**. Compare your screen to Figure 2.

2. Double-click the **Adobe Photoshop CS2 program icon**.

3. Click **File** on the menu bar, then click **New**.

   TIP If the Color Settings dialog box opens, click No. If a Welcome screen opens, click Close.

4. Double-click the number in the Width text box, type **500**, click the **Width list arrow**, then click **pixels** (if necessary).

5. Double-click the number in the Height text box, type **400**, click the **Height list arrow**, click **pixels** (if necessary), then verify a resolution of **72** pixels/inch.

6. Click **OK**.

7. Click the **arrow** ▶ at the bottom of the image window, click **Show**, then click **Document Sizes** (if is it not already displayed).

You started Photoshop for Macintosh, then created a file with custom dimensions. You changed the display at the bottom of the image window so the document size is visible.

LEARN HOW TO OPEN AND SAVE AN IMAGE

What You'll Do

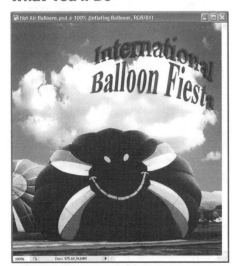

 In this lesson, you'll locate and open files using the File menu and Adobe Bridge, flag and sort files, then save a file with a new name.

Opening and Saving Files

Photoshop provides several options for opening and saving a file. Often, the project you're working on determines the techniques you use for opening and saving files. For example, you might want to preserve the original version of a file while you modify a copy. You can open a file, then immediately save it with a different filename, as well as open and save files in many different file formats. When working with graphic images you can open a Photoshop file that has been saved as a bitmap (.bmp) file, then save it as a JPEG (.jpg) file to use on a Web page.

Customizing How You Open Files

You can customize how you open your files by setting preferences. **Preferences** are options you can set that are based on your work habits. For example, you can use the Open Recent command on the File menu to instantly locate and open the files that you recently worked on, or you can allow others to preview your files as thumbnails. Figure 3 shows the Preferences dialog box options for handling your files in Windows.

TIP   In cases when the correct file format is not automatically determined, you can use the Open As command on the File menu (Win).

FIGURE 3
Preferences dialog box (Win)

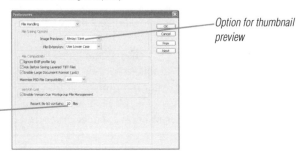

Option for thumbnail preview

Number of files to appear in Open Recent list

Browsing Through Files

You can easily find the files you're looking for by using **Adobe Bridge**: a stand-alone application that serves as the hub for the Adobe Creative Suite. See Figure 4. You can open Adobe Bridge (or just Bridge) by clicking the Go to Bridge button to the left of the **palette well**. The palette well contains three additional palettes. You can also open Bridge using the Start button (Win) or using the File menu when a Photoshop file is open. When you open Bridge, there are a series of palettes with which you can view the files on your hard drive as hierarchical files and folders. In addition to the Favorites and Folders palettes in the upper-left corner of the Bridge window, there are other important areas. Directly beneath the Favorites and Folders palettes is the Preview window, which displays a thumbnail of the currently selected file. Beneath the Preview window is a window containing the Metadata and Keywords palettes, which store

information about a selected file that can then be used as search parameters. You can use this tree structure to find the file you are searching for. When you locate a file, you can click its thumbnail to see information about its size, format, and creation

and modification dates. (Clicking a thumbnail selects the image. You can select multiple non-contiguous images by pressing and holding [Ctrl](Win) ⌘ (Mac) each time you click an image.) You can select contiguous images by clicking

FIGURE 4
Adobe Bridge window

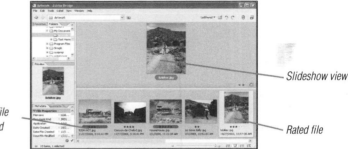

Slideshow view

Rated file with red label

Rated file

Using the File Info dialog box

You can use the File Info dialog box to identify a file, add a caption or other text, or add a copyright notice. The Description section allows you to enter printable text, as shown in Figure 5. For example, to add your name to an image, click File on the menu bar, click File Info, then click in the Description text box. (You can move from field to field by pressing [Tab] or by clicking in individual text boxes.) Type your name, course number, or other identifying information in the Description text box. You can enter additional information in the other text boxes, then save all the File Info data as a separate file that has an .XMP extension. To select the caption for printing, click File on the menu bar, then click Print with Preview. To print the filename, select the Labels check box. You can also print crop marks and registration marks. If you choose, you can even add a background color or border to your image. After you select the items you want to print, click Print.

FIGURE 5
File Info dialog box

Type information to be printed here

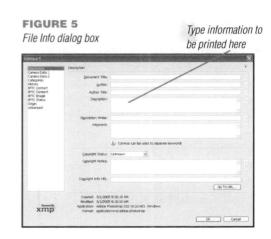

the first image, then pressing and holding [Shift] and clicking the last image in the group. You can open a file using Bridge by double-clicking its thumbnail, and find out information such as the file's format, and when it was created and edited. You can close Bridge by clicking File (Win) or Bridge (Mac) on the (Bridge) menu bar, then clicking Exit (Win) or Quit Bridge (Mac) or by clicking the window's Close button.

Understanding the Power of Bridge

In addition to allowing you to see all your images, Bridge can be used to rate (assign importance), sort (organize by name, rating, and other criteria), and label. Figure 4, on the previous page, contains images that are assigned a rating and shown in Filmstrip view. There are four views in Bridge (Thumbnails view, Filmstrip view, Details view, and Versions alternates view) that are controlled by buttons in the lower-right corner of the window. You can also see that several images have been assigned a color label. Any number of selected images can be assigned a color label by clicking Label on the menu bar, then clicking one of the five color options. You can see a list of only those labelled files by clicking the Unfiltered list arrow, then clicking an option for a rating or labels.

QUICKTIP

You can use Bridge to view thumbnails of all files on your computer. You can open any files for software installed on your computer by double-clicking its thumbnail.

Creating a PDF Presentation

Using Bridge you can create a PDF Presentation. Such a presentation can be viewed full-screen on any computer monitor, or in the Adobe Acrobat Reader as a PDF file. You can create such a presentation by opening Bridge, locating and selecting images using the file hierarchy, clicking Tools in the Bridge menu bar, pointing to Photoshop, then clicking PDF Presentation. The PDF Presentation dialog box, shown in Figure 6, opens and lists any figures you have selected. You can add images by clicking the Browse button.

Using Save As Versus Save

Sometimes it's more efficient to create a new image by modifying an existing one,

especially if it contains elements and special effects that you want to use again. The Save As command on the File menu creates a copy of the file, prompts you to give the duplicate file a new name, and then displays the new filename in the image's title bar. You use the Save As command to name an unnamed file or to save an existing file with a new name. For example, throughout this book, you will be instructed to open your data files and use the Save As command. Saving your data files with new names keeps them intact in case you have to start the lesson over again or you want to repeat an exercise. When you use the Save command, you save the changes you made to the open file.

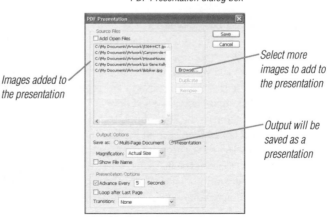

FIGURE 6
PDF Presentation dialog box

Images added to the presentation

Select more images to add to the presentation

Output will be saved as a presentation

Getting Started with Adobe Photoshop CS2   Chapter 1

FIGURE 7

Open dialog box for Windows and Macintosh

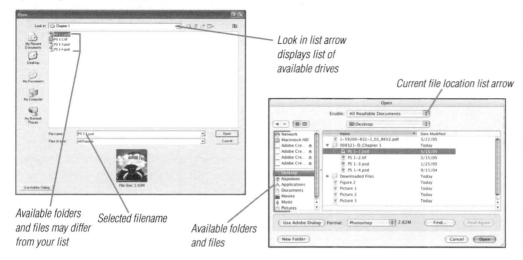

Look in list arrow
displays list of
available drives

Current file location list arrow

Available folders
and files may differ
from your list

Selected filename

Available folders
and files

Open a file using the File menu

1. Click **File** on the menu bar, then click **Open**.

2. Click the **Look in list arrow** (Win) or the **From list arrow** (Mac), navigate to the drive and folder where your Data Files are stored, then click **Open**.

3. Click **PS 1-1.psd** as shown in Figure 7, then click **Open**.

   TIP If you receive a message stating that some text layers need to be updated before they can be used for vector-based output, click Update (Mac).

You used the Open command on the File menu to locate and open a file.

Open a file using Folders palette in Adobe Bridge

1. Click the **Go to Bridge button** on the options bar, then click the **Folders palette tab** Folders (if necessary).

2. Navigate through the hierarchical tree to the drive and folder where your Chapter 1 Data Files are stored.

3. Drag the **slider** (at the bottom of the Bridge window) a third of the way between the Smallest thumbnail size buttton and the Largest thumbnail size button . Compare your screen to Figure 8.

4. Double-click the image of a butterfly, file **PS 1-2.tif**. The butterfly image opens and Adobe Bridge is no longer visible, but still open.

5. Close the Butterfly image in Photoshop.

You used the Folders palette tab in Adobe Bridge to locate and open a file. This feature makes it easy to see which file you want to use.

FIGURE 8

Adobe Bridge window

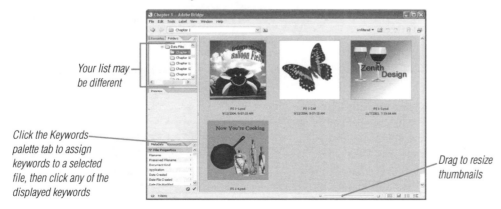

Your list may
be different

Click the Keywords
palette tab to assign
keywords to a selected
file, then click any of the
displayed keywords

Drag to resize
thumbnails

Lesson 2   Learn How to Open and Save an Image

Use the Save As command

1. Verify that the **PS 1-1.psd window** is active.

2. Click **File** on the menu bar, click **Save As**, then compare your Save As dialog box to Figure 9.

3. If the drive containing your Data Files is not displayed, click the **Save in list arrow** (Win) or the **Where list arrow** (Mac), then navigate to the drive and folder where your Chapter 1 Data Files are stored.

4. Select the current filename in the File name text box (Win) or Save As text box (Mac) (if necessary); type **Hot Air Balloons**, then click **Save**. Compare your image to Figure 10.

   TIP Click OK to close the Maximize Compatibility dialog box (if necessary).

You used the Save As command on the File menu to save the file with a new name. This command makes it possible for you to save a changed version of an image while keeping the original file intact.

Changing file formats
In addition to using the Save As command to duplicate an existing file, this is a handy way of changing one format into another. For example, you can open an image you created in a digital camera, then make modifications in the Photoshop format. To do this, open the .jpg file in Photoshop, click File on the menu bar, then click Save As. Name the file, click the Format list arrow, click Photoshop (*.PSD, *.PDD), then click OK.

FIGURE 9
Save As dialog box

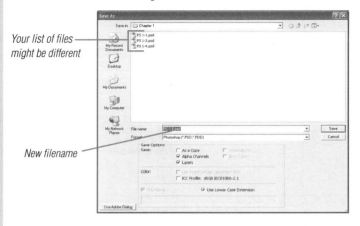

Your list of files might be different

New filename

FIGURE 10
Hot Air Balloons image

Duplicate file has new name

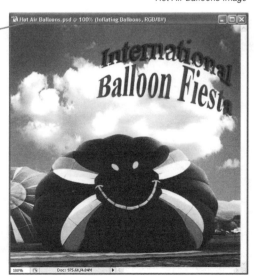

FIGURE 11

Images in Adobe Bridge

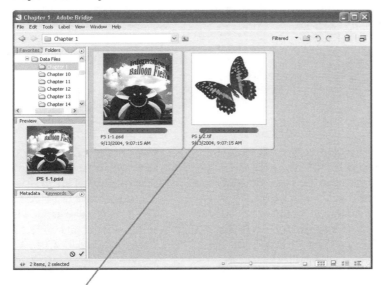

Purple labeled
files displayed

FIGURE 12

Flagged files

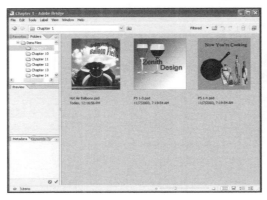

Rate and filter with Bridge

1. Click the **Go to Bridge button** on the options bar.

2. Click the **Folders palette tab** (if necessary), then click the drive and folder where your Chapter 1 Data Files are on the File Hierarchy tree (if necessary).

3. Click the butterfly image, file **PS 1-2.tif** to select it.

4. Press and hold **[Ctrl]** (Win) or **[⌘]** (Mac), click **PS 1-1.psd** (the image of the balloon), then release **[Ctrl]** (Win) or **[⌘]** (Mac).

5. Click **Label** on the menu bar, then click **Purple**. (If a warning box opens, click **OK**.)

6. Click the **Unfiltered list arrow**, then click **Show Purple Label**. See Figure 11.

7. Click the **Filtered list arrow**, then click **Show Unlabeled Items Only**. Compare your screen to Figure 12.

   The order of the flagged files is reordered.

8. Click the **Filtered list arrow**, then click **Show All Items**.

   TIP You can change the Bridge view at any time, depending on the type of information you need to see.

9. Click **File** (Win) or **Bridge** (Mac) on the (Bridge) menu bar, then click **Exit**.

You labeled files using Bridge, displayed only those labeled files, then displayed the unlabeled items. When finished, you displayed all the images in the selected folder, then closed Bridge.

USE ORGANIZATIONAL AND
MANAGEMENT FEATURES

What You'll Do

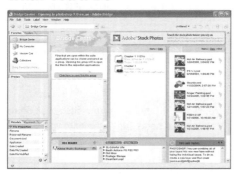

In this lesson, you'll learn how to use Version Cue and Bridge.

Learning about Version Cue

Version Cue is a file versioning and management feature of the Adobe Creative Suite that can be used to organize your work whether you work in groups or by yourself. Version Cue is accessed through Bridge. You can see Version Cue in Bridge in two different locations: the Favorites tab and the Folders tab. Figure 13 shows Version Cue in the Favorites tab of Bridge. You can also view Version Cue in the Folders tab by collapsing the Desktop, as shown in Figure 14.

Understanding Version Cue Workspaces

Regardless of where in Bridge you access it (the Favorites or Folders tab), Version Cue installs a **workspace** in which it stores projects and project files, and keeps track of file versions. The Version Cue Workspace can be installed locally on your own computer and can be made public or kept private. It can also be installed on a server and can be used by many users through a network.

FIGURE 13
Favorites tab in Bridge

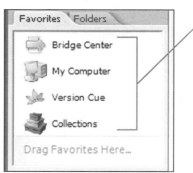

Your list of favorites may differ

FIGURE 14
Folders tab in Bridge

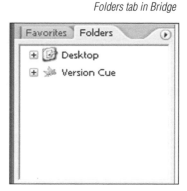

Using Version Cue's Administrative Functions

Once you log into Version Cue, you can control who uses the workspace and how it is used with the tabs at the top of the screen. The Home tab, which is shown in Figure 15, lets you add and edit users, create a project, and perform advanced tasks. The Users tab lets you easily identify the users that can share, access, or delete files and collaborate with coworkers on projects. The Projects tab allows you to create a project from a new or existing file. The Advanced tab lets you maintain the behavior and performance of Version Cue.

Understanding Bridge Center

You've already seen how you can use Bridge to find, identify, and sort files. But did you know that you can use Bridge Center to organize, open, save, and close files as a group? Bridge Center is available within Bridge, and is opened using the Favorites tab.

FIGURE 15

Version Cue CS2 Home tab

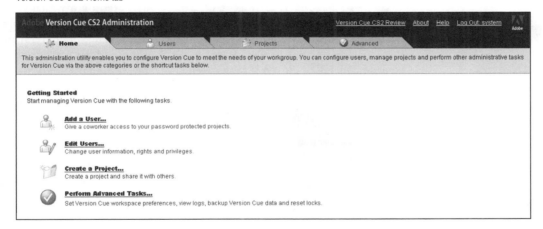

Using Adobe Stock Photos

You can view and try professional images using Adobe Stock Photos. Available through the Favorites pane in Bridge Center, an active Internet connection is all you need to browse through a wide variety of images to include in your Photoshop designs. You can download complimentary (comp) low-resolution versions of these images and place them in a Photoshop document to find the perfect fit for your design. Once you find the right image, you can purchase it in a high-resolution format. There are thousands of images to choose from, and you can look at previous downloads and purchases through your Adobe account.

EXAMINE THE PHOTOSHOP WINDOW

What You'll Do

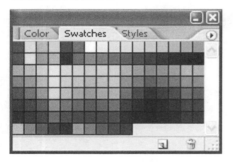

 In this lesson, you'll select a tool on the toolbox, use a shortcut key to cycle through the hidden tools, select and add a tool to the Tool Preset picker, use the Window menu to show and hide palettes in the workspace, and create a customized workspace.

Learning About the Workspace

The Photoshop **workspace** is the area within the program Photoshop window that includes the entire window, from the command menus at the top of your screen to the status bar (Win) at the bottom. Desktop items are visible in this area (Mac). The workspace is shown in Figure 16.

The **title bar** displays the program name (Win) and, if the active image window is maximized, the filename of the open file (for a new file, **Untitled-1**, because it has not been named). The title bar also contains a Close button, and Minimize, Maximize, and Restore buttons (Win).

The **menu bar** contains the program name (Mac) menu from which you can choose Photoshop commands. You can choose a menu command by clicking it or by pressing [Alt] plus the underlined letter in the menu name (Win). Some commands display shortcut keys on the right side of the menu. Shortcut keys provide an alternative way to activate menu commands. Some commands might appear dimmed, which means they are not currently available. An ellipsis after a command indicates additional choices.

Finding Tools Everywhere

The **toolbox** contains tools associated with frequently used Photoshop com-

---

DESIGNTIP **Overcoming information overload**

One of the most common experiences shared by first-time Photoshop users is information overload. There are just too many places and things to look at! When you feel your brain overheating, take a moment and sit back. Remind yourself that the active image area is the central area where you can see a composite of your work. All the tools and palettes are there to help you, not to add to the confusion.

---

mands. The face of a tool contains a graphical representation of its function; for example, the Zoom Tool shows a magnifying glass. You can place the pointer over each tool to display a tool tip, which tells you the name or function of that tool. Some tools have additional hidden tools, indicated by a small black triangle in the lower-right corner of the tool.

The **options bar**, located directly under the menu bar, displays the current settings for each tool. For example, when you click the Type Tool, the default font and font size appear on the options bar, which can be changed if desired. You can move the options bar anywhere in the workspace for easier access. The options bar also contains the Tool Preset picker. This is the left-most tool on the options bar and displays the active tool. You can click the list arrow on this tool to select another tool without having to use the toolbox. The options bar also contains the palette well, an area where you can assemble palettes for quick access.

QUICKTIP

The palette well is only available when your monitor resolution is greater than 800 pixels × 600 pixels.

Palettes are small windows used to verify settings and modify images. By default, palettes appear in stacked groups at the right side of the window. You can display a palette by simply clicking the palette's name tab, which makes it the active palette. Palettes can be separated and moved

FIGURE 16
Workspace

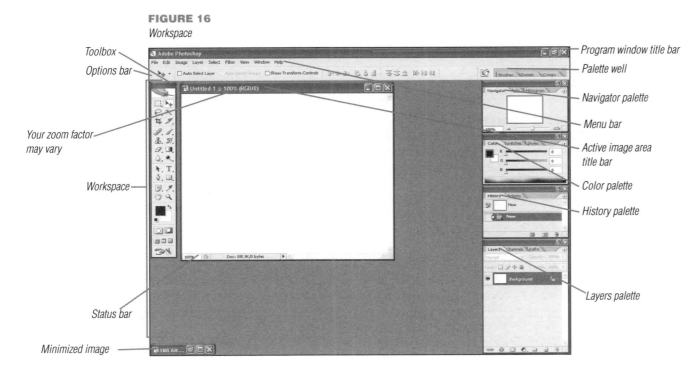

Toolbox
Options bar
Your zoom factor may vary
Workspace
Status bar
Minimized image

Program window title bar
Palette well
Navigator palette
Menu bar
Active image area title bar
Color palette
History palette
Layers palette

anywhere in the workspace by dragging their name tabs to new locations. Each palette contains a menu that you can view by clicking the list arrow in the upper-right corner of the palette.

QUICKTIP
You can reset palettes to their default locations at any time by clicking Window on the menu bar, pointing to Workspace, then clicking Reset Palette Locations.

The **status bar** is located at the bottom of the program window (Win) or work area (Mac). It displays information, such as the file size of the active window and a description of the active tool. You can display other information on the status bar, such as the current tool, by clicking the black triangle to view a pull-down menu with more options.

Rulers can help you precisely measure and position an object in the workspace. The rulers do not appear the first time you use Photoshop, but you can display them by clicking Rulers on the View menu.

Using Tool Shortcut Keys

Each tool has a corresponding shortcut key. For example, the shortcut key for the Type Tool is T. After you know a tool's shortcut key, you can select the tool on the toolbox by pressing its shortcut key. To select and cycle through a tool's hidden tools, you press and hold [Shift], then press the tool's shortcut key until the desired tool appears. See the Power User Shortcuts table at the end of each chapter for a description of tool shortcut keys.

Customizing Your Environment

Photoshop makes it easy for you to position elements you work with just where you want them. If you move elements around to make your environment more convenient, you can always return your workspace to its original appearance by resetting the default palette locations. Once you have your work area arranged the way you want it, you can create a customized workspace by clicking Window on the menu bar, pointing to Workspace, then clicking Save Workspace. If you want to open a named workspace, click Window on the menu bar, point to Workspace, then click the workspace you want to use.

Creating customized keyboard shortcuts

Keyboard shortcuts can make your work with Photoshop images faster and easier. In fact, once you discover the power of keyboard shortcuts, you may never use menus again. In addition to the keyboard shortcuts that are preprogrammed in Photoshop, you can create your own. To do this, click Edit on the menu bar, then click Keyboard Shortcuts. The Keyboard Shortcuts and Menus dialog box opens, as shown in Figure 17.

FIGURE 17
Keyboard Shortcuts and Menus dialog box

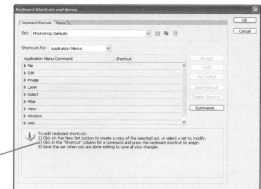

Instructions to edit shortcuts

Select a tool

1. Click the **Lasso Tool** ⟁ on the toolbox, press and hold the mouse button until a list of hidden tools appears, then release the mouse button. See Figure 18. Note the shortcut key, L, next to the tool name.

2. Click the **Polygonal Lasso Tool** ⟁ on the toolbox.

3. Press and hold **[Shift]**, press **[L]** three times to cycle through the Lasso tools, then release **[Shift]**. Did you notice how the options bar changes for each selected Lasso tool?

   TIP   You can return the tools to their default setting by clicking the Click to open the Tool Preset picker list arrow on the options bar, clicking the list arrow, then clicking Reset All Tools.

You selected the Lasso Tool on the toolbox and used its shortcut key to cycle through the Lasso tools. Becoming familiar with shortcut keys can speed up your work and make you more efficient.

FIGURE 18
Hidden tools

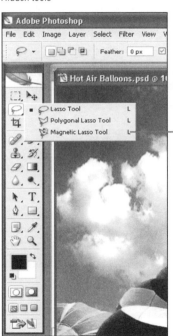

————— *Shortcut key*

DESIGNTIP   **Learning shortcut keys**

Don't worry about learning shortcut keys. As you become more familiar with Photoshop, you'll gradually pick up shortcuts for menu commands, such as saving a file, or toolbox tools, such as the Move Tool. You'll notice that as you learn to use shortcut keys, your speed while working with Photoshop will increase and you'll complete tasks with fewer mouse clicks.

Select a tool from the Tool Preset picker

1. Click the **Click to open the Tool Preset picker list arrow** ![icon] on the options bar.

   The name of a button is displayed in a tool tip, descriptive text that appears when you point to the button. Your Tool Preset picker list will differ, and may contain no entries at all. This list can be customized by each user.

2. Deselect the **Current Tool Only check box** (if necessary). See Figure 19.

3. Double-click **Magnetic Lasso 24 pixels** in the list.

You selected the Magnetic Lasso Tool using the Tool Preset picker. The Tool Preset picker makes it easy to access frequently used tools and their settings.

FIGURE 19
Using the Tool Preset picker

Active tool displays in Tool Preset picker button

Tool Preset picker list arrow opens palette

List arrow adds new tools and displays more options

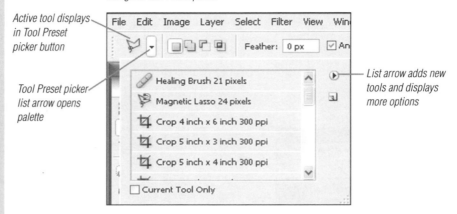

Using the Full Screen Mode

By default, Photoshop displays images in the Standard Screen Mode. This means that each image is displayed within its own window. You can choose from two other modes: Full Screen Mode with Menu Bar, and Full Screen Mode. And why would you want to stray from the familiar Standard Screen Mode? Perhaps your image is so large that it's difficult to see it all in Standard Mode, or perhaps you want a less cluttered screen. Maybe you just want to try something different. You can switch to Full Screen Mode with Menu Bar by clicking the Full Screen Mode with Menu Bar button (located near the bottom of the toolbox). When you click this button, the screen displays changes. Click the Hand Tool (or press the keyboard shortcut H), and you can reposition the active image, as shown in Figure 20.

FIGURE 20
Full Screen Mode with Menu Bar

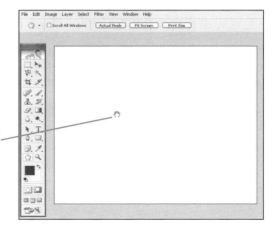

Use Hand pointer to relocate image

FIGURE 21
Move Tool added to Tool Preset picker

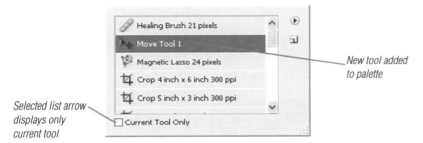

New tool added
to palette

Selected list arrow
displays only
current tool

FIGURE 22
Tool Preset picker list arrow menu

New Tool Preset...

Rename Tool Preset...
Delete Tool Preset

✔ Sort By Tool
✔ Show All Tool Presets
Show Current Tool Presets

Text Only
✔ Small List
Large List

Reset Tool
Reset All Tools

Preset Manager...

Reset Tool Presets...
Load Tool Presets...
Save Tool Presets...
Replace Tool Presets...

Art History
Brushes
Crop and Marquee
Text

Add a tool to the Tool Preset picker

1. Click the **Move Tool** ▸⊹ on the toolbox.

2. Click the **Click to open the Tool Preset picker list arrow** ▸⊹ ▾ on the options bar.

3. Click the **list arrow** ⊙ on the Tool Preset picker.

4. Click **New Tool Preset**, then click **OK** to accept the default name (Move Tool 1). Compare your list to Figure 21.

    TIP   You can display the currently selected tool alone by selecting the Current Tool Only check box.

You added the Move Tool to the Tool Preset picker. Once you know how to add tools to the Tool Preset picker, you can quickly and easily customize your work environment.

Modifying a tool preset

Once you've created tool presets, you'll probably want to know how they can be deleted and renamed. To delete any tool preset, select it on the Tool Preset picker palette. Click the list arrow on the Tool Preset picker palette to view the menu, shown in Figure 22, then click Delete Tool Preset. To rename a tool preset, click the same list arrow, then click Rename Tool Preset.

Show and hide palettes

1. Click **Window** on the menu bar, then verify that **Color** has a check mark next to it, then close the menu.

2. Click the **Swatches tab** next to the Color tab to make the Swatches palette active, as shown in Figure 23.

3. Click **Window** on the menu bar, then click **Swatches** to deselect it.

   TIP   You can hide all open palettes by pressing [Shift], then [Tab], then show them by pressing [Shift], then [Tab] again. To hide all open palettes, the options bar, and the toolbox, press [Tab], then show them by pressing [Tab] again.

4. Click **Window** on the menu bar, then click **Swatches** to redisplay the Swatches palette.

You used the Window menu to show and hide the Swatches palette. You might want to hide palettes at times in order to enlarge your work area.

FIGURE 23
Active Swatches palette

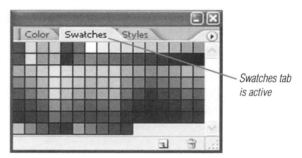

Swatches tab is active

DESIGNTIP   **Considering ethical implications**

Because Photoshop enables you to make so many dramatic changes to images, you should consider the ethical ramifications and implications of altering images. Is it proper or appropriate to alter an image just because you have the technical expertise to do so? Are there any legal responsibilities or liabilities involved in making these alterations? Because the general public is more aware about the topic of **intellectual property** (an image or idea that is owned and retained by legal control) with the increased availability of information and content, you should make sure you have the legal right to alter an image, especially if you plan on displaying or distributing the image to others. Know who retains the rights to an image, and if necessary, make sure you have written permission for its use, alteration, and/or distribution. Not taking these precautions could be costly.

FIGURE 24
Save Workspace dialog box

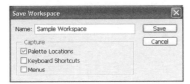

FIGURE 25
Resize Image Wizard dialog box

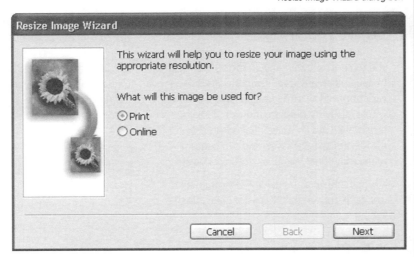

Create a customized workspace

1. Click and drag the **Toolbox title bar** so it appears to the right of the image.

2. Click **Window** on the menu bar, point to **Workspace**, then click **Save Workspace**.

3. Type **Sample Workspace** in the Name text box, then verify that only **Palette Locations** has a check mark beside it, as shown in Figure 24.

4. Click **Save**.

5. Click **Window** on the menu bar, then point to **Workspace**.

   The name of the new workspace appears on the Window menu.

6. Click **Reset Palette Locations**.

7. Click **Window** on the menu bar, point to **Workspace**, then click **Sample Workspace**.

8. Click **Window** on the menu bar, point to **Workspace**, then click **Reset Palette Locations**.

You created a customized workspace, reset the palette locations, tested the new workspace, then reset the palette locations again. Customized workspaces provide you with a work area that is always tailored to your needs.

Resizing an image

You may have created the perfect image, but the size may not be correct for your application. An image designed for a Web site, for example, might be too small for an image that will be printed in a newsletter. You can easily resize an image using the Resize Image Wizard (Win) or Resize Image Assistant (Mac). To use this feature, open the image you want to resize, click Help on the menu bar, then click Resize Image. The Resize Image Wizard dialog box, shown in Figure 25, opens. By answering each of the questions in the Wizard dialog boxes, you'll have your image resized in no time.

USE THE LAYERS AND HISTORY PALETTES

What You'll Do

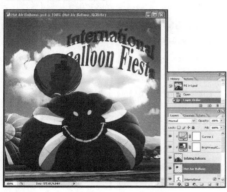

 In this lesson, you'll hide and display a layer, move a layer on the Layers palette, and then undo the move by deleting the Layer Order state on the History palette.

Learning About Layers

A **layer** is a section within an image that can be manipulated independently. Layers allow you to control individual elements within an image and create great dramatic effects and variations of the same image. Layers enable you to easily manipulate individual characteristics within an image. Each Photoshop file has at least one layer, and can contain many individual layers, or groups of layers.

You can think of layers in a Photoshop image as individual sheets of clear plastic that are in a stack. It's possible for your file to quickly accumulate dozens of layers. The **Layers palette** displays all the layers in an open file. You can use the Layers palette to create, copy, delete, display, hide, merge, lock, group or reposition layers.

> QUICKTIP
> In Photoshop, using and understanding layers is the key to success.

Setting preferences

The Preferences dialog box contains several topics, each with its own settings: General, File Handling, Display & Cursors, Transparency & Gamut, Units & Rulers, Guides, Grids & Slices, Plug-ins & Scratch Disks, Memory & Image Cache, and Type. To open the Preferences dialog box, click Edit (Win) or Photoshop (Mac) on the menu bar, point to Preferences, then click a topic that represents the settings you want to change. If you move palettes around the workspace, or make other changes to them, you can choose to retain those changes the next time you start the program. To always start a new session with default palettes, click General on the Preferences menu, deselect the Save Palette Locations check box, then click OK. Each time you start Photoshop, the palettes will be reset to their default locations and values.

Understanding the Layers Palette

The order in which the layers appear on the Layers palette matches the order in which they appear in the image; the topmost layer in the Layers palette is the topmost layer on the image. You can make a layer active by clicking its name on the Layers palette. When a layer is active, it is highlighted on the Layers palette, the name of the layer appears in parentheses in the image title bar. Only one layer can be active at a time. Figure 26 shows an image with its Layers palette. Do you see that this image contains five layers? Each layer can be moved or modified individually on the palette to give a different effect to the overall image. If you look at the Layers palette, you'll see that the Finger Painting layer is dark, indicating that it is currently active.

QUICKTIP

Get in the habit of shifting your eye from the image in the work area to the Layers palette. Knowing which layer is active will save you time and help you troubleshoot an image.

Displaying and Hiding Layers

You can use the Layers palette to control which layers are visible in an image. You can show or hide a layer by clicking the Indicates layer visibility button next to the layer thumbnail. When a layer is hidden, you are not able to merge it with another, select it, or print it. Hiding some layers can make it easier to focus on particular areas of an image.

Using the History Palette

Photoshop records each task you complete in an image on the **History palette**. This record of events, called states, makes it easy to see what changes occurred and the tools or commands that you used to make the modifications. The History palette, also shown in Figure 26, displays up to 20 states and automatically updates the list to display the most recently performed tasks. The list contains the name of the tool or command used to change the image. You can delete a state on the History palette by selecting it and dragging it to the Delete current state button. Deleting a state is equivalent to using the Undo command. You can also use the History palette to create a new image from any state.

QUICKTIP

When you delete a History state, you undo all the events that occurred after that state.

FIGURE 26
Layers and History palettes

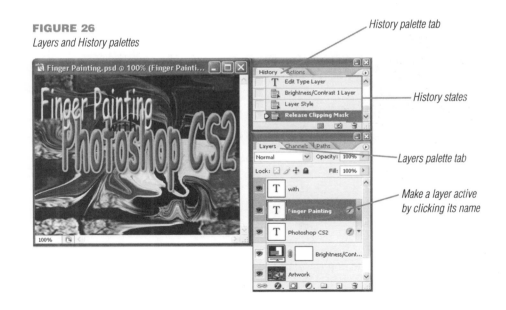

History palette tab

History states

Layers palette tab

Make a layer active by clicking its name

Hide and display a layer

1. Click the **Hot Air Balloon layer** on the Layers palette.

    TIP Depending on the size of the window, you might only be able to see the initial characters of the layer name.

2. Verify that the **Show Transform Controls** check box is not checked, then click the **Indicates layer visibility button** [ ] on the Hot Air Balloon layer to display the image, as shown in Figure 27.

    TIP By default, transparent areas of an image have a checkerboard display on the Layers palette.

3. Click the **Indicates layer visibility button** 👁 on the Hot Air Balloon layer to hide the image.

You made the Hot Air Balloon layer active on the Layers palette, then clicked the Indicates layer visibility button to display and hide a layer. Hiding layers is an important skill that can be used to remove distracting elements. Once you've finished working on specific layers, you can display the distracting layers.

FIGURE 27
Hot Air Balloon

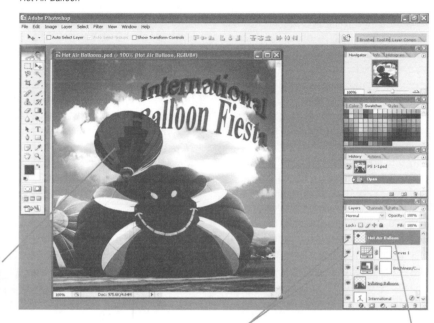

Visible Hot
Air Balloon
layer

Indicates layer
visibility button

Hot Air
Balloon
layer

FIGURE 28

Layer moved in Layers palette

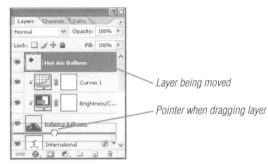

Layer being moved

Pointer when dragging layer

FIGURE 29

Result of moved layer

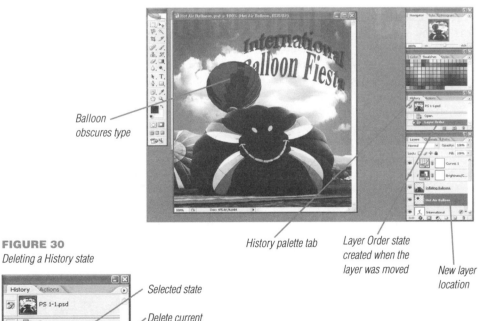

Balloon
obscures type

History palette tab

Layer Order state
created when the
layer was moved

New layer
location

FIGURE 30

Deleting a History state

Selected state

Delete current
state button

Pointer when deleting a History state

1. Click the **Indicates layer visibility button** on the Hot Air Balloon layer on the Layers palette.

2. Click and drag the **Hot Air Balloon layer** on the Layers palette, beneath the Inflating Balloons layer in the palette, as shown in Figure 28.

   The bottom of the Hot Air Balloon is hidden by the Inflating Balloons layer. See Figure 29.

3. Click **Layer Order** on the History palette, then drag it to the **Delete current state button** 🗑 on the History palette, as shown in Figure 30.

   TIP Each time you close and reopen an image, the History palette is cleared.

   The hot air balloon is no longer visible.

4. Click **File** on the menu bar, then click **Save**.

You moved the Hot Air Balloon layer so it was behind the Inflating Balloon layer, then returned it to its original position by dragging the Layer Order state to the Delete current state button on the History palette. You can easily undo what you've done using the History palette.

LEARN ABOUT PHOTOSHOP
BY USING HELP

What You'll Do

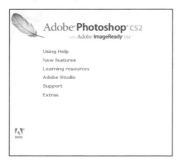

In this lesson, you'll open Help, then view and find information from the following Help links: Contents, Index, and Search.

Understanding the Power of Help

Photoshop features an extensive Help system that you can use to access definitions, explanations, and useful tips. Help information is displayed in a browser window, so you must have Web browser software installed on your computer to view the information; however, you do not need an Internet connection to use Photoshop Help.

Using Help Topics

The Home page of the Help window has six links in the right pane that you can use to retrieve information about Photoshop commands and features: Using Help, New Features, Learning Resources, Adobe Studio Support, and Extras. In the left pane, there are three palettes: Contents, Index, and Bookmarks as shown in Figure 31. The Getting Started link displays Contents, Index, and Bookmarks tabs in the left pane. The Contents palette tab allows you to browse topics by category; the Index palette tab provides the letters of the alphabet, which you can click to view keywords and topics alphabetically. The Search feature is located on the toolbar (above the left and right panes) in the form of a text box. You can search the Photoshop Help System by entering text in the Type in a word or phrase text box, then click Search.

FIGURE 31
Tabs in the Help Menu

Help tabs—

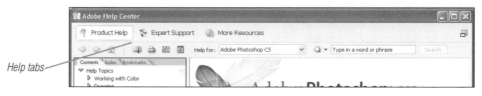

FIGURE 32

Contents section of the Help window

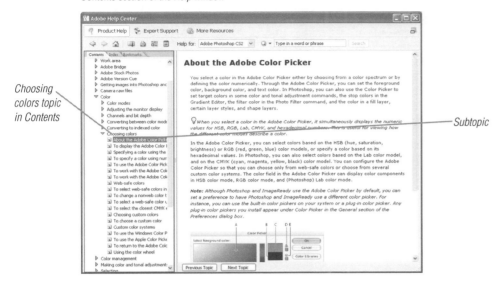

Choosing
colors topic
in Contents

Subtopic

1. Click **Help** on the menu bar, then click **Photoshop Help**.

   TIP   You can also open the Help window by pressing **[F1]** (Win) or ⌘ **[?]** (Mac).

2. If it's not already selected, click the **Contents tab** Contents , scroll down the left pane (if necessary), then click **Color**.

3. Click **Choosing colors**, then click **About the Adobe Color Picker** in the left pane. See Figure 32.

   TIP   You can maximize the window (if you want to take advantage of the full screen display).

You used the Photoshop Help command on the Help menu to open the Help window and viewed a topic in Contents.

Understanding the differences between monitor, images, and device resolution

Image resolution is determined by the number of pixels per inch (ppi) that are printed on a page. Pixel dimensions (the number of pixels along the height and width of a bitmap image) determine the amount of detail in an image, while image resolution controls the amount of space over which the pixels are printed. High resolution images show greater detail and more subtle color transitions than low resolution images. Device resolution or printer resolution is measured by the ink dots per inch (dpi) produced by printers. You can set the resolution of your computer monitor to determine the detail with which images will be displayed. Each monitor should be calibrated to describe how the monitor reproduces colors. Monitor calibration is one of the first things you should do because it determines whether your colors are being accurately represented, which in turn determines how accurately your output will match your design intentions.

Find information in the Index

1. Click the **Index tab** 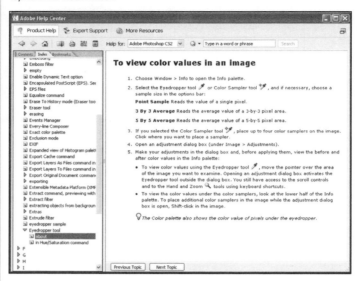 in the left pane of the Help window.

2. Click **E**, scroll down, then click **Eyedropper tool**, then click **about**. Compare your Help window to Figure 33.

You clicked an alphabetical listing and viewed an entry in the Index.

Create a Bookmark

1. Click the **Add a bookmark for the current help contents button**, then click **OK** in the New Bookmark dialog box.

2. Click the **Bookmarks tab** in the Help window. Compare your Help window to Figure 34.

You created a bookmark in the Help window.

FIGURE 33

Topics in the Index window

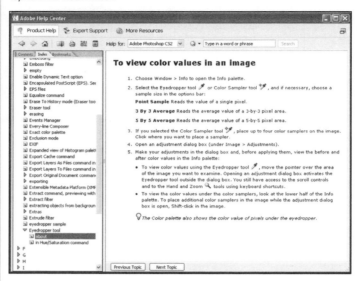

FIGURE 34

Topics added to Bookmark

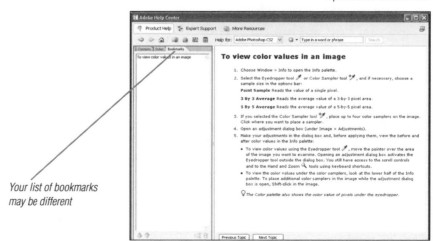

Your list of bookmarks may be different

FIGURE 35
Search topic in Help

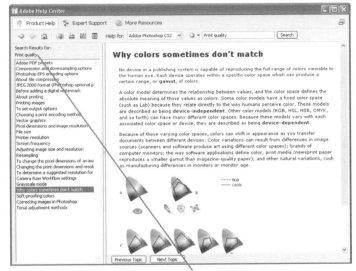

Search term

FIGURE 36
Create your own How To tips

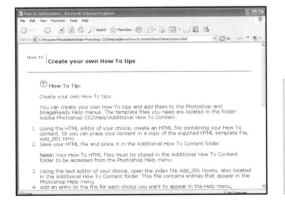

Find information using Search

1. Click the **Type in a word or phrase text box** in the Help window.

2. Type **print quality**, then click **Search**.

   > TIP   You can search for multiple words by inserting a space; do not use punctuation in the text box.

3. Scroll down the left pane (if necessary), click **Why colors sometimes don't match**, then compare your Help screen to Figure 35.

4. Click the **Close box** when you are finished reading the topic.

You entered a search term, viewed search results, then closed the Help window.

Creating customized How To's

Photoshop Help is pretty helpful, but perhaps there's a technique you've created, only to return later and think 'How did I do this?' Fortunately, you can create your own How To tips so you'll never wonder how you created a cool effect. To find out more, click Help on the menu bar, point to How to Create How Tos, then click Create your own How To tips. The information shown in Figure 36 walks you through the process.

VIEW AND PRINT AN IMAGE

What You'll Do

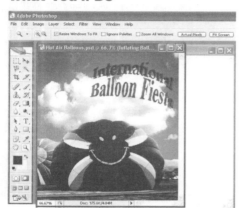

In this lesson, you'll use the Zoom Tool on the toolbox to increase and decrease your views of the image. You'll also change the page orientation settings in the Page Setup dialog box, and print the image.

Getting a Closer Look

When you edit an image in Photoshop, it is important that you have a good view of the area that you are focusing on. Photoshop has a variety of methods that allow you to enlarge or reduce your current view. You can use the Zoom Tool by clicking the image to zoom in on (magnify the view) or zoom out of (reduce the view) areas of your image. Zooming in or out enlarges or reduces your *view*, not the actual image. The maximum zoom factor is 1600%. The current zoom percentage appears in the document's title bar, on the Navigator palette, and on the status bar. When the Zoom Tool is selected, the options bar provides additional choices for changing your view as shown in Figure 37. For example, the Resize Windows To Fit check box automatically resizes the window whenever you magnify or reduce the view. You can also change the zoom percentage using the Navigator palette and the status bar by typing a new value in the zoom text box.

Printing Your Image

In many cases, a professional print shop might be the best option for printing a Photoshop image to get the highest quality. You can print a Photoshop image using a standard black-and-white or color printer. The printed image will be a composite of all visible layers. The quality of your printer and paper will affect the appearance of your output. The Page Setup dialog box displays options for printing, such as paper orientation. **Orientation** is the direction in which an image appears on the page. In **portrait orientation**, the image is printed with the shorter edges of the paper at the top and bottom. In **landscape orientation**, the image is printed with the longer edges of the paper at the top and bottom.

Use the Print command when you want to print multiple copies of an image. Use the Print One Copy command to print a single copy without making dialog box selections, and use the Print with Preview command when you want to handle color values using color management.

Understanding Color Handling in Printing

The Print dialog box that opens when you click Print with Preview on the File menu lets you determine how colors are output. You can click the Color Handling list arrow to choose whether to use color management, and whether Photoshop or the printing device should control this process. If you let Photoshop determine the colors, Photoshop performs any necessary conversions to color values appropriate for the selected printer. If you choose to let the printer determine the colors, the printer will convert document color values to the corresponding printer color values. In this scenario, Photoshop does not alter the color values. If no color management is selected, no color values will be changed when the image is printed.

Viewing an Image in Multiple Views

You can use the New Window command on the Window ➢ Arrange menu to open multiple views of the same image. You can change the zoom percentage in each view so you can spotlight the areas you want to modify, and then modify the specific area of the image in each view. Because you are working on the same image in multiple views, not in multiple versions, Photoshop automatically applies the changes you make in one view to all views. Although you can close the views you no longer need at any time, Photoshop will not save any changes until you save the file.

FIGURE 37
Zoom Tool options bar

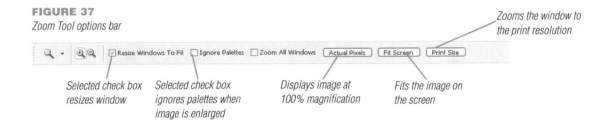

Zooms the window to the print resolution

Selected check box resizes window

Selected check box ignores palettes when image is enlarged

Displays image at 100% magnification

Fits the image on the screen

Use the Zoom Tool

1. Click the **Zoom Tool** 🔍 on the toolbox.

2. Select the **Resize Windows To Fit check box** ☐ Resize Windows To Fit (if it is not already selected) on the options bar.

3. Position the **Zoom In pointer** ⊕ over the center of the image, then click the image.

   | TIP   Position the pointer over the part of the image you want to keep in view.

4. Press **[Alt]** (Win) or **[option]** (Mac), then when the Zoom Out pointer appears, click the center of the image twice with the **Zoom Out pointer** ⊖.

5. Release **[Alt]** (Win) or **[option]** (Mac), then compare your image to Figure 38.

   The zoom factor for the image is 66.7%. Your zoom factor may differ.

You selected the Zoom Tool on the toolbox and used it to zoom in to and out of the image. The Zoom Tool makes it possible to see the detail in specific areas of an image, or to see the whole image at once, depending on your needs.

Using the Navigator palette

You can change the magnification factor of an image using the Navigator palette or the Zoom Tool on the toolbox. By double-clicking the Zoom text box on the Navigator palette, you can enter a new magnification factor, then press [Enter] (Win) or [return] (Mac). The magnification factor—shown as a percentage—is displayed in the lower-left corner of the Navigator palette, as shown in Figure 39. The red border in the palette, called the Proxy Preview Area, defines the area of the image that is magnified. You can drag the Proxy Preview Area inside the Navigator palette to view other areas of the image at the current magnification factor.

FIGURE 38
Reduced image

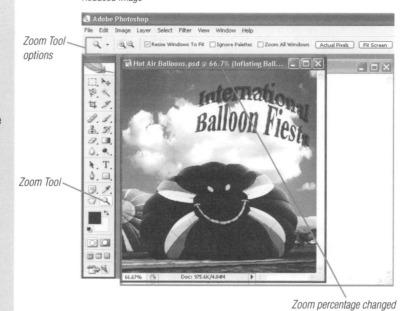

Zoom Tool options

Zoom Tool

Zoom percentage changed

FIGURE 39
Navigator palette

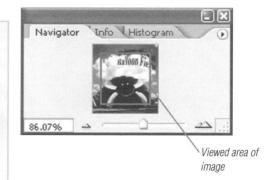

Viewed area of image

FIGURE 40
Page Setup dialog box

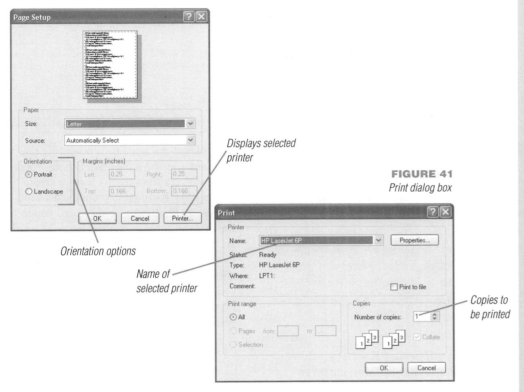

Displays selected printer

Orientation options

Name of selected printer

FIGURE 41
Print dialog box

Copies to be printed

Modify print settings

1. Click **File** on the menu bar, then click **Page Setup** to open the Page Setup dialog box, as shown in Figure 40.

    TIP If you have not selected a printer using the Print Center, a warning box might appear (Mac).

    Page setup and print settings vary slightly in Macintosh.

2. Click the **Landscape option button** in the Orientation section, then click **OK**.

    TIP Choose either Landscape option (Mac).

3. Click **File** on the menu bar, click **Print**, then click **Proceed** in the message box that opens. If a PostScript dialog box opens, click **OK** (Mac).

4. Make sure that the **All option button** is selected in the Print range section (Win) or Pages section (Mac), and that **1** appears in the Number of copies text box, then click **OK** (Win) or **Print** (Mac). See Figure 41.

You used the Page Setup command on the File menu to open the Page Setup dialog box, changed the page orientation, then printed the image. Changing the page orientation can make an image fit on a printed page better.

Creating a Proof Setup

You can create and save a Proof Setup, which lets you view your image to see how it will look when printed on a specific device. This feature lets you see how colors can be interpreted by different devices. By using this feature, you can decrease the chance that colors will vary from what you viewed on your monitor after they are printed. Create a custom proof by clicking View on the menu bar, pointing to Proof Setup, then clicking Custom. Specify the conditions in the Customize Proof Condition dialog box, then click OK. Each proof setup has the .PSF extension and can be loaded by clicking View on the menu bar, pointing to Proof Setup, clicking Custom, then clicking Load.

CLOSE A FILE
AND EXIT PHOTOSHOP

What You'll Do

New...	Ctrl+N
Open...	Ctrl+O
Browse...	Alt+Ctrl+O
Open As...	Alt+Shift+Ctrl+O
Open Recent	▶
Edit in ImageReady	Shift+Ctrl+M
Close	Ctrl+W
Close All	Alt+Ctrl+W
Close and Go To Bridge...	Shift+Ctrl+W
Save	Ctrl+S
Save As...	Shift+Ctrl+S
Save a Version...	
Save for Web...	Alt+Shift+Ctrl+S
Revert	F12
Place...	
Import	▶
Export	▶
Automate	▶
Scripts	▶
File Info...	Alt+Shift+Ctrl+I
Page Setup...	Shift+Ctrl+P
Print with Preview...	Alt+Ctrl+P
Print...	Ctrl+P
Print One Copy	Alt+Shift+Ctrl+P
Print Online...	
Jump To	▶
Exit	Ctrl+Q

 In this lesson, you'll use the Close and Exit (Win) or Quit (Mac) commands to close a file and exit Photoshop.

Concluding Your Work Session

At the end of your work session, you might have opened several files; you now need to decide which ones you want to save.

QUICKTIP

If you share a computer with other people, it's a good idea to reset Photoshop's preferences back to their default settings. You can do so when you start Photoshop by clicking Window on the menu bar, pointing to Workspace, then clicking Reset Palette Locations.

Closing Versus Exiting

When you are finished working on an image, you need to save and close it. You can close one file at a time, or close all open files at the same time by exiting the program. Closing a file leaves Photoshop open, which allows you to open or create another file. Exiting Photoshop closes the file, closes Photoshop, and returns you to the desktop, where you can choose to open another program or shut down the computer. Photoshop will prompt you to save any changes before it closes the files. If you do not modify a new or existing file, Photoshop will close it automatically when you exit.

QUICKTIP

To close all open files, click File on the menu bar, then click Close All.

Using Adobe online

Periodically, when you start Photoshop, an Update dialog box might appear, prompting you to search for updates or new information on the Adobe Web site. If you click Yes, Photoshop will automatically notify you that a download is available; however, you do not have to select it. You can also obtain information about Photoshop from the Adobe Photoshop Web site (*www.adobe.com/products/photoshop/main.html*), where you can link to downloads, tips, training, galleries, examples, and other support topics.

FIGURE 42

Closing a file using the File menu

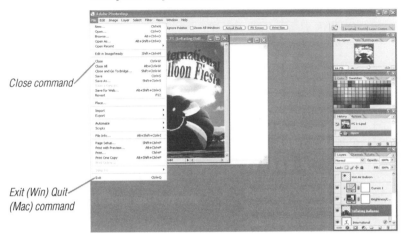

Close command

Exit (Win) Quit (Mac) command

DESIGNTIP   **Using a scanner and a digital camera**

If you have a scanner, you can import print images, such as those taken from photographs, magazines, or line drawings, into Photoshop. Remember that images taken from magazines are owned by others, and that you need permission to distribute them. There are many types of scanners, including flatbed or single-sheet feed. See your instructor to learn how to use the scanner in your facility. You can also use a digital camera to create your own images. A digital camera captures images as digital files and stores them on some form of electronic medium, such as a floppy disk or SmartMedia card. After you upload the images from your camera to your computer, you can work with images in Photoshop.

You can open a scanned or uploaded image (which usually has a .JPG extension or another graphics file format) by clicking File on the menu bar, then by clicking Open. All Formats is the default file type, so you should be able to see all available image files in the Open dialog box. Locate the folder containing your scanned or digital camera images, click the file you want to open, then click Open. A scanned or digital camera image contains all its imagery in a single layer. You can add layers to the image, but you can only save these new layers if you save the image as a Photoshop image (with the extension .PSD).

Close a file and exit Photoshop

1. Click **File** on the menu bar, then compare your screen to Figure 42.

2. Click **Close**.

    TIP   You can close an open file (without closing Photoshop) by clicking the Close button in the image window. Photoshop will prompt you to save any unsaved changes before closing the file.

3. If asked to save your work, click **Yes** (Win) or **Save** (Mac).

4. Click **File** on the menu bar, then click **Exit** (Win) or click **Photoshop** on the menu bar, then click **Quit Photoshop** (Mac).

    TIP   To exit Photoshop and close an open file, click the Close button in the program window. Photoshop will prompt you to save any unsaved changes before closing.

5. If asked to save your work, click **No**.

You closed the current file and exited the program by using the Close and Exit (Win) or Quit (Mac) commands.

Power User Shortcuts

Key: Menu items are indicated by ➤ between the menu name and its command. Blue bold letters are shortcuts for selecting tools on the toolbox.

to do this:	use this method:
Close a file	[Ctrl][W] (Win) ⌘[W] (Mac)
Create a new file	[Ctrl][N] (Win) ⌘[N] (Mac)
Create a workspace	Window ➤ Workspace ➤ Save Workspace
Drag a layer	✋
Exit Photoshop	[Ctrl][Q] (Win), ⌘[Q] (Mac)
Hide a layer	👁
Lasso Tool	⌇ or L
Open a file	[Ctrl][O] (Win), ⌘[O] (Mac)
Open Bridge	🖼
Open Help	[F1] (Win)
Open Preferences dialog box	[Ctrl][K] (Win) ⌘[K] (Mac)
Page Setup	[Shift][Ctrl][P] (Win) [Shift]⌘[P] (Mac)
Print File	File ➤ Print [Ctrl][P], (Win) ⌘[P] (Mac)

to do this:	use this method:
Reset preferences to default settings	[Shift][Alt][Ctrl] (Win) [Shift] option ⌘ (Mac)
Save a file	[Ctrl][S] (Win) ⌘[S] (Mac)
Show a layer	☐
Show hidden lasso tools	[Shift] L
Show or hide all open palettes	[Shift][Tab]
Show or hide all open palettes, the options bar, and the toolbox	[Tab]
Show or hide Swatches palette	Window ➤ Swatches
Use Save As	[Shift][Ctrl][S] (Win) [Shift]⌘[S] (Mac)
Zoom in	🔍 [⌘][+]
Zoom out	[Alt] 🔍 (Win) option 🔍 (Mac) [⌘][−]
Zoom Tool	🔍 or Z

In this chapter, you have learned the basics of Photoshop CS2: how to open and close a file, as well as how to start and exit Photoshop. You learned how to use Adobe Bridge, Version Cue, and Photoshop Help. You have also learned to identify some of the elements of the Photoshop window, how to use the Layers and History palettes, and how to move and delete layers.

What You Have Learned:

- How to open Photoshop CS2.
- How to open and save a file.
- How to identify elements of the Photoshop window.
- How to use organizational tools.
- How to move and delete layers.
- How to use the Adobe Help Center.
- How to view an image.
- How to close a file and quit Photoshop.

Key Terms

Adobe Bridge   A stand-alone application that serves as the hub for the Adobe Creative Suite.

Digital image   Picture in electronic form; it may be referred to as a file, document, picture, or image.

History palette   Records each task (state) completed during the current Photoshop session.

Layers palette   Displays all the layers in an open file, and can be used to create, copy, delete, display, hide, merge, lock, or reposition layers.

Options bar   Located directly under the menu bar, displays the current settings for the active tool.

Preferences   Options you can set that are based on your work habits.

Toolbox   Contains tools associated with frequently used Photoshop commands.

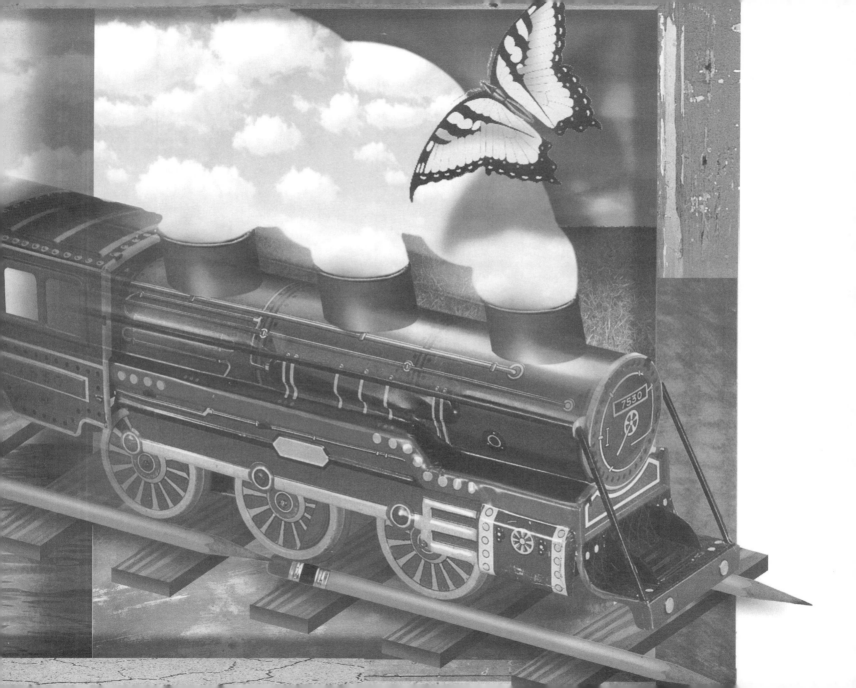

chapter

2

WORKING
WITH LAYERS

1. Examine and convert layers.

2. Add and delete layers.

3. Add a selection from one image to another.

4. Organize layers with layer groups and colors.

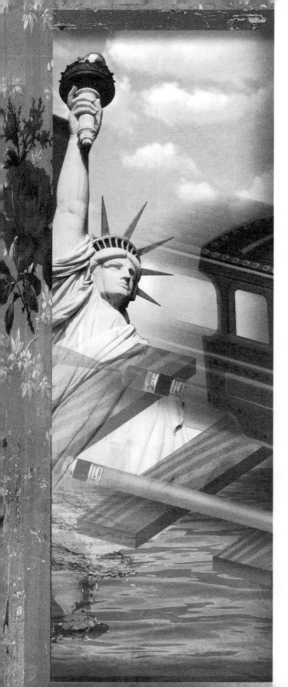

2 WORKING
WITH LAYERS

Layers Are Everything

You can use Photoshop to create sophisticated images because a Photoshop image can contain multiple layers. Each object created in Photoshop can exist on its own individual layer, making it easy to control the position and quality of each layer in the stack. Depending on your computer's resources, you can have a maximum of 8000 layers in each Photoshop image with each layer containing as much or as little detail as necessary.

QUICKTIP

The transparent areas in a layer do not increase file size.

Understanding the Importance of Layers

Layers make it possible to manipulate the tiniest detail within your image, which gives you tremendous flexibility when you make changes. By placing objects, effects, styles, and type on separate layers, you can modify them individually *without* affecting other layers. The advantage to using multiple layers is that you can isolate effects and images on one layer without affecting the others. The disadvantage of using multiple layers is that your file size might become very large. However, once your image is finished, you can dramatically reduce its file size by combining all the layers into one.

Using Layers to Modify an Image

You can add, delete, and move layers in your image. You can also drag a portion of an image, called a **selection**, from one Photoshop image to another. When you do this, a new layer is automatically created. Copying layers from one image to another makes it easy to transfer a complicated effect, a simple image, or a piece of type. You can also hide and display each layer, or change its opacity. **Opacity** is the ability to see through a layer so that layers beneath it are visible. You can continuously change the overall appearance of your image by changing the order of your layers, until you achieve just the look you want.

Tools You'll Use

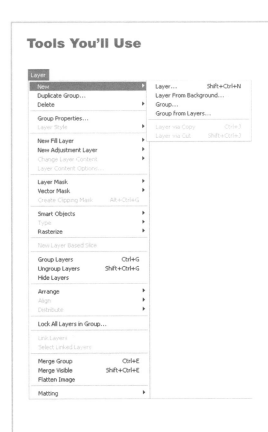

Opacity list arrow

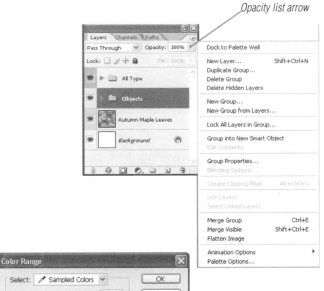

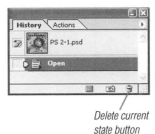

Color Range

Select: 🖉 Sampled Colors ▾

OK

Cancel

Fuzziness: 40

Load...

Save...

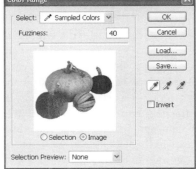

🖉 🖉 🖉

☐ Invert

○ Selection ⦿ Image

Selection Preview: None ▾

Delete current
state button

New Group

Name: Group 1

OK

Color: ■ Violet ▾

Cancel

Mode: Pass Through ▾ Opacity: 100 ▸ %

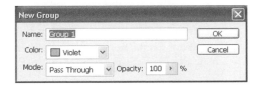

Layer Properties

Name: Layer 1

OK

Color: ☐ None ▾

Cancel

Color list arrow

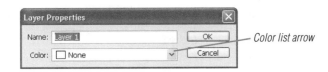

EXAMINE AND
CONVERT LAYERS

What You'll Do

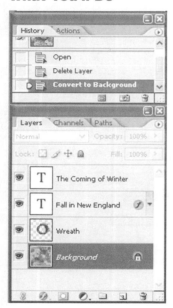

 In this lesson, you'll use the Layers palette to delete a Background layer and the Layer menu to create a Background layer from an image layer.

Learning About the Layers Palette

The **Layers palette** lists all the layer names within a Photoshop file and makes it possible for you to manipulate one or more layers. By default, this palette is located in the lower-right corner of the screen, but it can be moved to a new location by dragging the palette's tab. In some cases, the entire name of the layer might not appear on the palette. If a layer name is too long, an ellipsis appears, indicating that part of the name is hidden from view. You can view a layer's entire name by holding the pointer over the name until the full name appears. The **layer thumbnail** appears to the left of the layer name and contains a miniature picture of the layer's content, as shown in Figure 1. To the left of the layer thumbnail, you can add color, which allows you to easily identify layers. The Layers palette also contains common buttons, such as the Delete layer button and the Create new layer button.

QUICKTIP
You can hide or resize Layers palette thumbnails to improve your computer's performance. To remove or change the size of layer thumbnails, click the Layers palette list arrow, then click Palette Options to open the Layers Palette Options dialog box. Click the option button next to the desired thumbnail size, or click the None option button to remove thumbnails, then click OK. A paintbrush icon appears in place of a thumbnail.

Recognizing Layer Types

The Layers palette includes several types of layers: Background, type, and image (non-type). The Background layer—whose name appears in italics—is always at the bottom of the stack. Type layers—layers that contain text—contain the type layer icon in the layer thumbnail, and image layers display a thumbnail of their contents. In addition to dragging selections from one Photoshop image to another, you can also drag objects created in other applications, such as Adobe Illustrator, Adobe InDesign, or Macromedia Flash, onto a Photoshop image, which creates a layer containing the object you dragged from the other program window.

QUICKTIP

It is not necessary for a Photoshop image to have a Background layer. However, if you don't have a Background layer, the background will take on the properties of the layers and their opacities, which is more memory intensive than an object layer.

Organizing Layers

One of the benefits of using layers is that you can create different design effects by rearranging their order. Figure 2 contains the same layers as Figure 1, but they are arranged differently. Did you notice that the wreath is partially obscured by the gourds and the title text? This reorganization was created by dragging the Wreath layer below the Gourds layer and by dragging the Fall in New England layer below the Wreath layer on the Layers palette.

QUICKTIP

Did you notice the horizontal and vertical lines in the figures? Although you may find them distracting, these are moveable guides that you can use to help you place objects precisely. As you continue working in Photoshop, you'll find they are very useful—and soon you probably won't even notice them.

FIGURE 1
Image with multiple layers

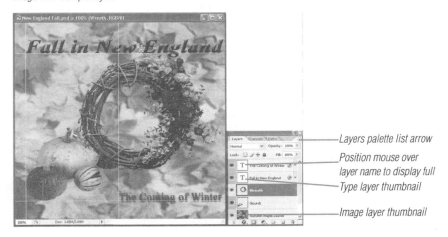

Layers palette list arrow

Position mouse over layer name to display full

Type layer thumbnail

Image layer thumbnail

FIGURE 2
Layers rearranged

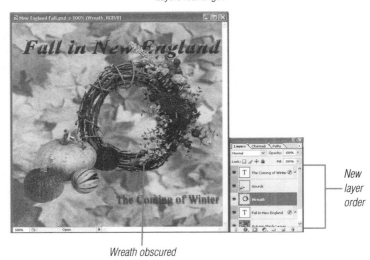

New layer order

Wreath obscured

Converting Layers

When you open an image created with a digital camera, you'll notice that the entire image appears in the Background layer. The Background layer of any image is the initial layer and is always located at the bottom of the stack. You cannot change its position in the stack, nor can you change its opacity or lighten or darken its colors. You can, however, convert a Background layer into an image layer (nontype layer), and you can convert an image layer into a Background layer. You need to modify the image layer *before* converting it to a Background layer. You might want to convert a Background layer into an image layer so that you can use the full range of editing tools on the layer content. You might want to convert an image layer into a Background layer after you have made all your changes and want it to be the bottom layer in the stack.

QUICKTIP

Before converting an image layer to a Background layer, you must first delete the existing Background layer. You can delete a Background layer by clicking it on the Layers palette, then dragging it to the Delete layer button on the Layers palette.

Using rulers and changing units of measurement

You can display horizontal and vertical rulers to help you better position elements. To display or hide rulers, click View on the menu bar, then click Rulers. (A check mark to the left of the Rulers command indicates that the Rulers are displayed.) In addition to displaying or hiding rulers, you can also choose from various units of measurement. Your choices include pixels, inches, centimeters, millimeters, points, picas, and percentages. Pixels, for example, display more tick marks and can make it easier to make tiny adjustments. You can change the units of measurement by clicking Edit [Win] or Photoshop [Mac] on the menu bar, pointing to Preferences, then clicking Units & Rulers. In the Preferences dialog box, click the Rulers list arrow, click the units you want to use, then click OK. The easiest way to change units of measurement, however, is shown in Figure 3. Once the rulers are displayed, right-click (Win) or [Ctrl]-click (Mac) either the vertical or horizontal ruler, then click the unit of measurement you want. The Info palette, located in the upper-right corner of the workspace, also displays your current coordinates. Regardless of the units of measurement in use, the X/Y coordinates are displayed in the Info palette.

FIGURE 3
Changing units of measurement

Right-click (Win) or [Ctrl]-click (Mac) to display measurement choices

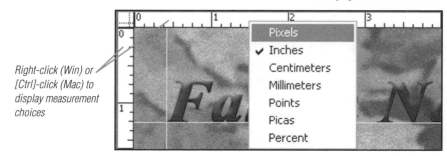

FIGURE 4
Warning box

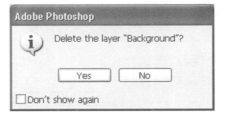

FIGURE 5
Background layer deleted

FIGURE 6
New Background layer added to Layers palette

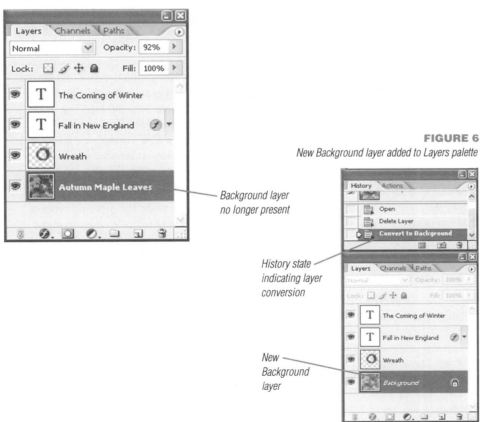

Background layer
no longer present

History state
indicating layer
conversion

New
Background
layer

Convert an image layer into a Background layer

1. Open PS 2-1.psd from the drive and folder where your Data Files are stored, then save it as **New England Fall**.

   TIP   If you receive a warning box about maximum compatibility, or a message stating that some of the text layers need to be updated before they can be used for vector-based output, click OK or click Update.

2. Click **View** on the menu bar, click **Rulers** if your rulers are not visible, then make sure that your rulers are displayed in pixels.

   TIP   If you are unsure which units of measurement are used, right-click (Win) or [Ctrl]-click (Mac) one of the rulers, then verify that Pixels is selected, or click Pixels (if necessary).

3. On the Layers palette, scroll down, click the **Background layer**, then click the **Delete layer button** 🗑.

4. Click **Yes** in the dialog box, as shown in Figure 4, then compare your Layers palette to Figure 5.

5. Click **Layer** on the menu bar, point to **New**, then click **Background From Layer**.

   The Autumn Maple Leaves layer has been converted into the Background layer. Did you notice that in addition to the image layer being converted to the Background layer that a state now appears on the History palette that says Convert to Background? See Figure 6.

6. Save your work.

You displayed the rulers, deleted the Background layer of an image, then converted an image layer into the Background layer. You can convert any layer into the Background layer, as long as you first delete the existing Background layer.

ADD AND
DELETE LAYERS

What You'll Do

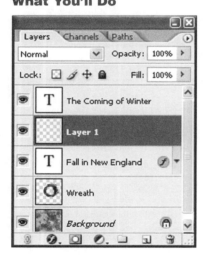

 In this lesson, you'll create a new layer using the New command on the Layer menu, delete a layer, and create a new layer using buttons on the Layers palette.

Adding Layers to an Image

Because it's so important to make use of multiple layers, Photoshop makes it easy to add and delete layers. You can create layers in three ways:

- Use the New command on the Layer menu.
- Use the New Layer command on the Layers palette menu.
- Click the Create a new layer button on the Layers palette.

Objects on new layers have a default opacity setting of 100%, which means that objects on lower layers are not visible. Each layer has the Normal (default) blending mode applied to it. (A **blending mode** is a feature that affects a layer's underlying pixels, and is used to lighten or darken colors.)

Merging layers

You can combine multiple image layers into a single layer using the merging process. Merging layers is useful when you want to combine multiple layers in order to make specific edits permanent. (This merging process is different from flattening in that it's selective. Flattening merges *all* visible layers.) In order for layers to be merged, they must be visible and next to each other on the Layers palette. You can merge all visible layers within an image, or just the ones you select. Type layers cannot be merged until they are **rasterized** (turned into a bitmapped image layer), or converted into uneditable text. To merge two layers, make sure that they are next to each other and that the Indicates layer visibility button is visible on each layer, then click the layer in the higher position on the Layers palette. Click Layer on the menu bar, then click Merge Down. The active layer and the layer immediately beneath it will be combined into a single layer. To merge all visible layers, click the Layers palette list arrow, then click Merge Visible. Most layer commands that are available on the Layers menu, such as Merge Down, are also available using the Layers palette list arrow.

Naming a Layer

Photoshop automatically assigns a sequential number to each new layer name, but you can rename a layer at any time. So, if you have four named layers and add a new layer, the default name of the new layer will be Layer 1. After all, calling a layer "Layer 12" is fine, but you might want to use a more descriptive name so it is easier to distinguish one layer from another. If you use the New command on the Layers menu, you can name the layer when you create it. You can rename a layer at any time by using either of these methods:

- Click the Layers palette list arrow, click Layer Properties, type the name in the Name text box, then click OK.
- Double-click the name on the Layers palette, type the new name, then press [Enter] (Win) or [return] (Mac).

Deleting Layers From an Image

You might want to delete an unused or unnecessary layer. You can use four methods to delete a layer:

- Click the name on the Layers palette, click the Layers palette list arrow, then click Delete Layer as shown in Figure 7.
- Click the name on the Layers palette, click the Delete layer button on the Layers palette, then click Yes in the warning box.
- Click the name on the Layers palette, press and hold [Alt] (Win) or [option] (Mac), then click the Delete layer button on the Layers palette.

- Drag the layer name on the Layers palette to the Delete layer button on the Layers palette.

You should be certain that you no longer need a layer before you delete it. If you delete a layer by accident, you can restore it during the current editing session by deleting the Delete Layer state on the History palette.

QUICKTIP

Photoshop always numbers layers sequentially, no matter how many layers you add or delete.

FIGURE 7
Layers palette menu

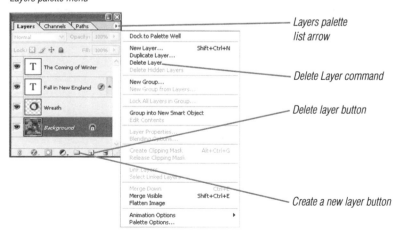

Layers palette list arrow

Delete Layer command

Delete layer button

Create a new layer button

Add a layer using the Layer menu

1. Click the **Fall in New England layer** on the Layers palette.

2. Click **Layer** on the menu bar, point to **New**, then click **Layer** to open the New Layer dialog box, as shown in Figure 8.

   A new layer will be added above the active layer.

   | TIP You can change the layer name in the New Layer dialog box before it appears on the Layers palette.

3. Click **OK**.

   The New Layer dialog box closes and the new layer appears above the Fall in New England layer on the Layers palette. The New Layer state is added to the History palette. See Figure 9.

   You created a new layer above the Fall in New England layer, using the New command on the Layer menu. The layer does not yet contain any content.

FIGURE 8
New Layer dialog box

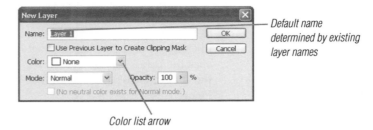

Default name determined by existing layer names

Color list arrow

FIGURE 9
New layer on Layers palette

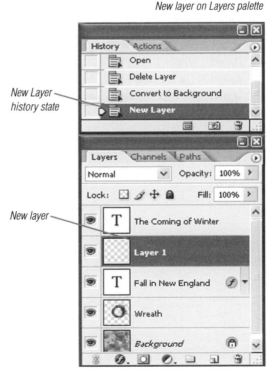

New Layer history state

New layer

Inserting a layer beneath the active layer

When you add a layer to an image either by using the Layer menu or clicking the Create a new layer button on the Layers palette, the new layer is inserted above the active layer. But there might be times when you want to insert the new layer beneath, or in back of, the active layer. You can do so easily, by pressing [Ctrl] (Win) or [Command] (Mac) while clicking the Create a new layer button on the Layers palette.

FIGURE 10
New layer with default settings

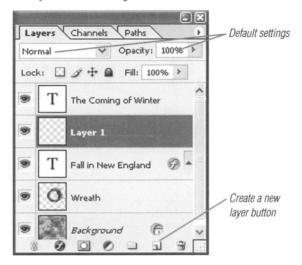

Default settings

Create a new
layer button

Right-clicking for everyone (Mac)

Mac users, are you feeling left out because you can't right-click? If so, you'll welcome this news: anyone (yes, even Mac users!) can right-click simply by replacing the mouse that came with your computer with any two-button mouse that uses a USB connector. OS X was designed to recognize two-button mice without having to add software. Once you've switched mice, just plug and play! You can then right-click using the (Win) instructions in the steps.

Delete a layer

1. Position the **Layer selection pointer** over Layer 1 on the Layers palette.

2. Drag **Layer 1** to the **Delete layer button** on the Layers palette.

    TIP You can also delete the layer by dragging the New Layer state on the History palette to the Delete current state button.

3. If the Delete the layer "Layer 1" dialog box opens, click the **Don't show again check box**, then click **Yes**.

    TIP Many dialog boxes let you turn off this reminder feature by selecting the Don't show again check box. Selecting these check boxes can improve your efficiency.

You used the Delete layer button on the Layers palette to delete a layer.

Add a layer using the Layers palette

1. Click the **Fall in New England layer** on the Layers palette, if it is not already selected.

2. Click the **Create a new layer button** on the Layers palette, then compare your Layers palette to Figure 10.

3. Save your work.

You used the Create a new layer button on the Layers palette to add a new layer.

ADD A SELECTION FROM ONE
IMAGE TO ANOTHER

What You'll Do

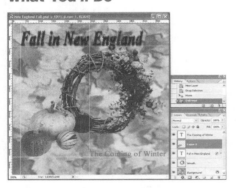

In this lesson, you'll use the Invert check box in the Color Range dialog box to make a selection, drag the selection to another image, and remove the fringe from a selection using the Defringe command.

Understanding Selections

Often the Photoshop file you want to create involves using an image or part of an image from another file. To use an image or part of an image, you must first select it. Photoshop refers to this as "making a selection." A selection is an area of an image surrounded by a **marquee**, a dashed line that surrounds the area you want to edit or move to another image, as shown in Figure 11. You can drag a marquee around a selection using four marquee tools: Rectangular Marquee, Elliptical Marquee, Single Row Marquee, and Single Column Marquee. Table 1 displays the four marquee tools and other selection tools. You can set options for each tool on the options bar when the tool you want to use is active.

Understanding the Extract and Color Range Commands

In addition to using selection tools, Photoshop provides other methods for incorporating imagery from other files. The **Extract command**, located on the Filter menu, separates an image from a background or surrounding imagery. You can use the **Color Range** command, located on the Select menu, to select a particular color contained in an existing image. Depending on the area you want, you can use the Color Range dialog box to extract a portion of an image.

Cropping an image

You might find an image that you really like, except that it contains a particular portion that you don't need. You can exclude, or **crop**, certain parts of an image by using the Crop Tool on the toolbox. Cropping hides areas of an image from view *without* losing resolution quality. To crop an image, click the Crop Tool on the toolbox, drag the pointer around the area you *want to keep*, then press [Enter] (Win) or [return] (Mac).

For example, you can select the Invert check box to choose one color and then select the portion of the image that is every color *except* that one. After you select all the imagery you want from another image, you can drag it into your open file.

Making a Selection and Moving a Selection

You can use a variety of methods and tools to make a selection, which can be used as a specific part of a layer or as the entire layer.

You use selections to isolate an area you want to alter. For example, you can use the Magnetic Lasso Tool to select complex shapes by clicking the starting point, tracing an approximate outline, then clicking the ending point. Later, you can use the Crop Tool to trim areas from a selection. When you use the Move Tool to drag a selection to the destination image, Photoshop places the selection in a new layer above the previously active layer.

Defringing Layer Contents

Sometimes when you make a selection, then move it into another image, the newly selected image can contain unwanted pixels that give the appearance of a fringe, or halo. You can remove this effect using a Matting command called Defringe. This command is available on the Layers menu and allows you to replace fringe pixels with the colors of other nearby pixels. You can determine a width for replacement pixels between 1 and 200. It's magic!

FIGURE 11
Marquee selections

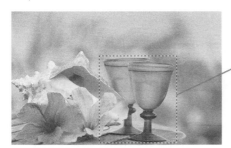

Area selected using the Rectangular Marquee Tool

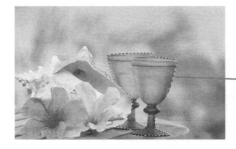

Specific element selected using the Magnetic Lasso Tool

TABLE 1: Selection Tools

tool	tool name	tool	tool name
⬚	Rectangular Marquee Tool	⬭	Lasso Tool
⬯	Elliptical Marquee Tool	⬙	Polygonal Lasso Tool
⚏	Single Row Marquee Tool	⬚	Magnetic Lasso Tool
⦙	Single Column Marquee Tool	⬚	Eraser Tool
⌗	Crop Tool	⬚	Background Eraser Tool
⚒	Magic Wand Tool	⬚	Magic Eraser Tool

Make a color range selection

1. Open PS 2-2.psd from the drive and folder where your Data Files are stored, save it as **Gourds**, click the **title bar**, then drag the window to an empty area of the workspace so that you can see both images.

   TIP When more than one file is open, each has its own set of rulers.

2. Click **Select** on the menu bar, then click **Color Range**.

   TIP If the background color is solid, you can select the Invert check box to pick only the pixels in the image area.

3. Click the **Image option button**, then type **0** in the Fuzziness text box (or drag the slider all the way to the left until you see 0).

4. Position the **Eyedropper pointer** 🖊 in the **white background** of the image in the Color Range dialog box, then click the **background**.

5. Select the **Invert check box**. Compare your dialog box to Figure 12.

6. Click **OK**, then compare your Gourds.psd image to Figure 13.

You opened a file and used the Color Range dialog box to select the image pixels by selecting the image's inverted colors. Selecting the inverse is an important skill in making selections.

Using the Place command

You can add an image from another image to a layer using the Place command. Place an image in a Photoshop layer by clicking File on the menu bar, then clicking Place. The placed artwork appears inside a bounding box at the center of the Photoshop image. The artwork maintains its original aspect ratio; however, if the artwork is larger than the Photoshop image, it is resized to fit.

FIGURE 12
Color Range dialog box

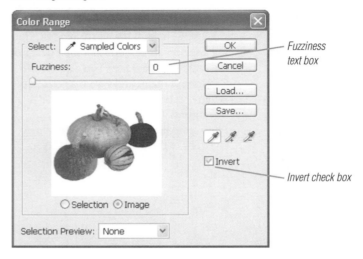

Fuzziness text box

Invert check box

FIGURE 13
Marquee surrounding selection

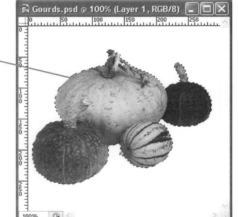

Marquee surrounds everything that is the inverse of the white background

FIGURE 14

Gourds image dragged to New England Fall image

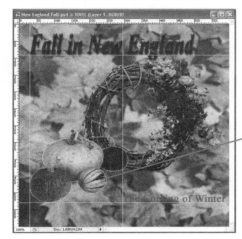

White fringe
surrounds object

FIGURE 15

Gourds layer defringed

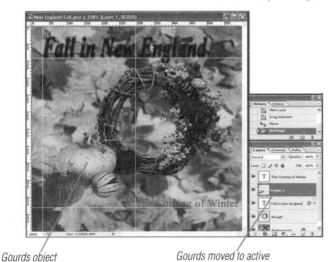

Gourds object
in image

Gourds moved to active
layer in image

Move a selection to another image

1. Click the **Move Tool** ⊕ on the toolbox.
2. Position the **Move Tool pointer** ▶⊕ any-where over the selection in the Gourds image.
3. Drag the selection to the New England Fall image, then release the mouse button.

   The Gourds image moves to the New England Fall file appearing on Layer 1.
4. If necessary, use the **Move Tool pointer** ▶⊕ to drag the gourds to the location at the lower-left corner of the wreath.
5. Click the **triangle** in the document window status bar ▶ , point to **Show**, then click **Document Sizes**. Compare your image to Figure 14.

You dragged a selection from one image to another. You displayed the document size in the window.

Defringe the selection

1. Click **Layer** on the menu bar, point to **Matting**, then click **Defringe**. Defringing a selection gets rid of the halo effect that sometimes occurs when objects are dragged from one image to another.
2. Type **2** in the Width text box, then click **OK**.
3. Save your work.
4. Close **Gourds.psd**, then compare the New England Fall image to Figure 15.

You removed the fringe from a selection.

ORGANIZE LAYERS WITH
LAYER GROUPS AND COLORS

What You'll Do

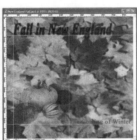

In this lesson, you'll use the Layers palette menu to create, name, and color a layer group, and then add layers to it. You'll add finishing touches to the image, save it as a copy, then flatten it.

Understanding Layer Groups

A **layer group** is a Photoshop feature that allows you to organize your layers on the Layers palette. A layer group contains individual layers. For example, you can create a layer group that contains all the type layers in your image. To create a layer group, you click the Layers palette list arrow, then click New Group. As with layers, it is helpful to choose a descriptive name for a layer group.

Organizing Layers into Groups

After you create a layer group, you simply drag layers on the Layers palette directly on top of the layer group. You can remove layers from a layer group by dragging them out of the layer group to a new location on the Layers palette or by deleting them. Some changes made to a layer group, such as blending mode or opacity changes, affect every layer in the layer group. You can choose to expand or collapse layer groups, depending on the amount of information you need to see. Expanding a layer group

Duplicating a layer

When you add a new layer by clicking the Create a new layer button on the Layers palette, the new layer contains default settings. However, you might want to create a new layer that has the same settings as an existing layer. You can do so by duplicating an existing layer to create a copy of that layer and its settings. Duplicating a layer is also a good way to preserve your modifications, because you can modify the duplicate layer and not worry about losing your original work. To create a duplicate layer, select the layer you want to copy, click the Layers palette list arrow, click Duplicate Layer, then click OK. The new layer will appear above the original.

shows all of the layers in the layer group, and collapsing a layer group hides all of the layers in a layer group. You can expand or collapse a layer group by clicking the triangle to the left of the layer group icon. Figure 16 shows one expanded layer group and one collapsed layer group.

Adding Color to a Layer

If your image has relatively few layers, it's easy to locate the layers. However, if your image contains many layers, you might need some help in organizing them. You can organize layers by color-coding them, which makes it easy to find the group you want, regardless of its location on the Layers palette. For example, you can put all type layers in red or put the layers associated with a particular portion of an image in blue. To color the Background layer, you must first convert it to a regular layer.

QUICKTIP

You can also color-code a layer group without losing the color-coding you applied to individual layers.

Flattening an Image

After you make all the necessary modifications to your image, you can greatly reduce the file size by flattening the image. **Flattening** merges all visible layers into a single Background layer and discards all hidden layers. Make sure that all layers that you want to display are visible before you flatten the image. Because flattening removes an image's individual layers, it's a good idea to make a copy of the original image *before* it is flattened. The status bar displays the file's current size and the size it will be when flattened. If you work on a Macintosh, you'll find this information in the lower-left corner of the document window.

FIGURE 16
Layer group

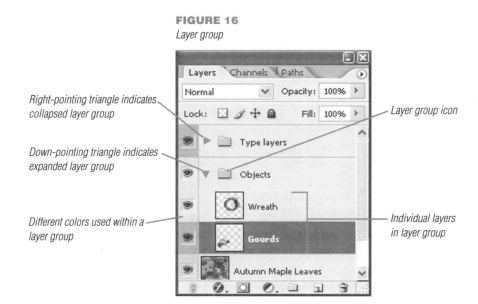

Right-pointing triangle indicates collapsed layer group

Down-pointing triangle indicates expanded layer group

Different colors used within a layer group

Layer group icon

Individual layers in layer group

Understanding Layer Comps

The ability to create a **layer comp**, a variation on the arrangement and visibility of existing layers, is a powerful tool that can make your work more organized. You can create a layer comp by clicking the Layer Comps tab on the palette well, then clicking the Create New Layer Comp button. The New Layer Comp dialog box, shown in Figure 17, opens, allowing you to name the layer comp and set parameters.

Using Layer Comps

Multiple layer comps, shown in Figure 18, make it easy to switch back and forth between variations on an image theme. Say, for example, that you want to show a client multiple arrangements of layers. The layer comp is an ideal tool for this.

FIGURE 17
New Layer Comp dialog box

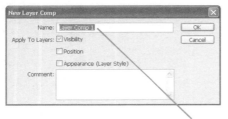

Type new comp name here

FIGURE 18
Multiple layer comps in image

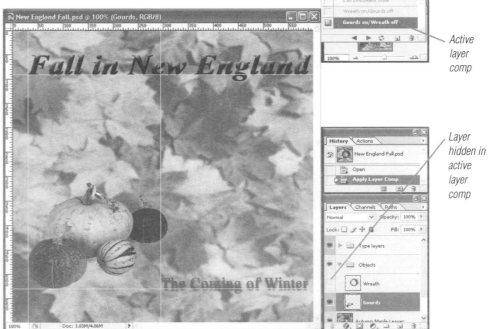

Active layer comp

Layer hidden in active layer comp

FIGURE 19
New Group dialog box

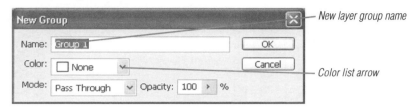

— New layer group name

— Color list arrow

FIGURE 20
New layer group on Layers palette

New layer group

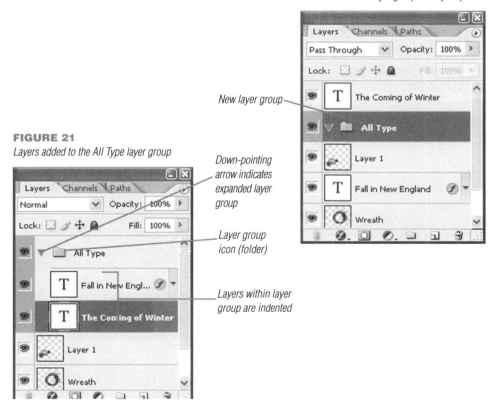

FIGURE 21
Layers added to the All Type layer group

Down-pointing
arrow indicates
expanded layer
group

Layer group
icon (folder)

Layers within layer
group are indented

Create a layer group

1. Verify that Layer 1 is active, click the **Layers palette list arrow** ▶, then click **New Group**.

   The New Group dialog box opens, as shown in Figure 19.

   TIP Photoshop automatically places a new layer group above the active layer.

2. Type **All Type** in the Name text box.

3. Click the **Color list arrow**, click **Red**, then click **OK**.

   The New Group dialog box closes. Compare your Layers palette to Figure 20.

You used the Layers palette menu to create a layer group, then named and applied a color to it. This new group will contain all the type layers in the image.

Move layers to the layer group

1. Click the **Fall in New England type layer** on the Layers palette, then drag it on to the **All Type layer group**.

2. Click the **The Coming of Winter type layer**, drag it on to the **All Type layer group**, then compare your Layers palette to Figure 21.

   TIP If the Coming of Winter layer is below the Fall in New England layer, move the layers to match Figure 21.

3. Click the **triangle** ▽ to the left of the layer group icon (folder) to collapse the layer group.

You created a layer group, then moved two layers into that layer group. Creating layer groups is a great organization tool, especially in complex images with many layers.

Rename a layer and adjust opacity

1. Double-click **Layer 1**, type **Gourds**, then press **[Enter]** (Win) or **[return]** (Mac).

2. Double-click the **Opacity text box** on the Layers palette, type **75**, then press **[Enter]** (Win) or **[return]** (Mac).

3. Drag the **Gourds layer** beneath the Wreath layer, then compare your image to Figure 22.

4. Save your work.

You renamed the new layer, adjusted opacity, and rearranged layers.

Create layer comps

1. Click the **Layer Comps tab** on the palette well.

2. Click the **Create New Layer Comp button** on the Layer Comps palette.

3. Type **Gourds on/Wreath off** in the Name text box, as shown in Figure 23, then click **OK**.

4. Click the **Indicates layer visibility button** on the Wreath layer.

5. Click the **Layer Comps tab** on the palette well (if necessary), then click the **Update Layer Comp button** on the Layer Comps palette. Compare your Layer Comps palette to Figure 24.

6. Save your work.

You created a Layer Comp in an existing image.

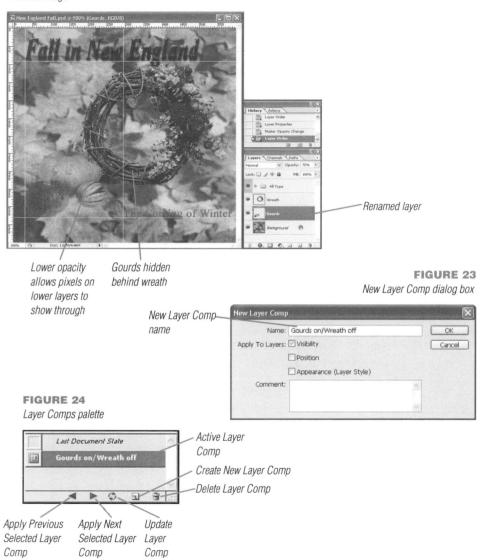

FIGURE 22
Finished image

Renamed layer

Lower opacity allows pixels on lower layers to show through

Gourds hidden behind wreath

FIGURE 23
New Layer Comp dialog box

New Layer Comp name

FIGURE 24
Layer Comps palette

Active Layer Comp

Create New Layer Comp

Delete Layer Comp

Apply Previous Selected Layer Comp

Apply Next Selected Layer Comp

Update Layer Comp

FIGURE 25
Save As dialog box

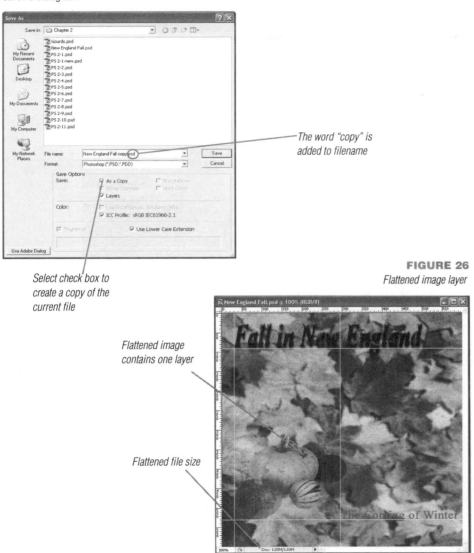

The word "copy" is added to filename

Select check box to create a copy of the current file

FIGURE 26
Flattened image layer

Flattened image contains one layer

Flattened file size

Flatten an image

1. Click **File** on the menu bar, then click **Save As**.

2. Click the **As a Copy check box** to add a checkmark, then compare your dialog box to Figure 25.

   TIP If "copy" does not display in the File name text box, click this text box and type copy to add it to the name.

3. Click **Save**.

   Photoshop saves and closes a copy of the file containing all the layers and effects.

4. Click **Layer** on the menu bar, then click **Flatten Image**.

5. Click **OK** in the warning box, if necessary, then save your work.

6. Compare your Layers palette to Figure 26.

7. Close all open images, then exit Photoshop.

You saved the file as a copy, and then flattened the image. The image now has a single layer.

Power User Shortcuts

to do this:	use this method:
Adjust layer opacity	Click Opacity list arrow on Layers palette, drag opacity slider or Double-click Opacity text box, type a percentage
Change measurements	Right-click (Win) or [Ctrl]-click (Mac) ruler
Color a layer	Layers palette list arrow, Layer Properties, Color list arrow
Create a layer comp	Click Layer Comps tab, ⬛
Create a layer group	⊙ , New Group
Delete a layer	🗑
Defringe a selection	Layer ➢ Matting ➢ Defringe

to do this:	use this method:
Flatten an image	Layer ➢ Flatten Image
Move Tool	▶⊕ or V
New Background layer from existing layer	Layer ➢ New ➢ Background From Layer
New layer	Layer ➢ New ➢ Layer or ⬛
Rename a layer	Double-click layer name, type new name
Select color range	Select ➢ Color Range
Show/Hide Rulers	View ➢ Rulers [Ctrl][R] (Win) ⌘[R] (Mac)
Update a layer comp	↻

Key: Menu items are indicated by ➢ between the menu name and its command. Blue bold letters are shortcuts for selecting tools on the toolbox.

In this chapter, you learned how make extensive use of the Layers palette, using layers to modify an image. You worked with Background layers and learned how to add and delete layers. You used a color range to make a selection. You created a selection in one image, dragged it into another image, then changed its appearance. You used layer groups and assigned colors to layer thumbnails.

What You Have Learned:

- How to change layer types.
- How to use commands on the Layers palette.
- How to create a selection.
- How to organize layers within the Layers palette.

Key Terms

Flattening   Merges all visible layers into a single Background layer and discards all hidden layers.

Layer comp   Variation on the arrangement and visibility of existing layers within an image that can be used to make your work more organized.

Layer group   Allows you to organize your layers on the Layers palette.

Layer thumbnail   Appears to the left of the layer name and contains a miniature picture of the layer's content.

Marquee   Area of an image that you want to edit or move to another image and is surrounded by a dashed line.

Opacity   Ability to see through a layer so that layers beneath it are visible.

Selection   Portion of an image that can be dragged within an image, or to another image.

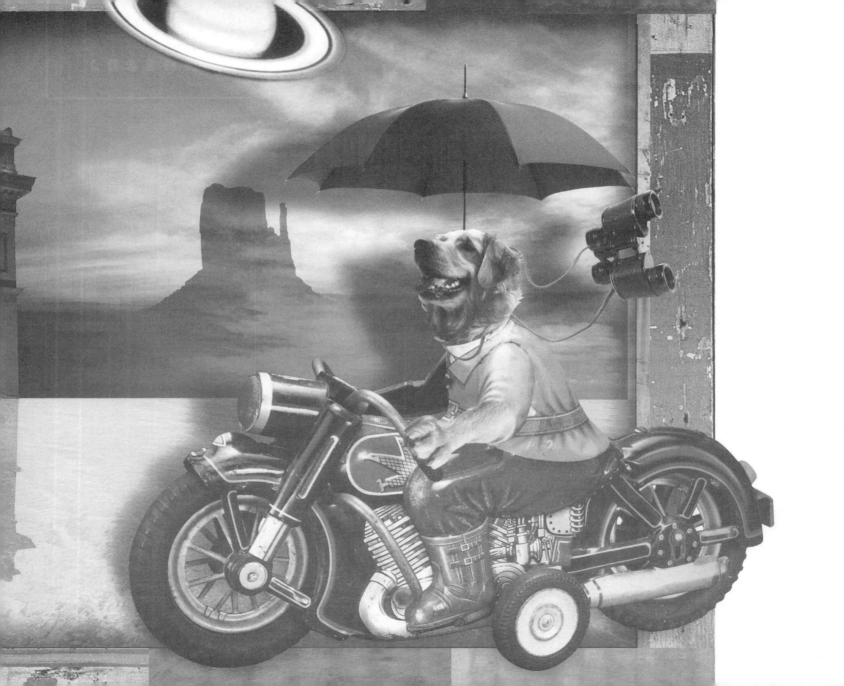

3

MAKING
SELECTIONS

1. Make a selection using shapes.

2. Modify a marquee.

3. Select using color and modify a selection.

4. Add a vignette effect to a selection.

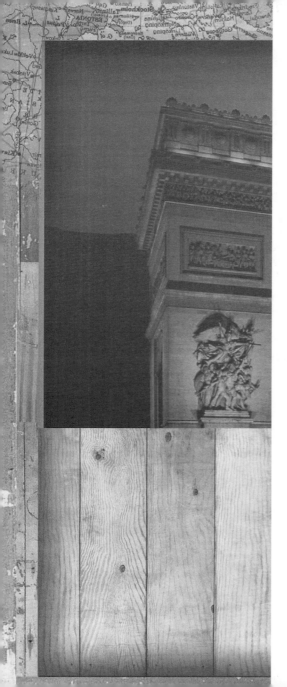

3 MAKING
SELECTIONS

Combining Images

Most Photoshop images are created using a technique called **compositing**—combining images from different sources. These sources include other Photoshop images, royalty-free images, pictures taken from digital cameras, and scanned artwork. How you get all that artwork into your Photoshop images is an art unto itself. You can include additional images by using tools on the toolbox and menu commands. And to work with all these images, you need to know how to select them—or exactly the parts you want to work with.

Understanding Selection Tools

The two basic methods you can use to make selections are using a tool or using color. You can use three freeform tools to create your own unique selections, four fixed area tools to create circular or rectangular selections, and a wand tool to make selections using color. In addition, you can use menu commands to increase

or decrease selections that you made with these tools, or you can make selections based on color.

Understanding Which Selection Tool to Use

With so many tools available, how do you know which one to use? After you know the different selection options, you'll learn how to look at images and evaluate selection opportunities. With experience, you'll learn how to identify edges that can be used to isolate imagery, and how to spot colors that can be used to isolate a specific object.

Combining Imagery

After you decide on an object that you want to place in a Photoshop image, you can add the object by cutting, copying, and pasting, dragging and dropping objects using the Move Tool, and using the **Clipboard**, the temporary storage area provided by your operating system.

Tools You'll Use

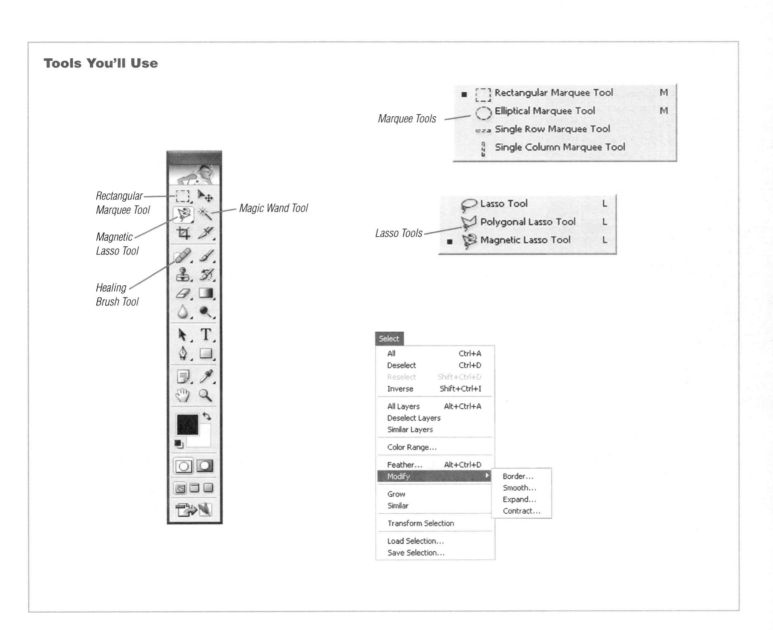

Marquee Tools

- ■ Rectangular Marquee Tool   M
- ○ Elliptical Marquee Tool   M
- Single Row Marquee Tool
- Single Column Marquee Tool

Rectangular Marquee Tool

Magnetic Lasso Tool

Healing Brush Tool

Magic Wand Tool

Lasso Tools

- Lasso Tool   L
- Polygonal Lasso Tool   L
- ■ Magnetic Lasso Tool   L

Select

All	Ctrl+A
Deselect	Ctrl+D
Reselect	Shift+Ctrl+D
Inverse	Shift+Ctrl+I
All Layers	Alt+Ctrl+A
Deselect Layers	
Similar Layers	
Color Range...	
Feather...	Alt+Ctrl+D
Modify ►	
Grow	
Similar	
Transform Selection	
Load Selection...	
Save Selection...	

- Border...
- Smooth...
- Expand...
- Contract...

MAKE A SELECTION
USING SHAPES

What You'll Do

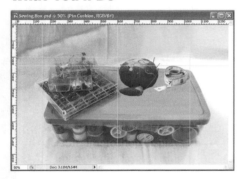

In this lesson, you'll make selections using a marquee tool and a lasso tool, position a selection with the Move Tool, deselect a selection, and drag a complex selection into another image.

Selecting by Shape

The Photoshop selection tools make it easy to select objects that are rectangular or elliptical in nature. It would be a boring world if every image we wanted fell into one of those categories so fortunately, they don't. While some objects are round or square, most are unusual in shape. Making selections can sometimes be a painstaking process because many objects don't have clearly defined edges. To select an object by shape, you need to click the appropriate tool on the toolbox, then drag the pointer around the object. The selected area is defined by a **marquee**, or series of dotted lines, as shown in Figure 1.

Creating a Selection

Drawing a rectangular marquee is easier than drawing an elliptical marquee, but with practice, you'll be able to create both types of marquees easily. Table 1 lists the tools you can use to make selections using shapes. Figure 2 shows a marquee surrounding an irregular shape.

> QUICKTIP
>
> A marquee is sometimes referred to as *marching ants* because the dots within the marquee appear to be moving.

Using Fastening Points

Each time you click one of the marquee tools, a fastening point is added to the image. A **fastening point** is an anchor within the marquee. When the marquee pointer reaches the initial fastening point (after making its way around the image), a very small circle appears on the pointer, indicating that you have reached the starting point. Clicking the pointer when this circle appears closes the marquee. Some fastening points, such as those in a circular marquee, are not visible, while others, such as those created by the Polygonal or Magnetic Lasso Tools, are visible.

Selecting, Deselecting, and Reselecting

After a selection is made, you can move, copy, transform, or make adjustments to it. A selection stays selected until you unselect, or **deselect**, it. You can deselect a selection by clicking Select on the menu bar, then clicking Deselect. You can reselect a deselected object by clicking Select on the menu bar, then clicking Reselect.

QUICKTIP

You can select the entire image by clicking Select on the menu bar, then clicking All.

FIGURE 1

Elliptical Marquee Tool used to create marquee

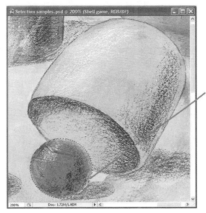

Elliptical Marquee Tool surrounds object

FIGURE 2

Marquee surrounding irregular shape

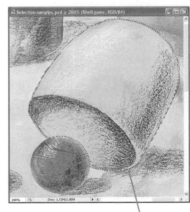

Marquee surrounding irregular shape

TABLE 1: Selection Tools by Shape

tool	button	effect
Rectangular Marquee Tool	⬚	Creates a rectangular selection. Press [Shift] while dragging to create a square.
Elliptical Marquee Tool	○	Creates an elliptical selection. Press [Shift] while dragging to create a circle.
Single Row Marquee Tool	⚏	Creates a 1-pixel-wide row selection.
Single Column Marquee Tool	⁞	Creates a 1-pixel-wide column selection.
Lasso Tool	♄	Creates a freehand selection.
Polygonal Lasso Tool	⟡	Creates straight line selections. Press [Alt] (Win) or [option] (Mac) to create freehand segments.
Magnetic Lasso Tool	⟡	Creates selections that snap to an edge of an object. Press [Alt] (Win) or [option] (Mac) to alternate between freehand and magnetic line segments.

Placing a Selection

You can place a selection in a Photoshop image in many ways. You can copy or cut a selection, then paste it to a different location in the same image or to a different image. You can also use the Move Tool to drag a selection to a new location.

QUICKTIP

You can temporarily change *any selected tool* into the Move Tool by pressing and holding [Ctrl] (Win) or [⌘] (Mac). When you're finished dragging the selection, release [Ctrl] (Win) or [⌘] (Mac), and the functionality of the originally selected tool returns.

Using Guides

Guides are non-printable horizontal and vertical lines that you can display on top of an image to help you position a selection. You can create an unlimited number of horizontal and vertical guides. You create a guide by displaying the rulers, positioning the pointer on either ruler, then clicking and dragging the guide into position. Figure 3 shows the creation of a vertical guide in a file that contains two existing guides. You delete a guide by selecting the Move Tool on the toolbox, positioning the pointer over the guide, then clicking and dragging it back to its

ruler. If the Snap feature is enabled, as you drag an object toward a guide, the object will be pulled toward the guide. To turn on the Snap feature, click View on the menu bar, then click Snap. A check mark appears to the left of the command if the feature is enabled.

QUICKTIP

Double-click a guide to open the Preferences dialog box to change guide colors, width, and other features.

FIGURE 3
Vertical guide added with two existing guides

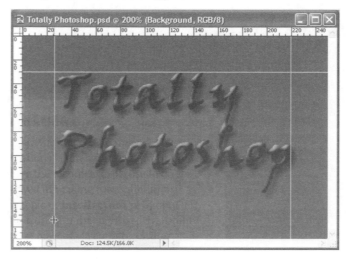

FIGURE 4
Rectangular Marquee Tool selection

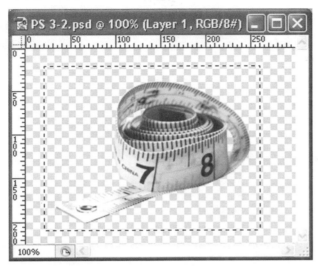

TABLE 2: Working with a Selection

if you want to	then do this
Move a selection (an image) using the mouse	Position the ⬚⊹ over the selection, then drag the marquee and its contents
Copy a selection to the Clipboard	Activate image containing the selection, click Edit ➤ Copy
Cut a selection to the Clipboard	Activate image containing the selection, click Edit ➤ Cut
Paste a selection from the Clipboard	Activate image where you want the selection, click Edit ➤ Paste
Delete a selection	Make selection, then press [Delete] (Win) or [delete] (Mac)
Deselect a selection	Press [Esc] (Win) or [D] (Mac)

Create a selection with the Rectangular Marquee Tool

1. Start Photoshop, open PS 3-1.psd from the drive and folder where your Data Files are stored, then save it as **Sewing Box**.

2. Display the rulers (if they are not already displayed) in pixels.

3. Open PS 3-2.psd, then display the rulers in pixels for this image (if they are not displayed).

4. Click the **Rectangular Marquee Tool** ⬚ on the toolbox.

5. Make sure the value in the Feather text box on the options bar is 0 px.

   Feathering determines the amount of blur between the selection and the pixels surrounding it.

6. Drag the **Marquee pointer** ┼ to select the tape measure from approximately **20 H/20 V** to **260 H/210 V**. See Figure 4.

   The first measurement refers to the horizontal ruler (H); the second measurement refers to the vertical ruler (V).

   | TIP You can also use the X/Y coordinates displayed in the lower-left corner of the Info palette.

7. Click the **Move Tool** ⬚⊹ on the toolbox, then drag the selection to any location in the Sewing Box image.

   The selection now appears in the Sewing Box image on a new layer (Layer 1).

   | TIP Table 2 describes methods you can use to work with selections in an image.

Using the Rectangular Marquee Tool, you created a selection in an image, then you dragged that selection into another image. This left the original image intact, and created a copy of the selection in the image you dragged it to.

Position a selection with the Move Tool

1. Verify that the **Move Tool** ⊹ is selected on the toolbox.

2. If you do not see guides in the Sewing Box image, click **View** on the menu bar, point to **Show**, then click **Guides**.

3. Drag the tape measure so that the top-right corner snaps to the ruler guides at approximately **1030 H/330 V**. Compare your image to Figure 5.

   Did you feel the snap to effect as you positioned the selection within the guides? This feature makes it easy to properly position objects within an image.

   > TIP   If you didn't feel the image snap to the guides, click View on the menu bar, point to Snap To, then click Guides.

4. Rename Layer 1 **Tape Measure**.

You used the Move Tool to reposition a selection in an existing image, then you renamed the layer.

FIGURE 5
Rectangular selection in image

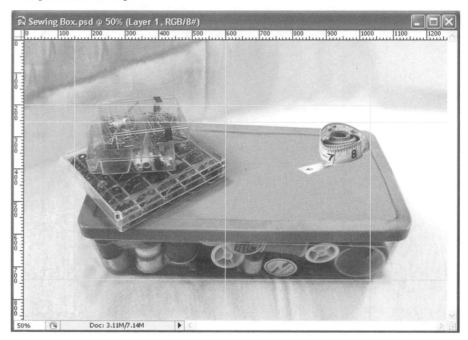

Using Smart Guides

Wouldn't it be great to be able to see a vertical or horizontal guide as you move an object? Using Smart Guides, you can do just that. Smart Guides are turned on by clicking View on the menu bar, pointing to Show, then clicking Smart Guides. Once this feature is turned on, horizontal and vertical purple guide lines appear automatically when you draw a shape or move an object. This feature allows you to align layer content as you move it.

FIGURE 6
Deselect command

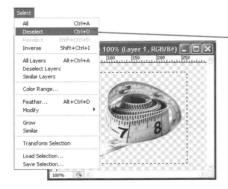

Shortcut can be
used instead of
clicking the menu

Deselect a selection

1. Click **Window** on the menu bar, then click
   PS 3-2.psd.

   TIP   If you can see the window of the
   image you want anywhere on the screen,
   you can just click it to make it active instead
   of using the Window menu.

2. Click **Select** on the menu bar, then click
   Deselect, as shown in Figure 6.

*You hid the active layer, then used the Deselect
command on the Select menu to deselect the
object you had moved into this image. When you
deselect a selection, the marquee no longer
surrounds it.*

FIGURE 7
Save Selection dialog box

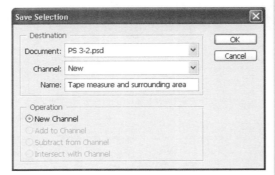

Saving and loading a selection

Any selection can be saved independently of the surrounding image, so that if you
want to use it again in the image, you can do so without having to retrace it using one
of the marquee tools. Once a selection is made, you can save it in the image by clicking Select on the menu bar, then clicking Save Selection. The Save Selection dialog
box opens, as shown in Figure 7; be sure to give the selection a meaningful name.
When you want to load a saved selection, click Select on the menu bar, then click Load
Selection. Click the Channel list arrow, click the named selection, then click OK.

Create a selection with the Magnetic Lasso Tool

1. Click the **Magnetic Lasso Tool** 🐾 on the toolbox, then change the settings on the options bar so that they are the same as those shown in Figure 8. Table 3 describes Magnetic Lasso Tool settings.

2. Open PS 3-3.psd from the drive and folder where your Data Files are stored.

3. Click the **Magnetic Lasso Tool pointer** 🐾 once anywhere on the edge of the pin cushion, to create your first fastening point.

   TIP   If you click on a spot that is not at the edge of the pin cushion, press [Esc] (win) or ⌘ [Z] (Mac) to undo the action, then start again.

4. Drag the **Magnetic Lasso Tool pointer** 🐾 slowly around the pin cushion (clicking at the top of each pin may be helpful) until it is almost entirely selected, as shown in Figure 9, then click directly over the initial fastening point.

   Don't worry about all the nooks and crannies surrounding the pin cushion: the Magnetic Lasso Tool will select those automatically. You will see a small circle next to the pointer when it is directly over the initial fastening point, indicating that you are closing the selection. The individual segments turn into a marquee.

   TIP   If you feel that the Magnetic Lasso Tool is missing some major details while you're tracing, you can insert additional fastening points by clicking the pointer while dragging. For example, click the mouse button at a location where you want to change the selection shape.

You created a selection with the Magnetic Lasso Tool.

FIGURE 8
Options for the Magnetic Lasso Tool

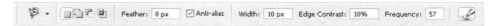

FIGURE 9
Creating a selection with the Magnetic Lasso Tool

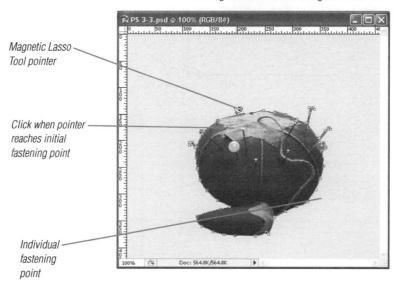

Magnetic Lasso Tool pointer

Click when pointer reaches initial fastening point

Individual fastening point

Mastering the art of selections

You might feel that it is difficult when you first start making selections. Making selections is a skill, and like most skills, it takes a lot of practice to become proficient. In addition to practice, make sure that you're comfortable in your work area, that your hands are steady, and that your mouse is working well. A non-optical mouse that is dirty will make selecting an onerous task, so make sure your mouse is well cared for and is functioning correctly.

FIGURE 10

Selection copied into image

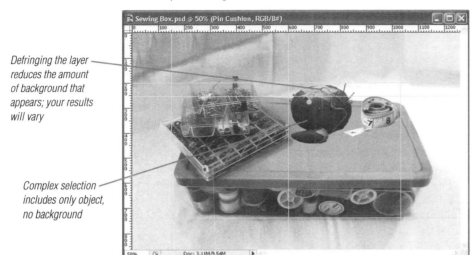

Defringing the layer reduces the amount of background that appears; your results will vary

Complex selection includes only object, no background

TABLE 3: Magnetic Lasso Tool settings

setting	description
Feather	The amount of blur between the selection and the pixels surrounding it. This setting is measured in pixels and can be a value between 0 and 250.
Anti-alias	The smoothness of the selection, achieved by softening the color transition between edge and background pixels.
Width	The interior width by detecting an edge from the pointer. This setting is measured in pixels and can have a value from 1 to 40.
Edge Contrast	The tool's sensitivity. This setting can be a value between 1% and 100%: higher values detect high-contrast edges.
Frequency	The rate at which fastening points are applied. This setting can be a value between 0 and 100: higher values insert more fastening points.

Move a complex selection to an existing image

1. Click the **Move Tool** ⯈⊹ on the toolbox.

   TIP You can also click the Click to open the Tool Preset picker list arrow on the options bar, then double-click the Move Tool.

2. Use the **Move Tool pointer** ⯈ₛₑ to drag the pin cushion selection to the Sewing Box image.

   The selection appears on a new layer (Layer 1).

3. Drag the object so that the left edge of the pin cushion snaps to the guide at approximately **600 Y** and the top of the pin cushion snaps to the guide at **200 X** using the coordinates on the info palette.

4. Use the Layer menu to defringe the new Layer 1 at a width of **1** pixel.

5. Close the PS 3-3.psd image without saving your changes.

6. Rename the new layer **Pin Cushion** in the Sewing Box image.

7. Save your work, then compare your image to Figure 10.

8. Click **Window** on the menu bar, then click **PS 3-2.psd.**

9. Close the PS 3-2.psd image without saving your changes.

You dragged a complex selection into an existing Photoshop image. You positioned the object using ruler guides and renamed a layer. You also defringed a selection to eliminate its white border.

MODIFY A
MARQUEE

What You'll Do

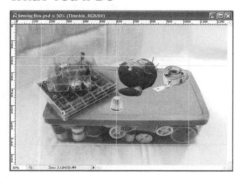

 In this lesson, you'll move and enlarge a marquee, drag a selection into a Photoshop image, then position a selection using ruler guides.

Changing the Size of a Marquee

Not all objects are easy to select. Sometimes, when you make a selection, you might need to change the size or shape of the marquee.

The options bar contains selection buttons that help you add to and subtract from a marquee, or intersect with a selection. The marquee in Figure 11 was modified into the one shown in Figure 12 by clicking the Add to selection button. After the Add to selection button is active, you can draw an additional marquee (directly adjacent to the selection), and it will be added to the current marquee.

One method you can use to increase the size of a marquee is the Grow command. After you make a selection, you can increase the marquee size by clicking Select on the menu bar, then by clicking Grow. The Grow command selects pixels adjacent to the marquee that have colors

similar to those specified by the Magic Wand Tool. (The Similar command selects both adjacent and non-adjacent pixels.)

QUICKTIP
While the Grow command selects adjacent pixels that have similar colors, the Expand command increases a selection by a specific number of pixels.

Modifying a Marquee

While a selection is active, you can modify the marquee by expanding or contracting it, smoothing out its edges, or enlarging it to add a border around the selection. These four commands: Border, Smooth, Expand, and Contract are sub-menus of the Modify command, which is found on the Select menu. For example, you might want to enlarge your selection. Using the Expand command, you can increase the size of the selection, as shown in Figure 13.

Moving a Marquee

After you create a marquee, you can move the marquee to another location in the same image or to another image entirely. You might want to move a marquee if you've drawn it in the wrong image or the wrong location. Sometimes it's easier to draw a marquee elsewhere on the page, and then move it to the desired location.

QUICKTIP

You can always hide and display layers as necessary to facilitate making a selection.

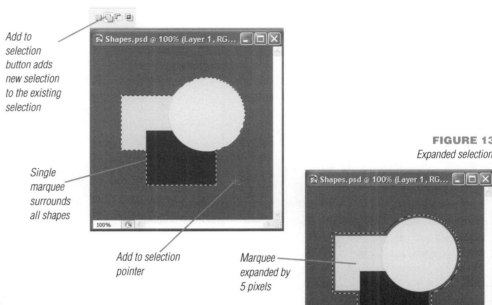

FIGURE 12
Selection with additions

Add to selection button adds new selection to the existing selection

Single marquee surrounds all shapes

Add to selection pointer

FIGURE 11
New selection

New selection button used to create a selection

Marquee surrounds rectangle

FIGURE 13
Expanded selection

Marquee expanded by 5 pixels

Adding and subtracting from a selection

Of course knowing how to make a selection is important, but it's just as important to know how to make alterations in an existing selection. Sometimes it's almost impossible to create that perfect marquee at first try. Perhaps your hand moved while you were tracing, or you just got distracted. Using the Add to selection, Subtract from selection, and Intersect with selection buttons (which appear with all selection tools), you can alter an existing marquee without having to start from scratch.

Move a marquee

1. Open PS 3-4.psd from the drive and folder where your Data Files are stored. Change the status bar display to show document sizes, then change the zoom factor to 200%.

2. Click the **Elliptical Marquee Tool** ○ on the toolbox.

   TIP The Elliptical Marquee Tool might be hidden under the Rectangular Marquee Tool.

3. Click the **New selection button** ▣ on the options bar (if it is not already selected).

4. Drag the **Marquee pointer** ╋ to select the area from approximately **150 X/50 Y** to **200 X/130 Y**. Compare your image to Figure 14.

5. Position the **pointer** ▷⋮⋮ in the center of the selection.

6. Drag the **Move pointer** ▶ so the marquee covers the thimble, at approximately **100 X/100 Y**, as shown in Figure 15.

   TIP You can also nudge a selection to move it, by pressing the arrow keys. Each time you press an arrow key, the selection moves one pixel in the direction of the arrow.

You created a marquee, then dragged the marquee to reposition it.

FIGURE 14
Selection in image

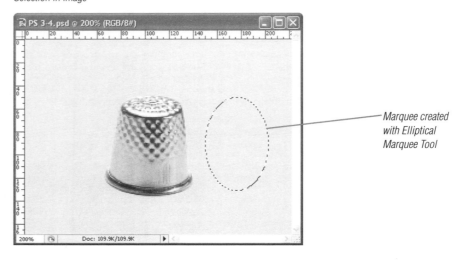

Marquee created
with Elliptical
Marquee Tool

FIGURE 15
Moved selection

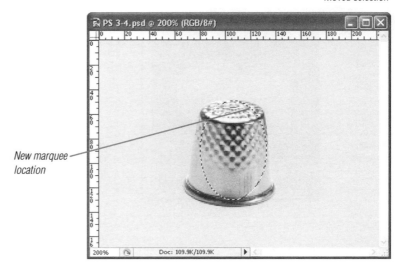

New marquee
location

FIGURE 16

Magic Wand settings

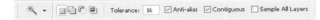

FIGURE 17

Smoothed selection

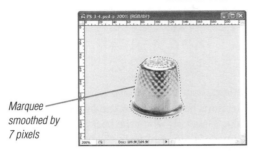

Marquee
smoothed by
7 pixels

FIGURE 18

Smoothed selection moved to the Sewing Box image

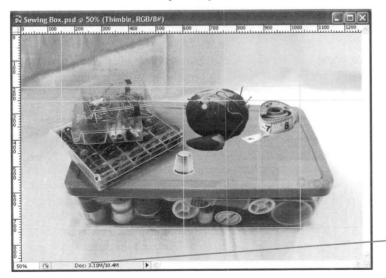

The document size
for your image
may differ

Enlarge a marquee

1. Click the **Magic Wand Tool** ✎ on the tool-box, then adjust your settings using Figure 16 as a guide.

2. Click **Select** on the menu bar, click **Similar**.

3. Click **Select** on the menu bar, point to **Modify**, then click **Expand**.

4. Type **1** in the Expand By text box of the Expand Selection dialog box, then click **OK**.

5. Click **Select** on the menu bar, point to **Modify**, then click **Smooth**.

6. Type **4** in the pixels text box, click **OK,** then compare your selection to Figure 17.

7. Click the **Move Tool** ▶♦ on the toolbox.

8. Position the **Move pointer** ▶✂ over the selection, then drag the thimble to the Sewing Box image.

9. Drag the thimble so that it is below and to the left of the pin cushion, centered on the guide at 600 X.

10. Defringe the thimble using a setting of **1** pixel.

11. Rename the new layer **Thimble**.

12. Save your work, then compare your image to Figure 18.

13. Make PS 3-4.psd active.

14. Close PS 3-4.psd without saving your changes.

You enlarged a selection marquee by using the Similar, Expand, and Smooth commands, then you dragged the selection into an existing image.

SELECT USING COLOR AND
MODIFY A SELECTION

What You'll Do

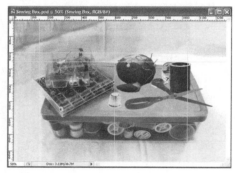

 In this lesson, you'll make selections using both the Color Range command and the Magic Wand Tool. You'll also flip a selection, then fix an image using the Healing Brush Tool.

Selecting with Color

Selections based on color can be easy to make, especially when the background of an image is different from the image itself. High contrast between colors is an ideal condition for making selections based on color. You can make selections using color with the Color Range command on the Select menu, or you can use the Magic Wand Tool on the toolbox.

Using the Magic Wand Tool

When you select the Magic Wand Tool, the following options are available on the options bar, as shown in Figure 19:

- The four selection buttons.

- The Tolerance setting, which allows you to specify whether similar pixels will be selected. This setting has a value from 0 to 255, and the lower the value, the closer in color the selected pixels will be.
- The Anti-alias check box, which softens the selection's appearance.
- The Contiguous check box, which lets you select pixels that are next to one another.
- The Sample All Layers check box, which lets you select pixels from multiple layers at once.

Knowing which selection tool to use

The hardest part of making a selection might be determining which selection tool to use. How are you supposed to know if you should use a marquee tool or a lasso tool? The first question you need to ask yourself is, "What do I want to select?" Becoming proficient in making selections means that you need to assess the qualities of the object you want to select, and then decide which method to use. Ask yourself: Does the object have a definable shape? Does it have an identifiable edge? Are there common colors that can be used to create a selection?

Using the Color Range Command

You can use the Color Range command to make the same selections as with the Magic Wand Tool. When you use the Color Range command, the Color Range dialog box opens. This dialog box lets you use the pointer to identify which colors you want to use to make a selection. You can also select the Invert check box to *exclude* the chosen color from the selection. The **fuzziness** setting is similar to tolerance, in that the lower the value, the closer in color pixels must be to be selected.

QUICKTIP

Unlike the Magic Wand Tool, the Color Range command does not give you the option of excluding contiguous pixels.

Transforming a Selection

After you place a selection in a Photoshop image, you can change its size and other qualities by clicking Edit on the menu bar, pointing to Transform, then clicking any of the commands on the submenu. After you select certain commands, small squares called **handles** surround the selection. To complete the command, you drag a handle until the image has the look you want, then press [Enter] (Win) or [return] (Mac). You can also use the Transform submenu to flip a selection horizontally or vertically.

Understanding the Healing Brush Tool

If you place a selection then notice that the image has a few imperfections, you can fix the image. You can fix imperfections such as dirt, scratches, bulging veins on skin, or wrinkles on a face using the Healing Brush Tool on the toolbox.

QUICKTIP

When correcting someone's portrait, make sure your subject looks the way he or she *thinks* they look. That's not always possible, but strive to get as close as you can to their ideal!

Using the Healing Brush Tool

This tool lets you sample an area, then paint over the imperfections. What is the result? The less-than-desirable pixels seem to disappear into the surrounding image. In addition to matching the sampled pixels, the Healing Brush Tool also matches the texture, lighting, and shading of the sample. This is why the painted pixels blend so effortlessly into the existing image. Corrections can be painted using broad strokes, or using clicks of the mouse.

QUICKTIP

To take a sample, press and hold [Alt] (Win) or [option] (Mac) while dragging the pointer over the area you want to duplicate.

FIGURE 19
Options for the Magic Wand Tool

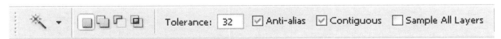

Select using color range

1. Open PS 3-5.psd from the drive and folder where your Data Files are stored.

2. Click **Select** on the menu bar, then click **Color Range**.

3. Click the **Image option button** (if it is not already selected).

4. Click the **Invert check box** to add a check mark.

5. Verify that your settings match those shown in Figure 20, then click **OK**.

6. Click anywhere in the gray area surrounding the sample image, then click **OK**.

   The Color Range dialog box closes and the spool of thread in the image is selected.

7. Click the **Move Tool** ⊹ on the toolbox.

8. Drag the selection into Sewing Box.psd, then position the selection as shown in Figure 21.

9. Rename the new layer **Thread**.

10. Activate PS 3-5.psd, then close this file without saving any changes.

You made a selection within an image using the Color Range command on the Select menu, and dragged the selection to an existing image.

FIGURE 20
Completed Color Range dialog box

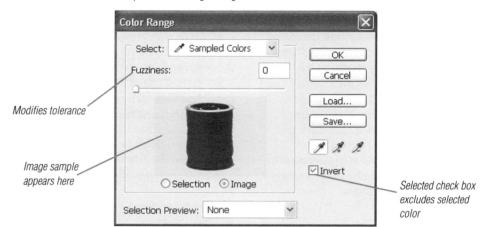

Modifies tolerance

Image sample appears here

Selected check box excludes selected color

FIGURE 21
Selection in image

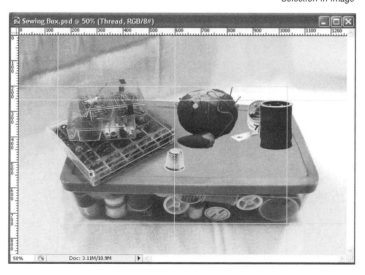

FIGURE 22

Magic Wand Tool settings

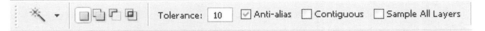

Select using the Magic Wand Tool

1. Open PS 3-6.psd from the drive and folder where your Data Files are stored.

2. Click the **Magic Wand Tool** ✺ on the toolbox.

3. Change the settings on the options bar to match those shown in Figure 22.

4. Click anywhere in the gray area of the image (such as **50 X/50 Y**).

   TIP Had you selected the Contiguous check box, the pixels within the handles *would not* have been selected. The Contiguous check box is a powerful feature of the Magic Wand Tool.

5. Click **Select** on the menu bar, then click **Inverse**. Compare your selection to Figure 23.

6. Click the **Move Tool** ▸ on the toolbox, then drag the selection into Sewing Box.psd.

You made a selection using the Magic Wand Tool, then dragged it into an existing image. The Magic Wand Tool is just one more way you can make a selection. One advantage of using the Magic Wand Tool is the Contiguous check box, which lets you choose pixels that are next to one another.

FIGURE 23

Selected area

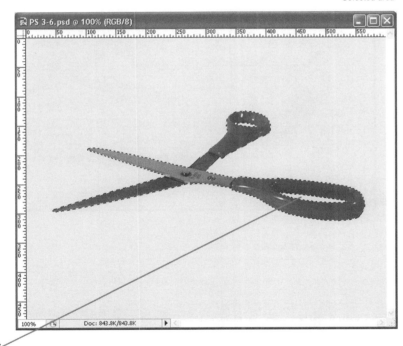

Selection excludes
background color

Flip a selection

1. Click **Edit** on the menu bar, point to **Transform**, then click **Flip Horizontal**.

2. Rename Layer 1 using the name **Scissors**.

3. Defringe **Scissors** using a **1** pixel setting.

4. Drag the flipped selection with the **Move Tool pointer** ▶⊹ so it is positioned as shown in Figure 24.

5. Make PS 3-6.psd the active file, then close PS 3-6.psd without saving your changes.

6. Save your work.

You flipped and repositioned a selection. Sometimes it's helpful to flip an object to help direct the viewer's eye to a desired focal point.

FIGURE 24
Flipped and positioned selection

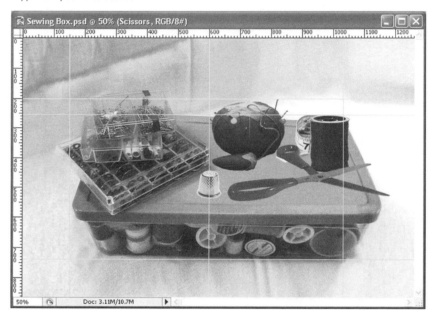

Getting Rid of Red Eye

When digital photos of your favorite people have that annoying red eye, what do you do? You use the Red Eye Tool to eliminate this effect. To do this, select the Red Eye Tool (which is grouped on the toolbox with the Spot Healing Brush Tool, the Healing Brush Tool, and the Patch Tool), then either click a red area of an eye or draw a selection over one red eye. When you release the mouse button, the red eye effect is removed.

FIGURE 25
Healing Brush Tool options

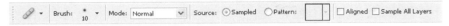

FIGURE 26
Healed area

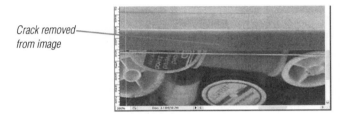

Crack removed—
from image

FIGURE 27
Image after using the Healing Brush Tool

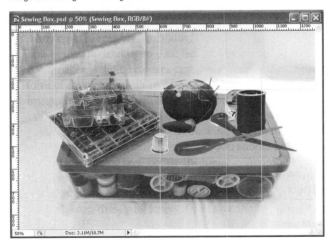

Fix imperfections with the Healing Brush Tool

1. Click the **Sewing Box layer** on the Layers palette, then click the **Zoom Tool** 🔍 on the toolbox.

2. Click the image with the **Zoom Tool pointer** ⊕ above the pink spool of thread, (in the box) at **750 X/600 Y** until the zoom factor is 200% and you can see the crack in the box.

3. Click the **Healing Brush Tool** 🖊 on the toolbox. Change the setting on the options bar to match those shown in Figure 25.

   > TIP   If you need to change the Brush settings, click the Brush list arrow on the options bar, then drag the sliders so the settings are 10 px diameter, 0% hardness, 1% spacing, 0° angle, 100% round-ness, and pen pressure size.

4. Press and hold **[Alt]** (Win) or **[option]** (Mac), click next to the crack at any location on the green lid, such as **700 X/580 Y**, then release **[Alt]** (Win) or **[option]** (Mac).

   You sampled an area of the box that is not cracked so that you can use the Healing Brush Tool to paint a damaged area with the sample.

5. Click the crack (at approximately **720 X/580 Y**).

6. Repeat steps 4 and 5, each time choosing a new source location, then clicking at a parallel location on the crack.

   Compare the repaired area to Figure 26.

7. Click the **Zoom Tool** 🔍 on the toolbox, press and hold **[Alt]** (Win) or **[option]** (Mac), click the center of the image with the **Zoom Tool pointer** ⊖ until the zoom factor is 50%, then release **[Alt]** (Win) or **[option]** (Mac).

8. Save your work, then compare your image to Figure 27.

You used the Healing Brush Tool to fix an imperfection in an image.

ADD A VIGNETTE EFFECT
TO A SELECTION

What You'll Do

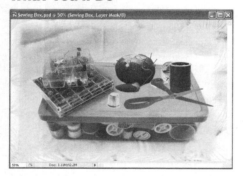

In this lesson, you'll create a vignette effect, using a layer mask and feathering.

Understanding Vignettes

Traditionally, a **vignette** is a picture or portrait whose border fades into the surrounding color at its edges. You can use a vignette effect to give an image an old-world appearance. You can also use a vignette effect to tone down an overwhelming background. You can create a vignette effect in Photoshop by creating a mask with a blurred edge. A **mask** lets you protect or modify a particular area and is created using a marquee.

Creating a Vignette

A **vignette effect** uses feathering to fade a marquee shape. The **feather** setting blurs the area between the selection and the surrounding pixels, which creates a distinctive fade at the edge of the selection. You can create a vignette effect by using a marquee or lasso tool to create a marquee in an image layer. After the selection is created, you can modify the feather setting (a 10- or 20-pixel setting creates a nice fade) to increase the blur effect on the outside edge of the selection.

Getting that Healing Feeling

The Spot Healing Brush Tool works in much the same way as the Healing Brush Tool in that it removes blemishes and other imperfections. Unlike the Healing Brush Tool, the Spot Healing Brush Tool does not require you to take a sample. When using the Spot Healing Brush Tool, you must choose whether you want to use a proximity match type (which uses pixels around the edge of the selection as a patch) or a create texture type (which uses all the pixels in the selection to create a texture that is used to fix the area). You also have the option of sampling all the visible layers or only the active layer.

FIGURE 28
Marquee in image

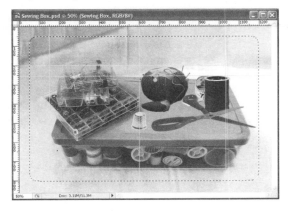

FIGURE 30
Vignette in image

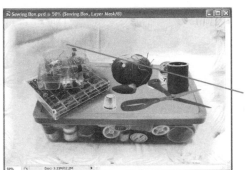

Vignette effect fades border

Lesson 4   Add a Vignette Effect to a Selection

FIGURE 29
Layers palette

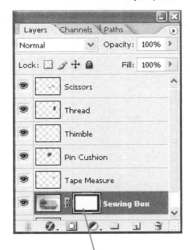

Feathered mask creates vignette effect

Create a vignette

1. Verify that the **Sewing Box layer** is selected.

2. Click the **Rectangular Marquee Tool** [⬚] on the toolbox.

3. Change the **Feather setting** on the options bar to **20px**.

4. Create a selection with the **Marquee pointer** ╬ from **50 X/50 Y** to **1200 X/800 Y**, as shown in Figure 28.

5. Click **Layer** on the menu bar, point to **Layer Mask**, then click **Reveal Selection**.

   The vignette effect is added to the layer.

   Compare your Layers palette to Figure 29.

6. Click **View** on the menu bar, then click **Rulers** to hide them.

7. Click **View** on the menu bar, then click **Clear Guides**.

8. Save your work, then compare your image to Figure 30.

9. Close the Sewing Box image, then exit Photoshop.

You created a vignette effect by adding a feathered layer mask. You also rearranged layers and defringed a selection. Once the image was finished, you hid the rulers and cleared the guides.

Power User Shortcuts

to do this:	use this method:
Copy selection	Click Edit ➤ Copy or [Ctrl][C] (Win) or ⌘[C] (Mac)
Create vignette effect	Marquee or Lasso Tool, create selection, click Layer ➤ Layer Mask ➤ Reveal Selection
Cut selection	Click Edit ➤ Cut or [Ctrl][X] (Win) or ⌘[X] (Mac)
Deselect object	Select ➤ Deselect or [Ctrl][D] (Win) or ⌘[D] (Mac)
Elliptical Marquee Tool	◯ or Shift M
Flip image	Edit ➤ Transform ➤ Flip Horizontal
Grow selection	Select ➤ Grow
Increase selection	Select ➤ Similar
Lasso Tool	◯ or Shift L
Magnetic Lasso Tool	◗ or Shift L
Move Tool	▶⊕ or V

to do this:	use this method:
Move selection marquee	Position pointer in selection, drag ▶⊕ to new location
Paste selection	Edit ➤ Paste or [Ctrl][V] (Win) or ⌘[V] (Mac)
Polygonal Lasso Tool	◗ or Shift L
Rectangular Marquee Tool	⬚ or Shift M
Reselect a deselected object	Select ➤ Reselect, or [Shift][Ctrl][D] (Win) or [Shift]⌘[D] (Mac)
Select all objects	Select ➤ All, or [Ctrl][A] (Win) or ⌘[A] (Mac)
Select using color range	Select ➤ Color Range, click in sample area
Select using Magic Wand	✳ or W, then click image
Single Column Marquee Tool	▯
Single Row Marquee Tool	⊏⊐

Key: Menu items are indicated by ➤ between the menu name and its command.

Compositing is one of the most important skills you can learn in Photoshop. If you can combine images, you will be able to take advantage of the many image sources at your disposal. You have learned several techniques to use to make a selection. You have learned to make selections by tracing the edges of objects, or by selecting using color, using menu commands and tools. You learned how to change the shape of a selection or move the marquee. You learned that you can drag the selected imagery from one file into another Photoshop file. You also learned how to fix imperfections in images and make a vignette.

What You Have Learned:

- How to make, move, and deselect a selection.
- How to change the shape of a marquee.
- How to make a selection using the Magic Wand Tool.
- How to create a vignette effect.

Key Terms

Compositing Technique in which images from different sources are combined.

Deselect Process of unselecting a marquee.

Fastening point Anchor point within the marquee.

Guides Non-printable horizontal and vertical lines that you can display on top of an image to help you position a selection.

Handles Small squares that surround a selection.

Vignette Picture or portrait whose border fades into the surrounding color at its edges.

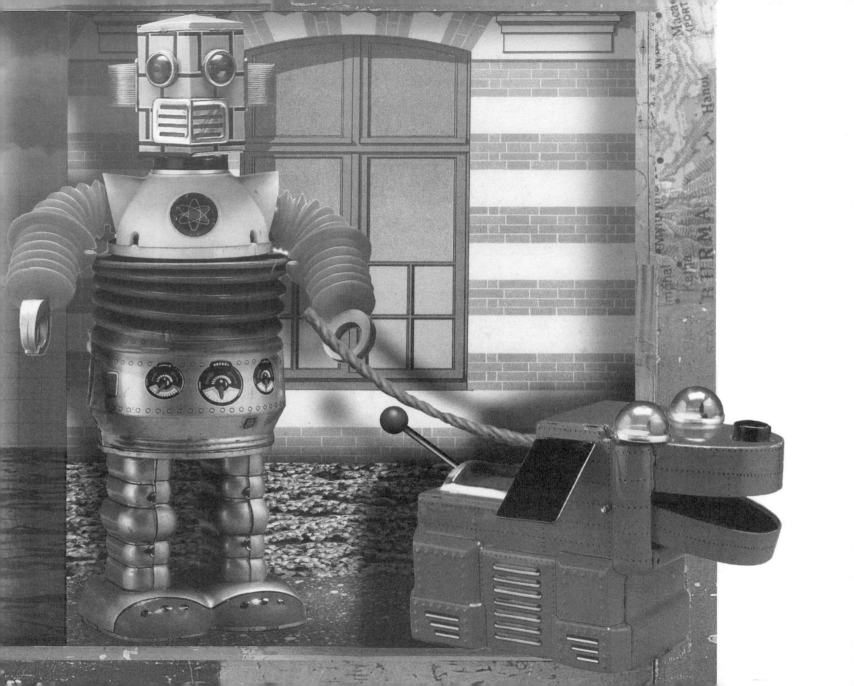

4

INCORPORATING COLOR
TECHNIQUES

1. Work with color to transform an image.

2. Use the Color Picker and the Swatches palette.

3. Place a border around an image.

4. Blend colors using the Gradient Tool.

5. Add color to a grayscale image.

6. Use filters, opacity, and blending modes.

7. Match colors.

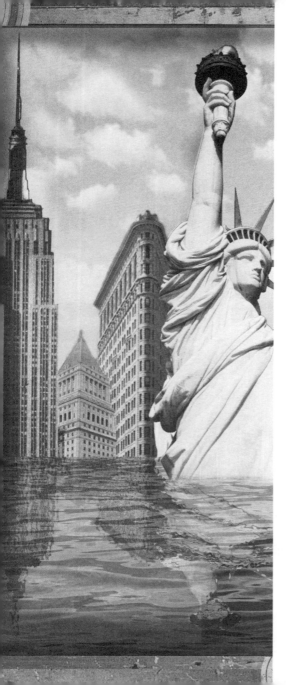

Using Color

Color can make or break an image. Sometimes colors can draw us into an image; other times they can repel us. We all know what colors we like, but when it comes to creating an image, it is helpful to have some knowledge of color theory and be familiar with color terminology.

Understanding how Photoshop measures, displays, and prints color can be valuable when you create new images or modify existing images. Some colors you choose might be difficult for a professional printer to reproduce or might look muddy when printed. As you become more experienced using colors, you will learn which colors can be reproduced well and which ones cannot.

Understanding Color Modes and Color Models

Photoshop displays and prints images using specific color modes. A **mode** is the amount of color data that can be stored in a given file format, based on an established model. A **model** determines how pigments combine to produce resulting colors. This is the way your computer or printer associates a name or numbers with colors. Photoshop uses standard color models as the basis for its color modes.

Displaying and Printing Images

An image displayed on your monitor, such as an icon on your desktop, is a **bitmap**, a geometric arrangement of different color dots on a rectangular grid. Each dot, called a **pixel**, represents a color or shade. Bitmapped images are *resolution-dependent* and can lose detail—often demonstrated by a jagged appearance—when highly magnified. When printed, images with high resolutions tend to show more detail and subtler color transitions than low-resolution images.

Tools You'll Use

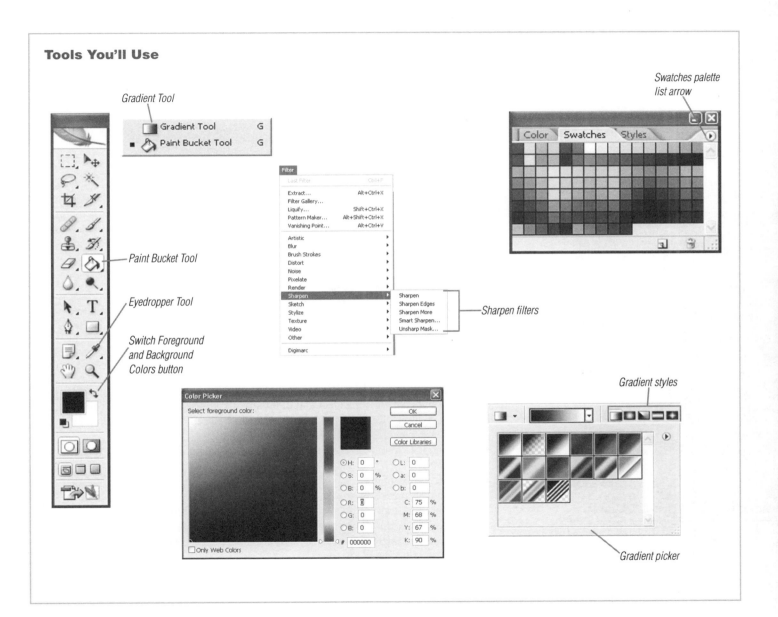

Gradient Tool

Gradient Tool   G
Paint Bucket Tool   G

Paint Bucket Tool

Eyedropper Tool

Switch Foreground and Background Colors button

Swatches palette list arrow

Sharpen filters

Gradient styles

Gradient picker

WORK WITH COLOR TO
TRANSFORM AN IMAGE

What You'll Do

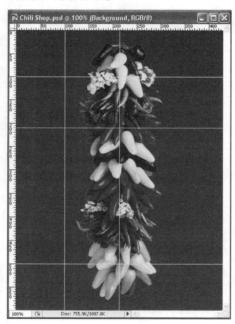

In this lesson, you'll use the Color palette, the Paint Bucket Tool, and the Eyedropper Tool to change the background color of an image.

Learning About Color Models

Photoshop reproduces colors using models of color modes. The range of displayed colors, or **gamut**, for each model available in Photoshop is shown in Figure 1. The shape of each color gamut indicates the range of colors it can display. If a color is out of gamut, it is beyond the color space that your monitor can display or that your printer can print. You select the color mode from the Mode command on the Image menu. The available Photoshop color models are L*a*b, HSB, RGB, CMYK, Bitmap, and Grayscale.

QUICKTIP

A color mode is used to determine which color model will be used to display and print an image.

DESIGNTIP   **Understanding the psychology of color**

Have you ever wondered why some colors make you react a certain way? You might have noticed that some colors affect you differently than others. Color is such an important part of our lives, and in Photoshop, it's key. Specific colors are often used in print and Web pages to evoke the following responses:
- Blue tends to instill a feeling of safety and stability and is often used by financial services.
- Certain shades of green can generate a soft, calming feeling, while others suggest youthfulness and growth.
- Red commands attention and can be used as a call to action; it can also distract a reader's attention from other content.
- White evokes the feeling of purity and innocence, looks cool and fresh, and is often used to suggest luxury.
- Black conveys feelings of power and strength, but can also suggest darkness and negativity.

L*a*b Model

The L*a*b model is based on one luminance (lightness) component and two chromatic components (from green to red, and from blue to yellow). Using the L*a*b model has distinct advantages: you have the largest number of colors available to you and the greatest precision with which to create them. You can also create all the colors contained by other color models, which are limited in their respective color ranges. The L*a*b model is device-independent—the colors will not vary, regardless of the hardware. Use this model when working with photo CD images so that you can independently edit the luminance and color values.

HSB Model

Based on the human perception of color, the HSB (Hue, Saturation, Brightness) model has three fundamental characteristics: hue, saturation, and brightness. The color reflected from or transmitted through an object is called **hue**. Expressed as a degree (between 0° and 360°), each hue is identified by a color name (such as red or green). **Saturation** (or *chroma*) is the strength or purity of the color, representing the amount of gray in proportion to hue. Saturation is measured as a percentage from 0% (gray) to 100% (fully saturated). **Brightness** is the measurement of relative lightness or darkness of a color and is measured as a percentage from 0% (black) to 100% (white). Although you can use the HSB model to define a color on the Color palette or in the Color Picker dialog box, Photoshop does not offer HSB mode as a choice for creating or editing images.

RGB Mode

Photoshop uses color modes to determine how to display and print an image. Each mode is based on established models used in color reproduction. Most colors in the visible spectrum can be represented by mixing various proportions and intensities of red, green, and blue (RGB) colored light. RGB colors are additive colors. **Additive colors** are used for lighting, video, and computer monitors; color is created by light passing through red, green, and blue phosphors. When the values of red, green, and blue are zero, the result is black; when the values are all 255, the result is white. Photoshop assigns each component of the RGB mode an intensity value. Your colors can vary from monitor to monitor even if you are using the exact RGB values on different computers.

FIGURE 1
Photoshop color gamuts

The gamuts of different color spaces
a. Lab color space encompasses all visible colors
b. RGB color space
c. CMYK color space

QUICKTIP

Colors you see onscreen often vary because color monitors use the RGB mode, which uses red, green, and blue phosphors to create a pixel. Variables such as the manufacturing technique used to apply phosphors to the glass, and the capabilities of your video adapter affect how your monitor displays color.

CMYK Mode

The light-absorbing quality of ink printed on paper is the basis of the CMYK (Cyan, Magenta, Yellow, Black) mode. Unlike the RGB mode—in which components are *combined* to create new colors—the CMYK mode is based on colors being partially *absorbed* as the ink hits the paper and being partially *reflected* back to your eyes. CMYK colors are **subtractive colors**—the *absence* of cyan, magenta, yellow, and black creates white. Subtractive (CMYK) and additive (RGB) colors are complementary colors; a pair from one model creates a color in the other. When combined, cyan, magenta, and yellow absorb all color and produce black. The CMYK mode—in which the lightest colors are assigned the highest percentages of ink colors—is used in four-color process printing. Converting an RGB image into a CMYK image produces a **color separation** (the commercial printing process

of separating colors for use with different inks). Note, however, that because your monitor uses RGB mode, you will not see the exact colors until you print the image, and even then the colors can vary depending on the printer and offset press.

Understanding the Bitmap and Grayscale Modes

In addition to the RGB and CMYK modes, Photoshop provides two specialized color modes: bitmap and grayscale. The **bitmap mode** uses black or white color values to represent image pixels, and is a good choice for images with subtle color gradations, such as photographs or painted images. The **grayscale mode** uses up to 256 shades of gray, assigning a brightness value from 0 (black) to 255 (white) to each pixel. Displayed colors can vary from monitor to monitor even if you use identical color settings on different computers.

Changing Foreground and Background Colors

In Photoshop, the **foreground color** is black by default and is used to paint, fill, and apply a border to a selection. The **background color** is white by default and is used

to make **gradient fills** (gradual blends of multiple colors) and fill in areas of an image that have been erased. You can change foreground and background colors using the Color palette, the Swatches palette, the Color Picker, or the Eyedropper Tool. One method of changing foreground and background colors is **sampling**, in which an existing color is used. You can restore the default colors by clicking the Default Foreground and Background Colors button on the toolbox, shown in Figure 2. You can apply a color to the background of a layer using the Paint Bucket Tool. When you click an image with the Paint Bucket Tool, the current foreground color on the toolbox fills the active layer.

FIGURE 2
Foreground and background color buttons

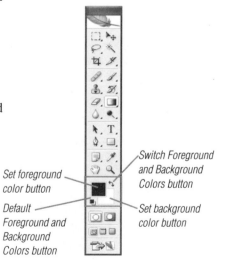

Set foreground color button

Default Foreground and Background Colors button

Switch Foreground and Background Colors button

Set background color button

FIGURE 3
Image with rulers displayed

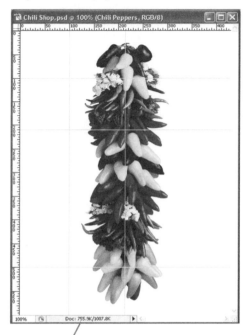

Your document size
may differ

FIGURE 4
Color Settings dialog box

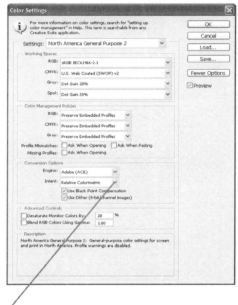

Intent list arrow

1. Start Photoshop, open PS 4-1.psd from the drive and folder where your Data Files are stored, then save it as **Chili Shop**.

2. Click the **Default Foreground and Background Colors button** on the toolbox.

3. Change the status bar so the document sizes display, if necessary.

    TIP Document sizes will not display in the status bar if the image window is too small. Drag the lower-right corner of the image window to expand the window and display the menu button and document sizes.

4. Display the rulers in pixels (if necessary), then compare your screen to Figure 3.

    TIP You can right-click (Win) or [control]-click (Mac) one of the rulers to choose Pixels, Inches, Centimeters, Millimeters, Points, Picas, or Percent as a unit of measurement, instead of using the Rulers and Units Preferences dialog box.

You set the default foreground and background colors and displayed rulers in pixels.

Creating a rendering intent

The use of a **rendering intent** determines how colors are converted by a color management system. A **color management** system is used to keep colors looking consistent as they move between devices. Colors are defined and interpreted using a **profile**. You can create a rendering intent by clicking Edit on the menu bar, then clicking Color Settings. Click the More Options button in the Color Settings dialog box, click the Intent list arrow shown in Figure 4, then click one of the four options. Since a **gamut** is the range of color that a color system can display or print, the rendering intent is constantly evaluating the color gamut and deciding whether or not the colors need adjusting. So, colors that fall inside the destination gamut may not be changed, or they may be adjusted when translated to a smaller color gamut.

Change the background color using the Color palette

1. Click the **Background layer** on the Layers palette.

2. Click the **Color palette tab** Color (if it is not already selected).

3. Drag each color slider on the Color palette until you reach the values shown in Figure 5.

   The active color changes to the new color. Did you notice that this image is using the RGB mode?

   TIP You can also double-click each component's text box on the Color palette and type the color values.

4. Click the **Paint Bucket Tool** on the toolbox.

   TIP If the Paint Bucket Tool is not visible on the toolbox, click the Gradient Tool on the toolbox, press and hold the mouse button until the list of hidden tools appears, then click the Paint Bucket Tool.

5. Click the image with the **Paint Bucket pointer** .

6. Drag the **Paint Bucket state** on the History palette onto the **Delete current state button** .

   TIP You can also undo the last action by clicking Edit on the menu bar, then clicking Undo Paint Bucket.

You set new values in the Color palette, used the Paint Bucket Tool to change the background to that color, then undid the change. You can change colors on the Color palette by dragging the sliders or by typing values in the color text boxes.

FIGURE 5
Color palette with new color

FIGURE 6
Info palette

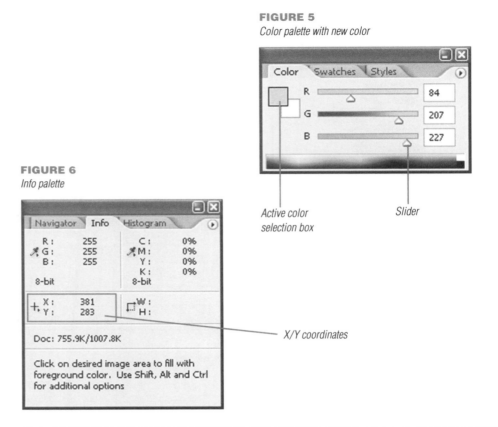

Active color selection box

Slider

X/Y coordinates

Using ruler coordinates

Photoshop rulers run along the top and left sides of the document window. Each point on an image has a horizontal and vertical location. These two numbers, called X and Y coordinates, appear on the Info palette (which is located behind the Navigator palette) as shown in Figure 6. The X coordinate refers to the horizontal location, and the Y coordinate refers to the vertical location. You can use one or both sets of guides to identify coordinates of a location, such as a color you want to sample. If you have difficulty seeing the ruler markings, you can increase the size of the image; the greater the zoom factor, the more detailed the measurement hashes.

FIGURE 7
New foreground color applied to Background layer

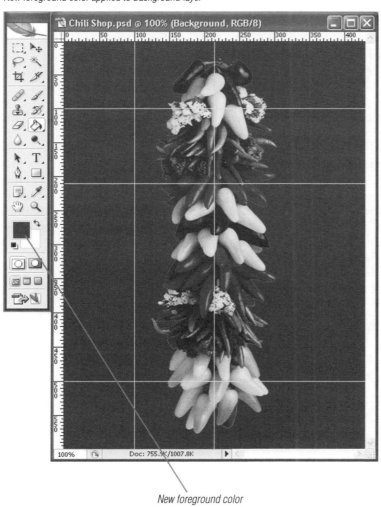

New foreground color

1. Click the **Background layer** on the Layers palette.
2. Click the **Eyedropper Tool** 🖊 on the toolbox.
3. Click the red pepper in the image at coordinates **215 X/210 Y** with the **Eyedropper pointer** 🖊, using the Info palette and the blue guides to help ensure accuracy.

   The Set foreground color button displays the red color that you clicked (or sampled).
4. Click the **Paint Bucket Tool** 🖌 on the toolbox.
5. Click the image, then compare your screen to Figure 7.

   TIP   Your color values on the Color palette might vary from the sample.
6. Save your work.

You used the Eyedropper Tool to sample a color as the foreground color, then used the Paint Bucket Tool to change the background color to the color you sampled. Using the Eyedropper Tool is a convenient way of sampling a color in any Photoshop image.

USE THE COLOR PICKER AND
THE SWATCHES PALETTE

What You'll Do

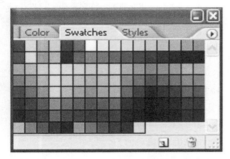

 In this lesson, you'll use the Color Picker and the Swatches palette to select new colors, then you'll add a new color to the background and to the Swatches palette.

Making Selections from the Color Picker

Depending on the color model you are using, you can select colors using the **Color Picker**, a feature that lets you choose a color from a color spectrum or lets you numerically define a custom color. You can change colors in the Color Picker dialog box by using the following methods:

- Drag the sliders along the vertical color bar.
- Click inside the vertical color bar.
- Click a color in the Color field.
- Enter a value in any of the text boxes.

Figure 8 shows a color in the Color Picker dialog box. A circular marker indicates the active color. The color slider displays the range of color levels available for the active color component. The adjustments you make by dragging or clicking a new color are reflected in the text boxes; when you choose a new color, the previous color appears below the new color in the preview area.

Using the Swatches Palette

You can also change colors using the Swatches palette. The **Swatches palette** is a visual display of colors you can choose from, as shown in Figure 9. You can add your own colors to the palette by sampling a color from an image, and you can also delete colors. When you add a swatch to the Swatches palette, Photoshop assigns a default name that has a sequential number, or you can name the swatch whatever you like. Photoshop places new swatches in the first available space at the end of the palette. You can view swatch names by clicking the Swatches palette list arrow, then clicking Small List. You can restore the default Swatches palette by clicking the Swatches palette list arrow, clicking Reset Swatches, then clicking OK.

FIGURE 8
Selecting a new color (pastel cyan) in the Color Picker dialog box

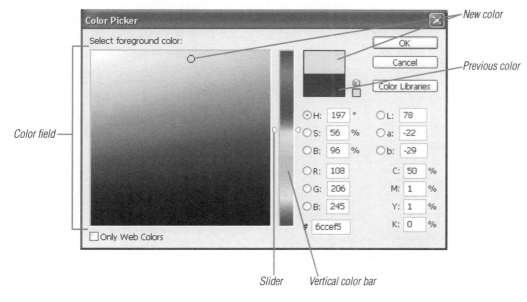

FIGURE 9
Selecting the pastel cyan color on the Swatches palette

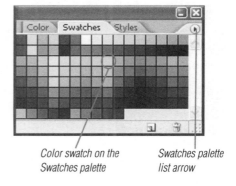

Select a color using the Color Picker dialog box

1. Click the **Set foreground color button** on the toolbox, then verify that the H: option button is selected in the Color Picker dialog box.

2. Click the **R: option button**.

3. Click the **bottom-right corner** of the Color field (purple), as shown in Figure 10.

   TIP   If the Warning: out-of-gamut for printing indicator appears next to the color, then this color exceeds the printable range.

4. Click **OK**.

You opened the Color Picker dialog box, selected a different color palette, and then selected a new color.

Select a color using the Swatches palette

1. Click the **Swatches palette tab** Swatches .

2. Click the **second swatch from the left in the first row** (RGB Yellow), as shown in Figure 11.

   Did you notice that the foreground color on the toolbox changed to a light, bright yellow?

3. Click the **Paint Bucket Tool** on the toolbox (if it is not already selected).

4. Click the image with the **Paint Bucket pointer**, then compare your screen to Figure 12.

You opened the Swatches palette, selected a color, and then used the Paint Bucket Tool to change the background to that color.

FIGURE 10
Color Picker dialog box

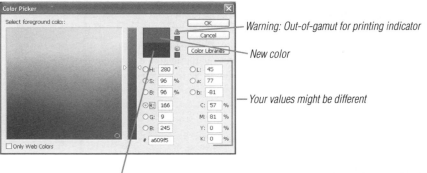

Warning: Out-of-gamut for printing indicator

New color

Your values might be different

Previous color

FIGURE 11
Swatches palette

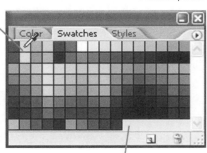

Second swatch from the left

Your swatches on the last row might be different

FIGURE 12
New foreground color applied to Background layer

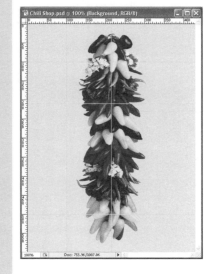

FIGURE 13

Swatch added to Swatches palette

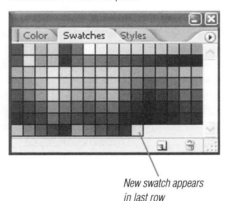

New swatch appears
in last row

1. Click the **Eyedropper Tool** on the toolbox.

2. Click the **light yellow pepper** at coordinates **215 X/65 Y**.

    TIP   When using both the Info palette and the Swatches palette, you'll have to rearrange the palettes so both are visible. Click the Minimize button on the palette tabs to reduce the size of either palette.

3. Click the empty area to the right of the last swatch in the bottom row of the Swatches palette with the **Paint Bucket pointer**.

4. Type **Light Yellow Pepper** in the Name text box.

5. Click **OK** in the Color Swatch Name dialog box.

    TIP   To delete a color from the Swatches palette, press [Alt] (Win) or [option] (Mac), position the pointer over a swatch, then click the swatch.

6. Save your work, then compare the new swatch on your Swatches palette to Figure 13.

You used the Eyedropper Tool to sample a color, and then added the color to the Swatches palette. Adding swatches to the Swatches palette makes it easy to reuse frequently used colors.

PLACE A BORDER AROUND AN IMAGE

What You'll Do

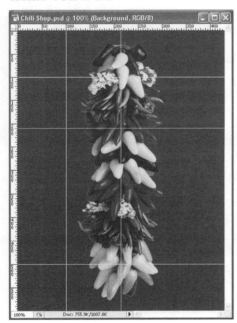

In this lesson, you'll add a border to an image.

Emphasizing an Image

You can emphasize an image by placing a border around its edges. This process is called **stroking the edges**. The default color of the border is the current foreground color on the toolbox. You can change the width, color, location, and blending mode of a border using the Stroke dialog box. The default stroke width is the setting last applied; you can apply a width from 1 to 16 pixels. The location option buttons in the dialog box determine where the border will be placed. If you want to change the location of the stroke, you must first delete the previously applied stroke, or Photoshop will apply the new border over the existing one.

Locking Transparent Pixels

As you modify layers, you can lock some properties to protect their contents. The ability to lock—or protect—elements within a layer is controlled from within the Layers palette, as shown in Figure 14. It's a good idea to lock transparent pixels when you add borders so that stray marks will

not be included in the stroke. You can lock the following layer properties:

- Transparency: Limits editing capabilities to areas in a layer that are opaque.
- Image: Makes it impossible to modify layer pixels using painting tools.
- Position: Prevents pixels within a layer from being moved.

QUICKTIP

You can lock transparency or image pixels only in a layer containing an image, not in one containing type.

FIGURE 14
Layers palette locking options

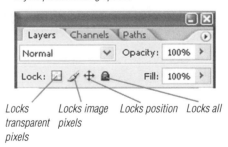

Locks transparent pixels   Locks image pixels   Locks position   Locks all

FIGURE 15
Locking transparent pixels

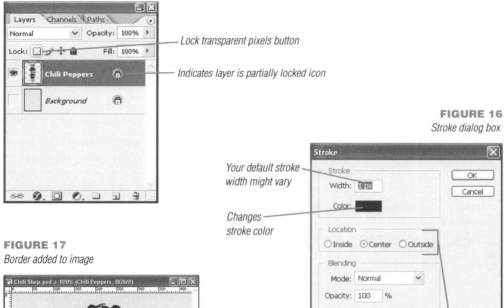

Lock transparent pixels button

Indicates layer is partially locked icon

FIGURE 16
Stroke dialog box

Your default stroke width might vary

Changes stroke color

Location options

FIGURE 17
Border added to image

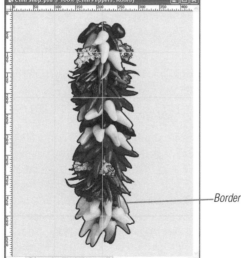

Border

Create a border

1. Click the **Indicates layer visibility button** 👁 on the Background layer on the Layers palette.

   TIP   You can click the Indicates layer visibility button to hide distracting layers.

2. Click the **Default Foreground and Background Colors button** ▪️.

   The foreground color will become the default border color.

3. Click the **Chili Peppers layer** on the Layers palette.

4. Click the **Lock transparent pixels button** ⊠ on the Layers palette. See Figure 15.

   The border will be applied only to the pixels on the edge of the chili peppers.

5. Click **Edit** on the menu bar, then click **Stroke** to open the Stroke dialog box. See Figure 16.

6. Type **3** in the Width text box, click the **Inside option button**, then click **OK**.

   TIP   Determining the correct border location can be confusing. Try different settings until you achieve the look you want.

7. Click the **Indicates layer visibility button** on the Background layer on the Layers palette.

8. Save your work, then compare your image to Figure 17.

You hid a layer, changed the foreground color to black, locked transparent pixels, then used the Stroke dialog box to apply a border to the image. The border makes the image stand out against the background color.

BLEND COLORS USING THE
GRADIENT TOOL

What You'll Do

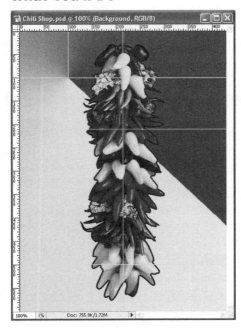

In this lesson, you'll create a gradient fill from a sampled color and a swatch, then apply it to the background.

Understanding Gradients

A **gradient** fill, or simply **gradient**, is a blend of colors used to fill a selection of a layer or an entire layer. A gradient's appearance is determined by its beginning and ending points, and its length, direction, and angle. Gradients allow you to create dramatic effects, using existing color combinations or your own colors. The Gradient picker, as shown in Figure 18, offers multi-color gradient fills and a few that use the current foreground or background colors on the toolbox.

FIGURE 18
Gradient picker

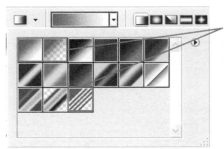

Gradient fills that use current foreground or background colors

Using the Gradient Tool

You use the Gradient Tool to create gradients in images. When you choose the Gradient Tool, five gradient styles become available on the options bar. These styles—Linear, Radial, Angle, Reflected, and Diamond—are shown in Figure 19. In each example, the gradient was drawn from 50 X/50 Y to 100 X/100 Y.

Customizing Gradients

Using the **gradient presets**—predesigned gradient fills that are displayed in the Gradient picker—is a great way to learn how to use gradients. But as you become more familiar with Photoshop, you might want to venture into the world of the unknown and create your own gradient designs. You can create your own designs by modifying an existing gradient using the Gradient Editor. You can open the Gradient Editor, shown in Figure 20, by clicking the selected gradient pattern that appears on the options bar. After it's open, you can use it to make the following modifications:

- Create a new gradient from an existing gradient.
- Modify an existing gradient.
- Add intermediate colors to a gradient.
- Create a blend between more than two colors.
- Adjust the opacity values.
- Determine the placement of the midpoint.

FIGURE 19
Sample gradients

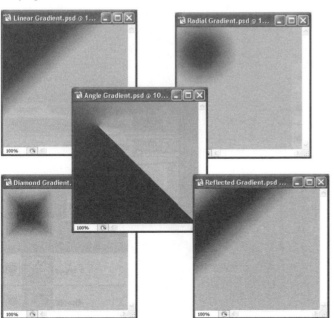

FIGURE 20
Gradient Editor dialog box

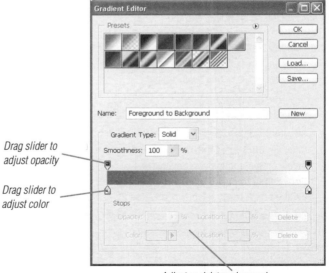

Drag slider to adjust opacity

Drag slider to adjust color

Adjust or delete colors and opacity values

Create a gradient from a sample color

1. Verify that the **Eyedropper Tool** 🖋 is selected.

2. Click a purple flower in the image at coordinates **245 X/450 Y**.

   TIP To accurately select the coordinates, adjust the zoom factor as necessary.

3. Click the **Switch Foreground and Background Colors button** ↺ on the toolbox.

4. Click **Light Yellow Pepper** on the Swatches palette (the new swatch you added) with the **Eyedropper pointer** 🖋.

5. Click the **Indicates layer visibility button** 👁 on the Chili Peppers layer.

6. Click the **Background** layer on the Layers palette to make it active, as shown in Figure 21.

7. Click the **Paint Bucket Tool** 🪣 on the toolbox, then press and hold the mouse button until the list of hidden tools appears.

8. Click the **Gradient Tool** 🔲 on the toolbox, then click the **Angle Gradient button** 🔲 on the options bar (if it is not already selected).

9. Click the **Click to open Gradient picker list arrow** on the options bar, then click **Foreground to Background** (the first gradient fill in the first row), as shown in Figure 22.

You sampled a color on the image to set the background color, changed the foreground color using an existing swatch, selected the Gradient Tool, and then chose a gradient fill and style.

FIGURE 21
Chili Peppers layer hidden

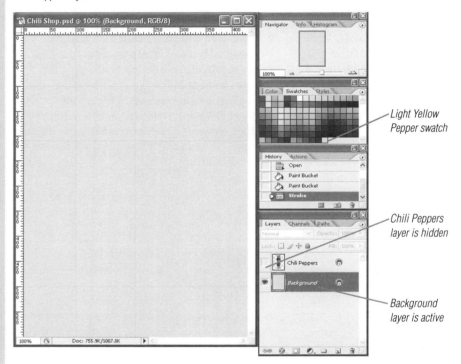

Light Yellow Pepper swatch

Chili Peppers layer is hidden

Background layer is active

FIGURE 22
Gradient picker

Click to open Gradient picker list arrow

Gradient styles

Foreground to Background (current foreground and background colors)

Gradient picker

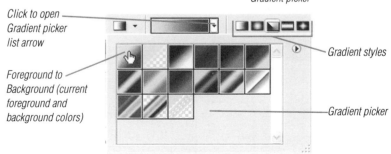

FIGURE 23
Gradient fill applied to Background layer

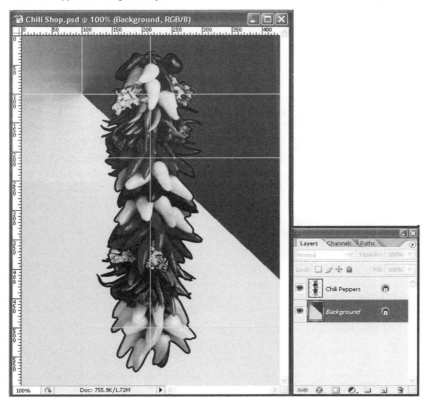

1. Click the **Click to open Gradient picker list arrow** to close the Gradient picker.

   TIP   You can also close the Gradient picker by pressing [Esc] (Win) or [esc] (Mac).

2. Drag the **Gradient pointer** -⁺- from **100 X/ 100 Y** to **215 X/210 Y** using the Info palette and the guides to help you create the gradient in the work area.

3. Click the **Indicates layer visibility button** on the Chili Peppers layer.

   The Chili Peppers layer appears against the new background, as shown in Figure 23.

   TIP   It is a good idea to save your work early and often in the creation process, especially before making significant changes or printing.

4. Save your work.

You applied the gradient fill to the background. You can create dramatic effects using the gradient fill in combination with foreground and background colors.

ADD COLOR TO A GRAYSCALE IMAGE

What You'll Do

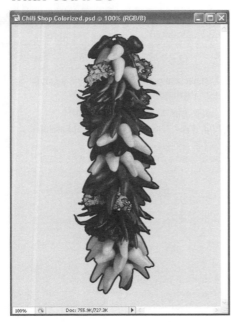

In this lesson, you'll convert an image to grayscale, change the color mode, then colorize a grayscale image using the Hue/Saturation dialog box.

Colorizing Options

Grayscale images can contain up to 256 shades of gray, assigning a brightness value from 0 (black) to 255 (white) to each pixel. Since the earliest days of photography, people have been tinting grayscale images with color to create a certain mood or emphasize an image in a way that purely realistic colors could not. To capture this effect in Photoshop, you convert an image to the Grayscale mode, then choose the color mode you want to work in before you continue. When you apply a color to a grayscale image, each pixel becomes a shade of that particular color instead of gray.

Converting Grayscale and Color Modes

When you convert a color image to grayscale, the light and dark values—called the **luminosity**—remain, while the color information is deleted. When you change from grayscale to a color mode, the foreground and background colors on the toolbox change from black and white to the previously selected colors.

Colorizing a Grayscale Image

In order for a grayscale image to be colorized, you must change the color mode to one that accommodates color. After you change the color mode, and then adjust settings in the Hue/Saturation dialog box, Photoshop determines the colorization range based on the hue of the currently selected foreground color. If you want a different colorization range, you need to change the foreground color.

QUICKTIP

A duotone is a grayscale image that uses two custom ink colors. The final output is dramatically affected by both the order in which the inks are printed and the screen angles that you use.

Tweaking adjustments

Once you have made your color mode conversion to grayscale, you may want to make some adjustments. You can fine-tune the Brightness/Contrast, filters, and blending modes in a grayscale image.

FIGURE 24
Gradient Map dialog box

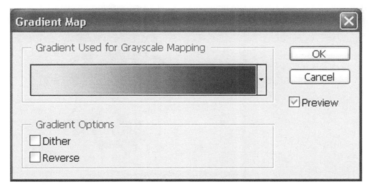

Applying a gradient effect

You can also use the Gradient Map to apply a colored gradient effect to a grayscale image. The Gradient Map uses gradient fills (the same ones displayed in the Gradient picker) to colorize the image, which can produce some stunning effects. You use the Gradient Map dialog box, shown in Figure 24, to apply a gradient effect to a grayscale image. You can access the Gradient Map dialog box using the Adjustments command on the Image menu.

Change the color mode

1. Open PS 4-2.psd from the drive and folder where your Data Files are stored, save it as **Chili Shop Colorized**, then turn off the ruler guides if they are displayed.

2. Click **Image** on the menu bar, point to **Mode**, then click **Grayscale**.

3. Click **Flatten** in the warning box.

   The color mode of the image is changed to grayscale, and the image is flattened so there is only a single layer. All the color information in the image has been discarded.

4. Click **Image** on the menu bar, point to **Mode**, then click **RGB Color**.

   The color mode is changed back to RGB color, although there is still no color in the image. Compare your screen to Figure 25.

You converted the image to Grayscale, which discarded the existing color information. Then you changed the color mode to RGB color.

FIGURE 25
Image with RGB mode

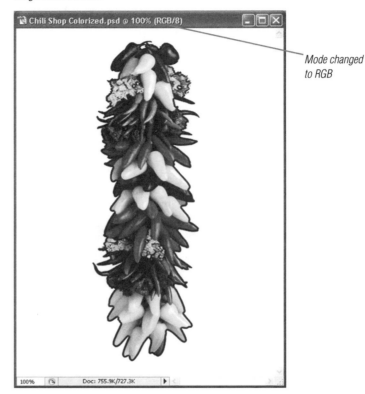

Mode changed
to RGB

Understanding the Hue/Saturation dialog box

The Hue/Saturation dialog box is an important tool in the world of color enhancement. Useful for both color and grayscale images, the saturation slider can be used to boost a range of colors. By clicking the Edit list arrow, you can isolate which colors (all, cyan, blue, magenta, red, yellow, or green) you want to modify. Using this tool requires patience and experimentation, but gives you great control over the colors in your image.

FIGURE 26
Hue/Saturation dialog box

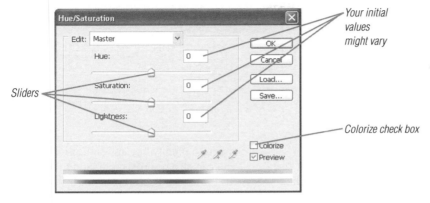

Your initial values might vary

Sliders

Colorize check box

FIGURE 27
Colorized image

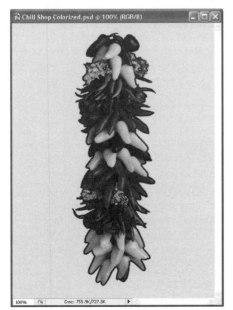

Colorize a grayscale image

1. Click **Image** on the menu bar, point to **Adjustments**, then click **Hue/Saturation** to open the Hue/Saturation dialog box, as shown in Figure 26.

2. Click the **Colorize check box** in the Hue/Saturation dialog box to add a check mark.

3. Drag the **Hue slider** until the text box displays **290**.

   TIP   You can also type values in the text boxes in the Hue/Saturation dialog box. Negative numbers must be preceded by a minus sign or a hyphen. Positive numbers can be preceded by an optional plus sign (+).

4. Drag the **Saturation slider** until the text box displays **40**.

5. Drag the **Lightness slider** until the text box displays **-15**.

6. Click **OK**.

7. Save your work, then compare your screen to Figure 27.

You colorized a grayscale image by adjusting settings in the Hue/Saturation dialog box.

Converting color images to grayscale

Like everything else in Photoshop, there is more than one way of converting a color image into one that is black & white. Changing the color mode to grayscale is the quickest method. You can also make this conversion through desaturation by clicking Image on the menu bar, pointing to Adjustments, then clicking Desaturate. Converting to Grayscale mode generally results in losing contrast, as does the desaturation method.

USE FILTERS, OPACITY,
AND BLENDING MODES

What You'll Do

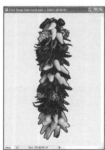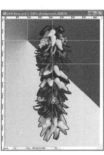

 In this lesson, you'll adjust the brightness and contrast in the Chili Shop colorized image, apply a Sharpen filter, and adjust the opacity of the lines applied by the filter. You'll also adjust the color balance of the Chili Shop image.

Manipulating an Image

As you work in Photoshop, you might realize that some images have fundamental problems that need correcting, while others just need to be further enhanced. For example, you might need to adjust an image's contrast and sharpness, or you might want to colorize an otherwise dull image. You can use a variety of techniques to change the way an image looks. For example, you have learned how to use the Adjustments command on the Image menu to modify hue and saturation, but you can also use this command to adjust brightness and contrast, color balance, and a host of other visual effects.

Understanding Filters

Filters are Photoshop commands that can significantly alter an image's appearance. Experimenting with Photoshop's filters is a fun way to completely change the look of an image. For example, the Watercolor filter gives the illusion that your image was

Fixing blurry scanned images

An unfortunate result of scanning a picture is that the image can become blurry. You can fix this, however, using the Unsharp Mask filter. This filter both sharpens and smoothes the image by increasing the contrast along element edges. Here's how it works: the smoothing effect removes stray marks, and the sharpening effect emphasizes contrasting neighboring pixels. Most scanners come with their own Unsharp Masks built into the TWAIN driver, but using Photoshop, you have access to a more powerful version of this filter. You can use Photoshop's Unsharp Mask to control the sharpening process by adjusting key settings. In most cases, your scanner's Unsharp Mask might not give you this flexibility. Regardless of the technical aspects, the result is a sharper image. You can apply the Unsharp Mask by clicking Filter on the menu bar, pointing to Sharpen, then click Unsharp Mask.

painted using traditional watercolors. Sharpen filters can appear to add definition to the entire image, or just the edges. Compare the different Sharpen filters applied in Figure 28. The **Sharpen More filter** increases the contrast of adjacent pixels and can focus a blurry image. Be careful not to overuse sharpening tools (or any filter), because you can create high-contrast lines or add graininess in color or brightness.

Choosing Blending Modes

A **blending mode** controls how pixels are made either darker or lighter based on underlying colors. Photoshop provides a variety of blending modes, listed in Table 1, to combine the color of the pixels in the current layer with those in layer(s) beneath it. You can see a list of blending modes by clicking the Add a layer style button on the Layers palette.

Understanding Blending Mode Components

You should consider the following underlying colors when planning a blending mode: **base color**, which is the original color of the image; **blend color**, which is the color you apply with a paint or edit tool; and **resulting color**, which is the color that is created as a result of applying the blend color.

Softening Filter Effects

Opacity can soften the line that the filter creates, but it doesn't affect the opacity of the entire layer. After a filter has been applied, you can modify the opacity and apply a blending mode using the Layers palette or the Fade dialog box. You can open the Fade dialog box by clicking Edit on the menu bar, then clicking the Fade command.

QUICKTIP

The Fade command appears only after a filter has been applied. When available, the command name includes the name of the applied filter.

Balancing Colors

As you adjust settings, such as hue and saturation, you might create unwanted imbalances in your image. You can adjust colors to correct or improve an image's appearance. For example, you can decrease a color by increasing the amount of its opposite color. You use the Color Balance dialog box to balance the color in an image.

FIGURE 28
Sharpen filters

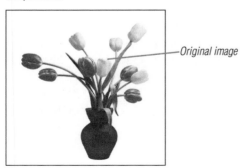
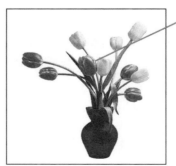
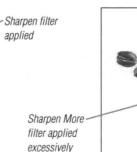
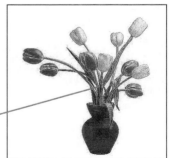

Original image

Sharpen filter applied

Sharpen More filter applied excessively

TABLE 1: Blending Modes

blending mode	description
Dissolve, Behind, and Clear modes	Dissolve mode creates a grainy, mottled appearance. The Behind mode paints on the transparent part of the layer—the lower the opacity, the grainier the image. The Clear mode paints individual pixels. All modes are available only when the Lock transparent pixels check box is *not* selected.
Multiply and Screen modes	Multiply mode creates semitransparent shadow effects. This mode assesses the information in each channel, then multiplies the value of the base color by the blend color. The resulting color is always *darker* than the base color. The Screen mode multiplies the value of the inverse of the blend and base colors. After it is applied, the resulting color is always *lighter* than the base color.
Overlay mode	Dark and light values (luminosity) are preserved, dark base colors are multiplied (darkened), and light areas are screened (lightened).
Soft Light and Hard Light modes	Soft Light lightens a light base color and darkens a dark base color. The Hard Light blending mode creates a similar effect, but provides greater contrast between the base and blend colors.
Color Dodge and Color Burn modes	Color Dodge mode brightens the base color to reflect the blend color. The Color Burn mode darkens the base color to reflect the blend color.
Darken and Lighten modes	Darken mode selects a new resulting color based on whichever color is darker—the base color or the blend color. The Lighten mode selects a new resulting color based on the lighter of the two colors.
Difference and Exclusion modes	The Difference mode subtracts the value of the blend color from the value of the base color, or vice versa, depending on which color has the greater brightness value. The Exclusion mode creates an effect similar to that of the Difference mode, but with less contrast between the blend and base colors.
Color and Luminosity modes	The Color mode creates a resulting color with the luminance of the base color, and the hue and saturation of the blend color. The Luminosity mode creates a resulting color with the hue and saturation of the base color, and the luminance of the blend color.
Hue and Saturation modes	The Hue mode creates a resulting color with the luminance of the base color and the hue of the blend color. The Saturation mode creates a resulting color with the luminance of the base color and the saturation of the blend color.

FIGURE 29

Brightness/Contrast dialog box

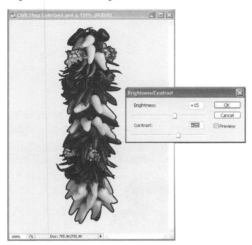

FIGURE 30

Shadow/Highlight dialog box

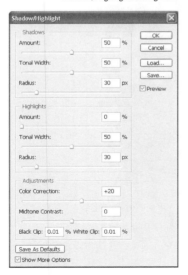

Adjust brightness and contrast

1. Click **Image** on the menu bar, point to **Adjustments**, then click **Brightness/Contrast** to open the Brightness/Contrast dialog box.

2. Drag the **Brightness slider** until **+15** appears in the Brightness text box.

3. Drag the **Contrast slider** until **+25** appears in the Contrast text box. Compare your screen to Figure 29.

4. Click **OK**.

You adjusted settings in the Brightness/Contrast dialog box. The image now looks much brighter, with a higher degree of contrast, which obscures some of the finer detail in the image.

Correcting shadows and highlights

The ability to correct shadows and highlights will delight photographers everywhere. This image correction feature (opened by clicking Image on the menu bar, pointing to Adjustments, then clicking Shadow/Highlight) lets you modify overall lighting and make subtle adjustments. Figure 30 shows the Shadow/Highlight dialog box with the Show More Options check box selected. Check out this one-stop shopping for adjustments!

Lesson 6   Use Filters, Opacity, and Blending Modes

Work with a filter, a blending mode, and an opacity setting

1. Click **Filter** on the menu bar, point to **Sharpen**, then click **Sharpen More**.

   The border and other features of the image are intensified.

2. Click **Edit** on the menu bar, then click **Fade Sharpen More** to open the Fade dialog box, as shown in Figure 31.

3. Drag the **Opacity slider** until **45** appears in the Opacity text box.

   The opacity setting softened the lines applied by the Sharpen More filter.

4. Click the **Mode list arrow**, then click **Dissolve**.

   The Dissolve setting blends the surrounding pixels.

5. Click **OK**.

6. Save your work, then compare your image to Figure 32.

You applied the Sharpen More filter, then adjusted the opacity and changed the color mode in the Fade dialog box. The image looks crisper than before, with a greater level of detail.

FIGURE 31
Fade dialog box

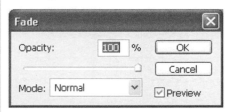

FIGURE 32
Image settings adjusted

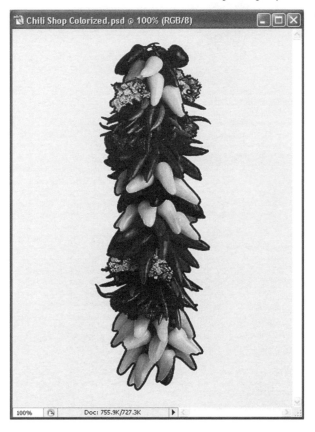

FIGURE 33

Color Balance dialog box

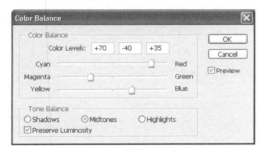

FIGURE 34

Image with colors balanced

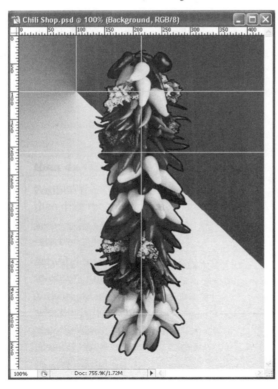

Adjust color balance

1. Switch to the Chili Shop image, with the Background layer active.

   The image you worked with earlier in this chapter becomes active.

2. Click **Image** on the menu bar, point to **Adjustments**, then click **Color Balance**.

3. Drag the **Cyan-Red slider** until **+70** appears in the first text box.

4. Drag the **Magenta-Green slider** until **–40** appears in the middle text box.

5. Drag the **Yellow-Blue slider** until **+35** appears in the last text box, as shown in Figure 33.

   Subtle changes were made in the color balance in the image.

6. Click **OK**.

7. Save your work, then compare your image to Figure 34.

You balanced the colors in the Chili Shop image by adjusting settings in the Color Balance dialog box.

MATCH COLORS

What You'll Do

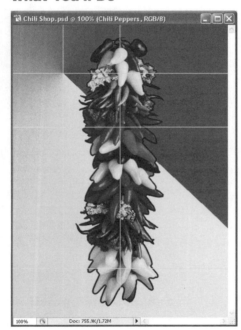

In this lesson, you'll make selections in source and target images, then use the Match Color command to replace the target color.

Finding the Right Color

If it hasn't happened already, at some point you'll be working on an image and wish you could grab a color from another image to use in this one. Just as you can use the Eyedropper Tool to sample any color in the current image for the foreground and background, you can sample a color from any other image to use in the current one. Perhaps the skin tones in one image look washed out: you can use the Match Color command to replace those tones with skin tone colors from another image. Or maybe the jacket color in one image would look better using a color in another image.

Using Selections to Match Colors

Remember that this is Photoshop, where everything is about layers and selections.

To replace a color in one image with one you've matched from another, you work with—you guessed it—layers and selections.

Suppose you've located the perfect color in another image. The image you are working with is the **target**, and that image that contains your perfect color is the **source**. By activating the layer on which the color lies in the source image, and making a selection around the color, you can have Photoshop match the color in the source and replace a color in the target. To accomplish this, you use the Match Color command, which is available through the Adjustments command on the Image menu.

FIGURE 35
Selection in source image

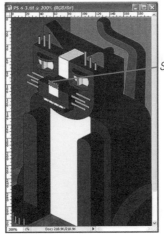

Selected area

FIGURE 37
Image with matched color

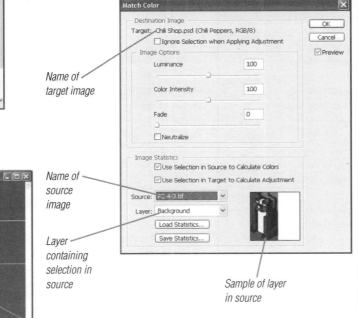

Name of source image

Layer containing selection in source

Modified selection (your selection may look slightly different)

FIGURE 36
Match Color dialog box

Name of target image

Sample of layer in source

1. Click the **Chili Peppers layer** on the Layers palette, then zoom into the center of the image.

2. Click the **Magic Wand Tool** on the toolbox.

3. Verify that the **Contiguous check box** on the options bar is selected, then set the **Tolerance** to **160**.

4. Click the image with the **Magic Wand pointer** on a yellow pepper at approximately **260 X/260 Y**.

5. Open PS 4-3.tif from the drive and folder where your Data Files are stored, zoom into the image if necessary, change the tolerance to **40** then click the purple part of cat's nose (at 60 X/100 Y) with the **Magic Wand pointer**. Compare your selection to Figure 35.

6. Activate the **Chili Shop image**, click **Image** on the menu bar, point to **Adjustments**, then click **Match Color**.

7. Click the **Source list arrow**, then click **PS 4-3.tif**. Compare your settings to Figure 36.

8. Click **OK**.

9. Deselect the selection, zoom out to 100%, turn off the rulers, save your work, then compare your image to Figure 37.

10. Close all open images, then exit Photoshop.

You used the Match Color dialog box to replace a color in one image with a color from another image. The Match Color dialog box makes it easy to sample colors from other images, giving you even more options for incorporating color into an image.

Power User Shortcuts

to do this:	use this method:
Apply a sharpen filter	Filter ➤ Sharpen
Balance colors	Image ➤ Adjustments ➤ Color Balance
Change color mode	Image ➤ Mode
Choose a background color from the Swatches palette	[Ctrl]Color swatch (Win) ⌘ Color swatch (Mac)
Delete a swatch from the Swatches palette	[Alt], click swatch (Win) [option], click swatch (Mac)
Eyedropper Tool	🖊 or I
Fill with background color	[Shift][Backspace] (Win) ⌘[delete] (Mac)
Fill with foreground color	[Alt][Backspace] (Win) option [delete] (Mac)
Gradient Tool	▭
Guide pointer	╫ or ╪
Hide a layer	👁

to do this:	use this method:
Hide or show rulers	[Ctrl][R] (Win) ⌘[R] (Mac)
Hide or show the Color Palette	[F6] (Win)
Lock transparent pixels check box on/off	/
Make Swatches palette active	Swatches
Paint Bucket Tool	🪣 or G
Return background and foreground colors to default	◼ or D
Show a layer	▢
Show hidden Paint Bucket/ Gradient Tools	[Shift] G
Switch between open files	[Ctrl][Tab] (Win) [control tab] (Mac)
Switch Foreground and Background Colors	↰ or X

Key: Menu items are indicated by ➤ between the menu name and its command. Blue bold letters are shortcuts for selecting tools on the toolbox.

Color plays such an important part of our lives. So much of your work with Photoshop involves choosing, applying, and working with color. There are a variety of ways you can select a color: from the Color Picker dialog box, the Swatches palette, or from an existing color in an image. You can also add a colorful border to an object, and blend multiple colors to create interesting effects. With Photoshop, you can turn a color image into one that displays shades of gray, then colorize it, or replace a color within an image with a color from another image.

What You Have Learned:

- How to change foreground and background colors
- How to change a color using the Color palette
- How to sample a color using the Eyedropper Tool
- How to select a color from the Color Picker dialog box and the Swatches palette
- How to add a color to the Swatches palette
- How to add a border to an image
- How to create a gradient and apply a gradient fill
- How to change a color image to a grayscale image
- How to add color to a grayscale image
- How to adjust brightness and contrast
- How to apply a filter and change a blending mode
- How to change the opacity setting
- How to adjust color balance
- How to replace a color in one image with a color from another image

Key Terms

Background color   Used to make gradual blends of multiple colors and fill in areas of an image that have been erased; white by default.

Brightness   Measurement of relative lightness or darkness of a color and is measured as a percentage from 0% (black) to 100% (white).

Color Picker   Used to select colors from a color spectrum or lets you numerically define a custom color.

Foreground color   Used to paint, fill, or apply a border to a selection; black by default.

Hue   Color reflected from or transmitted through an object.

Luminosity   Light and dark values remaining in a color image converted to grayscale.

Sampling   Method of changing foreground and background colors, in which an existing color in an image is used.

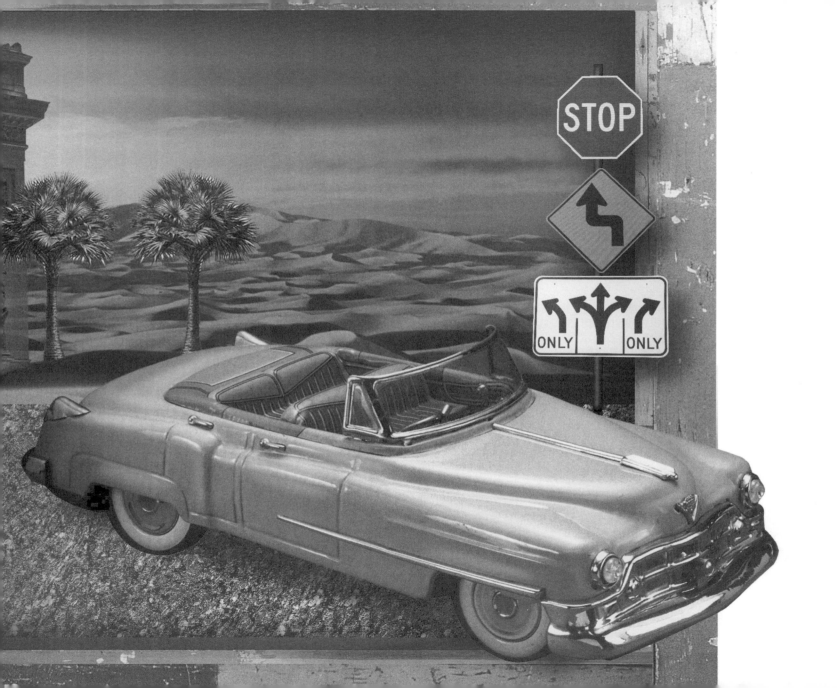

5

PLACING TYPE IN
AN IMAGE

1. Learn about type and how it is created.

2. Change spacing and adjust baseline shift.

3. Use the Drop Shadow style.

4. Apply anti-aliasing to type.

5. Modify type with the Bevel and Emboss style.

6. Apply special effects to type using filters.

7. Create text on a path.

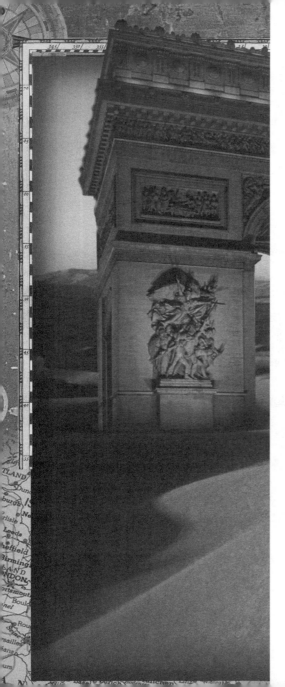

5 PLACING TYPE IN
AN IMAGE

Learning About Type

Text plays an important design role when combined with images for posters, magazine and newspaper advertisements, and other graphics materials that need to communicate detailed information. In Photoshop, text is referred to as **type**. You can use type to express the ideas conveyed in a file's imagery or to deliver an additional message. You can manipulate type in many ways to reflect or reinforce the meaning behind an image. As in other programs, type has its own unique characteristics in Photoshop. For example, you can change its appearance by using different fonts (also called typefaces) and colors.

Understanding the Purpose of Type

Type is typically used along with imagery to deliver a message quickly and with flare. Because type is used sparingly (typically

there's not a lot of room for it), its appearance is very important; color and imagery are often used to *complement* or *reinforce* the message within the text. Type should be limited, direct, and to the point. It should be large enough for easy reading, but should not overwhelm or distract from the central image. For example, a vibrant and daring advertisement should contain just enough type to interest the reader, without demanding too much reading.

Getting the Most Out of Type

Words can express an idea, but the appearance of the type is what drives the point home. After you decide on the content you want to use and create the type, you can experiment with its appearance by changing its **font** (characters with a similar appearance), size, and color. You can also apply special effects that make it stand out, or appear to pop off the page.

Tools You'll Use

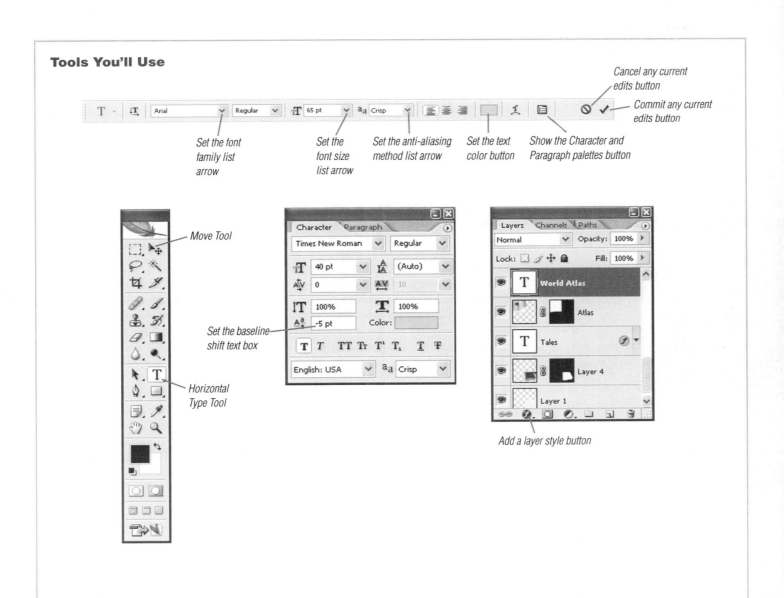

Cancel any current edits button

Commit any current edits button

Set the font family list arrow

Set the font size list arrow

Set the anti-aliasing method list arrow

Set the text color button

Show the Character and Paragraph palettes button

Move Tool

Horizontal Type Tool

Set the baseline shift text box

Add a layer style button

LEARN ABOUT TYPE AND
HOW IT IS CREATED

What You'll Do

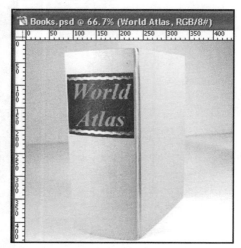

In this lesson, you'll create a type layer, then change the alignment, font family, size, and color of the type.

Introducing Type Types

Outline type is mathematically defined, which means that it can be scaled to any size without losing its sharp, smooth edges. Some programs, such as Adobe Illustrator, create outline type. **Bitmap type** is composed of pixels, and, like images, can develop jagged edges when enlarged. The type you create in Photoshop is initially outline type, but it is converted into bitmap type when you apply special filters. Using the type tools and the options bar, you can create horizontal or vertical type and modify font size and alignment. You use the Color Picker dialog box to change type color. When you create type in Photoshop, it is automatically placed on a new type layer on the Layers palette.

QUICKTIP

Keeping type on separate layers makes it much easier to modify and change positions within the image.

Getting to Know Font Families

Each **font family** represents a complete set of characters, letters, and symbols for a particular typeface. Font families are generally divided into three categories: serif, sans serif, and symbol. Characters in **serif fonts** have a tail, or stroke, at the end of some characters. These tails make it easier for the eye to recognize words. For this reason, serif fonts are generally used in text passages. **Sans serif fonts** do not have tails and are commonly used in headlines.

Symbol fonts are used to display unique characters (such as $, ÷, or ™). Table 1 lists commonly used serif and sans serif fonts. After you select the Horizontal Type Tool, you can change font families using the options bar.

Measuring Type Size

The size of each character within a font is measured in **points**. **PostScript**, a programming language that optimizes printed text and graphics, was introduced by Adobe in 1985. In PostScript measurement, one inch is equivalent to 72 points or six picas. Therefore, one pica is equivalent to 12 points. In traditional measurement, one inch is equivalent to 72.27 points. The default Photoshop type size is 12 points. In Photoshop, you have the option of using PostScript or traditional character measurement.

Acquiring Fonts

Your computer probably has many fonts installed on it, but no matter how many fonts you have, you probably can use more. Fonts can be purchased from private companies, individual designers, computer stores, catalog companies, on CD-ROM or over the Internet. Using your browser and your favorite search engine, you can locate Web sites that let you purchase or download fonts. Many Web sites offer specialty fonts, such as the Web site shown in Figure 1. Other Web sites offer these fonts free of charge or for a nominal fee.

TABLE 1: Commonly Used Serif and Sans Serif Fonts

serif fonts	sample	sans serif fonts	sample
Lucida Handwriting	*Adobe Photoshop*	Arial	Adobe Photoshop
Rockwell	Adobe Photoshop	Bauhaus	Adobe Photoshop
Times New Roman	Adobe Photoshop	Century Gothic	Adobe Photoshop

FIGURE 1
Font Web site

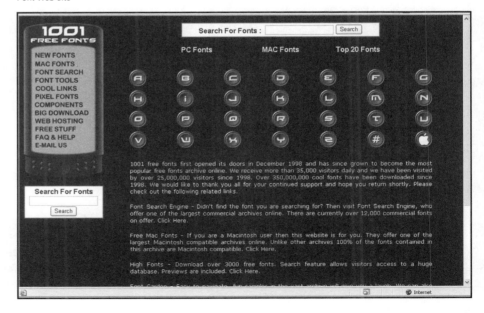

Create and modify type

1. Start Photoshop, open PS 5-1.psd from the drive and folder where your Data Files are stored, update the text layers, then save the file as **Books**.

2. Display the document size in the status bar, and the rulers in pixels (if they are not already displayed).

   TIP   You can quickly display the rulers by pressing [Ctrl][R] (Win) or [⌘][R] (Mac).

3. Click the **Default Foreground and Background Colors button** ▪️◻ on the toolbox.

4. Click the **Horizontal Type Tool** T. on the toolbox.

5. Click the **Set the font family list arrow** on the options bar, click **Arial** (a sans-serif font), click the **Set the font style list arrow**, then click **Italic**.

   TIP   If Arial is not available, make a reasonable substitution.

6. Click the **Center text button** ≣ on the options bar (if it is not already selected).

7. Click the **Set the font size list arrow** on the options bar, then click **24 pt** (if it is not already selected).

8. Click the image with the **Horizontal Type pointer** ⥊ in the center of the brown area of the spine just below the gold leaf at **160 X/130 Y**, then type **World**, press **[Shift] [Enter]** (Win) or **[shift][return]** (Mac), then type **Atlas**, as shown in Figure 2.

   TIP   Type should be short enough to be able to be read in a glance.

You created a type layer by using the Horizontal Type Tool on the toolbox and modified the font family, alignment, and font size.

FIGURE 2
New type in image

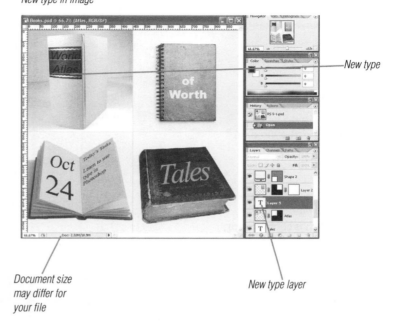

——New type

Document size
may differ for
your file

New type layer

Using the active layer palette background (Macintosh)

Icons used in Macintosh to identify type layers are similar to those found in Windows. In Macintosh, the active layer has the same Type and Layer style buttons. The active layer's background color is the same color as the Highlight Color. (In Windows, the active layer's background color is navy blue.)

FIGURE 3

Type with new color

Type with
new color

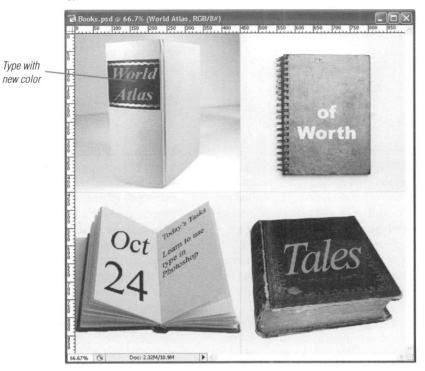

Change type color using an existing image color

1. Press **[Ctrl][A]** (Win) or **⌘ [A]** (Mac) to select all the text.

2. Click the **Set the font family list arrow** on the options bar, scroll down, then click **Times New Roman**.

   TIP Click in the Set the font family text box and you can select a different font by typing the first few characters of the font name. Scroll through the fonts by clicking in the Set the font family text box, then pressing the [UpArrow] or [DownArrow].

3. Click the **Set the font style list arrow**, then click **Bold Italic**.

4. Click the **Set the text color button** ▬ on the options bar.

   TIP Drag the Color Picker dialog box out of the way if it blocks your view of the image.

   As you position the pointer over the image, the pointer automatically becomes an Eyedropper pointer.

5. Click the image with the **Eyedropper pointer** 🖋 anywhere in the letter "T" in the book in the lower-right corner at approximately **600 X/610 Y**.

   The new color is now the active color in the Color Picker dialog box.

6. Click **OK** in the Color Picker dialog box.

7. Click the **Commit any current edits button** ✔ on the options bar.

   Clicking the Commit any current edits button accepts your changes and makes them permanent in the image.

8. Save your work, then compare your image to Figure 3.

You changed the font family, modified the color of the type by using an existing image color, and committed the current edits.

Using the Swatches palette to change type color

You can also use the Swatches palette to change type color. Select the type, then click a color on the Swatches palette. The new color that you click will appear in the Set foreground color button on the toolbox and will be applied to type that is currently selected.

CHANGE SPACING AND
ADJUST BASELINE SHIFT

What You'll Do

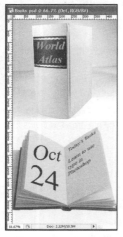

In this lesson, you'll adjust the spacing between characters and change the baseline of type.

Adjusting Spacing

Competition for readers on the visual landscape is fierce. To get and maintain an edge over other designers, Photoshop provides tools that let you make adjustments to your type, thereby making your type more distinctive. These adjustments might not be very dramatic, but they can influence readers in subtle ways. For example, type that is too small and difficult to read might make the reader impatient (at the very least), and he or she might not even look at the image (at the very worst). You can make finite adjustments, called **type spacing**, to the space between characters and between lines of type. Adjusting type spacing affects the ease with which words are read.

Understanding Character and Line Spacing

Fonts in desktop publishing and word processing programs use proportional spacing, whereas typewriters use monotype spacing. In **monotype spacing**, each character occupies the same amount of space. This means that wide characters such as "o" and "w" take up the same real estate on the page as narrow ones such as "i" and "l". In **proportional spacing**, each character can take up a different amount of space, depending on its width. **Kerning** controls the amount of space between characters and can affect several characters, a word, or an entire paragraph. **Tracking** inserts a *uniform* amount of space between selected characters. Figure 4 shows an example of type before and after it has been kerned.

The second line of text takes up less room and has less space between its characters, making it easier to read. You can also change the amount of space, called **leading**, between lines of type, to add or decrease the distance between lines of text.

Using the Character Palette

The **Character palette**, shown in Figure 5, helps you manually or automatically control type properties such as kerning, tracking, and leading. You open the Character palette from the options bar.

Adjusting the Baseline Shift

Type rests on an invisible line called a **baseline**. Using the Character palette, you can adjust the **baseline shift**, the vertical distance that type moves from its baseline.

You can add interest to type by changing the baseline shift.

QUICKTIP

Clicking the Set the text color button on either the options bar or the Character palette opens the Color Picker dialog box.

FIGURE 4
Kerned characters

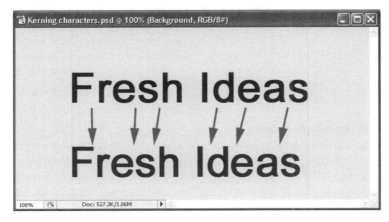

FIGURE 5
Character palette

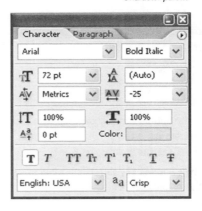

Kern characters

1. Click the **World Atlas type layer** on the Layers palette (if it is not already selected).

2. Click the **Horizontal Type Tool** T. on the toolbox.

3. Click the **Toggle the Character and Paragraph palettes button** 📖 on the options bar to open the Character palette.

   > TIP You can close the Character palette by clicking the Close button in the upper-right corner of its title bar or by clicking the Toggle the Character and Paragraph palettes button.

4. Click between "o" and "r" in the word "World."

   > TIP You can drag the Character palette out of the way if it blocks your view.

5. Click the **Set the kerning between two characters list arrow** `Metrics ▾` on the Character palette, then click **–25**.

   The spacing between the two characters decreases.

6. Click between "A" and "t" in the word "Atlas."

7. Click the **Set the kerning between two characters list arrow** `Metrics ▾`, then click **–25**, as shown in Figure 6.

8. Click the **Commit any current edits button** ✓ on the options bar.

You modified the kerning between characters by using the Character palette.

FIGURE 6
Kerned type

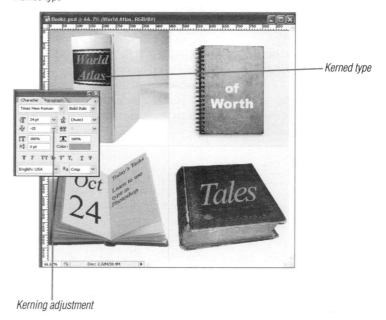

Kerned type

Kerning adjustment

Correcting spelling errors

Are you concerned that your gorgeous image will be ruined by misspelled words? Photoshop understands your pain and has included a spelling checker to make sure you are never plagued by incorrect spellings. If you want, the spelling checker will check the type on the current layer, or all the layers in the image. First, make sure the correct dictionary for your language is selected. English: USA is the default, but you can choose another language by clicking the Set the language on selected characters for hyphenation and spelling list arrow at the bottom of the Character palette. To check spelling, click Edit on the menu bar, then click Check Spelling. The spelling checker will automatically stop at each word not already appearing in the dictionary. One or more suggestions might be offered, which you can either accept or reject.

FIGURE 7
Color Picker dialog box

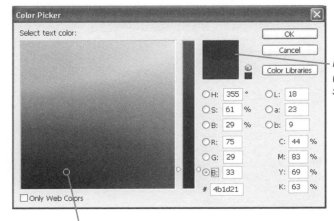

New foreground color
(your color may differ slightly)

Selects the new
foreground color

FIGURE 8
Type with baseline shifted

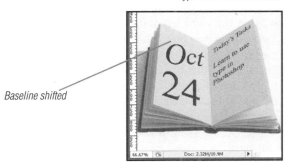

Baseline shifted

Shift the baseline

1. Double-click the **layer thumbnail** on the Oct type layer, then use the **Horizontal Type Pointer** to select the "O".

2. Click the **Set the text color button** ▮▮ on the options bar.

3. Click anywhere in the maroon area in the World Atlas type, such as 210 X/180 Y, compare your Color Picker dialog box to Figure 7, then click **OK**.

4. Double-click **36** in the Set the font size text box on the Character palette, type **45**, double-click **0** in the Set the baseline shift text box on the Character palette, then type **–5**.

5. Click the **Commit any current edits button** ✓ on the options bar.

6. Click the **Toggle the Character and Paragraph palettes button** 🗒 on the options bar.

7. Save your work, then compare your screen to Figure 8.

You changed the type color, then adjusted the baseline of the first character in a word, to make the first character stand out.

USE THE DROP
SHADOW STYLE

What You'll Do

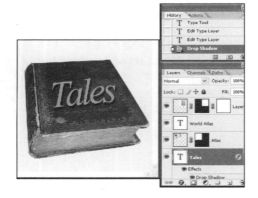

 In this lesson, you'll apply the drop shadow style to a type layer, then modify drop shadow settings.

Adding Effects to Type

Layer styles (effects which can be applied to a type or image layer) can greatly enhance the appearance of type and improve its effectiveness. A type layer is indicated by the appearance of the T icon in the layer's thumbnail box. When a layer style is applied to any layer, the Indicates layer effects icon (*f*) appears in that layer when it is active. The Layers palette is a great source of information. You can see which effects have been applied to a layer by clicking the arrow to the left of the Indicates layer effects icon on the Layers palette if the layer is active or inactive. Figure 9 shows a layer that has two type layer styles applied to it. Layer styles are linked to the contents of a layer, which means that if a type layer is moved or modified, the layer's style will still be applied to the type.

QUICKTIP

Type layer icons in the Macintosh version of Photoshop are similar though not identical to those in the Windows version.

Using the Drop Shadow

One method of placing emphasis on type is to add a drop shadow to it. A **drop shadow** creates an illusion that another colored layer of identical text is behind the selected type. The drop shadow default color is black, but it can be changed to another color using the Color Picker dialog box, or any of the other methods for changing color.

Applying a Style

You can apply a style, such as a drop shadow, to the active layer, by clicking Layer on the menu bar, pointing to Layer Style, then clicking a style. (The settings in the Layer Style dialog box are "sticky," meaning that they display the settings that you last used.) An alternative method to using the menu bar is to select the layer that you want to apply the style to, click the Add a layer style button on the Layers palette, then click a style. Regardless of which method you use, the Layer Style dialog box opens. You use this dialog box to add all kinds of effects to type. Depending on which style you've chosen, the Layer Style dialog box displays options appropriate to that style.

QUICKTIP
You can apply styles to objects as well as to type.

Controlling a Drop Shadow

You can control many aspects of a drop shadow's appearance, including its angle, its distance behind the type, and the amount of blur it contains. The **angle** determines where the shadow falls relative to the text, and the **distance** determines how far the shadow falls from the text. The **spread** determines the width of the shadow

text, and the **size** determines the clarity of the shadow. Figure 10 shows samples of two different drop shadow effects. The first line of type uses the default background color (black), has an angle of 160 degrees, distance of 10 pixels, a spread of 0%, and a size of five pixels. The second line of type uses a blue background color, has an angle of 120 degrees, distance of 20 pixels, a spread of 10%, and a size of five pixels. As you modify the drop shadow, the preview window displays the changes.

FIGURE 9
Effects in type layer

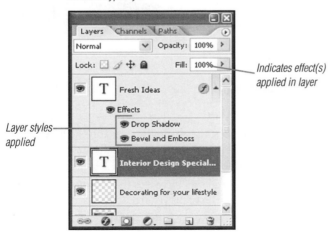

Indicates effect(s) applied in layer

Layer styles applied

FIGURE 10
Sample drop shadows

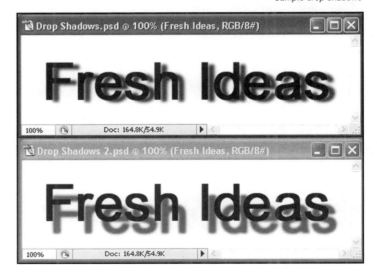

Add a drop shadow

1. Click the **layer thumbnail** on the Tales type layer.

2. Click the **Add a layer style button** 🦋 on the Layers palette.

3. Click **Drop Shadow**.

4. Compare your Layer Style dialog box to Figure 11.

   The default drop shadow settings are applied to the type. Table 2 describes the drop shadow settings.

   > TIP   You can also open the Layer Style dialog box by double-clicking a layer on the Layers palette.

You created a drop shadow by using the Add a layer style button on the Layers palette and the Layer Style dialog box.

FIGURE 11
Type color changed

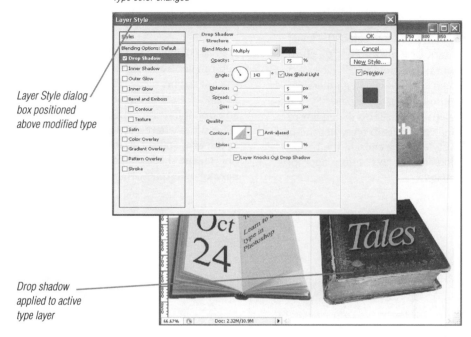

Layer Style dialog box positioned above modified type

Drop shadow applied to active type layer

TABLE 2: Drop Shadow Settings

setting	scale	explanation
Angle	0–360 degrees	At 0 degrees, the shadow appears on the baseline of the original text. At 90 degrees, the shadow appears directly below the original text.
Distance	0–30,000 pixels	A larger pixel size increases the distance from which the shadow text falls relative to the original text.
Spread	0–100%	A larger percentage increases the width of the shadow text.
Size	0–250 pixels	A larger pixel size increases the blur of the shadow text.

FIGURE 12

Layer Style dialog box

Angle text box —

Distance text box —

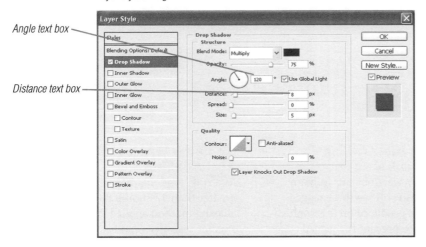

FIGURE 13

Drop shadow added to type layer

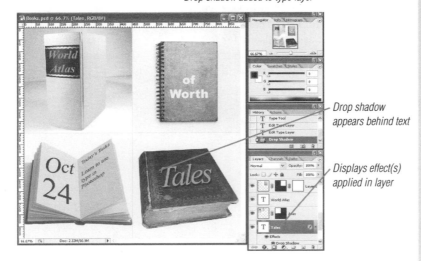

Drop shadow
appears behind text

Displays effect(s)
applied in layer

Modify drop shadow settings

1. Double-click the number in the Angle text box, then type **120**. Each style in the Layer Styles dialog box shows different options in the center section. These options are displayed as you click each style (in the left column).

   TIP   You can also set the angle by dragging the dial slider in the Layer Style dialog box.

2. Double-click the number in the Distance text box, then type **8**. See Figure 12.

   TIP   You can create your own layer style in the Layer Style dialog box, by selecting style settings, clicking New Style, typing a new name or accepting the default, then clicking OK. The new style appears as a preset in the Styles list of the Layer Style dialog box.

3. Click **OK**, then compare your screen to Figure 13.

4. Click the **list arrow to the right of the Indicates layer effects icon** ▲ on the Tales layer to close the list.

5. Save your work.

You used the Layer Style dialog box to modify the settings for the drop shadow.

APPLY ANTI-ALIASING
TO TYPE

What You'll Do

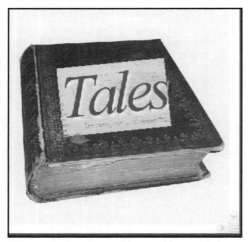

In this lesson, you'll view the effects of the anti-aliasing feature, then use the History palette to return the type to its original state.

Eliminating the "Jaggies"

In the good old days of dot-matrix printers, jagged edges were obvious in many print ads. You can still see these jagged edges in designs produced on less sophisticated printers. To prevent the jagged edges (sometimes called "jaggies") that often accompany bitmap type, Photoshop offers an anti-aliasing feature. **Anti-aliasing** partially fills in pixel edges with additional colors, resulting in smooth-edge type and an increased number of colors in the image. Anti-aliasing is useful for improving the display of large type in print media; however, this can cause a file to become large.

Knowing When to Apply Anti-Aliasing

As a rule, type that has a point size greater than 12 should have some anti-aliasing method applied. Sometimes, smaller type sizes can become blurry or muddy when anti-aliasing is used. As part of the process, anti-aliasing adds intermediate colors to your image in an effort to reduce the jagged edges. As a designer, you need to weigh the following factors when determining if you should apply anti-aliasing: type size versus file size and image quality.

Understanding Anti-Aliasing

Anti-aliasing improves the display of type against the background. You can use five anti-aliasing methods: None, Sharp, Crisp, Strong, and Smooth. An example of each method is shown in Figure 14. The **None** setting applies no anti-aliasing, and can result in type that has jagged edges. The **Sharp** setting displays type with the best possible resolution. The **Crisp** setting gives type more definition and makes type appear sharper. The **Strong** setting makes type appear heavier, much like the bold attribute. The **Smooth** setting gives type more rounded edges.

QUICKTIP

Generally, the type used in your image should be the messenger, not the message. As you work with type, keep in mind that using more than two fonts in one image might be distracting or make the overall appearance look unprofessional.

FIGURE 14
Anti-aliasing effects

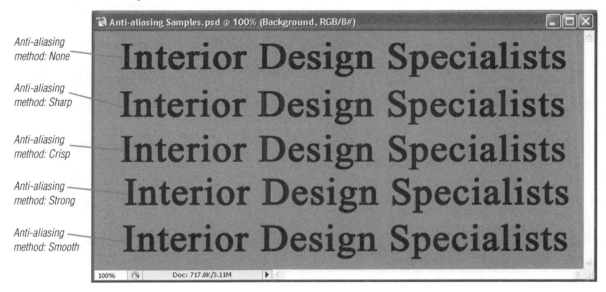

Anti-aliasing method: None

Anti-aliasing method: Sharp

Anti-aliasing method: Crisp

Anti-aliasing method: Strong

Anti-aliasing method: Smooth

Apply anti-aliasing

1. Double-click the **layer thumbnail** on the Tales layer.

2. Click the **Set the anti-aliasing method list arrow** Crisp ▾ on the options bar.

3. Click **Strong**, then compare your work to Figure 15.

4. Click the **Commit any current edits button** ✓ on the options bar.

You applied the Strong anti-aliasing setting to see how the setting affected the appearance of type.

FIGURE 15
Effect of None anti-aliasing

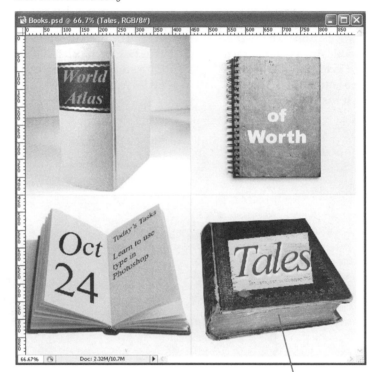

FIGURE 15
Effect of None anti-aliasing

Type appearance altered

Different strokes for different folks

You're probably already aware that you can use different methods to achieve the same goals in Photoshop. For instance, if you want to see the type options bar, you can either double-click a type layer or single-click it, then click the Horizontal Type Tool. The method you use determines what you'll see in the History palette. Using the double-clicking method, a change in the anti-aliasing method will result in the following history state 'Edit Type Layer'. Using the single-clicking method to change to the anti-alias method to Crisp results in an 'Anti Alias Crisp' history state.

FIGURE 16

Deleting a state from the History palette

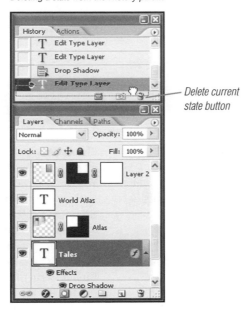

Delete current
state button

Undo anti-aliasing

1. Click the **Edit Type Layer state** listed at the bottom of the History palette, then drag it to the **Delete current state button** <img> ; as shown in Figure 16.

   TIP   Various methods of undoing actions are reviewed in Table 3.

2. Save your work.

You deleted a state in the History palette to return the type to its original appearance. The History palette offers an easy way of undoing previous steps.

TABLE 3: Undoing Actions

method	description	keyboard shortcut
Undo	Edit ≻ Undo	[Ctrl][Z] (Win) ⌘ [Z] (Mac)
Step Backward	Click Edit on the menu bar, then click Step Backward	[Alt][Ctrl][Z] (Win) [option] ⌘ [Z] (Mac)
History palette	Drag state to the Delete current state button on the History palette	[Alt] 🗑 (Win) [option] 🗑 (Mac)

MODIFY TYPE WITH THE
BEVEL AND EMBOSS STYLE

What You'll Do

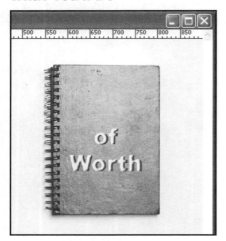

In this lesson, you'll apply the Bevel and Emboss style, then modify the Bevel and Emboss settings.

Using the Bevel and Emboss Style

You use the Bevel and Emboss style to add combinations of shadows and highlights to a layer and make type appear to have dimension and shine. You can use the Layer menu or the Layers palette to apply the Bevel and Emboss style to the active layer. Like all Layer styles, the Bevel and Emboss style is linked to the type layer that it is applied to.

Understanding Bevel and Emboss Settings

You can use two categories of Bevel and Emboss settings: structure and shading. **Structure** determines the size and physical properties of the object, and **shading** determines the lighting effects. Figure 17 contains several variations of Bevel and Emboss structure settings. The shading used in the Bevel and Emboss style determines how and where light is projected on

Filling type with imagery

You can use the imagery from a layer in one file as the fill pattern for another image's type layer. To create this effect, open a multi-layer file that contains the imagery you want to use (the source), then open the file that contains the type you want to fill (the target). In the source file, activate the layer containing the imagery you want to use, use the Select menu to select all, then use the Edit menu to copy the selection. In the target file, press [Ctrl] (Win) or ⌘ (Mac) while clicking the type layer to which the imagery will be applied, then click Paste Into on the Edit menu. The imagery will appear within the type.

the type. You can control a variety of settings, including the angle, altitude, and gloss contour, to create a unique appearance. The **Angle** setting determines where the shadow falls relative to the text, and the **Altitude** setting affects the amount of visible dimension. For example, an altitude of 0 degrees looks flat, while a setting of 90 degrees has a more three-dimensional appearance. The **Gloss Contour** setting determines the pattern with which light is reflected, and the **Highlight Mode** and **Shadow Mode** settings determine how pigments are combined. When the Use Global Light check box is selected, *all the type* in the image will be affected by your changes.

FIGURE 17
Bevel and Emboss style samples

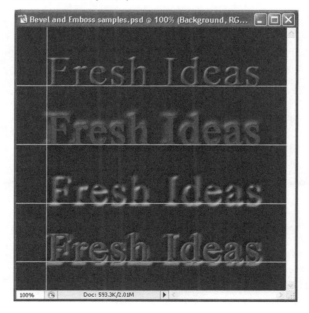

Add the Bevel and Emboss style with the Layer menu

1. Click the **of Worth layer** on the Layers palette.

2. Click **Layer** on the menu bar, point to **Layer Style**, click **Bevel and Emboss,** then click **Bevel and Emboss** in the Styles column (if it is not already selected).

3. Review the Layer Style dialog box shown in Figure 18, then move the Layer Style dialog box (if necessary), so you can see the of Worth type.

You applied the Bevel and Emboss style by using the Layer menu. This gave the text a more three-dimensional look.

FIGURE 18
Layer Style dialog box

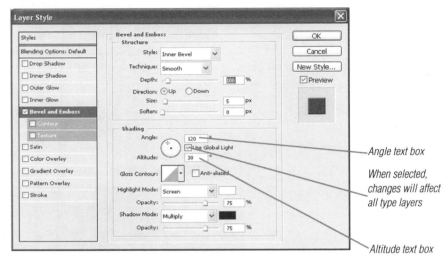

Angle text box

When selected, changes will affect all type layers

Altitude text box

Warping type

You can add dimension and style to your type by using the Warp Text feature. After you select the type layer you want to warp, click the Horizontal Type Tool on the toolbox. Click the Create warped text button on the options bar to open the Warp Text dialog box. (If a warning box opens telling you that your request cannot be completed because the type layer uses a faux bold style, click the Toggle the Character and Paragraph palettes button on the options bar, click the Character palette list arrow, click Faux Bold to deselect it, then click the Create warped text button again.) You can click the Style list arrow to select from 15 available styles. After you select a style, you can modify its appearance by dragging the Bend, Horizontal Distortion, and Vertical Distortion sliders.

TABLE 4: Bevel and Emboss Structure Settings

sample	style	technique	direction	size	soften
1	Inner Bevel	Smooth	Up	5	1
2	Outer Bevel	Chisel Hard	Up	5	8
3	Emboss	Smooth	Down	10	3
4	Pillow Emboss	Chisel Soft	Up	10	3

Modify Bevel and Emboss settings

1. Double-click the number in the Angle text box, then type **163**.

   Some of the Bevel and Emboss settings are listed in Table 4. You can use the Layer Style dialog box to change the structure by adjusting style, technique, direction, size, and soften settings.

2. Double-click the **Altitude text box**, then type **20**.

3. Click **OK**, then compare your type to Figure 19.

4. Save your work.

You modified the default settings for the Bevel and Emboss style. Experimenting with different settings is crucial to achieve the effect you want.

FIGURE 19
Bevel and Emboss style applied to type

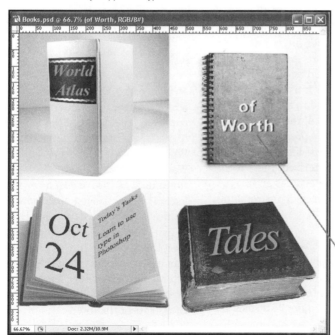

Bevel and Emboss style applied to layer

APPLY SPECIAL EFFECTS TO
TYPE USING FILTERS

What You'll Do

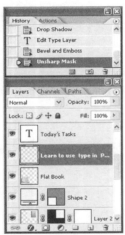

In this lesson, you'll rasterize a type layer, then apply a filter to it to change its appearance.

Understanding Filters

Like an image layer, a type layer can have one or more filters applied to it to achieve special effects and make your text look unique. Some filter dialog boxes have preview windows that let you see the results of the particular filter before it is applied to the layer. Other filters must be applied to the layer before you can see the results. Before a filter can be applied to a type layer, the type layer must first be **rasterized**, or converted to an image layer. After it is rasterized, the type characters *can no longer be edited* because it is composed of pixels, just like artwork. When a type layer is rasterized, the T icon in the layer thumbnail becomes an image thumbnail while the Effects icons remain on the type layer.

Creating Special Effects

Filters enable you to apply a variety of special effects to type, as shown in Figure 20. Notice that none of the original type layers on the Layers palette in Figure 20 display the T icon in the layer thumbnail because the layers have all been rasterized.

QUICKTIP

Because you cannot edit type after it has been rasterized, you should save your original type by making a copy of the layer *before* you rasterize it, then hide it from view.

Producing Distortions

Distort filters let you create waves or curves in type. Some of the types of distortions you can produce include Glass, Pinch, Ripple, Shear, Spherize, Twirl, Wave, and Zigzag. These effects are sometimes used as the basis of a corporate logo. The Twirl dialog box, shown in Figure 21, lets you determine the amount of twirl effect you want to apply. By dragging the Angle slider, you control how much twirl effect is added to a layer. Most filter dialog boxes have Zoom In and Zoom Out buttons that make it easy to see the effects of the filter.

Using Textures and Relief

Many filters let you create the appearance of textures and **relief** (the height of ridges within an object). One of the Stylize filters, Wind, applies lines throughout the type, making it appear shredded. The Wind dialog box, shown in Figure 22, lets you determine the kind of wind and its direction. The Texture filter lets you choose the type of texture you want to apply to a layer: Brick, Burlap, Canvas, or Sandstone.

Blurring Imagery

The Gaussian Blur filter softens the appearance of type by blurring its edge pixels. You can control the amount of blur applied to the type by entering high or low values in the Gaussian Blur dialog box. The higher the blur value, the blurrier the effect.

QUICKTIP

Be careful: too much blur applied to type can make it unreadable.

FIGURE 20
Sample filters applied to type

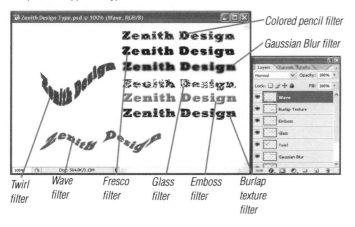

Twirl filter — Wave filter — Fresco filter — Glass filter — Emboss filter — Burlap texture filter

Colored pencil filter — Gaussian Blur filter

FIGURE 21
Twirl dialog box

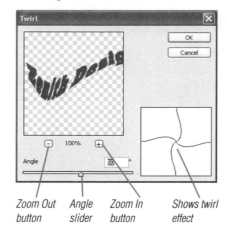

Zoom Out button — Angle slider — Zoom In button — Shows twirl effect

FIGURE 22
Wind dialog box

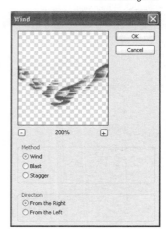

Rasterize a type layer

1. Click the **Learn to use type in Photoshop** layer on the Layers palette.

2. Click **Filter** on the menu bar, point to **Sharpen**, then click **Unsharp Mask**.

3. Click **OK** to rasterize the type and close the warning box shown in Figure 23.

   > TIP You can also rasterize a type layer by clicking Layer on the menu bar, pointing to Rasterize, then clicking Type.

   The Unsharp Mask dialog box opens.

You rasterized a type layer in preparation for filter application.

FIGURE 23
Warning box

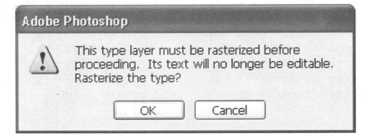

DESIGNTIP   **Using multiple filters**

Sometimes, adding one filter doesn't achieve the effect you had in mind. You can use multiple filters to create a unique effect. Before you try your hand at filters, though, it's a good idea to make a copy of the original layer. That way, if things don't turn out as you planned, you can always start over. You don't even have to write down which filters you used, because you can always look at the History palette to see which filters you applied.

FIGURE 24
Unsharp Mask dialog box

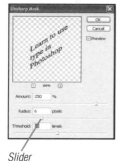

Slider

FIGURE 25
Type with Gaussian Blur filter

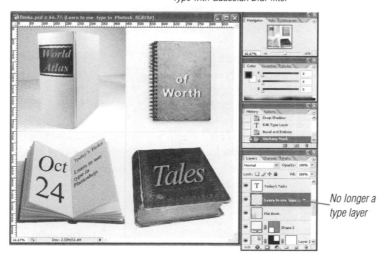

No longer a
type layer

Modify filter settings

1. Drag the default background patterns in the preview window of the dialog box to position the type so it is visible.

2. Drag the sliders in the Unsharp Mask dialog box until **250** appears in the Amount text box, **6** appears in the Radius pixels text box, and **85** appears in the Threshold levels text box, as shown in Figure 24.

3. Click **OK**.

4. Save your work. Compare your modified type to Figure 25.

You modified the Unsharp Mask filter settings to modify the appearance of the layer.

Creating a neon glow
Want to create a really cool effect that takes absolutely no time at all, and works on both type and objects? You can create a neon glow that appears to surround an object. You can apply the Neon Glow filter (one of the Artistic filters) to any flattened image. This effect works best by starting with any imagery—either type or objects—that has a solid color background. Flatten the image so there's only a Background layer. Click the Magic Wand Tool on the toolbox, then click the solid color (in the background). Click Filter on the menu bar, point to Artistic, then click Neon Glow. Adjust the glow size, the glow brightness, and color, if you wish, then click OK. (An example of this technique is used in the Design Project at the end of this chapter.)

CREATE TEXT
ON A PATH

What You'll Do

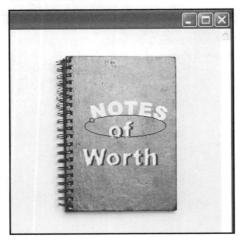

In this lesson, you'll create a shape, then add type to it.

Understanding Text on a Path

Although it is possible to create some cool type effects by adding layer styles such as bevel, emboss, and drop shadow, you can also create some awesome warped text. Suppose you want type to conform to a shape, such as an oval or a free-form you've drawn? No problem—just create the shape and add the text!

Creating Text on a Path

You start by creating a shape using one of the Photoshop shape tools on the toolbox, and then adding type to that shape (which is called a path). Add type to a shape by clicking the Horizontal Type Tool. When the pointer nears the path, you'll see that it changes to the Type Tool pointer. Click the path when the Type Tool pointer displays and begin typing. You can change fonts, font sizes, add styles, and any other interesting effects you've learned to apply with type. As you will see, the type is on a path!

QUICKTIP

Don't worry when you see the outline of the path on the screen. The path won't print, only the type will.

FIGURE 26
Type on a path

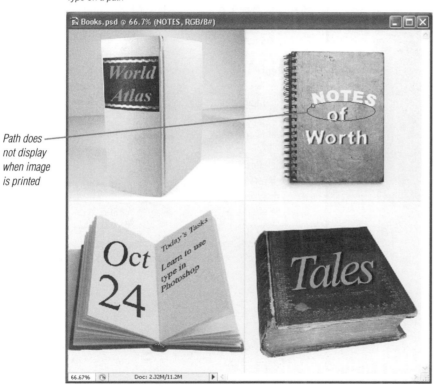

R Books.psd @ 66.7% (NOTES, RGB/8#)

World Atlas

NOTES of Worth

Today's Tasks
Learn to use type in Photoshop

Oct 24

Tales

Path does not display when image is printed

66.67%   Doc: 2.32M/11.2M

Create a path and add type

1. Click the **Rectangle Tool** on the toolbox.

2. Click the **Ellipse Tool** on the options bar.

3. Click the **Paths button** on the options bar.

4. Drag the **Paths pointer** to encircle the word "of" from **610 X/190 Y** to **780 X/240 Y**.

5. Click the **Horizontal Type Tool** T on the toolbox.

6. Change the font to **Arial Black**, the font size to **20** pt, then verify that the **Left align text button** is selected.

   TIP You can change to any point size by typing the number in the Set the font size text box.

7. Click the **Horizontal Type pointer** at approximately **620 X/205 Y** on the left edge of the ellipse.

8. Change the font color by sampling the white of Worth type, turn on the Caps Lock, then type **NOTES**.

9. Commit any current edits, then turn off the Caps Lock.

10. Hide the rulers and save your work. Compare your image to Figure 26.

11. Close the Books.psd file and exit Photoshop.

You created a path using a shape tool, then added type to it.

Power User Shortcuts

to do this:	use this method:
Apply anti-alias method	Crisp ⌄
Apply Bevel and Emboss style	𝑓., Bevel and Emboss
Apply blur filter to type	Filter ➢ Blur ➢ Gaussian Blur
Apply Drop Shadow style	𝑓., Drop Shadow
Change font family	Times New Roman... ⌄
Change font size	60 pt ⌄
Change type color	▬
Close type effects	▽
Commit current edits	✓
Display/hide rulers	[Ctrl][R] (Win) or ⌘[R] (Mac)
Erase a History state	Select state, drag to 🗑

to do this:	use this method:
Horizontal Type Tool	T. or T
Kern characters	Metrics ⌄
Move Tool	►⊕ or V
Open Character palette	▤
Save image changes	[Ctrl][S] (Win) or ⌘[S] (Mac)
See type effects (active layer)	►
See type effects (inactive layer)	►
Select all text	[Ctrl][A] (Win) or ⌘[A] (Mac)
Shift baseline of type	A$^a_\uparrow$
Warp type	𝒯

Key: Menu items are indicated by ➢ between the menu name and its command. Blue bold letters are shortcuts for selecting tools on the toolbox.

You can manipulate type in many ways to reflect or reinforce the meaning behind an image. The appearance of type is very important; color and imagery are often used to *complement* the type. You can also change the appearance of type by using different fonts (also called typefaces) and colors. You can use filters and layer styles to create the illusion that type has special effects. Type is typically used along with imagery to deliver a message quickly and with flare. Type should be limited, direct, and to the point. It should be large enough for easy reading, but should not overwhelm or distract from the central image. After you decide on the content you want to use and create the type, you can experiment with its appearance by changing its font, size, and color. You can also apply special effects that make type stand out, or appear to pop off the page.

What You Have Learned:

- How to create and modify type
- How to change the type color
- How to adjust spacing between characters
- How to make characters look higher/lower than other characters
- How to add depth to characters with a drop shadow
- How to give characters an embossed appearance
- How to apply a filter to type
- How to create type on a non-horizontal/vertical line

Key Terms

Baseline shift   Vertical distance that type moves from its baseline.

Bitmap type   Composed of pixels, and can develop jagged edges when enlarged.

Character palette   Helps you control type properties such as kerning, tracking, and leading.

Drop shadow   Creates an illusion that another colored layer of identical text is behind the selected type.

Layer styles   Effects which can be applied to a type or image layer that can greatly enhance its appearance.

Rasterized   Process of converting a type layer into an image layer.

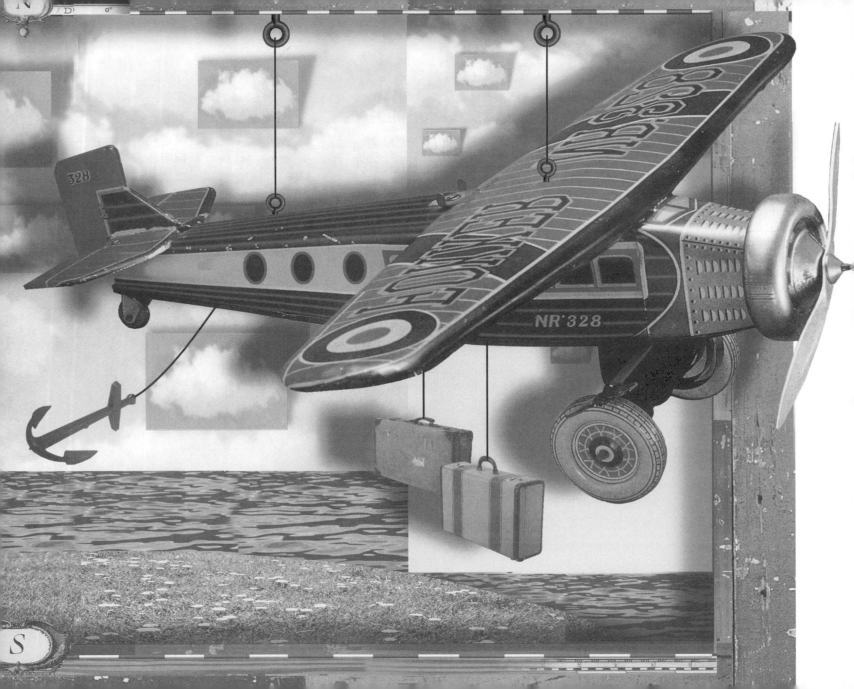

chapter

6

USING PAINTING
TOOLS

1. Paint and patch an image.

2. Create and modify a brush tip.

3. Use the Smudge Tool.

4. Use a library and an airbrush effect.

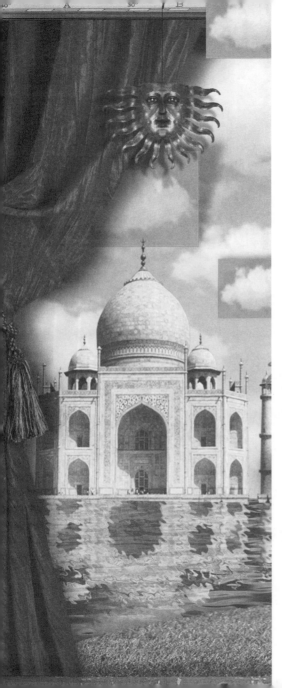

6 USING PAINTING
TOOLS

Painting Pixels

In addition to the color-enhancing techniques you've already learned, Photoshop has a variety of painting tools that let you modify colors. Unlike the tools an oil painter might use to *apply* pigment to a canvas, such as a brush or a palette knife, these virtual painting tools let you *change* existing colors and pixels.

Understanding Painting Tools

In most cases, you use a painting tool by selecting it, then choosing a brush tip. Just like a real brush, the brush size and shape determines how colors are affected. You paint the image by applying the brush tip to an image, which is similar to the way pigment is applied to a real brush and then painted on a canvas. In Photoshop, the results of the painting process can be deeper, richer colors, bleached or blurred colors, or filter-like effects in specific areas. You can select the size and shape of a brush tip, and control the point at which the brush stroke fades.

Learning About Brush Libraries

Brushes that are used with painting tools are stored within a brush library. Each **brush library** contains a variety of brush tips that you can use, rename, delete, or customize. After you select a tool, you can select a brush tip from the default brush library, which is automatically available from the Brush Preset picker list arrow. Photoshop comes with the following additional brush libraries:

- Assorted Brushes
- Basic Brushes
- Calligraphic Brushes
- Drop Shadow Brushes
- Dry Media Brushes
- Faux Finish Brushes
- Natural Brushes
- Natural Brushes 2
- Special Effect Brushes
- Square Brushes
- Thick Heavy Brushes
- Wet Media Brushes

Tools You'll Use

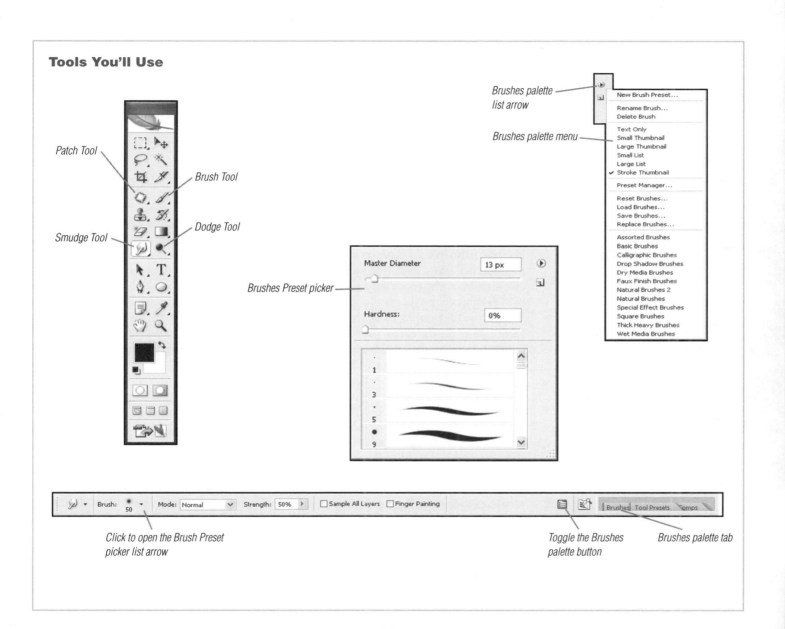

Patch Tool

Brush Tool

Smudge Tool

Dodge Tool

Brushes palette list arrow

Brushes palette menu

New Brush Preset...

Rename Brush...
Delete Brush

Text Only
Small Thumbnail
Large Thumbnail
Small List
Large List
✓ Stroke Thumbnail

Preset Manager...

Reset Brushes...
Load Brushes...
Save Brushes...
Replace Brushes...

Assorted Brushes
Basic Brushes
Calligraphic Brushes
Drop Shadow Brushes
Dry Media Brushes
Faux Finish Brushes
Natural Brushes 2
Natural Brushes
Special Effect Brushes
Square Brushes
Thick Heavy Brushes
Wet Media Brushes

Master Diameter   13 px

Brushes Preset picker

Hardness: 0%

Brush: 50   Mode: Normal   Strength: 50%   ☐ Sample All Layers   ☐ Finger Painting   Brushes Tool Presets Comps

Click to open the Brush Preset picker list arrow

Toggle the Brushes palette button

Brushes palette tab

PAINT AND
PATCH AN IMAGE

What You'll Do

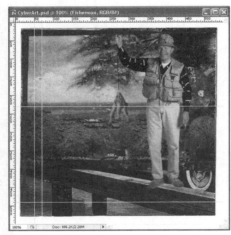

In this lesson, you'll use the Sharpen Tool to give pixels more definition, the Burn Tool to increase darker areas, then use fade settings to paint an area. You'll also use the Patch Tool to hide unnecessary imagery.

Using Painting Tools

As you've probably realized, you can use many methods to achieve similar effects in Photoshop. No method is necessarily better than another. Like a mask that hides a specific area, Photoshop painting tools can be used to enhance specific areas of a layer. You can use the painting tools, shown in Table 1, to create the effects shown in Figure 1. Unlike a mask that is applied to a defined area within a layer, or a filter that is applied to an entire layer, the effects of painting tools are applied to whatever areas the pointer contacts. In some ways, Photoshop painting tools function very similarly to real painting brushes; in others, they go far beyond traditional tools to let you achieve some incredible effects.

Understanding Fade Options

When you dip a real brush in paint and then stroke the brush across canvas, the brush stroke begins to fade as more of the pigment is left on the canvas than on the brush. This effect can be duplicated in Photoshop using fade options. Fade options are brush settings that determine how and when colors fade toward the end of brush strokes. Fade option settings are measured in steps. A **step** is equivalent to one mark of the brush tip and can be any value from 1–9999. The larger the step value, the longer the fade. You can set fade options for most of the painting tools using the Size Jitter Control option on several of the Brush Tip Shape options within the Brushes palette.

QUICKTIP

To picture a brush fade, imagine a skid mark left by a tire. The mark starts out strong and bold, then fades out gradually or quickly, depending on conditions. This effect is analogous to a brush fade.

Learning About the Patch Tool

Photoshop offers many tools to work with damaged or unwanted imagery. One such tool is the Patch Tool. Although this is not a painting tool, you might find as you work in Photoshop, you have to combine a variety of tool strategies to achieve the effect you want. The Patch Tool is located on the toolbox and is hidden under the Healing Brush Tool. You can use this tool to cover a selected area with pixels from another area, or a pattern. Both the Patch Tool and the Healing Brush Tool match the texture, lighting, and shading of the sampled pixels so your repaired area will look seamless. The Healing Brush Tool, however, also matches the transparency of the pixels.

QUICKTIP

As you drag a selection made with the Patch Tool, look at the selection and you'll see what the pixels will be replaced with.

Using the Patch Tool

The Patch Tool provides a quick and easy way to repair or remove an area within an image. You can use the Patch Tool in the following ways:

- Select the area you want to fix, click the Source option button on the options bar, then drag the selection over the area you want to replicate.
- Select the area you want replicated, click the Destination option button on the options bar, then drag the selection over the area you want to fix.

QUICKTIP

There's not necessarily one "right tool" for any given job: there might be several methods of completing a task. It's up to you to figure out which tool can be used to do the job. Remember, many Photoshop tasks might take several tries before you get the results you want. Hang in there and just keep trying.

FIGURE 1
Painting samples

TABLE 1: Painting Tools

tool	button	effect
Smudge Tool		Smears colors across an image as if you dragged your finger across wet ink. (Hidden under the Blur Tool.)
Sharpen Tool		Increases contrast between pixels, giving a sharp, crisp look. (Hidden under the Blur Tool.)
Blur Tool		Decreases contrast between pixels, giving a soft, blurred look.
Dodge Tool		Lightens underlying pixels, giving a lighter, underexposed appearance.
Burn Tool		Darkens underlying pixels, giving a richer, overexposed appearance. (Hidden under the Dodge Tool.)
Sponge Tool		Increases or decreases the purity of a color by saturating or desaturating the color. (Hidden under the Dodge Tool.)

Use the Sharpen Tool

1. Start Photoshop, open PS 6-1.psd from the drive and folder where your Data Files are stored, then save it as **CyberArt**.

2. Display the rulers in pixels (if they are not already displayed) and make sure the document size displays in the status bar.

3. Click the **Sharpen Tool** △ on the toolbox.

   | TIP Look under the Blur Tool if the Sharpen Tool is hidden.

4. Click the **Click to open the Brush Preset picker list arrow** ⁝ ⁻ on the options bar.

5. Scroll down the list, and double-click **19** (Hard Round 19 pixels).

6. Drag the **Brush pointer** ◯ from **20 X/20 Y** to **530 X/20 Y**, to sharpen across the top area of the image.

7. Press and hold **[Shift]**, click the image in the lower-right corner at **530 X/530 Y**, then release **[Shift]**.

   | TIP Instead of dragging to create a line from point to point, you can click a starting point, press and hold [Shift], click an ending point, then release [Shift] to create a perfectly straight line.

8. Press and hold **[Shift]**, click the image in the lower-left corner at **20 X/530 Y**, then release **[Shift]**.

9. Press and hold **[Shift]**, click the image in the upper-left corner at **20 X/20 Y**, then release **[Shift]**. Compare your image to Figure 2.

You used the Sharpen Tool to focus on the pixels around the perimeter of the image. The affected pixels now appear sharper and crisper.

FIGURE 2
Results of Sharpen Tool

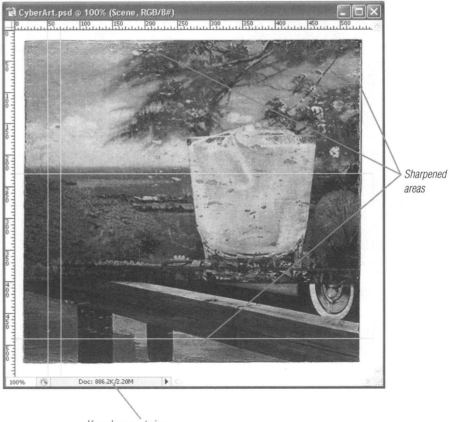

Sharpened areas

Your document size may be different

FIGURE 3
Results of Burn Tool

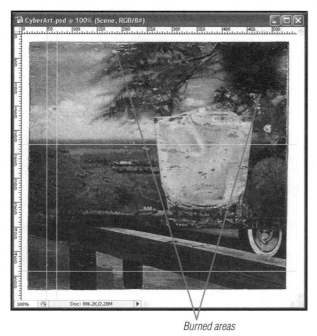

Burned areas

Painting with a pattern

Suppose you have an area within an image that you want to replicate on a new or existing layer. You can create a tiled effect using the desired area and the Pattern Stamp Tool. To create this effect, select the Rectangular Marquee Tool using a 0 pixel feather setting, then drag the outline around an area in your image. With this area outlined, click Edit on the menu bar, click Define Pattern, type a name in the Name text box, then click OK. Deselect the marquee, click the Pattern Stamp Tool on the toolbox, click the Click to open Pattern picker list arrow on the options bar, then click the new pattern. Each time you click the pointer on a layer, the new pattern will be applied. You can delete a custom pattern by right-clicking the pattern swatch in the Pattern picker, then clicking Delete Pattern.

Burn an area

1. Click the **Burn Tool** on the toolbox.

   TIP Look under the Dodge Tool if the Burn Tool is hidden.

2. Click the **Click to open the Brush Preset picker list arrow** on the options bar, then scroll to and double-click **27** (Soft Round 27 pixels).

   TIP You can change any brush tip size at any time. Press [[] to increase the brush tip or []] to decrease the brush tip in increments of 10.

3. Drag the **Brush pointer** from **20 X/25 Y** to **550 X/25 Y**.

   Did you notice that the area you painted became darker? It looks as though the edges are burned.

4. Drag the **Brush pointer** back and forth throughout the upper-right corner from **400 X/25 Y** to **530 X/120 Y**. Compare your image to Figure 3.

You used the Burn Tool to tone down the pixels in the upper-right corner of the image. This technique increases the darker tones, changing the mood of the image.

Set fade options and paint an area

1. Click the **Eyedropper Tool** on the toolbox.

2. Use the **Eyedropper pointer** to click the image at **50 X/490 Y**, as shown in Figure 4.

3. Click the **Brush Tool** on the toolbox.

4. Click the **Click to open the Brush Preset picker list arrow** on the options bar, then double-click **19** (Hard Round 19 pixels).

5. Click the **Toggle the Brushes palette button** on the options bar.

6. Click **Shape Dynamics** on the Brushes palette (if it is not already selected), then adjust your settings using Figure 5 as a guide.

   The Brushes palette will automatically close when you begin painting. Available fade options and their locations on the Brushes palette are described in Table 2.

   TIP Click the option name on the Brushes palette to see the option settings. Selecting an option's check box turns the option on, but doesn't display the settings.

7. Press and hold **[Shift]**, drag the **Brush pointer** from **25 X/25 Y** to **525 X/25 Y**, then release **[Shift]**.

8. Use the **Brush pointer** to click the image at **25 X/40 Y**, press and hold **[Shift]**, click the image at **25 X/520 Y**, then release **[Shift]**, as shown in Figure 6.

You modified the fade options, then painted areas using the Brush tool.

FIGURE 4
Location to sample

FIGURE 6
Areas painted with fade

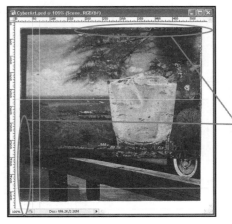

Faded areas

FIGURE 5
Brushes palette

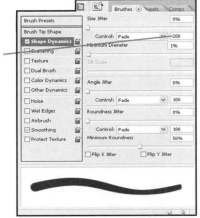

Indicates how many steps it takes for fade to occur

TABLE 2: Fade Options

option	description	on Brushes palette
Size Jitter	Decreases the brush stroke size toward the end of the stroke.	Shape Dynamics
Opacity Jitter	Decreases the brush stroke opacity toward the end of the stroke.	Other Dynamics
Color	Causes the foreground color to shift to the background color toward the end of the stroke. Available in the following tools: Brush , and Pencil .	Color Dynamics

FIGURE 7
Marquee surrounding source area

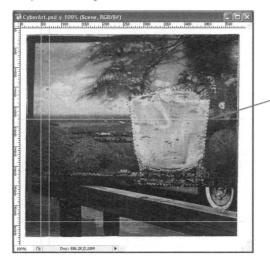

Selection to be patched

FIGURE 8
Results of Patch Tool

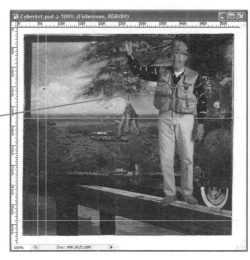

The location of your fisherman
may vary

Patch an area

1. Click the **Patch Tool** ⟳ on the toolbox.

   TIP   Look under the Healing Brush Tool if the Patch Tool is hidden.

2. Drag the **Patch Tool pointer** ⟲ around the periphery of the glass, being sure to complete the loop so you create the selection as shown in Figure 7.

3. Click the **Source option button** on the options bar, if it's not already selected.

4. Drag the selection so that the outline of the left edge of the glass (the outline source) is at approximately **60 X/170 Y**.

   TIP   You can reverse steps using the History palette, then retry until you're satisfied with the results.

   The selection is replaced with imagery from the location that you defined with the selection. As you drag, you'll see the pixels that will be replacing the selection. When finished, the horizon should be aligned.

5. Click **Select** on the menu bar, then click **Deselect**.

6. Click the **Fisherman layer** on the Layers palette and display the layer.

7. Click the **Move Tool** ⤢ on the toolbox, then press the arrow keys as needed until the right side of the man covers any remnants of the glass. Compare your image to Figure 8.

   Selecting and patching are difficult skills to master. Your results might differ.

8. Click the **Scene layer** on the Layers palette.

9. Save your work.

You used the Patch Tool to cover an area within an image. The tool makes it possible to correct flaws within an image using existing imagery.

CREATE AND MODIFY
A BRUSH TIP

What You'll Do

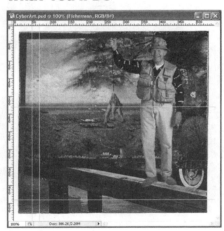

In this lesson, you'll create a brush tip and modify its settings, then you'll use it to paint a border. This new brush tip will be wide and have a distinctive shape that adds an element of mystery to the image.

Understanding Brush Tips

You use brush tips to change the size and pattern of the brush used to apply color. Brushes are stored within libraries. In addition to the default brushes that are available from the Brush Preset picker list, you can also select a brush tip from one of 12 brush libraries. You can access these additional libraries, shown in Figure 9, by clicking the Brush Preset picker list arrow on the options bar.

Learning About Brush Tip Modifications

You can adjust the many brush tip settings that help determine the shape of a brush. One factor that influences the shape of a brush stroke is jitter. **Jitter** is the randomness of dynamic elements such as size, angle, roundness, hue, saturation, brightness, opacity, and flow. The number beneath the brush tip indicates the diameter, and the image of the tip changes as its values are modified. Figure 10 shows some of the types of modifications that

you can make to a brush tip using the Brushes palette. The shape of the brush tip pointer reflects the shape of the brush tip. As you change the brush tip, its pointer also changes.

FIGURE 9
Brush tip libraries

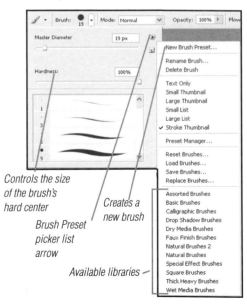

Controls the size of the brush's hard center

Brush Preset picker list arrow

Creates a new brush

Available libraries

QUICKTIP
You can open the Brushes palette to change a brush tip by clicking the Brushes palette tab in the palette well, or by clicking the Toggle the Brushes palette button on the options bar.

Creating a Brush Tip

You can create your own brush tip by clicking the Brushes palette list arrow, then clicking New Brush Preset to open the Brush Name dialog box, where you can type a descriptive name in the Name text box. All the options on the Brushes palette are available to you as you adjust the settings. As you select settings, a sample appears at the bottom of the palette. You can delete the current brush tip by selecting it from the Brush Preset picker, clicking the Brush Preset picker list arrow, clicking Delete Brush, then clicking OK in the warning box. You can also right-click (Win) or [Ctrl]-click (Mac) a brush tip on the Brushes palette, then click Delete Brush.

FIGURE 10
Brush Presets on the Brushes palette

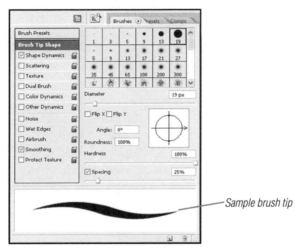

Sample brush tip

FIGURE 11
Tinted image

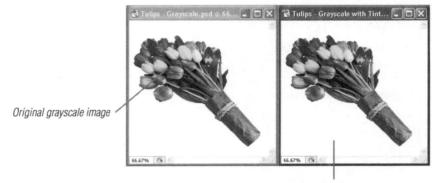

Original grayscale image

After tinting has been applied

Applying a tint

You can use brush tips to apply a tint to a grayscale image. By changing the mode of a grayscale image to RGB color, you can use painting tools to tint an image. After you change the image mode, create a new layer, click the Mode list arrow in the New Layer dialog box, click Color, select colors from the Swatches palette, then apply tints to the new layer. See Figure 11 for an example.

Lesson 2   Create and Modify a Brush Tip

Create a brush tip

1. Click the **Brush Tool** ✐. on the toolbox.

2. Click the **Brushes palette tab** `Brushes` in the palette well.

3. Click the **arrow** ▶ to the right of the tab, then click **Clear Brush Controls**.

4. Click the **Brushes palette tab arrow** ▶ again, then click **New Brush Preset**.

5. Type **Custom oval brush tip** to replace the current name, then click **OK**.

6. Click **Brush Tip Shape** on the Brushes palette, then adjust your settings using Figure 12 as a guide.

7. Click the **Brushes palette tab** `Brushes` to close the palette.

   | TIP   A newly added brush tip generally is added at the bottom of the Brushes palette.

   The new brush tip appears on the options bar or by opening the Brushes palette and scrolling to the bottom.

You cleared the current brush settings, and then created a brush tip using the Brushes palette. You modified its settings to create a custom brush tip for painting a border.

FIGURE 12
Brush Tip Shape settings

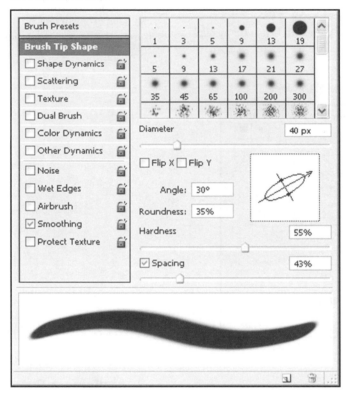

FIGURE 13
Painted image

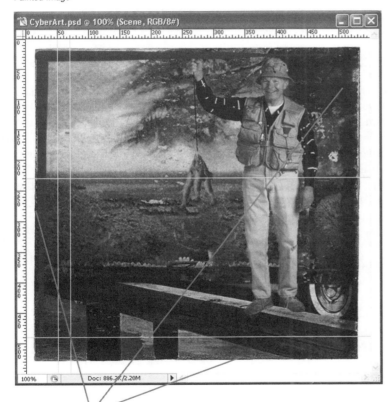

Effects of the custom brush tip

1. Click the **Mode list arrow** on the options bar, then click **Multiply**.

   TIP   The Multiply blend mode creates semi-transparent shadow effects and multiplies the value of the base color by the blend color.

2. Double-click the **Opacity text box**, then type **75**.

3. Click the **Toggle the Brushes palette button** on the options bar, then click **Shape Dynamics**.

4. Click the **Control list arrow** under the Size Jitter section, then click **Fade**.

5. Type **400** in the list box to the right of the Control list arrow.

6. Click the **Brushes palette tab** Brushes to close the palette.

7. Use the **Brush pointer** to click the image near the upper-right corner at **515 X/25 Y**, press and hold **[Shift]**, click the image near the lower-right corner at **515 X/515 Y**, then release **[Shift]**.

8. Save your work, then compare your image to Figure 13.

Using the newly created brush tip, you painted areas of the image. You also made adjustments to the opacity and fade settings to make the brush stroke more dramatic.

USE THE
SMUDGE TOOL

What You'll Do

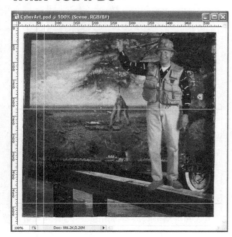

In this lesson, you'll smudge pixels to create a surreal effect in an image.

Blurring Colors

You can create the same finger-painted look in your Photoshop image that you did as a kid using paints in a pot. Using the Smudge Tool, you can create the effect of dragging your finger through wet paint. Like the Brush Tool, the Smudge Tool has many brush tips that you can select from the Brushes palette, or you can create a brush tip of your own.

> **QUICK**TIP
>
> You can use the Smudge Tool to minimize defects in an image.

Smudging Options

Figure 14 shows an original image and three examples of Smudge Tool effects. In each example, the same brush tip is used with different options on the options bar. If you select the Smudge Tool with the default settings, your smudge effect will be similar to the image shown in the upper-right corner of Figure 14.

Using Finger Painting

The image in the lower-right corner of Figure 14 shows the effect with the Finger Painting check box selected *prior* to the smudge stroke. The image in the upper-right corner did not have the Finger Painting check box selected. The image in the lower-left corner had the Finger Painting option off, but had the Use All Layers check box selected. The Use All Layers check box enables your smudge stroke to affect all the layers beneath the current layer.

QUICKTIP

The Finger Painting option uses the foreground color at the beginning of each stroke. Without the Finger Painting option, the color under the pointer is used at the beginning of each stroke.

FIGURE 14
Smudge samples

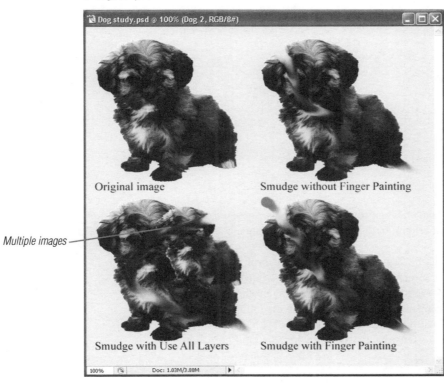

Original image

Smudge without Finger Painting

Multiple images

Smudge with Use All Layers

Smudge with Finger Painting

Modify smudge settings

1. Click the **Smudge Tool** 🖐 on the toolbox.

   | TIP The Smudge Tool might be hidden under the Sharpen Tool.

2. Click the **Click to open the Brush Preset picker list arrow** on the options bar.

3. Double-click **46 (Spatter 46 pixels)**.

   | TIP This brush tip is located in the middle of the list.

4. Select the **Finger Painting check box** ☐ Finger Painting on the options bar (if it is not already selected).

5. Make sure your settings match those shown in Figure 15.

You modified the existing smudge settings, to prepare to smudge the image.

FIGURE 15
Smudge Tool options bar

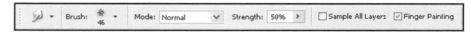

FIGURE 16
Graphics tablet

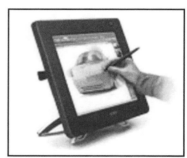

Using a graphics tablet

If you really want to see Photoshop take off when you use brush tools, try using a graphics tablet. This nifty item might set you back several hundred dollars, but you'll love what you get in return.

Figure 16 shows the Wacom CintiQ 18SX graphics tablet, with a cordless, battery-free tablet and an 18.1" hi-res screen. The stand makes it possible to rotate, incline, or use the tablet on your lap. (You can learn more about the product at www.wacom.com.) The benefits of using a graphics tablet include the following:

- Over 1000 levels of pressure sensitivity
- The ability to use the 19 pressure-sensitive tools already included in Photoshop
- Programmable menu buttons
- The ability to move even faster than when you use shortcut keys

And as an added bonus, you'll probably experience fewer problems with repetitive stress injuries.

FIGURE 17
Smudged area

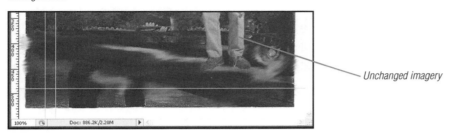

Unchanged imagery

FIGURE 18A
Original image

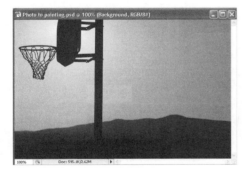

FIGURE 18B
Painted image

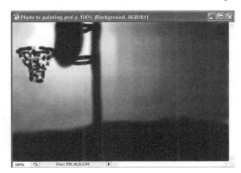

Smudge an image

1. Verify that the Scene layer is active.

2. Drag the **Smudge Tool pointer** (zigzagging from right to left) from **0 X/400 Y** to **530 X/500 Y**.

   Dragging the pointer back and forth as you move from left to right creates an interesting smudge effect. The degree and effect of your smudging will vary.

   An area on the current layer is smudged. Did you notice that the fisherman layer is unchanged?

3. Save your work, then compare your image to Figure 17.

You used the Smudge Tool to smear the pixels in the bottom third of the image. That area now has a dreamy quality.

Turning a photo into a "painting"

You can create a painting-like appearance using a photographic image and a few simple Photoshop brush tools. Take an image, like the one shown in Figure 18A, and make any necessary color adjustments. Define the entire image as a pattern by clicking Edit on the menu bar, then clicking Define Pattern. Click the Pattern Stamp Tool, click the Create new fill or adjustment layer button on the Layers palette, then click Solid Color. Choose white from the Color Picker, then lower the opacity so you can see the image. Create another new layer, then use the Pattern Stamp Tool and the new pattern you created to paint over the existing image. Figure 18B shows the same image after the painting treatment.

USE A LIBRARY AND AN
AIRBRUSH EFFECT

What You'll Do

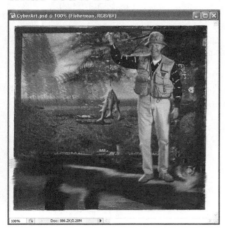

In this lesson, you'll sample an area of the image, then use brush tips from a library to create additional effects. You'll also use an airbrush effect to apply gradual tones.

Learning About the Airbrush Effect

You might have heard of professional photographers using an airbrush to minimize or eliminate flaws in faces or objects. In Photoshop, the effect simulates the photographer's technique by applying gradual tones to an image. Airbrushing creates a diffused effect on the edges of pixels. The airbrush effect is located on the options bar and on the Brushes palette. You can apply the airbrush effect with any brush tip size, using the Brush Tool, History Brush Tool, Dodge Tool, Burn Tool, and Sponge Tool. The **flow** setting determines how much paint is sprayed while the mouse button is held.

> QUICKTIP
> When using the airbrush effect, you can accumulate color by holding the mouse button without dragging.

Restoring pixel data

You can use the History Brush Tool to restore painted pixels. The History Brush Tool makes a copy of previous pixel data, and then lets you paint with that data, making this tool another good source for undoing painting errors. The Art History Brush Tool also lets you re-create imagery using pixel data, but with more stylized effects. This tool has many more options than the History Brush Tool, including Style, Area, and Tolerance. Style controls the shape of the paint stroke. Area controls the area covered by the brush tip (a higher area value covers a larger area). Tolerance controls the region where the paint stroke is applied, based on color tolerance. A greater spacing value causes paint strokes to occur in areas that differ in color from the original area. Some of the Art History Brush Tool options are shown in Figure 19.

Using Brush Tip Libraries

Photoshop comes with 12 brush libraries that can replace or be appended to the current list of brushes. All the libraries are stored in a folder called Brushes. Each of the libraries is stored in its own file (having the extension .abr). Eight of the libraries are shown in Figure 20. Four of the brush libraries are available in the Adobe Photoshop Only folder. When you use the Load Brushes command, the brush tips are added to the end of the brushes list. When you click the name of a brush tip library from the Brush Preset picker

list, you are given the option of replacing the existing brush tips with the contents of the library, or appending the brush tips to the existing list.

QUICKTIP

You can restore the default brush tip settings by clicking the list arrow on the Brushes palette, clicking Reset Brushes, then clicking OK.

Managing the Preset Manager

The **Preset Manager** is a Photoshop feature that allows you to manage libraries of preset brushes, swatches, gradients, styles, patterns, contours, custom shapes, and tools. You can display the Preset Manager by clicking Edit on the menu bar, and then clicking Preset Manager. Options for the Preset Manager are shown in Figure 21. You can delete or rename individual elements for each type of library. Changes that you make in the Preset Manager dialog box are reflected on the corresponding palettes.

FIGURE 19
Art History Brush Tool options

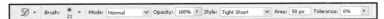

FIGURE 20
Load dialog box

4 additional libraries are available in this folder

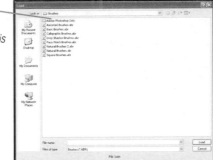

FIGURE 21
Preset Manager dialog box

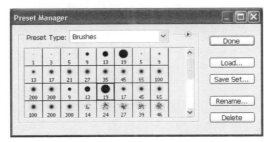

Load a brush library

1. Click the **Eyedropper Tool** ✐. on the toolbox.

2. Use the **Eyedropper pointer** ✐ to click the image at **50 X/230 Y** (at the intersection of the guides).

3. Click the **Brush Tool** ✐. on the toolbox.

4. Click the **Click to open the Brush Preset picker list arrow** on the options bar.

5. Click the **Brush Preset picker list arrow,** then click **Load Brushes,** as shown in Figure 22.

6. Navigate to the Brushes folder (if it is not already selected), then click **Faux Finish Brushes.abr**, as shown in Figure 23.

   TIP This brush library is located in the Brushes folder. The Brushes folder is located in/Program Files/Adobe/Adobe Photoshop CS2/Presets/Brushes (Win) and the Presets folder in the Adobe Photoshop CS2 folder in Applications (Mac).

7. Click **Load**.

8. Click the **Click to open the Brush Preset picker list arrow** on the options bar, scroll to the bottom of the list of brush tips, then double-click **75 (Veining Feather 1)** near the bottom of the list.

The active brush tip is from the Faux Finish Brushes library.

You sampled a specific location in the image, then loaded the Faux Finish Brushes library. You selected a brush tip from this new library, which you will use to paint an area.

FIGURE 22
Load Brushes command

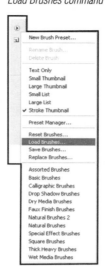

FIGURE 23
Load dialog box

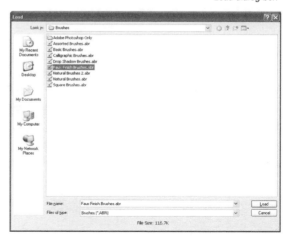

FIGURE 24
Brush Tool options

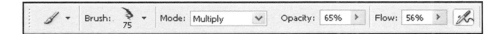

Create an airbrush effect

1. Click the **Set to enable airbrush capabilities button** on the options bar.

2. Change the settings on the options bar so they match those shown in Figure 24.

3. Drag the **Brush pointer** back and forth over the areas of the image containing the sky (from approximately **30 X/50 Y** to **250 X/200 Y**).

4. Hide the rulers.

5. Clear the guides.

6. Click the **Fisherman layer** on the Layers palette.

7. Click the **Add a layer style button** on the Layers palette.

8. Click **Bevel and Emboss,** then click **OK** to accept the existing settings.

9. Save your work, then compare your image to Figure 25.

10. Close the image and exit Photoshop.

You used an airbrush effect to paint the sky in the image. You applied the Bevel and Emboss style to a layer to add finishing touches.

FIGURE 25
Results of Airbrush option and style

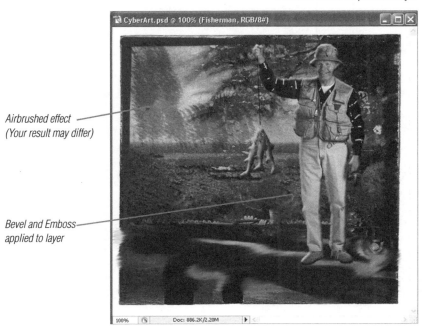

Airbrushed effect
(Your result may differ)

Bevel and Emboss
applied to layer

Power User Shortcuts

to do this:	use this method:
Apply tint to grayscale image	Image ➤ Mode ➤ RGB Color, choose color, choose paint tool, then apply color from Swatches palette
Blur an image	◌ or Shift R
Burn an image	◌ or Shift O
Create a brush tip	Brushes ◥, ⊙, click New Brush Preset
Define a pattern	Edit ➤ Define Pattern, type name, click OK
Delete brush tip	⊙, then click Delete Brush
Dodge an image	◉ or Shift O
Load brush library	Click painting tool, ⌗, ⊙, click Load Brushes, choose a library

to do this:	use this method:
Paint a straight line	Press and hold [Shift] while dragging pointer
Paint an image	✎ or Shift B
Patch a selection	◌ or Shift J
Restore default brushes	⌗, ⊙, click Reset Brushes
Select Fade options	Brushes ◥, then click Shape Dynamics
Sharpen an image	△ or Shift R
Smudge an image	◌ or Shift R

Key: Menu items are indicated by ➤ between the menu name and its command. Bold blue letters are shortcuts for selecting tools on the toolbox.

With painting tools, you can give your image a quality that looks as though your work came off of an artist's easel. Using an assortment of brush libraries, you can create many interesting effects. Painting tools give you the ability to change brush sizes, shapes, and even the length in which a brush stroke fades. You can use the Patch Tool and the Healing Brush Tool to make repairs to specific areas within an image.

What You Have Learned:

- How to change the brush size
- How to paint in a straight line
- How to sharpen and burn pixels
- How to set fade options
- How to patch an area
- How to create and modify a brush tip
- How to smudge pixels
- How to load a brush library

Key Terms

Brush library   A variety of brush tips that you can use, rename, delete, or customize.

Flow   Airbrush effect setting that determines how much paint is sprayed while the mouse button is held.

Jitter   The randomness of dynamic elements such as size, angle, roundness, hue, saturation, brightness, opacity, and flow.

Preset Manager   Feature that allows you to manage libraries of preset brushes, swatches, gradients, styles, patterns, contours, custom shapes, and tools.

Step   One mark of the brush tip that determines the brush stroke length for a fade.

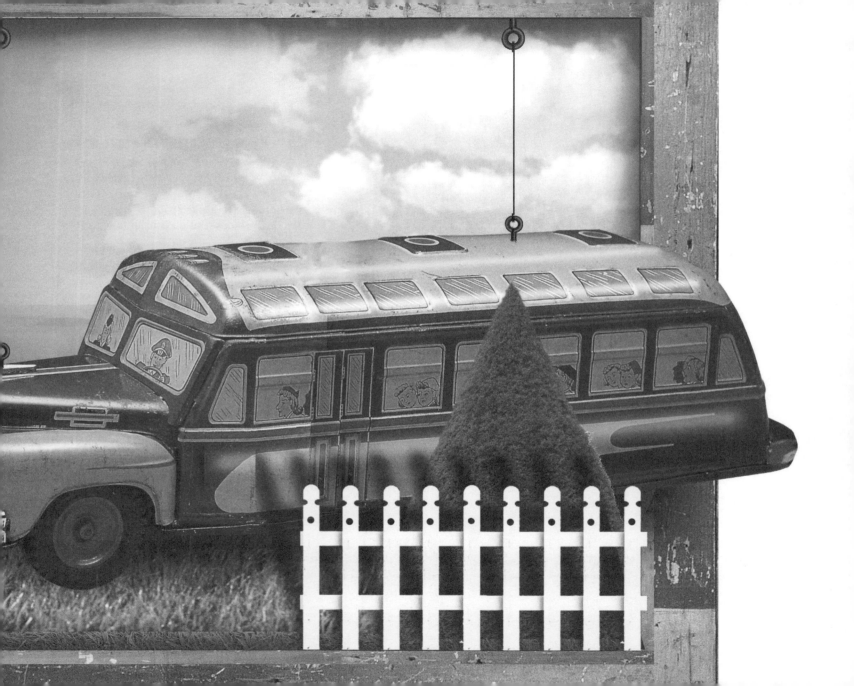

7

WORKING WITH SPECIAL
LAYER FUNCTIONS

1. Use a layer mask with a selection.

2. Work with layer masks and layer content.

3. Control pixels to blend colors.

4. Eliminate a layer mask.

5. Use an adjustment layer.

6. Create a clipping mask.

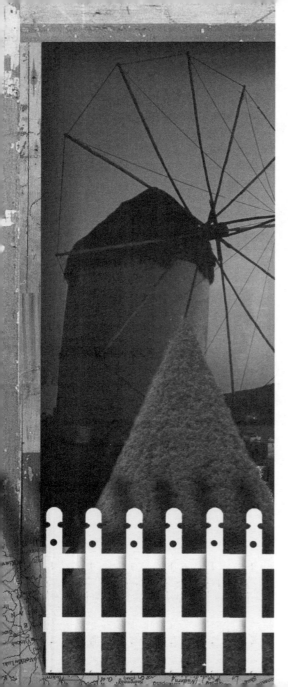

chapter 7 WORKING WITH SPECIAL
LAYER FUNCTIONS

Designing with Layers

Photoshop is rich with tools and techniques for creating and enhancing images. After the imagery is in place, you can hide and modify objects to create special effects. When used in conjunction with other relatively simple techniques, such as merging layers or duplicating layers, the results can be dramatic.

Modifying Specific Areas Within a Layer

You can use special layer features to modify the entire image or a single layer of an image. For example, suppose that you have an image with objects in multiple layers. Perhaps you want to include certain elements from each layer, but you also want to hide some imagery in the finished image. You can *define* the precise area you want to manipulate in each layer, and then accurately adjust its appearance to exactly what you want, without permanently altering the original image. You can turn your changes on or off, align images, blend and adjust color, and combine elements to enhance your image.

Tools You'll Use

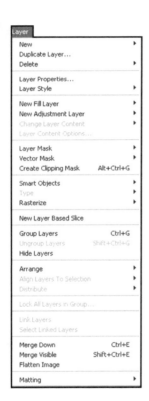

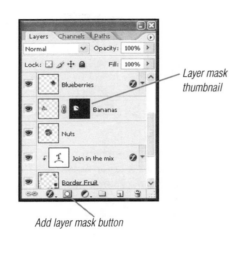

Layer mask thumbnail

Add layer mask button

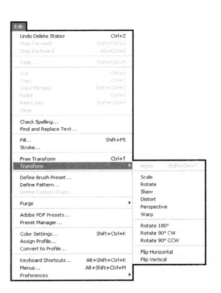

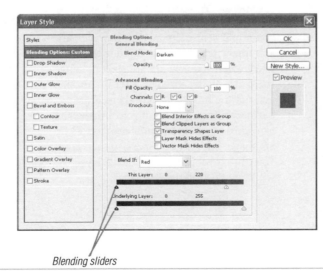

Blending sliders

USE A LAYER MASK WITH
A SELECTION

What You'll Do

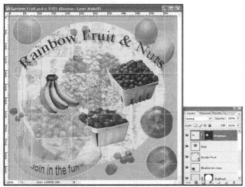

In this lesson, you'll use the Elliptical Marquee Tool to make a selection and create a layer mask on the Rainbow layer and on the Bananas layer. You'll select the Brush Tool and a brush tip, and then paint on the layer mask to hide pixels.

About Layer Masks

You can hide or reveal a selection within a layer by using a layer mask. A **layer mask** can cover an entire layer or specific areas within a layer. When a layer contains a mask, a layer mask thumbnail appears on the Layers palette to the left of the layer name. As you hide or reveal portions of a layer, the layer mask thumbnail mirrors the changes you make to the object. Some Photoshop features are permanent after you implement them. Masks, however, are extremely flexible—you can hide their effect when you view the image, or change them at will. Because you alter the mask and not the image, no actual pixels are harmed in the creation of your image. You can add an unlimited number of masks to an image, but only one mask to each layer. You can also continue to edit the layer without affecting the layer mask.

QUICKTIP

You can think of a mask as a type of temporary eraser. When you erase pixels from an image, they're gone. A mask can be used to cover pixels—either temporarily or permanently. You can also think of a mask as a cropping tool that offers flexible shapes.

Creating a Layer Mask

You can use tools on the toolbox to create the area you want to mask. You can apply a mask to the selection, or you can apply the mask to everything except the selection. You can also feather a selection (control the softness of its edges) by typing pixel values in the Feather text box on the options bar.

QUICKTIP

The term "mask" has its origin in printing. Traditionally, a mask was opaque material or tape used to block off an area of the artwork that you did not want to print.

Painting a Layer Mask

After you add a layer mask to a layer, you can reshape it with the Brush Tool and a specific brush size, or tip. Photoshop offers dozens of brush tips, so you can paint just the area you want. For example, you can create a smooth transition between the hidden and visible areas using a soft-edged brush. Here are some important facts about painting a layer mask:

- When you paint the image with a black foreground, the size of the mask *increases*, and each brush stroke hides pixels on the image layer. *Paint with black to hide pixels*.
- When you paint an object using white as the foreground color, the size of the mask *decreases*, and each brush stroke restores pixels of the layer object. *Paint with white to reveal pixels*.

In Figure 1, the School Bus layer contains a layer mask. The area where the bus intersects with the camera has been painted in black so that the bus appears to be driving through the lens of the camera.

Correcting and Updating a Mask

If you need to make a slight correction to an area, you can just switch the foreground and background colors and paint over the mistake. The layer mask thumbnail on the Layers palette automatically updates itself to reflect changes you make to the mask.

FIGURE 1
Example of a layer mask

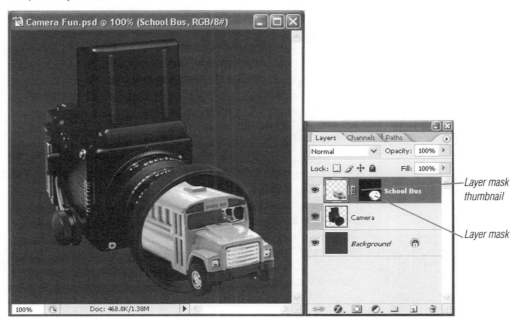

Create a layer mask using the Layer menu

1. Start Photoshop, open PS 7-1.psd from the drive and folder where your Data Files are stored, then save it as **Rainbow Fruit**.

   TIP If you see a message stating that some text layers need to be updated before they can be used for vector-based output, click Update (Mac).

2. Click the **Default Foreground and Background Colors button** ▣ on the toolbox.

3. Display the rulers in pixels (if they are not already displayed).

4. Click the **Washout layer** on the Layers palette.

5. Click the **Elliptical Marquee Tool** ○ on the toolbox.

   TIP Look under the Rectangular Marquee Tool if the Elliptical Marquee Tool is hidden.

6. Change the Feather setting to **0 px** (if this is not the current setting).

7. Drag the **Marquee pointer** ─┼─ from **30 X/20 Y** to **550 X/540 Y**, to create a marquee that includes the text, bananas, and blueberries using the guides, then compare your image to Figure 2.

8. Click **Layer** on the menu bar, point to **Layer Mask**, then click **Reveal Selection**.

   TIP You can deselect a marquee by clicking Select on the menu bar, then clicking Deselect or by clicking in another area of the image with the marquee tool that you are using; or by right-clicking the object, then clicking Deselect in the shortcut menu.

You used the Elliptical Marquee Tool to create a selection, and created a layer mask on the Washout layer using the Layer Mask command on the Layer menu.

FIGURE 2
Elliptical selection on the Rainbow layer

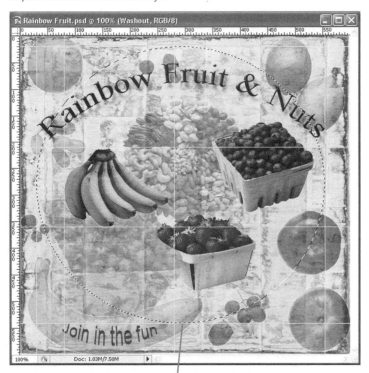

Elliptical marquee selection

Creating a selection from a Quick Mask

Once you have created a selection, you can click the Edit in Quick Mask Mode button ▣ on the toolbox to create a mask that can be saved as a selection. When you click the Edit in Quick Mask Mode button, a red overlay displays. Use any painting tools to form a shape in and around the selection. When your mask is finished, click the Edit in Standard Mode button ▣ on the toolbox, and the shape will be outlined by a marquee. you can then save the selection for future use, or use any other Photoshop tools and effects on it.

FIGURE 3
Elliptical selection on the Bananas layer

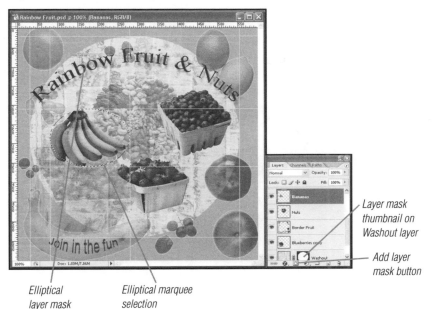

Layer mask
thumbnail on
Washout layer

Add layer
mask button

Elliptical
layer mask

Elliptical marquee
selection

FIGURE 4
Layer mask icons on the Layers palette

Layer mask
thumbnail on
Bananas layer

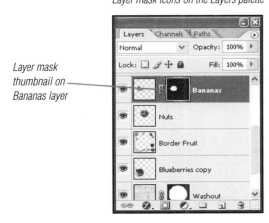

Create a layer mask using the Layers palette

1. Click the **Bananas layer** on the Layers palette.

2. Drag the **Marquee pointer** ╋ from approximately **80 X/210 Y** to **280 X/360 Y** (to surround the bunch of bananas), as shown in Figure 3.

3. Click the **Add layer mask button** on the Layers palette.

   The lower-left edge of the Bananas layer is obscured by the layer mask. The layer mask thumbnail appears to the right of the layer thumbnail.

   TIP You can press and hold [Alt] (Win) or [option] (Mac) while clicking the Add mask layer button to add a mask that *hides* the selection, rather than reveals it.

4. Click the **layer mask thumbnail** on the Bananas layer to ensure that the layer mask is active, then compare your Layers palette to Figure 4.

   TIP You can tell whether the layer mask or the layer object is active by the outline surrounding the thumbnail.

You used the Elliptical Marquee Tool to create a selection, and then used the Add layer mask button on the Layers palette to create a layer mask on the Bananas layer.

Paint a layer mask

1. Click the **Zoom Tool** 🔍 on the toolbox.

2. Select the **Resize Windows To Fit check box** on the options bar.

3. Click on the bananas at approximately **150 X/300 Y** with the **Zoom pointer** ⊕ until the bananas are centered and the zoom factor is 200%.

4. Click the **Brush Tool** 🖌. on the toolbox.

5. Click the **Click to open the Brush Preset picker list arrow** on the options bar, then double-click the **Hard Round 9 pixels brush tip**.

6. Change the Painting Mode in the options bar to **Normal** and the Opacity to **100%** (if necessary).

7. Verify that Black is the foreground color and White is the background color.

   > TIP Learning to paint a layer mask can be challenging. It's important to make sure the correct layer (and thumbnail) is active before you start painting, to know whether you're adding to or subtracting from the mask, and to set your foreground and background colors correctly.

8. Drag the **Brush pointer** ○ along the leftmost banana until it is completely hidden. Compare your screen to Figure 5.

   > TIP Select a different brush tip if the brush is too big or too small.

You used the Zoom Tool to keep a specific portion of the image in view as you increased the zoom percentage, selected a brush tip, and painted pixels on the layer mask to hide a banana.

FIGURE 5
Layer mask painted

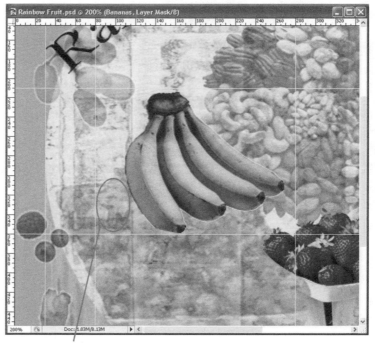

Painted area

FIGURE 6
Modified layer mask

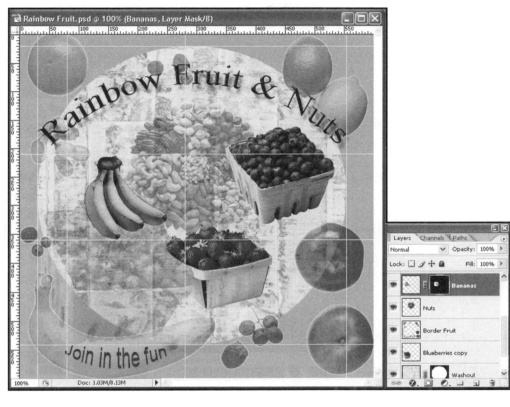

Modify the layer mask

1. Drag the **Brush pointer** ○ along the right edge of the object, until the right-most banana is no longer visible and you revealed the nuts.

   TIP As you paint, a new History state is created each time you release the mouse button.

2. Click the **Zoom Tool** 🔍 on the toolbox.

3. Press **[Alt]** (Win) or **[option]** (Mac), click at **150 X/300 Y** with the **Zoom pointer** 🔍 until the zoom factor is 100%, then release **[Alt]** (Win) or **[option]** (Mac).

4. Save your work, then compare your screen to Figure 6.

You painted pixels to hide the right-most banana, then reset the zoom percentage to 100%.

Editing a layer mask versus editing a layer
Modifying a layer mask can be tricky because you have to make sure that you've selected the layer mask and not the layer thumbnail. Even though the active thumbnail is surrounded by an outline, it can be difficult to see. To make sure whether the layer mask or layer thumbnail is selected, click each one so you can see the difference, then make sure the one you want is selected. You'll know if you've selected the wrong item as soon as you start painting!

WORK WITH LAYER MASKS
AND LAYER CONTENT

What You'll Do

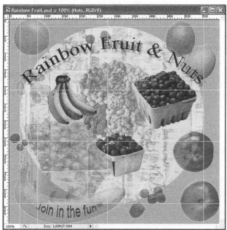

In this lesson, you'll select three layers simultaneously align the images on three layers, and then deselect the layers. You'll also scale the strawberries on the Strawberries layer and rotate the nuts on the Nuts layer.

Understanding Layers and Their Masks

The ability to repeatedly alter the appearance of an image without ever disturbing the actual pixels on the layer image makes a layer mask a powerful editing tool. By default, Photoshop links the mask to the layer. This means that if you move the layer, the mask moves as well.

Understanding the Link Icon

The link icon automatically appears when you create a layer mask. When you create a layer mask, the link icon appears *between* the layer thumbnail and the layer mask thumbnail, indicating that the layer and the layer mask are linked together. To unlink the layer mask from its layer, you click the link icon. The Unlink Mask state displays in the History palette. You can re-link a mask to its layer by clicking the space between the layer and mask thumbnails. The Link Mask state displays in the History palette.

Selecting Multiple Layers

You can select more than one layer on the Layers palette so that multiple layers can

behave as one. Selecting multiple layers in Photoshop is analogous to grouping objects in other programs. You select multiple layers or layer sets by clicking a layer on the Layers palette. To select contiguous layers (layers that are next to one another on the Layers palette), press and hold [Shift] while clicking additional layers on the Layers palette. To select non-contiguous layers, press and hold [Ctrl] (Win) or ⌘ (Mac) while clicking additional layers on the Layers palette. When selecting multiple layers make sure that you click the layer, *not the layer mask*. You can make multiple selections that include the active layer and any other layers on the Layers palette, even if they are in different layer sets. You can select entire layer sets along with a single layer or with other layer sets.

QUICKTIP

When you move multiple selections of layers, the relocation of layers affects the object's appearance in your image, as well as the layers' position on the Layers palette. This means that you can link two layers and then align them in your image. You can also select two non-contiguous layers and then move them simultaneously as a unit to the top of the Layers palette where they will become contiguous.

Working with Layers

After you select multiple layers, you can perform actions that affect the selection such as moving their content as a single unit in your image. To deselect multiple layers, click any layer (within the selection) on the Layers palette with [Ctrl] for each layer you want to deselect. When you deselect each layer, each one returns to its independent state. You can also turn off a layer's display while it is part of a selection of layers by clicking the layer's Indicates layer visibility button.

QUICKTIP

To move a layer mask from one layer to another, make sure that the layer mask that you want to move is active, and that the destination layer doesn't already have a layer mask. Drag the layer mask thumbnail from the layer containing the layer mask onto the layer where you want to move the mask.

Aligning Selected Layers

Suppose you have several type layers in your image and need to align them by their left edges. Rather than individually moving and aligning numerous layers, you can precisely position selected layers in your image. You can align the content in the image by first selecting layers on the Layers palette, then choosing one of six subcommands from the Align command on the Layer menu.

Photoshop aligns layers relative to each other or to a selection border. So, if you have four type layers and want to align them by their left edges, Photoshop will align them relative to the leftmost pixels in those layers only, not to any other (nonselected) layers on the Layers palette or to other content in your image.

Distributing Selected Layers

To distribute (evenly space) the content on layers in your image, you must first select three or more layers, verify that their opacity settings are 50% or greater, and then select one of the six options from the Distribute command on the Layer menu. Photoshop spaces out the content in your image relative to pixels in the selected layers. For example, imagine an image that is 700 pixels wide and has four type layers that are 30 pixels wide each and span a range between 100 X and 400 Y. If you select the four type layers and click the Horizontal Centers command on the Distribute Layers menu, Photoshop will distribute them evenly, but only between 100 X and 400 Y. To distribute the type layers evenly across the width of your entire image, you must first move the left and right layers to the left and right edges of your image, respectively.

QUICKTIP

By activating the Move Tool on the toolbox you can use the 12 align and distribute buttons on the options bar to align and distribute layers.

Transforming Objects

You can **transform** (change the shape, size, perspective, or rotation) of an object or objects on a layer, using one of 11 transform commands on the Edit menu. When you use some of the transform commands, eight selection handles surround the contents of the active layer. When you choose a transform command, a transform box appears around the object you are transforming. A **transform box** is a rectangle that surrounds an image and contains handles that can be used to change dimensions. You can pull the handles with the pointer to start transforming the object. After you transform an object, you can apply the changes by clicking the Commit transform (Return) button on the options bar, or by pressing [Enter] (Win) or [return] (Mac). You can use transform commands individually or in a chain. After you choose your initial transform command, you can try out as many others as you like before you apply the changes by pressing [Enter] (Win) or [return] (Mac). If you attempt another command (something other than another transform command) before pressing [Enter] (Win) or [return] (Mac), a warning box will appear. Click Apply to accept the transformation you made to the layer.

QUICKTIP

You can transform selected layers using the same transform commands that you use to transform individual layers. For example, you might want to scale or rotate selected layers. Photoshop transforms selected layers when any of the selected layers are active.

Select and align layers

1. Verify that the Bananas layer on the Layers palette is active.

2. Press and hold **[Ctrl]** (Win) or ⌘ (Mac), click the **Nuts layer** on the Layers palette, then release **[Ctrl]**.

3. Press and hold **[Ctrl]** (Win) or ⌘ (Mac), click the **Blueberries layer** on the Layers palette, release **[Ctrl]**, then compare your Layers palette to Figure 7.

4. Click **Layer** on the menu bar, point to **Align**, then click **Vertical Centers**.

    The centers of the Blueberries and Nuts layers are aligned with the center of the Bananas layer. Compare your image to Figure 8.

5. Press and hold **[Ctrl]** (Win) or ⌘ (Mac), click the **Nuts layer** and the **Blueberries layer** on the Layers palette, then release **[Ctrl]** (Win) or ⌘ (Mac).

    The objects are no longer selected and retain their new locations.

You selected three layers on the Layers palette, aligned the objects on those layers by their vertical centers using the Align command on the Layer menu, then you deselected the layers.

Grouping layers

You can quickly turn multiple selected layers into a group. Select as many layers as you'd like—even if they are not contiguous, click Layer on the menu bar, then click Group Layers. Each of the selected layers will be placed in a Group (which looks like a layer set) in the Layers palette. You can ungroup the layers by selecting the group in the Layers palette, clicking Layers on the menu bar, then clicking Ungroup Layers.

FIGURE 7
Blueberries layer and Nuts layer linked to Bananas layer

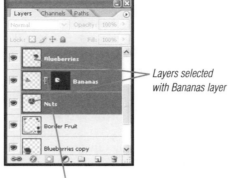

Layers selected
with Bananas layer

Indicates that the layer and
the layer mask are linked
together

FIGURE 8
Aligned layers

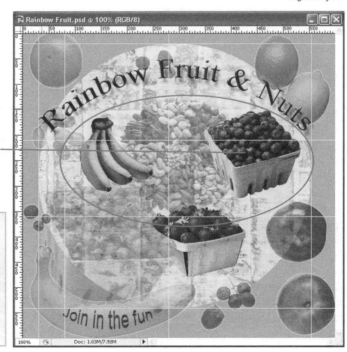

Center pixel of blueberries
and nuts layers aligned
with center pixel of
bananas layer

FIGURE 9
Strawberries layer scaled

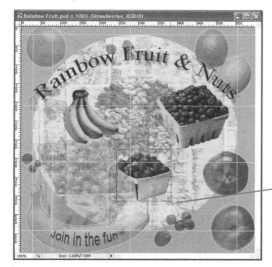

Drag handle to
resize

FIGURE 10
Nuts layer rotated

Nuts layer rotated
90 degrees
counterclockwise

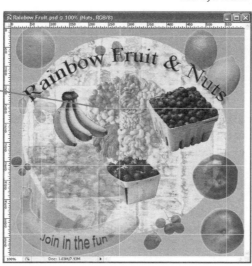

Transform a layer using scale

1. Click the **Strawberries layer** on the Layers palette.

2. Click **Edit** on the menu bar, point to **Transform**, then click **Scale**.

3. Position the **Scaling pointer** over the bottom-right sizing handle using the ruler pixel measurements at approximately **430 X/480 Y**, drag to **380 X/460 Y** up and to the left, as shown in Figure 9, then release the mouse button.

4. Click the **Commit transform (Return) button** ✔ on the options bar.

   The strawberries image is reduced.

You resized the Strawberries layer using the Scale command. This command makes it easy to resize an object while maintaining its proportions.

Transform a layer using rotate

1. Make the Nuts layer active on the Layers palette.

2. Click **Edit** on the menu bar, point to **Transform**, then click **Rotate 90° CCW**.

3. View the transformation.

4. Save your work, then compare your image to Figure 10.

You rotated the Nuts layer 90° counterclockwise using the Rotate 90° CCW command. You can use this command to change the orientation of an object on a layer.

CONTROL PIXELS
TO BLEND COLORS

What You'll Do

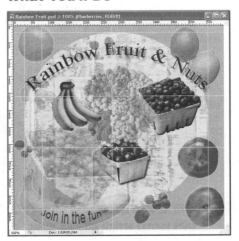

 In this lesson, you'll apply styles to layers using the Layer Style dialog box. You'll also work with blending modes to blend pixels on various layers.

Blending Pixels

You can control the colors and form of your image by blending pixels on one layer with pixels on another layer. You can control *which* pixels from the active layer are blended with pixels from lower layers on the Layers palette. You can control how the pixels are blended by specifying which color pixels you want to change. If you set the Blend If color to Red, then all pixels on the layer that are red will be blended based on your new settings. Blending options are found in the Layer Style dialog box. You can control *how* these pixels are blended by choosing a color as the Blend If color, and using the This Layer and Underlying

Layer sliders. The **Blend If** color determines the color range for the pixels you want to blend. You use the **This Layer** sliders to specify the range of pixels that will be blended on the active layer. You use the **Underlying Layer** sliders to specify the range of pixels that will be blended on all the lower—but still visible—layers. The color channels available depend on the color mode. For example, an RGB image will have Red, Green, and Blue color channels available.

QUICKTIP

Color channels contain information about the colors in an image.

Using duplicate layers to blend pixels

You can create interesting effects by duplicating layers. To duplicate a layer, click the layer you want to duplicate to activate it, click the Layers palette list arrow, click Duplicate Layer, then click OK. The duplicate layer is given the same name as the active layer with "copy" attached to it. (You can also create a duplicate layer by dragging the layer to the Create a new layer button on the Layers palette.) You can modify the duplicate layer by applying effects or masks to it. In addition, you can alter an image's appearance by moving the original and duplicate layers to different positions on the Layers palette.

Using Color Sliders

The colors that are outside the pixel range you set with the color sliders will not be visible, and the boundary between the visible and invisible pixels will be sharp and hard. You can soften the boundary by creating a gradual transition between the visible and invisible pixels. Normally, you determine the last visible color pixel by adjusting its slider position, just as you can set opacity by dragging a slider on the Layers palette. Photoshop allows you to split the color slider in two. When you move the slider halves apart, you create a span of pixels for the visible boundary. Figure 11 shows two objects before they are blended and Figure 12 shows the two objects after they are blended. Do you see how the blended pixels conform to the shape of the underlying pixels?

QUICKTIP

A slider that displays a hand when the pointer covers its label is sometimes referred to as a scrubby slider because it lets you change the value without actually having to drag the slider.

FIGURE 11
Pixels before they are blended

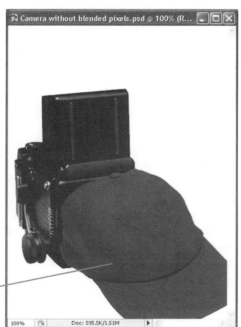

All red cap pixels are visible (unblended)

FIGURE 12
Pixels after they are blended

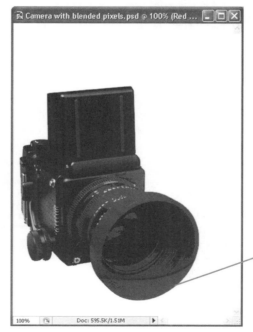

Red cap pixels blended using sliders in the Layer Style dialog box

Blend pixels with a color range

1. Double-click the **Strawberries thumbnail** on the Layers palette to open the Layer Style dialog box.

   TIP   Move the Layer Style dialog box if it obscures your view of the strawberries.

2. Click to highlight the **Blending Options: Custom bar** at the top of the list (if necessary).

3. Select the **Drop Shadow check box**.

4. Click the **Blend If list arrow**, then click **Red**.

5. Drag the right (white) **This Layer slider** to **220**, as shown in Figure 13.

   TIP   Slider position determines number of visible pixels for the color channel you've selected.

6. Click **OK**, then view the fade-out effect on the Strawberries layer.

   TIP   If you want to really observe the fade-out effect, you can delete and then add the last state on the History palette.

You opened the Layer Style dialog box for the Strawberries layer, applied the Drop Shadow style, selected Red as the Blend If color, and then adjusted the This Layer slider to change the range of visible pixels. The result is that you blended pixels on the Strawberries layer so that red pixels outside a specific range will not be visible.

FIGURE 13
Layer Style dialog box

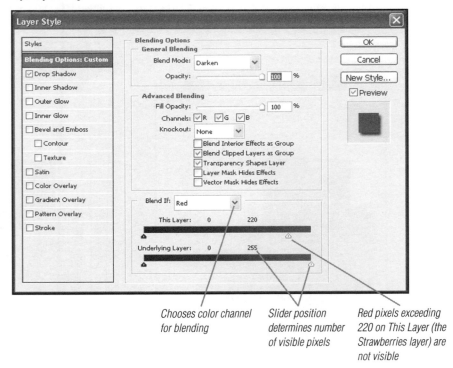

Chooses color channel for blending

Slider position determines number of visible pixels

Red pixels exceeding 220 on This Layer (the Strawberries layer) are not visible

FIGURE 14

Transition range for visible pixels

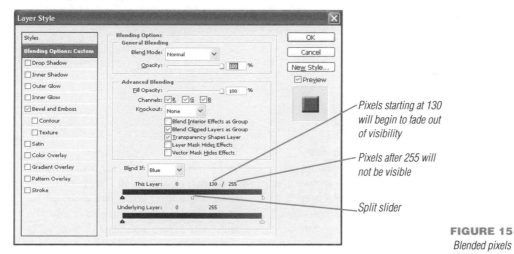

Pixels starting at 130
will begin to fade out
of visibility

Pixels after 255 will
not be visible

Split slider

FIGURE 15

Blended pixels

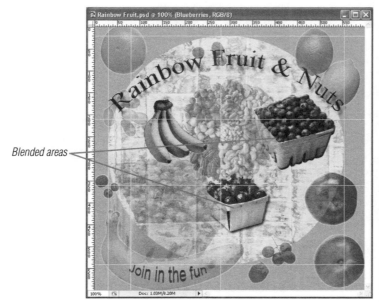

Blended areas

Split sliders to select a color range

1. Double-click the **Blueberries thumbnail** on the Layers palette to open the Layer Style dialog box.

2. Click to highlight the **Blending Options: Default bar** at the top of the list (if necessary), then click the **Bevel and Emboss check box**.

3. Click the **Blend Mode list arrow**, then click **Dissolve**.

4. Click the **Blend If list arrow**, then click **Blue**.

5. Press and hold **[Alt]** (Win) or **[option]** (Mac), click the right **This Layer slider**, drag the left half of the **Right slider** to **130**, then release **[Alt]** (Win) or **[option]** (Mac).

   TIP Pressing [Alt] (Win) or [option] (Mac) splits the slider into two halves.

6. Compare your dialog box to Figure 14, then click **OK**.

7. Save your work, then compare your image to Figure 15.

You opened the Layer Style dialog box for the Blueberries layer, applied the Bevel and Emboss style to the layer and changed the blending mode to Dissolve, specifying the blue pixels as the color to blend. To fine-tune the blend, you split the right This Layer slider and set a range of pixels that smoothed the transition between visible and invisible pixels.

ELIMINATE
A LAYER MASK

What You'll Do

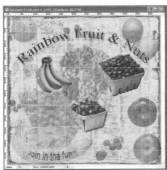

In this lesson, you'll use the Layer menu to temporarily disable a layer mask, and discard a layer mask using the Layers palette.

Disposing of Layer Masks

As you have seen, layer masks enable you to radically change an image's appearance. However, you might not want to keep every layer mask you create, or you might want to turn the layer mask on or off, or you might want to apply the layer mask to the layer and move on to another activity. You can enable or disable the layer mask (turn it on or off), or remove it from the Layers palette by deleting it from the layer entirely or by permanently applying it to the layer.

Disabling a Layer Mask

Photoshop allows you to temporarily disable a layer mask from a layer to view the layer without the mask. When you disable a layer mask, Photoshop indicates that the layer mask is still in place, but not currently visible, by displaying a red X over the layer mask thumbnail, as shown in Figure 16. Temporarily disabling a layer mask has many advantages. For example, you can create duplicate layers and layer masks, apply different styles and effects to them, and then enable and disable (show and hide) layer masks individually until you decide which mask gives you the look you want.

> **QUICK**TIP
>
> The command available for a layer mask changes depending on whether the layer is visible or not. If the layer mask is enabled, the Disable Layer Mask command is active on the Layer menu. If the layer mask is disabled, the Enable Layer Mask command is active.

Removing Layer Masks

If you are certain that you don't want a layer mask, you can permanently remove it. Before you do so, Photoshop gives you two options:

- You can apply the mask to the layer so that it becomes a permanent part of the layer.
- You can discard the mask and its effect completely.

QUICKTIP

Each layer mask increases the file size, so it's a good idea to perform some routine maintenance as you finalize your image. Remove any unnecessary, unwanted layer masks, and then apply the layer masks you want to keep.

If you apply the mask, the layer will retain the *appearance* of the mask effect, but it will no longer contain the actual layer mask. If you discard the mask entirely, you delete the effects you created with the layer mask, and return the layer to its original state.

QUICKTIP

You can toggle between selecting the layer mask and the entire layer by pressing [Ctrl][\] (Win) or [⌘][\] (Mac) to select the layer mask, and pressing [Ctrl][~] (Win) or [⌘][~] (Mac) to select the entire layer.

Working with Smart Objects

Just as multiple layers can be selected, you can combine multiple objects into a Smart Object. This combination, which has a visible indicator in the lower-right corner of the layer thumbnail, makes it possible to scale, rotate, and warp layers without losing image quality. Once the layers you want to combine are selected, you can create a Smart Object by clicking Layer on the menu bar, pointing to Smart Objects, then clicking Group into New Smart Object; or by clicking the Layers palette list arrow, then clicking Group into New Smart Object.

FIGURE 16
Layer mask disabled

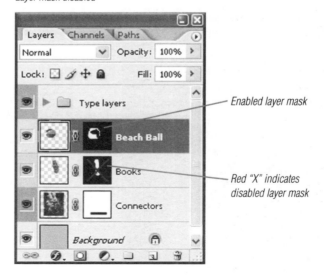

Enabled layer mask

Red "X" indicates disabled layer mask

Disable and enable a layer mask

1. Click the **Bananas layer** on the Layers palette.

2. Click **Layer** on the menu bar, click **Layer Mask,** then click **Disable**. See Figure 17.

   TIP You can also disable a layer mask by pressing [Shift] and then clicking the layer mask thumbnail, and then enable it by pressing [Shift] and clicking the layer mask thumbnail again.

3. Drag the **Disable Layer Mask history state** to the **Delete current state button** 🗑 on the History palette.

   TIP Before you remove a layer mask, verify that the layer mask, not just the layer, is active. Otherwise, if you use the Delete layer button on the Layers palette to remove the mask, you will delete the layer, not the layer mask.

You disabled and enabled the layer mask on the Bananas layer, using commands on the Layer menu.

FIGURE 17
Layer mask disabled

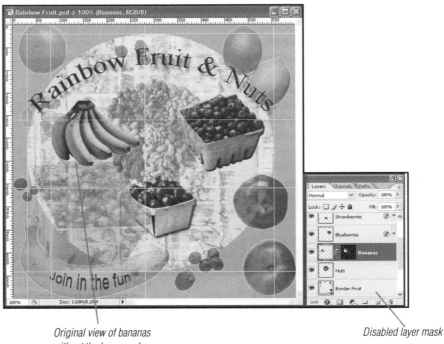

Original view of bananas
without the layer mask

Disabled layer mask

FIGURE 18
Warning box

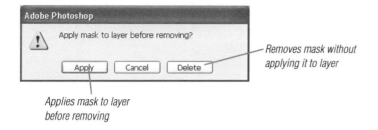

Removes mask without
applying it to layer

Applies mask to layer
before removing

Remove a layer mask

1. Click the **layer mask thumbnail** on the Washout layer on the Layers palette.

2. Click the **Delete layer button** 🗑 on the Layers palette, then compare your warning box to Figure 18.

3. Click **Delete** to remove the mask without first applying it to the Washout layer. Compare your screen to Figure 19.

4. Click **Edit** on the menu bar, then click **Undo Delete Layer Mask**.

5. Save your work.

You used the Delete layer button on the Layers palette to delete a layer mask, chose the Delete option in the warning box to remove the mask without applying it to the Washout layer, and then undid the action to restore the layer mask on the Washout layer.

FIGURE 19
Washout layer with layer mask removed

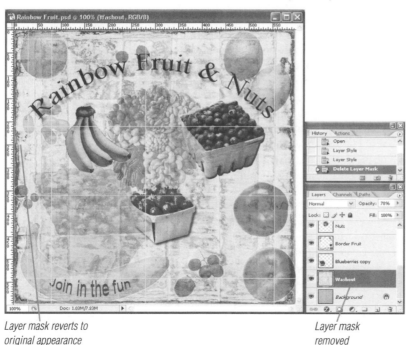

Layer mask reverts to
original appearance

Layer mask
removed

USE AN ADJUSTMENT LAYER

What You'll Do

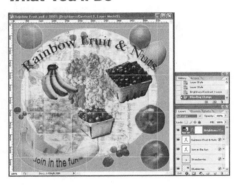

In this lesson, you'll create an adjustment layer, choose Brightness/Contrast as the type of adjustment layer, adjust brightness and contrast settings for the layer, and then use the Layers palette to change the blending mode of the adjustment layer.

Understanding Adjustment Layers

An **adjustment layer** is a special layer that acts as a color filter for a single layer or for all the layers beneath it. Just as you can use a layer mask to edit the layer content without permanently deleting pixels on the image, you can create an adjustment layer to adjust color and tone. If you were to make changes directly on the original layer, the changes would be irreversible. (You could use the Undo feature or the History palette to undo your changes, but only in the current Photoshop session.) However, the color changes you make to the adjustment layer exist only in the adjustment layer.

Creating an Adjustment Layer

You can create an adjustment layer by selecting the layer you want to adjust, then using the Layer menu to click a new adjustment layer command or by clicking the Create new fill or adjustment layer button on the Layers palette. When you create an adjustment layer, you must specify which of the color adjustments you want to use. Color adjustments

made directly on a layer or using an adjustment layer are described in Table 1.

> **QUICK**TIP
>
> If you use the Create new fill or adjustment layer button on the Layers palette, you'll see three additional menu items: Solid Color, Gradient, and Pattern. You use these commands to create fill layers, which fill a layer with a solid color.

Modifying an Adjustment Layer

You can change the adjustment layer settings by double-clicking the layer thumbnail on the adjustment layer. Photoshop identifies the type of adjustment layer on the Layers palette by including the type of adjustment layer in the layer name.

Using Multiple Adjustment Layers

You can use as many adjustment layers as you want, but you must create them one at a time. At first glance, this might strike you as a disadvantage, but when you're working on an image, you'll find it to be an advantage. By adding one or more adjustment layers, you can experiment with a variety of colors and tones, then hide and show each one to determine the one that best suits your needs. Adjustment layers can also contain layer masks, which allow you to fine-tune your alterations by painting just the adjustment layer mask.

Merging Adjustment Layers

You can merge adjustment layers with any *visible* layers in the image, including linked layers. You cannot, however, merge one adjustment layer with another adjustment layer. Merging adjustment layers reduces file size and ensures that your adjustments will be permanent.

TABLE 1: Color Adjustments

color adjustment	description	color adjustment	description
Levels	Sets highlights and shadows by increasing the tonal range of pixels, while preserving the color balance.	Gradient Map	Maps the equivalent grayscale range of an image to colors of a specific gradient fill.
Curves	Makes adjustments to an entire tonal range, using three variables: highlights, shadows, and midtones.	Photo Filter	Similar to the practice of adding a color filter to a camera lens to adjust the color balance and color temperature.
Color Balance	Changes the overall mixture of color.	Shadow/Highlight	Used to correct images with silhouetted images due to strong backlighting, as well as brightening up areas of shadow in an otherwise well-lit image. (Available on the Image > Adjustments menu.)
Brightness/Contrast	Makes simple adjustments to a tonal range.		
Hue/Saturation	Changes position on the color wheel (hue) or purity of a color (saturation).	Invert	Converts an image's brightness values to the inverse values on the 256-step color-values scale.
Match Color	Changes the brightness, color saturation, and color balance in an image.	Threshold	Converts images to high-contrast, black-and-white images.
Replace Color	Replaces specific colors using a mask.	Equalize	Redistributes brightness values of pixels so that they evenly represent the entire range of brightness levels.
Selective Color	Increases or decreases the number of process colors in each of the additive and subtractive primary color components.	Posterize	Specifies the number of tonal levels for each channel.
Channel Mixer	Modifies a color channel, using a mix of current color channels.	Variations	Adjusts the color balance, contrast, and saturation of an image, and shows alternative thumbnails.

Create and set an adjustment layer

1. Click the **Rainbow Fruit & Nuts layer** on the Layers palette.

2. Click **Layer** on the menu bar, point to **New Adjustment Layer**, then click **Brightness/Contrast**. Compare your dialog box to Figure 20.

   TIP   You can also create a new adjustment layer by clicking the Create new fill or adjustment layer button on the Layers palette, then selecting a color adjustment.

3. Click **OK**.

4. Type **−15** in the Brightness text box.

5. Type **30** in the Contrast text box.

6. Click **OK**. Compare your Layers palette to Figure 21.

   Did you notice that the new adjustment layer appears on the Layers palette above the Rainbow Fruit & Nuts layer and its thumbnail is directly above that of the previous layer? The new layer is named Brightness/Contrast 1 because you chose Brightness/Contrast as the type of color adjustment.

You created a Brightness/Contrast adjustment layer on the Rainbow Fruit & Nuts layer, then adjusted settings in the Brightness/Contrast dialog box.

FIGURE 20
New Layer dialog box

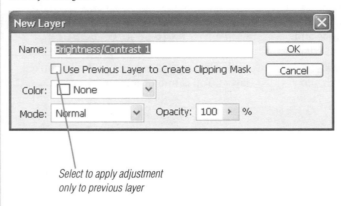

Select to apply adjustment
only to previous layer

FIGURE 21
Adjustment layer on Layers palette

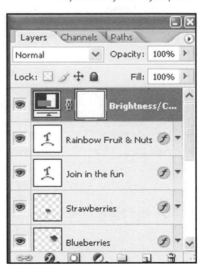

FIGURE 22
Result of adjustment layer

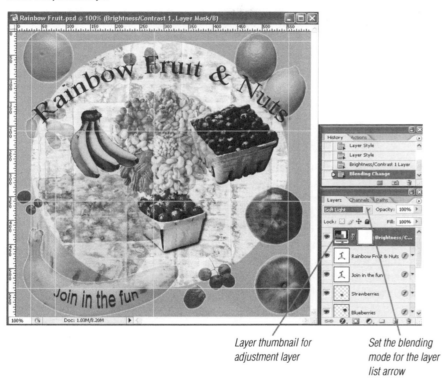

Layer thumbnail for
adjustment layer

Set the blending
mode for the layer
list arrow

Set the blending mode

1. Make sure that the Brightness/Contrast 1 layer is the active layer.

2. Click the **Set the blending mode for the layer list arrow** on the Layers palette, then click **Soft Light**.

3. Save your work, then compare your image to Figure 22.

You changed the blending mode for the adjustment layer to Soft Light, using the Layers palette.

Modifying an adjustment layer

What if you've created an adjustment layer that affects all the layers beneath it, and then you decide you want it to only affect the previous layer? Do you have to delete this adjustment layer and start over? Certainly not. To toggle an adjustment layer between applying to all the layers beneath it and only the layer immediately beneath it, position the pointer between the adjustment layer and the layer beneath it. Press [Alt] (Win) and [option] (Mac), then click between the two layers.

CREATE A CLIPPING MASK

What You'll Do

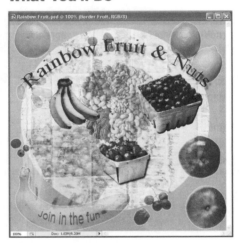

In this lesson, you'll create a clipping mask, adjust the opacity of the base layer, remove and restore the clipping mask, then flatten the image.

Understanding Clipping Masks

A **clipping mask** (sometimes called a *clipping group*) is a group of two or more contiguous layers that are linked for the purpose of masking. Clipping masks are useful when you want one layer to act as the mask for other layers, or if you want an adjustment layer to affect only the layer directly beneath it. The bottom layer in a clipping mask is called the **base layer**, and it serves as the group's mask. For example, you can use a type layer as the base of a clipping mask so that a pattern appears through the text on the base layer, as shown in Figure 23. (On the left side of the figure is the imagery used as the pattern in the type.) The properties of the base layer determine the opacity and visible imagery of a clipping mask. You can, however, adjust the opacity of the individual layers in a clipping mask.

> **QUICK**TIP
> You can merge layers in a clipping mask with an adjustment layer, as long as the layers are visible.

Creating a Clipping Mask

To create a clipping mask, you need at least two layers: one to create the shape of the mask, and the other to supply the content for the mask. You can use a type or an image layer to create the clipping mask shape, and when the shape is the way you want it, you can position the pointer between the two layers, then press [Alt] (Win) or [option] (Mac). The pointer changes to two circles with a left-pointing arrowhead. Simply click the line between the layers to create the clipping mask. You can tell if a clipping mask exists by looking at the Layers palette. A clipping mask is indicated when one or more layers are indented and appear with a down arrow icon, and the base layer is underlined.

Removing a Clipping Mask

When you create a clipping mask, the layers in the clipping mask are grouped together. To remove a clipping mask, press and hold [Alt] (Win) or [option] (Mac), position the clipping mask pointer over the line separating the grouped layers on the Layers palette, then click the mouse. You can also select the base layer, click Layer on the menu bar, and then click Release Clipping Mask.

FIGURE 23
Result of clipping mask

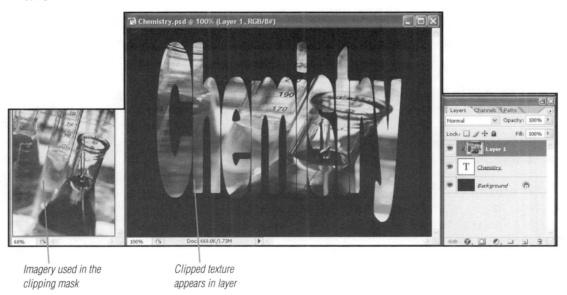

Imagery used in the clipping mask

Clipped texture appears in layer

Create a clipping mask

1. Click the **Join in the fun layer** on the Layers palette to make it the active layer.

2. Drag the **active layer** below the **Nuts layer** on the Layers palette.

3. Press and hold **[Alt]** (Win) or **[option]** (Mac), then point with the **Clipping mask pointer** ◄🐽 to the line between the Border Fruit and the Join in the fun layers. Compare your Layers palette to Figure 24.

4. Click the line between the two layers with the **Clipping mask pointer** ◄🐽, then release **[Alt]** (Win) or **[option]** (Mac).

   The Join in the fun layer (member) is filled with the images from the Border fruit layer (base).

5. Verify that the clipping icon (a small downward pointing arrow) appears in the Join in the fun layer, then compare your Layers palette to Figure 25.

6. Make sure the Join in the fun layer is active, click the **Opacity list arrow** on the Layers palette, drag the slider to 100%, then press **[Enter]** (Win) or **[return]** (Mac).

You created a clipping mask, using the Border Fruit layer as the base and the Join in the fun layer as a member of the clipping mask to make the banana peel appear as the fill of the Join in the fun layer, and then you adjusted the opacity of the Join in the fun layer.

FIGURE 24
Creating a clipping mask

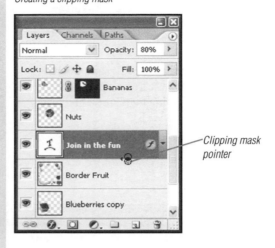

Clipping mask pointer

FIGURE 25
Clipping mask on Layers palette

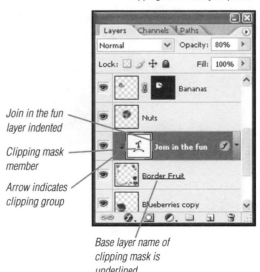

Join in the fun layer indented

Clipping mask member

Arrow indicates clipping group

Base layer name of clipping mask is underlined

FIGURE 26
Finished product

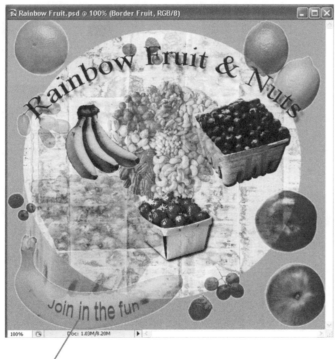

*Join in the fun layer
text filled in*

1. Click the **Border Fruit layer** on the Layers palette.

2. Hide the rulers and guides.

3. Click **Layer** on the menu bar, then click **Release Clipping Mask**.

4. Click **Edit** on the menu bar, then click **Undo Release Clipping Mask**. Compare your screen to Figure 26.

5. Click **File** on the menu bar, click **Save As**, then, using the name given, select the **As a Copy check box**.

6. Type **copy** after the original filename if it does not automatically appear in the File name text box, then click **Save**.

7. Click **Layer** on the menu bar, then click **Flatten Image**.

8. Save your work, then close the file and exit Photoshop.

You removed the clipping mask by using the Release command on the Layer menu, restored the clipping mask by using the Undo command on the Edit menu, saved a copy of the image, and then flattened the file.

Power User Shortcuts

to do this:	use this method:
Activate layer	Press and hold [Ctrl][~] (Win) or ⌘[~] (Mac)
Activate layer mask	Press and hold [Ctrl][\] (Win) or ⌘[\] (Mac)
Add an adjustment layer	◔.
Align linked layers by vertical centers	Layer ➤ Align ➤ Vertical Centers
Blend pixels on a layer	Double-click a layer thumbnail, click Blend If list arrow, choose color, drag This Layer and Underlying Layer sliders
Brush Tool	✎. or B
Change brush tip	Select Brush Tool, right-click (Win) or control (Mac), then click
Create a clipping mask	Press and hold [Alt] (Win) or option (Mac), move the pointer to the line between two layers, then click
Create a layer mask	▣

to do this:	use this method:
Create a layer mask that hides the selection	Press and hold [Alt] (Win) or option (Mac) ➤ ▣
Create a layer mask that reveals the selection	Layer ➤ Layer Mask ➤ Reveal Selection
Delete layer	🗑
Disable layer mask	Layer ➤ Layer Mask ➤ Disable
Next or previous brush tip in palette	[,] or [.]
Remove a clipping mask	Click a layer in the group ➤ Layer ➤ Release Clipping Mask
Remove a link	Click 🔗
Scale a layer	Edit ➤ Transform ➤ Scale
Rotate a layer 90° to the left	Edit ➤ Transform ➤ Rotate 90° CCW
Select first or last brush tip in palette	[Shift][,] or [Shift][.]

Key: Menu items are indicated by ➤ between the menu name and its command. Blue bold letters are shortcuts for selecting tools on the toolbox.

One of the most powerful editing tools that Photoshop has to offer is the ability to create and modify masks. Once a mask is placed on a layer, you can edit its shape using the Brush Tool. Mask pixels can be painted in, or painted away, so that your image looks exactly the way you want it to. A mask is automatically linked to its layer, so that when you move a masked layer, the mask moves with the layer content. You can also select multiple layers and move them as a group. Multiple layers can be aligned and distributed when they are selected as a group. Once you are satisfied with the results of a mask, you can choose to disable it, delete it, or apply it to the layer.

An adjustment can be used to make color adjustments to a layer without permanently affecting the pixels on the layer. An adjustment layer can affect all the layers beneath it, or just the immediate layer beneath it. This feature makes it possible for you to try your changes without permanently changing the layer's content. Like masks, you can disable an adjustment layer, delete it, or apply it by merging it with its layer.

What You Have Learned:

- How to create a layer mask to hide pixels
- How to paint on a layer mask
- How to link and unlink a mask
- How to select multiple layers
- How to align and distribute layers
- How to transform layer objects
- How to blend pixels
- How to disable and remove a layer mask
- How to create and modify an adjustment layer
- How to create a clipping mask

Key Terms

Adjustment layer   A special layer that lets you make color modifications without permanently changing the actual layer.

Base layer   The bottom layer in a clipping mask, or group; serves as the group's mask.

Blend If color   Determines the color range for the pixels you want to blend.

Clipping mask   A group of two or more contiguous layers that are linked for the purpose of masking.

Layer mask   A feature that can cover an entire layer, or specific areas within a layer, and can be used to change dimensions when transforming the object.

This Layer slider   Specifies the range of pixels that will be blended on the active layer.

Transform Box   A rectangle that surrounds an image and contains handles.

Transform   Changes the shape, size, perspective, or rotation of an object.

Underlying Layer slider   Specifies the range of pixels that will be blended on all the lower layers.

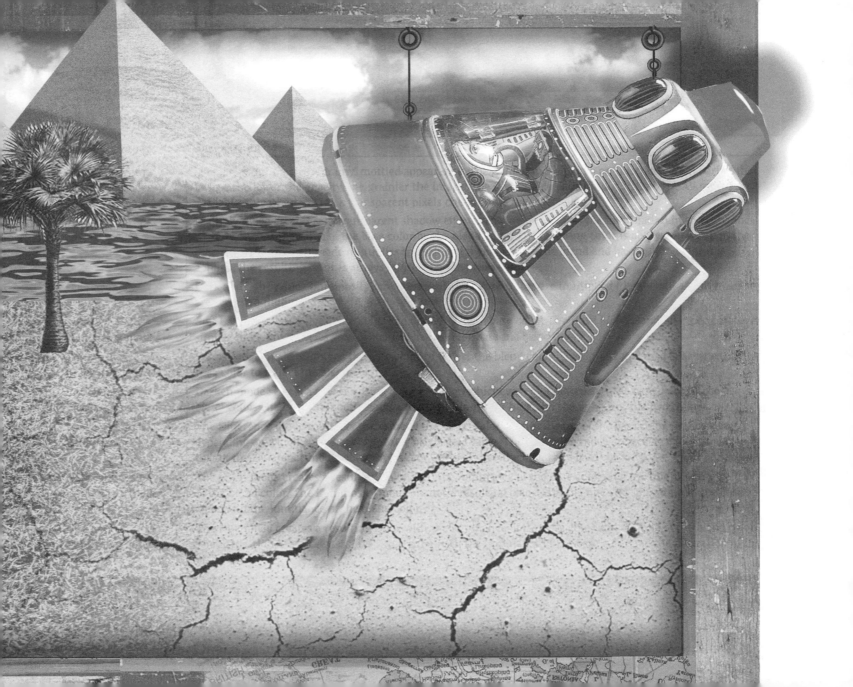

chapter

8

CREATING SPECIAL
EFFECTS WITH
FILTERS

1. Learn about filters and how to apply them.

2. Create an effect with an Artistic filter.

3. Add unique effects with Stylize filters.

4. Alter images with Distort and Noise filters.

5. Alter lighting with a Render filter.

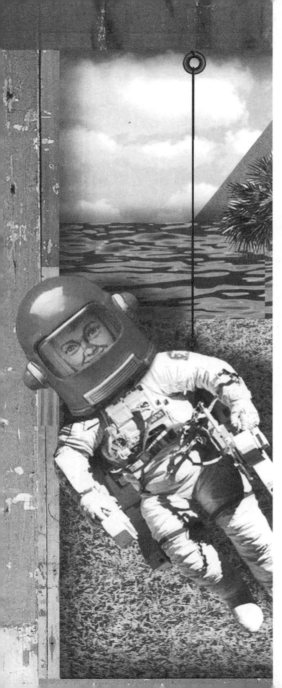

chapter **8 CREATING SPECIAL**
EFFECTS WITH
FILTERS

Understanding Filters

You've already seen some of the filters that Photoshop offers. Filters alter the look of an image by altering pixels in a particular pattern or format, across a layer or a selection. This results in a unique, customized appearance. You use filters to apply special effects, such as realistic textures, distortions, changes in lighting, and blurring. Although you can use several types of filters and options, and can apply them to multiple layers in an image, the most important thing to remember when using filters is subtlety.

Applying Filters

You can apply filters to any layer (except the Background layer) using commands on the Filter menu. Most filters have their own dialog box, where you can adjust filter settings and preview the effect before applying it. The preview window in the dialog box allows you to evaluate the precise effect of the filter on your selection. You can zoom in and out and pan the image in the dialog box to get a good look before making a final decision. Other filters—those whose menu command is not followed by an ellipsis (...)—apply their effects instantly as soon as you click the command.

> **QUICK**TIP
>
> Does your computer have enough RAM? You'll know for sure when you start using filters because they are very memory-intensive.

Tools You'll Use

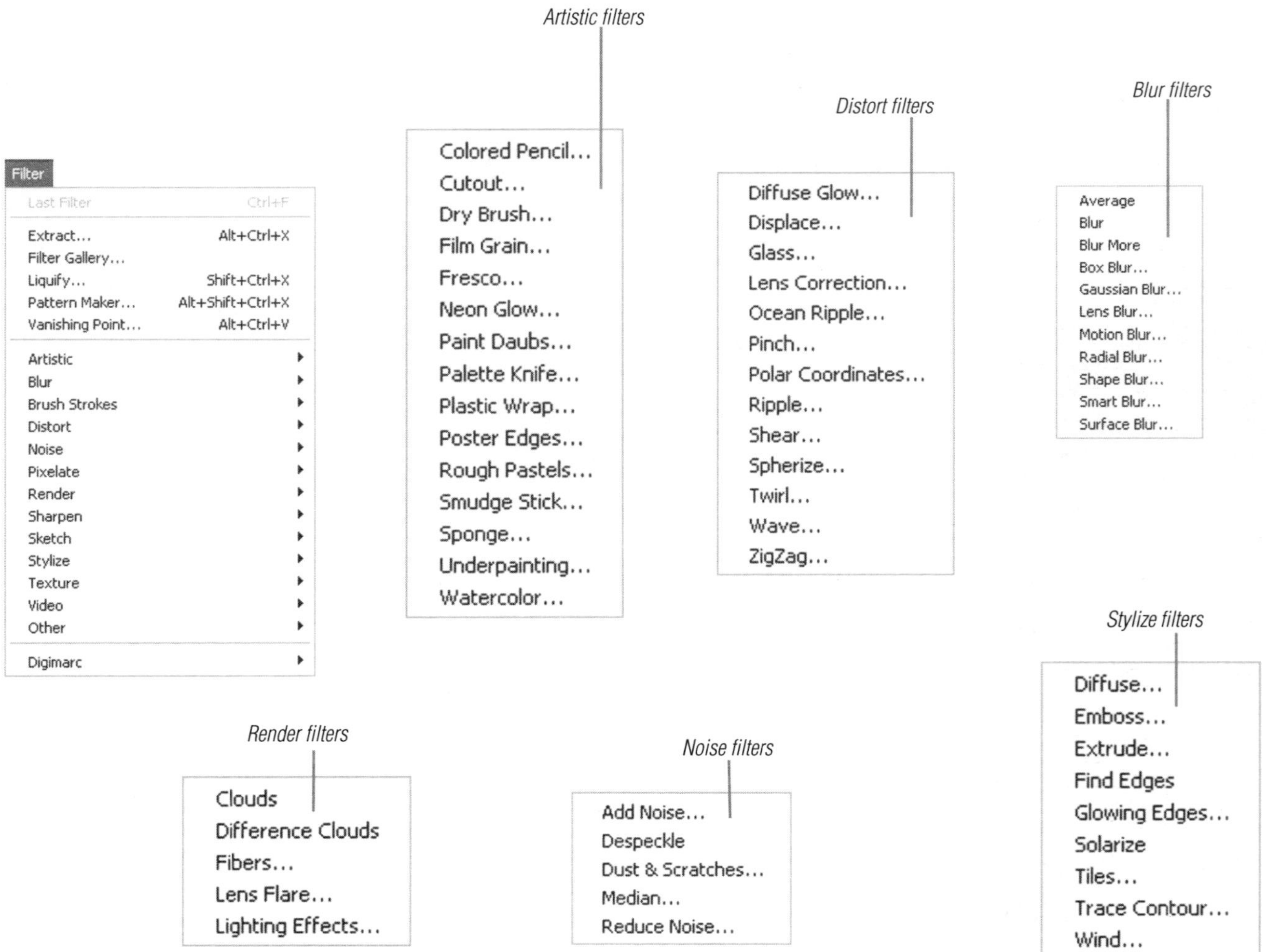

Artistic filters

Distort filters

Blur filters

Filter

Last Filter	Ctrl+F
Extract...	Alt+Ctrl+X
Filter Gallery...	
Liquify...	Shift+Ctrl+X
Pattern Maker...	Alt+Shift+Ctrl+X
Vanishing Point...	Alt+Ctrl+V
Artistic	▶
Blur	▶
Brush Strokes	▶
Distort	▶
Noise	▶
Pixelate	▶
Render	▶
Sharpen	▶
Sketch	▶
Stylize	▶
Texture	▶
Video	▶
Other	▶
Digimarc	▶

Colored Pencil...
Cutout...
Dry Brush...
Film Grain...
Fresco...
Neon Glow...
Paint Daubs...
Palette Knife...
Plastic Wrap...
Poster Edges...
Rough Pastels...
Smudge Stick...
Sponge...
Underpainting...
Watercolor...

Diffuse Glow...
Displace...
Glass...
Lens Correction...
Ocean Ripple...
Pinch...
Polar Coordinates...
Ripple...
Shear...
Spherize...
Twirl...
Wave...
ZigZag...

Average
Blur
Blur More
Box Blur...
Gaussian Blur...
Lens Blur...
Motion Blur...
Radial Blur...
Shape Blur...
Smart Blur...
Surface Blur...

Stylize filters

Diffuse...
Emboss...
Extrude...
Find Edges
Glowing Edges...
Solarize
Tiles...
Trace Contour...
Wind...

Render filters

Clouds
Difference Clouds
Fibers...
Lens Flare...
Lighting Effects...

Noise filters

Add Noise...
Despeckle
Dust & Scratches...
Median...
Reduce Noise...

LEARN ABOUT FILTERS AND
HOW TO APPLY THEM

What You'll Do

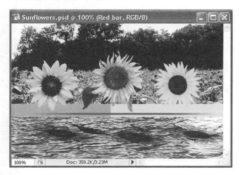

▶ *In this lesson, you'll apply the Motion Blur filter to the Red bar layer.*

Understanding the Filter Menu

The Filter menu sorts filters into categories and subcategories. Many filters are memory-intensive, so you might need to wait several seconds while Photoshop applies the effect. Using filters might slow down your computer's performance. Figure 1 shows samples of several filters.

Learning About Filters

You can read about filters all day long, but until you apply one yourself, it's all academic. When you do, here are a few tips to keep in mind.

- Distort filters can completely reshape an image; they are highly resource-demanding.
- Photoshop applies most of the Pixelate filters as soon as you click the command, without opening a dialog box.

- Digimarc filters notify users that the image is copyright-protected.

QUICKTIP

Some imported files may require rasterizing before they can be used in Photoshop. These files have vector artwork. During rasterization, the mathematically defined lines and curves of vector art are converted into pixels or bits of a bitmap image.

Applying a Filter

You can apply a filter by clicking its category and name under the Filter menu. When you click a Filter menu name, a dialog box opens displaying a sample of each filter in the category. You can also apply one or more filters using the Filter Gallery.

FIGURE 1

Examples of filters

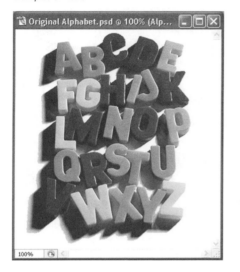

Original Alphabet.psd @ 100% (Alp...

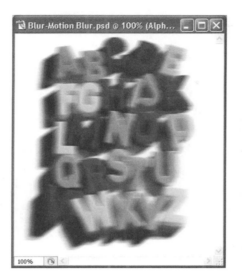

Blur-Motion Blur.psd @ 100% (Alph...

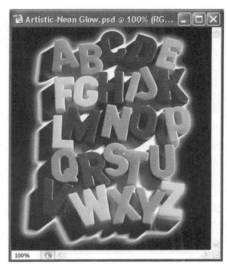

Artistic-Neon Glow.psd @ 100% (RG...

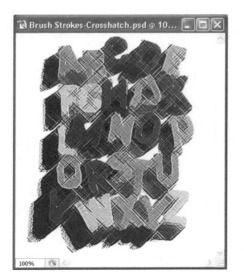

Brush Strokes-Crosshatch.psd @ 10...

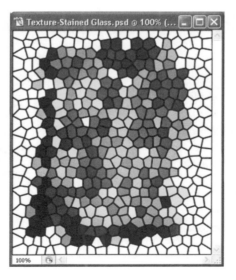

Texture-Stained Glass.psd @ 100% (...

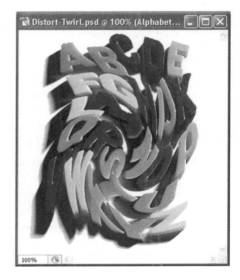

Distort-Twirl.psd @ 100% (Alphabet...

Lesson 1   Learn About Filters and How to Apply Them

You will be amazed by how many filters there are, how much they can do for an image, and just how much fun they can be. Table 1 describes each filter category.

Understanding the Filter Gallery

The **Filter Gallery** is a feature that lets you see the effects of each filter *before* its application. You can also use the Filter Gallery to apply filters (either individually, or in groups), rearrange filters, and change individual filter settings. The Filter Gallery is opened by clicking Filter on the menu bar, then clicking Filter Gallery. In Figure 2, the Mosaic Tiles filter (in the Texture category) is applied to the active layer, which has been enlarged for easier viewing in the preview window.

FIGURE 2
Filter Gallery dialog box

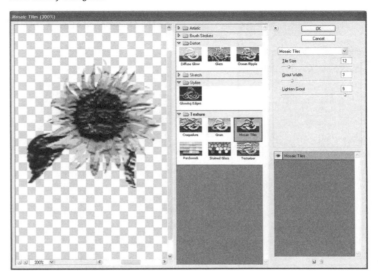

TABLE 1: Filter Categories			
category	**use**	**category**	**use**
Artistic	Replicates traditional fine arts effects.	Sharpen	Refocuses blurry objects by increasing contrast in adjacent pixels.
Blur	Simulates an object in motion; can use to retouch photographs.	Sketch	Applies a texture, or simulates a fine arts hard-drawn effect.
Brush Strokes	Mimics fine arts brushwork and ink effects.		
Distort	Reshapes an image.	Stylize	Produces a painted or impressionistic effect.
Noise	Gives an aged look; can use to retouch photographs.	Texture	Gives the appearance of depth or substance.
		Video	Restricts color use to those that are acceptable for television reproduction and smooth video images.
Pixelate	Adds small honeycomb shapes based on similar colors.	Other	Creates unique filters, modifies masks, or makes quick color adjustments.
Render	Transforms three-dimensional shapes; simulates light reflections.	Digimarc	Embeds a digital watermark that stores copyright information.

FIGURE 3
Current Layers palette

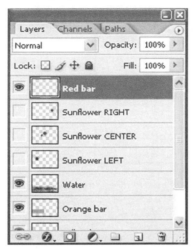

Learning about Motion filters

When you apply a Blur filter, keep in mind how you want your object to appear—as if it's moving. Blur filters smooth the transitions between different colors. The effect of the Blur More filter is four times stronger than the Blur filter. The Gaussian Blur filter produces more of a hazy effect. The direction of the blur is determined by the Angle setting—a straight horizontal path has an angle set to zero. The Motion Blur filter simulates taking a picture of an object in motion, and the Radial Blur filter simulates zooming or rotation. You can use the Smart Blur filter to set exactly how the filter will blur the image.

Open a Blur filter

1. Start Photoshop, open PS 8-1.psd from the drive and folder where your Data Files are stored, then save it as **Sunflowers**.

   TIP   If you see a message stating that some text layers need to be updated before they can be used for vector-based output, click Update.

2. Click the **Default Foreground and Background Colors button** on the toolbox to display the default settings.

   TIP   It's a good habit to check Photoshop settings and display the rulers before you begin your work if you'll need these features.

3. Click the **Indicates layer visibility button** on the Sunflower LEFT layer on the Layers palette.

4. Click the **Indicates layer visibility button** on the Sunflower RIGHT layer on the Layers palette.

5. Click the **Indicates layer visibility button** on the Sunflower CENTER layer on the Layers palette.

6. Click the **Red bar layer** on the Layers palette to make it active. Compare your Layers palette to Figure 3.

7. Click **Filter** on the menu bar, point to **Blur**, then click **Motion Blur**.

   TIP   The last filter applied to a layer appears at the top of the Filter menu.

You set default foreground and background colors, hid three layers, then opened the Motion Blur dialog box.

Apply a Blur filter

1. Position the red bar in the preview window with the **Hand pointer** 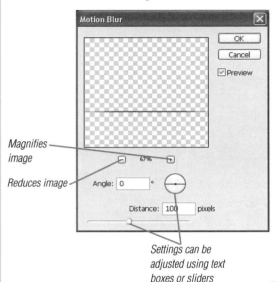, reducing or enlarging the image with the buttons beneath the preview window so it displays in the center.

   The red bar image is repositioned from the lower area to the center of the preview window.

2. Verify that **0** is in the Angle text box.

   TIP In this case, increasing the angle results in a thicker bar.

3. Type **100** in the Distance text box, then compare your dialog box to Figure 4.

   TIP You can also adjust the settings in the Motion Blur dialog box by dragging the Angle radius slider and Distance slider.

4. Click **OK**.

   The Motion Blur filter is applied to the Red bar layer and the Motion Blur state appears on the History palette.

You repositioned the Red bar layer in the preview window and then applied a Motion Blur filter to the layer.

FIGURE 4
Motion Blur dialog box

Magnifies image

Reduces image

Settings can be adjusted using text boxes or sliders

Reducing blur with the Smart Sharpen Filter
You can use the Smart Sharpen Filter to remove or reduce blurriness. This filter can be used to remove blur effects in images created by Gaussian Blur, Lens Blur, or Motion Blur filters. The Smart Sharpen Filter is available by clicking Filter on the menu bar, pointing to Sharpen, then clicking Smart Sharpen. Using the Smart Sharpen dialog box, you can change the amount as a percentage and the radius in pixels of the settings. You can choose the type of blur to be removed from the image.

Getting some perspective
In the real world, the perspective of objects that are moved away from you changes as well. If you use Photoshop to stretch the top of a skyscraper, to maintain proper perspective the modified shape should change so it appears to get taller and narrower. Using a grid, the Vanishing Point filter lets you do this by defining the area to modify so you can drag objects around corners and into the distance while maintaining the correct perspective. The sky's the limit! The Vanishing Point feature is opened by clicking Filter on the menu bar, then clicking Vanishing Point.

FIGURE 5

Motion Blur filter applied to layer

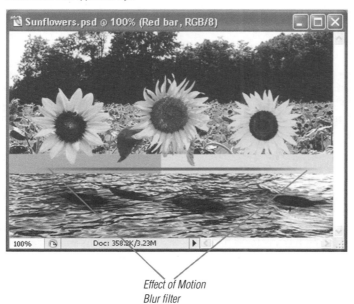

Effect of Motion
Blur filter

1. Click the **Indicates layer visibility button** on the Sunflower RIGHT layer on the Layers palette.

2. Click the **Indicates layer visibility button** on the Sunflower CENTER layer on the Layers palette.

3. Click the **Indicates layer visibility button** on the Sunflower LEFT layer on the Layers palette.

4. Save your work, then compare your image to Figure 5.

You restored the visibility of three layers. The ability to turn layers on and off while working on an image means you can decrease distracting elements and concentrate on specific objects.

CREATE AN EFFECT WITH
AN ARTISTIC FILTER

What You'll Do

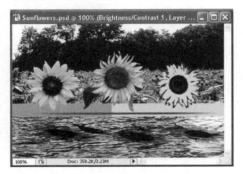

In this lesson, you'll apply the Poster Edges filter from the Artistic category to the Sunflower RIGHT layer and adjust the contrast and brightness of the layer.

Learning About Artistic Filters
You can dramatically alter an image by using Artistic filters. **Artistic filters** are often used for special effects in television commercials and other multimedia venues.

Using Artistic Filters
There are 15 Artistic filters. Figure 6 shows examples of some of the Artistic filters. The following list contains the names of each of the Artistic filters and their effects.

- Colored Pencil has a colored pencil effect and retains important edges.
- Cutout allows high-contrast images to appear in silhouette and has the effect of using several layers of colored paper.

- Dry Brush simplifies an image by reducing its range of colors.
- Film Grain applies even color variations throughout an object.
- Fresco paints an image with short, rounded dabs of color.
- Neon Glow adds a glow effect to selected objects.
- Paint Daubs gives an image a painterly effect.
- Palette Knife reduces the level of detail in an image, revealing underlying texture.
- Plastic Wrap accentuates surface details and makes the contents of a layer appear to be covered in plastic.

Learning about third-party plug-ins
A plug-in is any external program that adds features and functionality to another while working from within that program. Plug-ins enable you to obtain and work in additional file types and formats, add dazzling special effects, or provide efficient shortcut modules. You can purchase Photoshop plug-ins from third-party companies, or download them from freeware sites. To locate Photoshop plug-ins, you can use your favorite Internet search engine, or search for plug-ins on Adobe's Web site: *www.adobe.com*.

- Poster Edges reduces the number of colors in an image.
- Rough Pastels makes an image look as if it is stroked with colored pastel chalk on a textured background.
- Smudge Stick softens an image by smudging or smearing darker areas.

- Sponge creates highly textured areas, making an object look like it was painted with a sponge.
- Underpainting paints the image on a textured background.
- Watercolor simplifies the appearance of an object, making it look like it was painted with watercolors.

Adjusting Filter Effects

You can change the appearance of a filter by using any of the functions listed under the Adjustments command on the Image menu. For example, you can modify the color balance or the brightness/contrast of a layer before or after you apply a filter to it.

FIGURE 6

Examples of Artistic filters

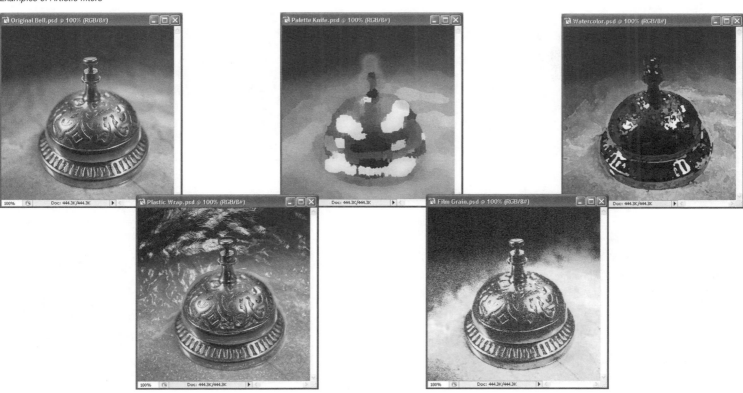

Apply an Artistic filter with the Filter Gallery

1. Click the **Sunflower RIGHT layer** on the Layers palette.

2. Click **Filter** on the menu bar, click **Filter Gallery**, then move the image so that it is visible in the preview window (if necessary).

   The Filter Gallery displays thumbnails of each filter in the current category, so you can see a quick overview of what effects are available.

   TIP The settings available for a filter in the Filter Gallery are the same as those in the individual dialog box that opens when you click the category name in the menu.

3. Click the **triangle to the left of the Artistic folder** ▷, then click **Poster Edges**.

4. Type **5** in the Edge Thickness text box.

   The Edge Thickness determines the settings of the edges within the image.

5. Type **3** in the Edge Intensity text box.

   The Edge Intensity setting gives the edges more definition.

6. Type **3** in the Posterization text box, then compare your dialog box to Figure 7.

   The Posterization setting controls the number of unique colors the filter will reproduce in the image.

7. Click **OK**, then compare your image to Figure 8.

Using the Filter Gallery, you applied the Poster Edges filter to the Sunflower RIGHT layer. The right-most sunflower now looks less realistic than the flowers next to it, and has poster effects.

FIGURE 7
Poster Edges filter in Filter Gallery dialog box

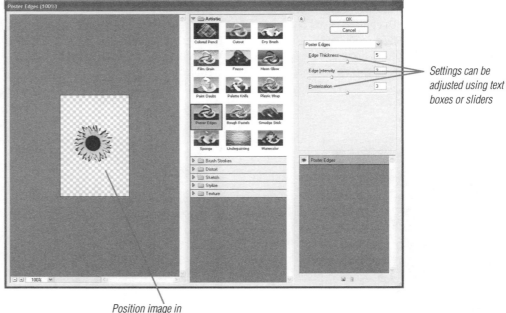

Settings can be adjusted using text boxes or sliders

Position image in preview window

FIGURE 8
Poster Edges filter applied to layer

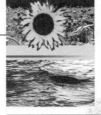

Effect of Poster Edges filter

FIGURE 9
Image adjusted

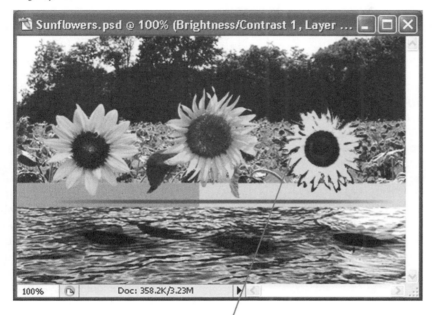

Sunflowers.psd @ 100% (Brightness/Contrast 1 , Layer ...

100%   Doc: 358.2K/3.23M

Brightness and contrast
adjusted on layer

Adjust the filter effect

1. Click **Layer** on the menu bar, point to **New Adjustment Layer**, then click **Brightness/Contrast**.

2. Select the **Use Previous Layer to Create Clipping Mask check box**, then click **OK**.

   The effects of the adjustment layer will be limited to the active layer.

3. Type **20** in the Brightness text box.

4. Type **15** in the Contrast text box, then click **OK**.

5. Save your work, then compare your image to Figure 9.

You adjusted the brightness and contrast of the Sunflower RIGHT layer.

ADD UNIQUE EFFECTS
WITH STYLIZE FILTERS

What You'll Do

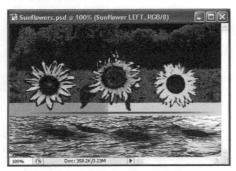

 In this lesson, you'll apply a solarize filter to the Sunflower field layer and a Wind filter to the Orange bar layer. You'll also apply the Poster Edges filter to a layer using the Filter Gallery.

Learning About Stylize Filters

Stylize filters produce a painted or impressionistic effect by displacing pixels and heightening the contrast within an image. Figure 10 shows several Stylize filters. Several commonly used Stylize filters and their effects are listed below:

- The Diffuse filter breaks up the image so that it looks less focused. The Darken Only option replaces light pixels with dark pixels, and the Lighten Only option replaces dark pixels with light pixels.

- The Wind filter conveys directed motion.
- The Extrude filter converts the image into pyramids or blocks.

Applying a Filter to a Selection

Instead of applying a filter to an entire layer, you can specify a particular area of a layer to which you want to apply a filter. You need to first define the area by using a marquee tool, and then apply the desired filter. If you want to apply a filter to a layer that contains a mask, be sure to select the layer name, not the layer mask thumbnail.

Detecting a watermark

Before you can embed a watermark, you must first register with Digimarc Corporation. When Photoshop detects a watermark in an image, it displays the copyright image © in the image file's title bar. To check if an image has a watermark, make the layer active, click Filter on the menu bar, point to Digimarc, then click Read Watermark.

FIGURE 10

Examples of Stylize filters

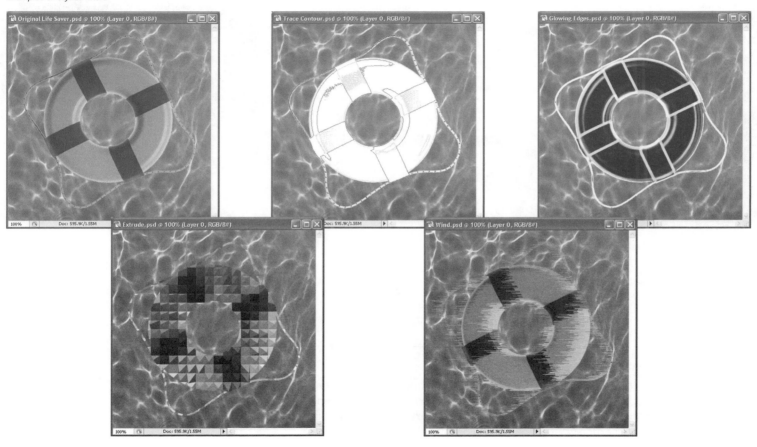

Apply a Stylize filter

1. Click the **Sunflower field layer** on the Layers palette.

2. Click **Filter** on the menu bar, point to **Stylize** as shown in Figure 11, then click **Solarize**.

3. Compare your image to Figure 12.

You applied the Solarize filter to the Sunflower field layer.

FIGURE 11
Stylize options on the Filter menu

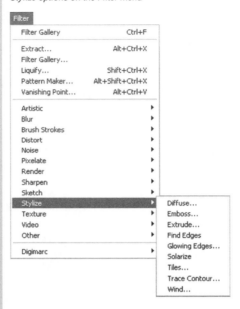

FIGURE 12
Effect of Solarize filter

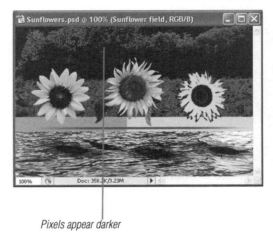

Pixels appear darker

DESIGNTIP   **Using filters to reduce file size**

If you apply a filter to a small area, you can view the effect while conserving your computer's resources. For example, you can test several filters on a small area and then decide which one you want to apply to one or more layers. Alternatively, you can apply a filter to a large portion of a layer, such as applying a slight Motion Blur filter to a grassy background. Your viewers will not notice an appreciable difference when they look at the grass, but by applying the filter, you reduce the number of green colors Photoshop must save in the image, which reduces the size of the file.

FIGURE 13
Elliptical Marquee selection

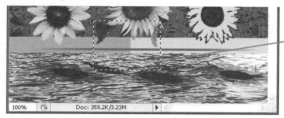

Marquee surrounds
the box

FIGURE 14
Wind dialog box

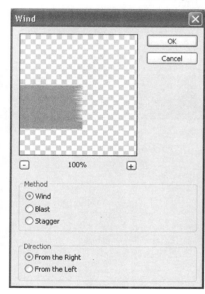

FIGURE 15
Effect of Wind filter

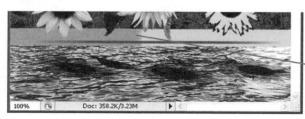

Wind filter applied
to orange bar

Lesson 3   Add Unique Effects with Stylize Filters

1. Click the **Orange bar layer** on the Layers palette.

2. Click the **Rectangular Marquee Tool** ⬚ on the toolbox.

3. Change the Feather setting to **0 px** (if it is not already set to 0).

4. Draw a rectangle around an area that includes the right side of the bar (from approximately 140 X/140 Y to 250 X/225 Y) using the **Marquee pointer** ┼, as shown in Figure 13.

5. Click **Filter** on the menu bar, point to **Stylize**, then click **Wind**.

6. Verify that the **Wind option button** is selected in the Method section of the Wind dialog box.

7. Click the **From the Right option button** in the Direction section of the Wind dialog box (if it is not already selected), then compare your dialog box to Figure 14.

8. Click **OK**.

9. Deselect the marquee, then compare your image to Figure 15.

You used the Rectangular Marquee Tool to select a specific area on the Orange bar layer, then applied the Wind filter to the selection.

Apply a previously used filter

1. Click the **Sunflower CENTER layer** on the Layers palette.

2. Click **Filter** on the menu bar, then click **Filter Gallery**. Compare your Filter Gallery dialog box to Figure 16.

3. Click **OK**.

   The filter last applied using the Filter Gallery is applied to the active layer.

You applied the Poster Edges filter to a layer using the Filter Gallery.

FIGURE 16
Last filter applied on Filter Gallery

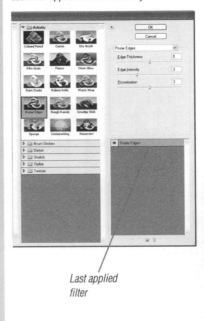

Last applied filter

FIGURE 17
Combining filters

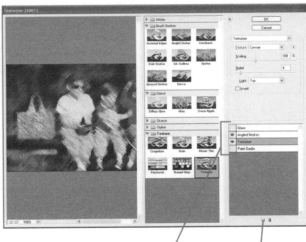

Multiple filters applied to image   Adds new filter layer

Using the Filter Gallery to combine effects

The Filter Gallery offers more than just another way of applying a single filter. Using this feature, you can apply multiple filters. And using the same principles as on the Layers palette, you can rearrange the filter layers and control their visibility. Figure 17 shows an image to which four different filters have been applied, but only the effects of two are visible. Each time you apply, reorder, or turn off one of the filters, the preview image is updated, so you'll always know how your image is being modified.

FIGURE 18
Solarize filter applied to multiple layers

Solarize filter applied to
all Sunflowers layers

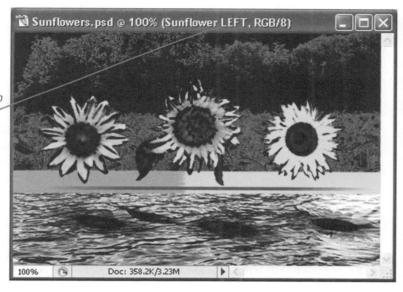

1. Click the **Sunflower LEFT layer** on the Layers palette.

2. Click **Filter** on the menu bar, then click the first instance of **Filter Gallery**.

   The Sunflower LEFT and Sunflower CENTER layers have the same filter applied.

3. Save your work, then compare your image to Figure 18.

You used the last filter applied on the Filter Gallery to apply the Solarize filter to the Sunflower LEFT layer and the Sunflower CENTER layer.

ALTER IMAGES WITH DISTORT
AND NOISE FILTERS

What You'll Do

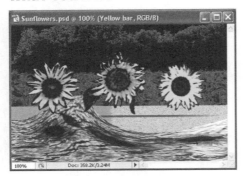

In this lesson, you'll apply the Twirl filter to the Water layer and the Noise filter to the Yellow bar layer.

Understanding Distort and Noise Filters

Distort filters use the most memory, yet even a minimal setting can produce dramatic results. They create a 3-D effect or reshape an object. The Diffuse Glow filter mutes an image, similar to how classic film cinematographers layered cheesecloth or smeared Vaseline on the lens of a movie camera when filming leading ladies. Others, such as the Ocean Ripple, Glass, Wave, and Ripple filters make an object appear as if it is under or in water. The Twirl filter applies a circular effect to a layer. By adjusting the angle of the twirl, you can make images look as if they are moving or spinning. Figure 19 shows the diversity of the Distort filters.

Noise filters give an image an appearance of texture. You can apply them to an image layer or to the Background layer. If you want to apply a Noise filter to a type layer, you must rasterize it to convert it to an image layer. You can apply effects to the rasterized type layer; however, you can no longer edit the text.

Optimizing Memory in Photoshop

Many of the dynamic features in Photoshop are memory-intensive, particularly layer masks and filters. In addition to significantly increasing file size, they require a significant quantity of your computer memory to take effect. Part of the fun of working in Photoshop is experimenting with different styles and effects; however, doing so can quickly consume enough memory to diminish Photoshop's performance, or can cause you to not be able to work in other programs while Photoshop is running. You can offset some of the resource loss by freeing up memory as you work in Photoshop, and by adjusting settings in the Preferences dialog box.

Understanding Memory Usage

Every time you change your image, Photoshop stores the previous state in its buffer, which requires memory. You can control some of the memory that Photoshop uses by lowering the number of states available on the History palette. To change the number of states, open the Preferences dialog box, select the General topic, then enter a number in the History States text box. You can also liberate the memory used to store Undo commands, History states, and items on the clipboard by clicking Edit on the menu bar, pointing to Purge, then clicking the area you want to purge. It's a good idea to use the Purge command after you've tried out several effects during a session, but be aware that you cannot undo the Purge command. For example, if you purge the History states, they will no longer appear on the History palette.

Controlling Memory Usage

Factors such as how much memory your computer has, the average size file you work with, and your need to multitask (have other programs open) can determine how Photoshop uses the memory currently allotted to it. To change your memory settings, click Edit on the menu bar, point to Preferences, then click Memory & Image Cache (Win). If you are using a Macintosh, click Photoshop on the menu bar, point to Preferences, click Memory & Image Cache, then change the amount of memory allocated to Photoshop in the Maximum Use by Photoshop text box. You should carefully consider your program needs before changing the default settings. For additional tips on managing resources, search the Adobe Web site Support Knowledgebase: *www.adobe.com/support*.

FIGURE 19
Examples of Distort filters

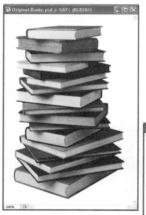
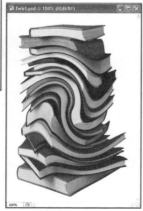
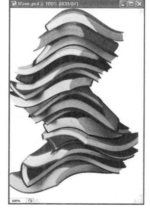
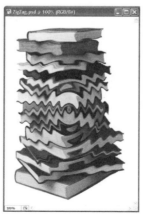
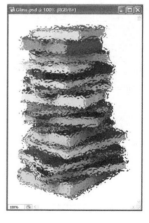

Apply a Twirl filter

1. Click the **Water layer** on the Layers palette.

2. Click **Filter** on the menu bar, point to **Distort**, then click **Twirl**.

3. Drag the **Angle slider** to **145**, as shown in Figure 20.

   | TIP   The selection is rotated more sharply in the center of the selection than at the edges.

4. Click **OK**.

5. Click the **Red bar layer** on the Layers palette, drag it beneath the Water layer, then compare your image to Figure 21.

You applied a Twirl filter to the Water layer. You moved the Red bar layer beneath the water to complete the effect.

FIGURE 20
Twirl dialog box

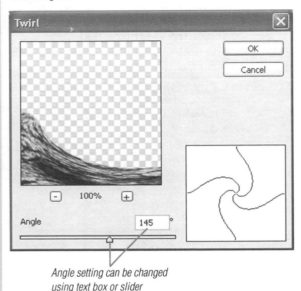

Angle setting can be changed using text box or slider

FIGURE 21
Twirl filter applied to Water layer

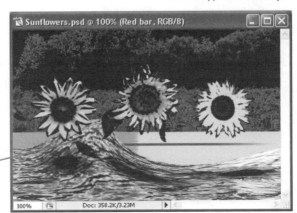

Effect of Twirl filter

Correction lens distortion

Some distortions occur as a result of the camera lens. You can use the Lens Correction filter to counteract barrel (convex appearance), pincushion (concave appearance), and perspective distortions. You can also correct for chromatic aberrations and lens vignetting. These distortions can occur as a result of the focal length or f-stop in use. The Lens Correction filter can also be used to rotate an image, or fix perspectives caused by camera tilt. Click Filter on the menu bar, point to Distort, and then click Lens Correction.

FIGURE 22
Add Noise dialog box

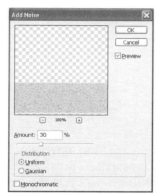

FIGURE 23
Add Noise filter applied to type layer

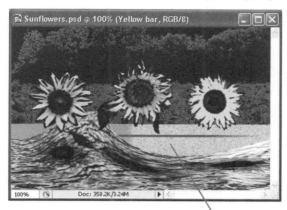

Effect of Add
Noise filter

FIGURE 24
Reduce Noise dialog box

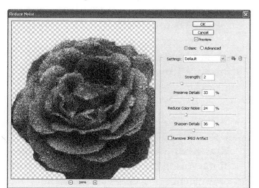

Apply a Noise filter

1. Click the **Yellow bar layer** on the Layers palette.

2. Click **Filter** on the menu bar, point to **Noise**, then click **Add Noise**.

3. Drag the **Amount slider** to **30** (or type the value in the text box), then compare your dialog box to Figure 22.

   TIP The Uniform setting distributes color values using random numbers between 0 and a specified value, while the Gaussian setting distributes color values along a bell-shaped curve for a speckled effect.

4. Click **OK**.

   Flecks of noise are visible in the layer.

5. Save your work, then compare your image to Figure 23.

You applied a Noise filter to the active layer.

Reducing noise
While some images look better when you've added some noise, others can benefit from a little noise reduction. You can quiet things down using the Reduce Noise dialog box shown in Figure 24. Here you can adjust the strength, details, and color noise, and can also sharpen the image.

Lesson 4   Alter Images with Distort and Noise Filters

ALTER LIGHTING WITH
A RENDER FILTER

What You'll Do

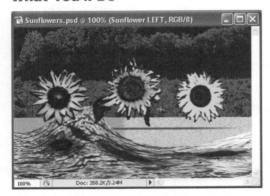

In this lesson, you'll add a lighting effect to the Sunflower LEFT layer.

Understanding Lighting Effects

The Lighting Effects filter in the **Render** category off the Filter menu allows you to set an atmosphere or highlight elements in your image. You can select the style and type of light, adjust its properties, and texturize it. The preview window displays an ellipse that shows the light settings and allows you to position the light relative to your image, so that it looks like the light in the image is coming from a specific source. You can drag the handles on each circle, ellipse, or bar to change the direction and distance of the light sources. Figure 25 shows how you can position the light using the Soft Spotlight style.

Adjusting Light by Setting the Style and Light Type

You can choose from over a dozen lighting styles, including spotlights, floodlights, and full lighting, as shown in Figure 25. After you select a style, you choose the type of light—Directional, Omni, or Spotlight,

and set its intensity and focus. Directional lighting washes the surface with a constant light source, Omni casts light from the center, and Spotlight directs light outward from a single point. As shown in Figure 26, you can adjust the brightness of the light by using the Intensity slider. You can use the Focus slider to adjust the size of the beam of light filling the ellipse. The light source begins where the radius touches the edge of the ellipse. The Light type color swatch lets you modify the color of the light. You can also create custom lighting schemes and save them for use in other images. Custom lighting schemes will appear in the Style list.

Adjusting Surrounding Light Conditions

You can adjust the surrounding light conditions using the Gloss, Material, Exposure, or Ambience properties, as shown in Figure 26. The Gloss property controls the amount of surface reflection on the lighted surfaces. The Material property controls the parts of an image that reflect the light source color. The Exposure property lightens or darkens the ellipse (the area displaying the light source). The Ambience property controls the balance between the light source and the overall light in an image. The Properties color swatch changes the ambient light around the spotlight.

Adding Texture to Light

The Texture Channel allows you to add 3-D effects to the lighting filter. The Texture Channel controls how light reflects off an image. If a channel is selected and the 'White is High' check box is also selected, white parts of the channel will be raised. To use this option, you select one of the three RGB color channels, then drag the Height slider to the relief setting you want. You

can also choose whether the black or white areas appear highest in the relief. Figure 27 shows a lighting effect texture with black colors highest.

QUICKTIP

You can add additional light sources by dragging the light bulb icon onto the preview window, and then adjusting each new light source that you add.

FIGURE 25
Lighting Effects dialog box

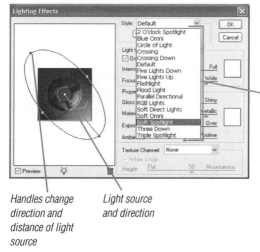

Handles change direction and distance of light source

Light source and direction

FIGURE 26
Settings in the Lighting Effects dialog box

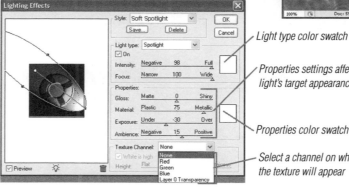

Light type color swatch

Properties settings affect light's target appearance

Properties color swatch

Select a channel on which the texture will appear

FIGURE 27
Texture added to lighting effect

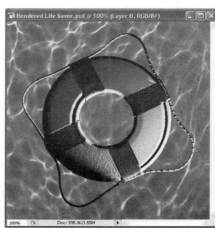

Light styles

Select lighting settings

1. Click the **Sunflower LEFT layer** on the Layers palette.

2. Click **Filter** on the menu bar, point to **Render**, then click **Lighting Effects**.

3. Click the **Style list arrow**, then click **Flashlight**.

   The preview window displays the newly selected style.

4. Click the **Light type list arrow**, then click **Omni** (if it is not already selected).

5. Verify that the **On check box** is selected.

   The preview window shows the settings for the Spotlight light source.

6. Drag the center handle of the flashlight so it is directly over the sunflower in the preview box.

   As you drag the ellipse handle, the preview window automatically displays the change in the lighting direction and distance.

7. Drag any one of the handles on the edge of the flashlight so the spotlight is larger than the sunflower.

8. Adjust the slider settings as shown in Figure 28 in the Lighting Effects dialog box.

   │ TIP   Lighting effects must include at least one light source.

You selected a lighting style and type, then changed the direction and distance of the lighting.

FIGURE 28
Light direction and source repositioned

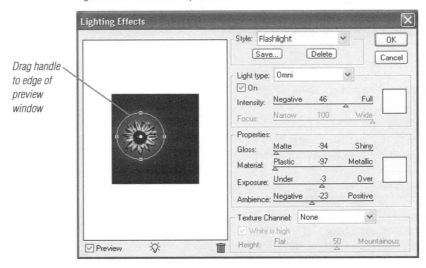

Drag handle to edge of preview window

FIGURE 29

Lighting Effects filter applied to Sunflower LEFT layer

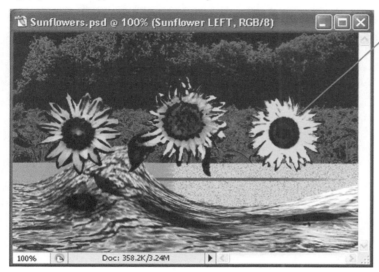

Shadow created
by Lighting
Effects filter

Apply a lighting effect

1. Click **OK**.

   The light appears brightest in the center of the flower.

   TIP   When there are multiple sources of light, you can delete a light source ellipse by dragging its center point over the Delete icon in the Lighting Effects dialog box.

2. Save your work, then compare your image to Figure 29. Your results may vary, depending on your settings in the Lighting Effects dialog box.

3. Close the file, then exit Photoshop.

You applied a lighting effect to the Sunflower LEFT layer.

Creating custom lighting effects

As you modify a style in the Lighting Effects dialog box, you can save the settings as a new style with a unique name. To create a custom style, choose your settings, then click the Save button beneath the Style list arrow. Enter a new name in the Save as dialog box, then click OK. The new style name will appear in the Style list. You can delete an entry by selecting it from the Style list, then clicking the Delete button.

Power User Shortcuts

to do this:	use this method:	to do this:	use this method:
Apply a filter	Filter ➤ Filter category ➤ Filter name	Descend one layer at a time on the Layers palette	[Alt][[] (Win) or option [[] (Mac)
Apply last filter	[Ctrl][F] (Win) or ⌘[F] (Mac)	Fades effect of previous filter	[Ctrl][Shift][F] (Win) or ⌘[Shift][F] (Mac)
Apply last filter, but set new options	[Ctrl][Alt][F] (Win) or ⌘ option [F] (Mac)	Open Filter Gallery	Filter ➤ Filter Gallery
Ascend one layer at a time on the Layers palette	[Alt][]] (Win) or option []] (Mac)		

Key: Menu items are indicated by ➤ between the menu name and its command.

You can apply a filter using the Filter menu or the Filter Gallery. With the Filter Gallery, you can apply multiple filters at once, and see how each filter will affect your image. Applying one or more filters can make your image look dramatic. Because there are so many different types of filters, you'll have a lot of fun figuring out which filter gives you which effect. Filters can be applied to an entire layer or to a selection.

Nearly every filter has a variety of settings that you can modify to give you just the look you want. Stylize filters, for example, produce an impressionistic effect for displacing pixels and heightening contrast. Noise filters give an image the appearance of texture. Perhaps the most dramatic of all the filters is Lighting Effects in the Render filter category. There are so many filters that you'll have to experiment to see just what each one does.

What You Have Learned:

- How to apply a filter using the Filter menu
- How to use the Filter Gallery
- How to use Artistic filters and adjust filter effects
- How to apply a Stylize filter
- How to apply a filter to a selection
- How to apply a previously used filter
- How to alter lighting with a Render filter

Key Terms

Artistic filters　Filters that replicate natural or traditional media effects.

Distort filters　Used to create three-dimensional or other reshaping effects.

Filter Gallery　A feature that lets you see the effects of each filter before it is applied to a layer.

Noise filters　Add or remove pixels with randomly distributed color levels.

Render filters　Transform three-dimensional shapes and simulated light reflections in an image.

Stylize filters　Produce a painted or impressionistic effect.

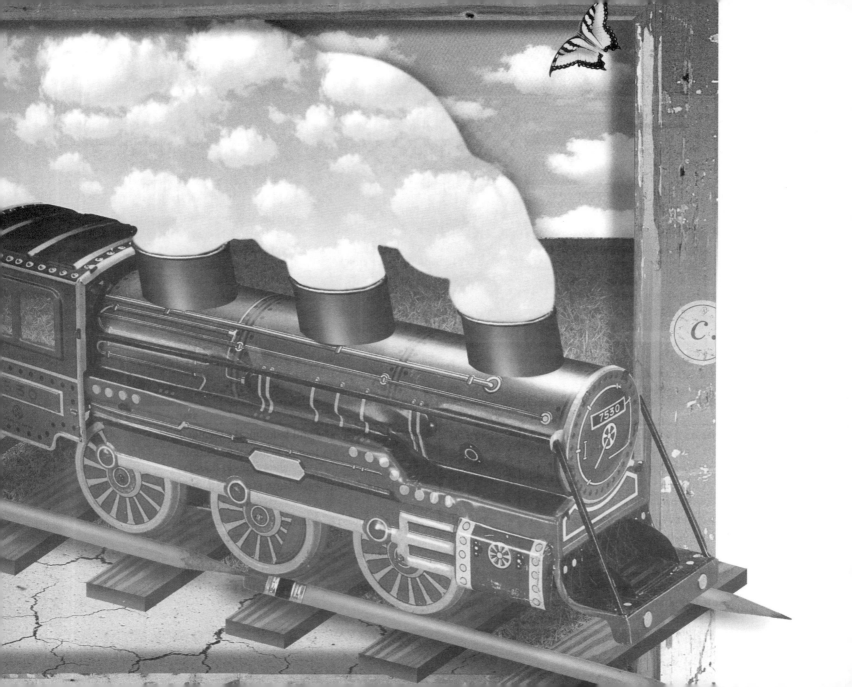

CHAPTER

9

ENHANCING SPECIFIC
SELECTIONS

1. Create an alpha channel.

2. Use Extract to isolate an object.

3. Erase areas in an image to enhance appearance.

4. Use the Clone Stamp Tool to make repairs.

5. Use the Magic Wand Tool to select objects.

6. Learn how to create snapshots.

7. Create multiple-image layouts.

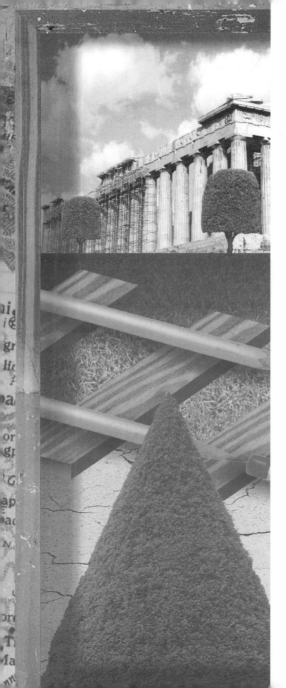

9 ENHANCING SPECIFIC
SELECTIONS

Modifying Objects

As you have most likely figured out by now, a great part of the power of Photoshop resides in its ability to isolate graphics and text objects and make changes to them. This chapter focuses on several of the techniques used to isolate graphics objects and then make changes that enhance their appearance.

Using Channels

Nearly every image you open or create in Photoshop is separated into **channels**. Photoshop uses channels to house the color information for each layer and layer mask in your image. The number of color information channels depends on the color mode of the image. You can also create specific channels for layer masks.

> **QUICK**TIP
>
> Photoshop creates default channels based on the image mode, but you can create additional channels to gain more control of an image.

Fixing Imperfections

From time to time, you'll probably work with flawed images. Flawed images are not necessarily "bad," they just might contain imagery that does not fit your needs. Photoshop offers several ways to repair an image's imperfections. You can use the following methods—or combinations of these methods—to fix areas within an image that are less than ideal:

- Isolate areas using the Extract feature.
- Erase areas using a variety of eraser tools.
- Take a sample and then paint that sample over an area using the Clone Stamp Tool.

Creating Snapshots

The Snapshot command lets you make a temporary copy of any state of an image. The snapshot is added to the top of the History palette and lets you work on a new version of the image. Snapshots are like the states found on the History palette but offer a few more advantages:

- You can name a snapshot to make it easy to identify and manage.
- You can compare changes to images easily. For example, you can take a snapshot before and after changing the color of a selection.
- You can recover your work easily. If your experimentation with an image doesn't satisfy your needs, you can select the snapshot to undo all the steps from the experiment.

Using Automation Features

After you complete an image that you want to share, you can create an image that contains various sizes of the same image, or several different images. The Picture Package feature, for example, makes it possible to print images in a variety of sizes and shapes on a single sheet. Another example is a contact sheet, a file that displays thumbnail views of a selection of images, so that you can easily catalog and preview them without opening each individual file.

Tools You'll Use

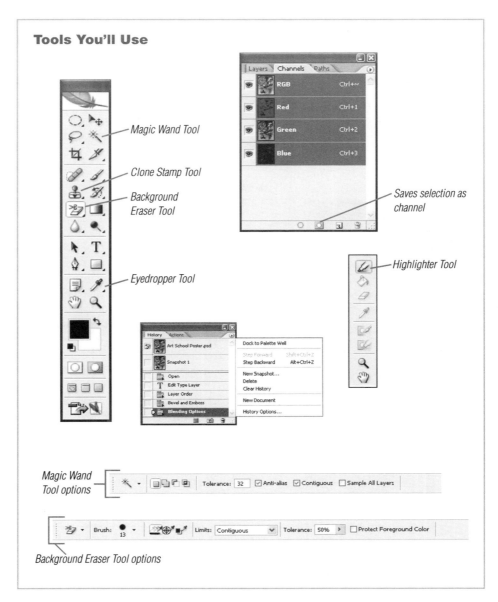

CREATE AN ALPHA CHANNEL

What You'll Do

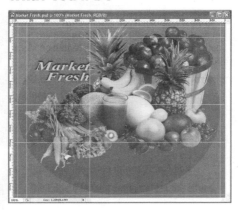

 In this lesson, you'll view the colors in the default color mode on the Channels palette. You'll also create a selection, save it as an alpha channel, and then change the color of the alpha channel.

Defining Channels

Photoshop automatically creates channel information in a new image and uses channels to store color information about images. Channels are created at the same time the image is created, and the number of channels is determined by the image mode. For example, a CMYK image has at least four channels (one each for cyan, magenta, yellow, and black), whereas an RGB image has three channels (one each for red, green, and blue). Every Photoshop image has at least one channel, and can have a maximum of 24 color channels. The color channels contained in an image are known as **default channels**, which Photoshop creates automatically. You can add specific color information by adding an **alpha channel** or a **spot channel**. You use an alpha channel to create and store masks, which let you manipulate, isolate, and protect parts of an image. A spot channel contains information about special pre-mixed inks used in CMYK color printing. The default number of channels is determined by the color mode you select in the New dialog box that opens when you create

a new file, as shown in Figure 1. You can add channels to images displayed in all color modes, except the bitmap modes.

Understanding Alpha Channels

You create alpha channels on the Channels palette. You can create an alpha channel that masks all or specific areas of a layer. For example, you can create a selection and then convert it into an alpha channel. Photoshop superimposes the color in an alpha channel onto the image; however, an alpha channel might appear in grayscale on the Channels palette thumbnail. You can use alpha channels to preserve a selection, to experiment with, to use later, to create special effects, such as screens or shadows, or to save and reuse in other images. Photoshop supports the following formats for saving an alpha channel: PSD, PDF, PICT, TIFF, and Raw. If you use other formats, you might lose some channel information. You can copy the alpha channel to other images and instantly apply the same information. Alpha channels do not print—they will not be visible in print media.

QUICKTIP

Adding alpha channels increases the size of the file based on the mode that you select for the image.

Understanding the Channels Palette

The Channels palette lists all the default channels contained in a layer and manages all the image's channels. To access this palette, click the Channels tab next to the Layers tab, as shown in Figure 2. The top channel is a **composite channel**—a combination of all the other default channels. The additional default channels, based on the existing color mode, are shown below the composite channel, followed by spot color channels, and finally by the alpha channels.

Channels have many of the same properties as layers. You can hide channels in the same way as you hide layers, by clicking a button in the column to the left of the thumbnail on the Channels palette. Each channel has a thumbnail that mirrors the changes you make to the image's layers. You can also change the order of channels by dragging them up or down on the Channels palette.

The thumbnails on the Channels palette might appear in grayscale. To view the channels in their actual color, click Edit on the menu bar, point to Preferences, click Display & Cursors, select the Color Channels in Color check box, then click OK. The default channels will appear in the color mode colors; an alpha channel will appear in the color selected in the Channel Options dialog box. You open the Channel Options dialog box by double-clicking the alpha channel on the Channels palette.

FIGURE 1
New dialog box

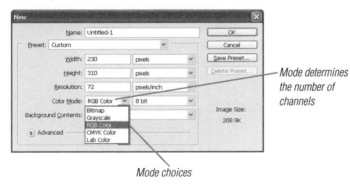

Mode determines the number of channels

Mode choices

FIGURE 2
Channels on the Channels palette

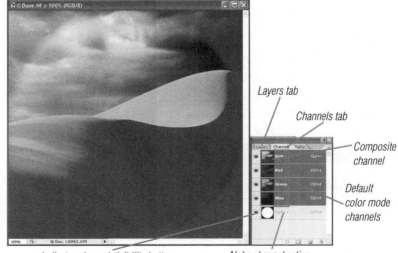

Layers tab

Channels tab

Composite channel

Default color mode channels

Indicates channel visibility button

Alpha channel active

View the Channels palette

1. Start Photoshop, open PS 9-1.psd from the drive and folder where your Data Files are stored, update the text layers, then save it as **Market Fresh**.

2. Click the **Default Foreground and Background Colors button** on the toolbox to display the default settings.

3. Display the rulers in pixels, then change the zoom factor to **100**%.

4. Click **Edit** (Win) or **Photoshop** (Mac) on the menu bar, point to **Preferences**, click **Display & Cursors**, verify that there is a check mark in the **Color Channels in Color check box**, then click **OK** to verify that the default color channels are displayed in color.

5. Click the **Channels tab** Channels next to the Layers tab on the Layers palette, then compare your Channels palette to Figure 3.

   The Channels palette is active and displays the four channels for RGB color mode: RGB (composite), Red, Green, and Blue.

You opened the Channels palette, and verified that colors are displayed in the default color channels. This allows you to see the actual colors contained in each channel when working with images.

FIGURE 3
Channels palette

Changes to the composite channel affect the entire layer

Displays the Channels palette

Your thumbnails might appear in grayscale

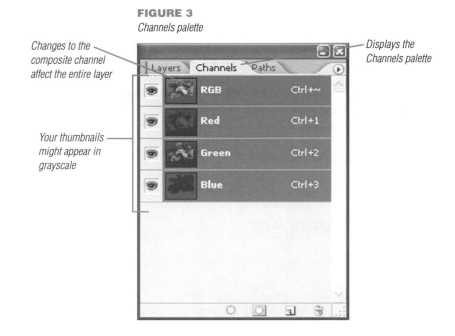

Changing alpha channel colors
You can change the color that the alpha channel displays (to alter the appearance of the image) by picking a color in the Channel Options dialog box. To open the Channel Options dialog box, double-click the alpha channel (which appears at the bottom of the Channels panel once it is created), click the color box, select a color in the Color Picker dialog box, then click OK. Click an option button in the Channel Options dialog box to choose whether the color includes or excludes the selected area, then click OK.

FIGURE 4
Selection created

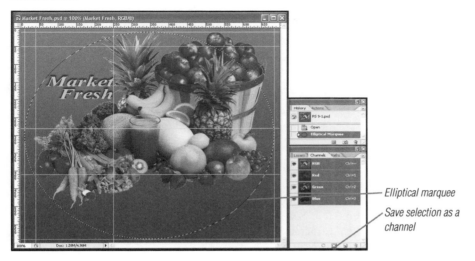

Elliptical marquee

Save selection as a channel

FIGURE 5
Alpha channel created

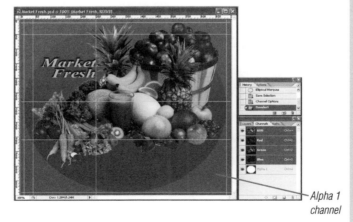

Alpha 1 channel

Create an alpha channel from a selection

1. Click the **Elliptical Marquee Tool** ⬭ on the toolbox, then set the Feather setting on the options bar to **0 px** (if it is not already set to 0).

2. Drag the **Marquee pointer** ✛ from approximately **10 X/10 Y** to **685 X/590 Y**, then compare your image to Figure 4.

3. Click the **Save selection as channel button** ◻ on the Channels palette.

4. Double-click the **Alpha 1 thumbnail** on the Channels palette, then click the **color box** in the Channel Options dialog box.

5. Verify that the **Red option button** is selected in the Color Picker dialog box (R=255, G=0, B=0), then click **OK**.

6. Verify that the opacity setting is **50%** and that the **Masked Areas option button** is selected, then click **OK**.

7. On the Channels palette, click the **RGB layer**, then click the **Indicates channel visibility button** ▢ for the Alpha 1 channel to view the alpha channel.

   The combination of the red alpha channel color overlaying blue produces pink.

8. Click **Select** on the menu bar, click **Deselect**, then compare your image to Figure 5.

9. Save your work.

You used the Elliptical Marquee Tool to create a selection and then saved the selection as an alpha channel. You also verified the alpha channel color and reviewed the results by viewing the alpha channel.

USE EXTRACT TO
ISOLATE AN OBJECT

What You'll Do

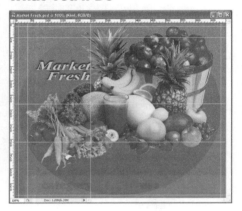

In this lesson, you'll create a duplicate layer, and use the Extract feature to extract the kiwi from the Fruit and Vegetables layer so that you can adjust its color. You'll also adjust the color of the extracted kiwi by applying a Gradient Map to it.

Isolating Objects

You can use the **Extract feature** to isolate a foreground object from its background. This feature lets you define the object you want to extract, even if its edge is vaguely defined. When you extract an object from a layer, Photoshop deletes the non-extracted portion of the image's background to underlying transparency. It's always a good idea to first copy the original layer and then extract an object from the duplicate layer. This preserves the original layer, which you can use as a reference, and helps you to avoid losing any of the original image information. After you extract an image, you can modify the extracted object layer as you wish.

QUICKTIP
The Extract feature is great for objects that you want to look blurry, in motion, or translucent.

Using the Extract Feature

You isolate objects using tools in the Extract dialog box (see Table 1). You first trace the edge of the object you want to extract with the Edge Highlighter Tool, then you select everything inside of the edge with the Fill Tool. If you make a mistake, you can use the eraser to erase the erroneous parts or you can click Undo on the Edit menu to delete the entire action. It takes practice to become proficient at using the Edge Highlighter Tool. If you do not draw a continuous edge around the object, Photoshop might not fill in the area accurately. You can edit portions of the edge as often as necessary. Depending on the size of the brush tip you select, the dimensions of your extracted object will vary.

TABLE 1: Extraction Tools

tool	name	use
	Edge Highlighter Tool	Paints an edge around the object you want to extract.
	Fill Tool	Fills the extracted object.
	Eraser Tool	Deletes highlighted edges or filled areas.
	Eyedropper Tool	Active when Force Foreground check box is selected; samples a color in the image or in the Color Picker dialog box.
	Cleanup Tool	Makes mask transparent; press keyboard numbers 1–9 (increasing transparency) to change pressure of tool.
	Edge Touchup Tool	Deletes edges of extracted object to sharpen edge; press keyboard numbers 1–9 (increasing transparency) to change pressure of tool.
	Zoom Tool	Changes view of object in dialog box.
	Hand Tool	Positions image in dialog box.

Isolate an object

1. Click the **Layers tab** Layers on the Layers palette.

2. Click the **Fruit and Vegetables layer** on the Layers palette, click the **Layers palette list arrow** Channels, then click **Duplicate Layer**.

3. Type **Kiwi** in the As text box, then click **OK** to close the Duplicate Layer dialog box.

   The new layer appears above the Fruit and Vegetables layer on the Layers palette, and is now the active layer.

4. Click the **Channels tab** Channels, click the **Indicates layer visibility** button for the Alpha channel if any layer is not visible, then click the **Layers tab** Layers.

5. Click **Filter** on the menu bar, then click **Extract**.

6. Click the **Zoom Tool** in the Extract dialog box, then click the **center of the kiwi** three times.

7. Click the **Edge Highlighter Tool** in the Extract dialog box.

8. Double-click the **Brush Size text box** on the right side of the Extract dialog box, then type **5**.

9. Drag the **Brush pointer** around the inner edge of the kiwi, avoiding the celery leaf (if possible).

10. Click the **Fill Tool** in the Extract dialog box, click the **center of the kiwi**, then compare your dialog box to Figure 6.

   The kiwi is surrounded by the green highlighted border and filled in blue.

You created and named a duplicate layer of the Fruit and Vegetables layer, opened the Extract dialog box, used the Edge Highlighter Tool to outline the kiwi, and filled in the kiwi using the Fill Tool.

FIGURE 6
Extract dialog box

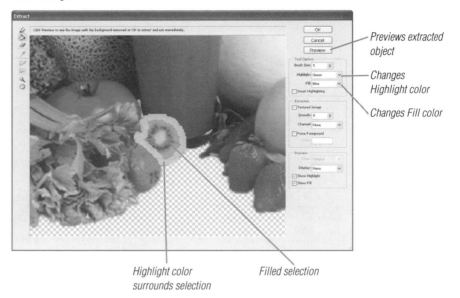

Previews extracted object

Changes Highlight color

Changes Fill color

Highlight color surrounds selection

Filled selection

Using Extract on a complex object

You may be wondering why the Extract feature is located on the Filter menu. This is because this feature is used not only to isolate objects, but it also *filters out* background imagery. Let's say you want to extract a woman who has bushy hair—the kind you can see through. Use a larger brush tip and trace on the outside edge of the object you want to extract. If your object has a well-defined edge (even in only a few places), turn on the Smart Highlighting feature. This feature highlights just the edge. It ignores the current brush size and applies a highlight wide enough to cover the edge. In our example, only the woman and her hair will be extracted, not the pieces of sky between individual strands of hair.

FIGURE 7
Layer containing the extracted object

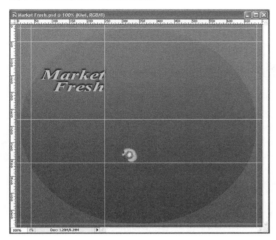

FIGURE 9
Extracted object with a Gradient Map applied

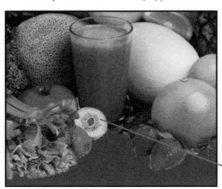

*Gradient Map adjustment
on the extracted object*

FIGURE 8
Sample gradients

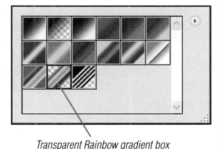

Transparent Rainbow gradient box

Extract an object

1. Click **Preview** in the upper-right corner of the Extract dialog box.

   The highlighted kiwi appears on the layer with a transparent background.

2. Click **OK**.

3. Click the **Indicates layer visibility button** 👁 on the Fruit and Vegetables, Apples, and Pineapple layers on the Layers palette. See Figure 7.

You previewed the extracted kiwi in the Extract dialog box, then viewed the layer containing the extracted object.

Enhance an extracted object

1. Click **Image** on the menu bar, point to **Adjustments**, then click **Gradient Map**.

2. Select the **Reverse check box**, click the **Gradient list arrow**, click the **Transparent Rainbow gradient box**, as shown in Figure 8, then click **OK**.

3. Click the **Indicates layer visibility button** ☐ on the Fruit and Vegetables, Apples, and Pineapple layers on the Layers palette.

4. Save your work, then compare your image to Figure 9.

You adjusted the color for the extracted kiwi by applying a Gradient Map to the layer, then viewed the color-adjusted image.

Lesson 2   Use Extract to Isolate an Object

ERASE AREAS IN AN IMAGE
TO ENHANCE APPEARANCE

What You'll Do

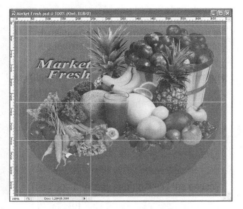

In this lesson, you'll use the Background Eraser Tool to delete pixels on the Fruit and Vegetables layer, then adjust the brightness and contrast of the isolated object.

Learning How to Erase Areas

As you have learned, the Extract feature automatically discards the area of an image that is *not* highlighted and filled. But there may be times when you want to simply erase an area *without* going through the extraction process. Photoshop provides three eraser tools that can accommodate all your expunging needs. Figure 10 shows samples of the effects of each eraser tool. The specific use for each eraser tool is reflected in its options bar, as shown in Figure 11.

Understanding Eraser Tools

The **Eraser Tool** has the opposite function of a brush. Instead of brushing *on* pixel color, you drag it *off*. When you erase a layer that has a layer beneath it, and the Lock transparent pixels button is not selected, you'll expose the color on the underlying layer when you erase. If there is no underlying layer, you'll expose transparency. If the Lock transparent pixels button *is* selected, you'll expose the current background color on the toolbox, regardless of the color of an underlying layer.

Setting options for eraser tools

Each eraser tool has its own options bar. You can select the brush mode for the Eraser Tool, and the brush tip and size for both the Eraser Tool and Background Eraser Tool. Depending on the tool, you can also set the **tolerance**—how close a pixel color must be to another color to be erased with the tool. The lower the tolerance, the closer the color must be to the selection. You can also specify the opacity of the eraser strength. A 100% opacity erases pixels to complete transparency. To set options, click an eraser tool on the toolbox, then change the tolerance and opacity settings using the text boxes and list arrows on the options bar.

The **Magic Eraser Tool** grabs similarly colored pixels based on the tool settings, and then exposes background color in the same way as the Eraser Tool. However, instead of dragging the eraser, you click the areas you want to change. The Magic Eraser Tool erases all pixels on the current layer that are close in color value to where you first click or just those pixels that are contiguous to that area.

The **Background Eraser Tool** contains small crosshairs in the brush tip. When you click, the tool selects a color in the crosshairs, then erases that particular color anywhere within the brush tip size. The Background Eraser Tool exposes the color of the layer beneath it, or it exposes transparency if there is no layer beneath it. You can preserve objects in the foreground,

while eliminating the background (it works best with a large brush tip size). The Background Eraser Tool will sample the background colors of the current layer as you drag the tool in your image—you can watch the current background color change on the toolbox.

FIGURE 10
Examples of eraser tools

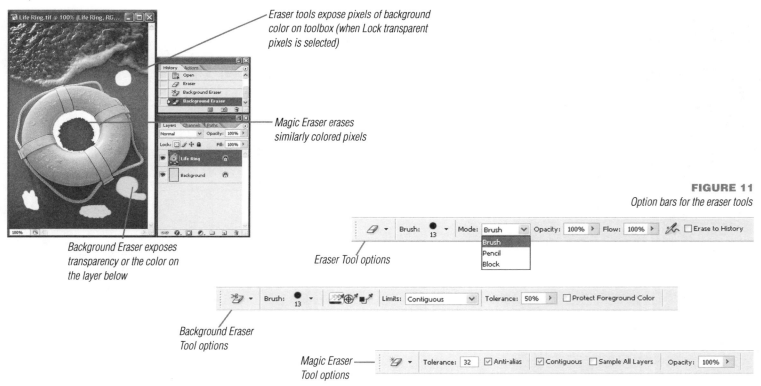

Eraser tools expose pixels of background color on toolbox (when Lock transparent pixels is selected)

Magic Eraser erases similarly colored pixels

Background Eraser exposes transparency or the color on the layer below

Eraser Tool options

Background Eraser Tool options

Magic Eraser Tool options

FIGURE 11
Option bars for the eraser tools

Use the Background Eraser Tool

1. Click the **Indicates layer visibility button** 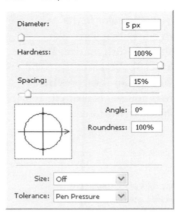 on the Kiwi layer to hide the layer.

2. Click the **Fruit and Vegetables layer** to make it the active layer.

3. Click the **Zoom Tool** on the toolbox.

4. Click the **center of the kiwi** with the **Zoom pointer** until the zoom factor is 300%.

5. Click the **Background Eraser Tool** on the toolbox.

   TIP Look under the Eraser Tool if the Background Eraser Tool is hidden. To cycle through the eraser tools, press and hold [Shift], then press [E].

6. Click the **Click to open the Brush Preset picker list arrow** on the options bar, set the Diameter to **5 px**, the Hardness to **100%**, and the Spacing to **15%** as shown in Figure 12.

7. Press **[Enter]** (Win) or **[return]** (Mac).

8. Keeping the crosshairs of the **Brush tip pointer** on the kiwi, drag the brush tip over the kiwi until it is completely erased, as shown in Figure 13.

   TIP As you drag the pointer, background colors change on the toolbox when the pointer moves over a different colored pixel in the layer beneath it.

You hid the Kiwi layer, zoomed in on the Fruit and Vegetables layer, selected a brush tip for the Background Eraser Tool, and erased the kiwi on the Fruit and Vegetables layer.

FIGURE 12
Brush Preset picker

FIGURE 13
Selection erased on layer

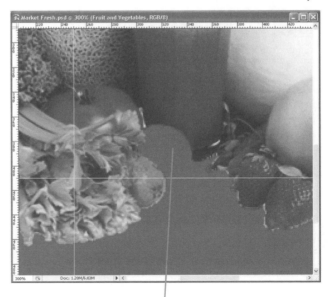

*Erased area exposes pixels
on Background layer*

FIGURE 14

Object adjusted in image

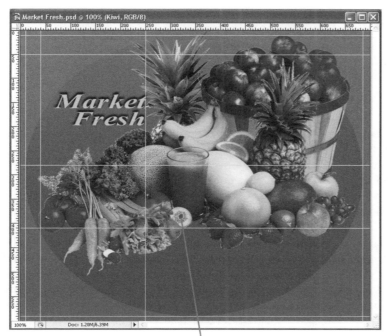

Equalize adjustment
applied to Kiwi layer

1. Click the **Kiwi layer** on the Layers palette and make the layer visible.

2. Click the **Zoom Tool** 🔍 on the toolbox.

3. Press and hold **[Alt]** (Win) or **[option]** (Mac), click the center of the kiwi with the **Zoom pointer** 🔍 until the zoom factor is 100%, then release **[Alt]** (Win) or **[option]** (Mac).

4. Click **Image** on the menu bar, point to **Adjustments**, then click **Equalize**.

    The Equalize command evens out the brightness and contrast values in the kiwi.

5. Save your work, then compare your image to Figure 14.

You adjusted the color of the kiwi by equalizing the colors, then viewed the color-adjusted image.

Redistributing brightness values

The Equalize command changes the brightness values of an image's pixels so they more evenly display the entire range of brightness levels. Photoshop changes the brightest and darkest values by remapping them so that the brightest values appear as white and the darkest values appear as black, then it redistributes the intermediate pixel values evenly throughout the grayscale. You can use this command to "tone down" an image that is too bright. Conversely, you could use it on a dark image that you want to make lighter.

USE THE CLONE STAMP TOOL
TO MAKE REPAIRS

What You'll Do

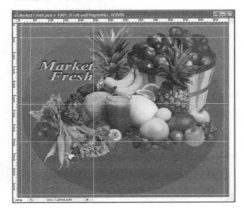

In this lesson, you'll use the Clone Stamp Tool to sample an undamaged portion of an image and use it to cover up a flaw on the image.

Touching Up a Damaged Area

Let's face it, many of the images you'll want to work with will have a visual flaw of some kind, such as a scratch, or an object obscuring what would otherwise be a great shot. While you cannot go back in time and move something out of the way, you can often use the Clone Stamp Tool to remove an object or cover up a flaw.

Using the Clone Stamp Tool

The Clone Stamp Tool can copy a sample (a pixel selection) in an image, and then paste it over what you want to cover up. The size of the sample taken with the Clone Stamp Tool depends on the brush tip size you choose on the Brushes palette. Figure 15 shows the Clone Stamp Tool in action. In addition to using the Clone Stamp Tool to touch up images, you can use it to copy one image onto another. Using the Clone Stamp Tool to copy an image differs from copying an image because you have extensive control over how much of the cloned area you expose and at what opacity.

FIGURE 15
Clone Stamp Tool in action

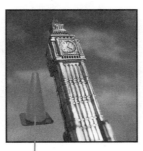

Object to be deleted

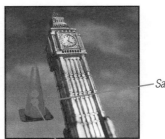

—*Sampled area*

Sampled area applied twice to hide portions of the object

FIGURE 16
Comparing images

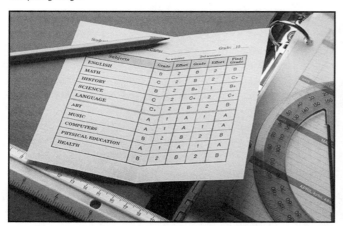

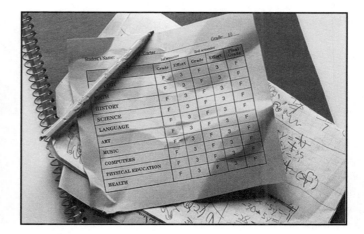

DESIGNTIP   **Perfecting your analytical skills**

An important step in making an adjustment to any image is to examine it critically and figure out what is wrong. An area that you select for fixing does not necessarily have to look bad or appear wrong. An image might be "wrong" because it simply does not convey the right meaning or mood. Compare the two images in Figure 16. They contain basically the same elements but express entirely different ideas. The figure on the left conveys a more positive image than the one on the right; clearly the grades are better for the student on the left, however, this is also reflected in the lighter colored paper, which is in pristine condition. The elements that you choose for your content should depend on what you want to convey. For example, if you want to convey a positive mood, using the elements in the image on the right would be inappropriate for your image. Choosing the right content in the beginning can save you a lot of time in the end. It is much easier and quicker to reach a destination if you know where you are going before you begin the journey.

Sample an area to clone

1. Click the **Fruit and Vegetables layer** on the Layers palette.
2. Click the **Zoom Tool** 🔍 on the toolbox.
3. Click the **center of the far-left tomato** with the **Zoom pointer** ⊕ until the zoom factor is 200% so you can clearly see the fly.
4. Click the **Clone Stamp Tool** 🖫, on the toolbox.
5. Click the **Click to open the Brush Preset picker list arrow** on the options bar, then double-click the **Hard Round 13 pixels brush tip**.
6. Verify that the Opacity setting on the options bar is **100%**.
7. Position the **Brush pointer** ○ at approximately **60 X/400 Y**, as shown in Figure 17.
8. Press **[Alt]** (Win) or **[option]** (Mac), click once, then release **[Alt]** (Win) or **[option]** (Mac).

   The sample is collected and is ready to be applied to the fly.

You selected the Fruit and Vegetables layer, set the zoom percentage, selected a brush tip for the Clone Stamp Tool, and sampled an undamaged portion of the tomato.

FIGURE 17
Defining the area to be sampled

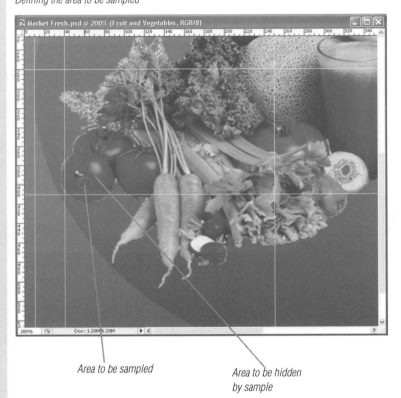

Area to be sampled

Area to be hidden by sample

FIGURE 18

Clone Stamp Tool positioned over defect

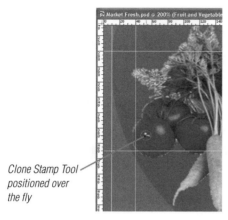

Clone Stamp Tool
positioned over
the fly

FIGURE 19

Defect corrected

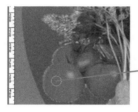

Clone Stamp Tool sample
area covers the fly

FIGURE 20

Corrected image

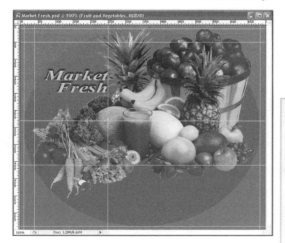

Use the Clone Stamp Tool to fix an imperfection

1. Position the **Brush pointer** ⬡ *directly* over the fly, as shown in Figure 18.

2. Click the **fly**, then compare your image to Figure 19.

   TIP   Select a different brush size if your brush is too small or too large, and then reapply the stamp.

3. Click the **Zoom Tool** 🔍 on the toolbox.

4. Press and hold **[Alt]** (Win) or **[option]** (Mac), click the **center of the tomato** with the **Zoom pointer** 🔍 until the zoom factor is 100%, then release **[Alt]** (Win) or **[option]** (Mac).

5. Save your work, then compare your image to Figure 20.

You fixed the damaged area of the tomato by covering up the fly.

Using pressure-sensitive tablets

For specialized painting that gives you maximum control when you create an image, you can purchase a pressure-sensitive stylus or tablet. A pressure-sensitive device mimics the force you'd use with an actual brush; you paint softer when you press lightly and paint darker when you press harder. You can set the stylus or tablet pressure for the Magnetic Lasso, Magnetic Pen, Pencil, Brush, Airbrush, Eraser, Clone Stamp, Pattern Stamp, History Brush, Art History Brush, Smudge, Blur, Sharpen, Dodge, Burn, and Sponge Tools.

USE THE MAGIC WAND
TOOL TO SELECT OBJECTS

What You'll Do

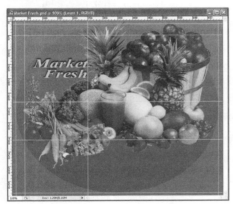

In this lesson, you'll open a new image, use the Magic Wand Tool to select an image in the new image, and move it to the Market Fresh image. You'll also readjust the Eyedropper Tool sample size, reselect and move the image so you can compare the selection difference, then delete the incomplete layer and position the complete layer in the Market Fresh image.

Understanding the Magic Wand Tool

You can use the Magic Wand Tool to select an object by selecting the color range of the object. The **Magic Wand Tool** lets you choose pixels that are similar to the ones where you first click in an image. You can control how the Magic Wand Tool behaves by specifying tolerance settings and whether or not you want to select only contiguous pixels on the options bar. The Magic Wand Tool options bar is shown in Figure 21.

Learning About Tolerance

The tolerance setting determines the range of colors you select with the Magic Wand Tool. For example, if you select a low tolerance and then click an image of the sky, you will only select a narrow range of blue pixels and probably not the entire sky. However, if you set a higher tolerance, you can expand the range of blue pixels selected by the Magic Wand Tool. Each time you click the Magic Wand Tool, you can choose from one of four buttons on the options bar to select a new area, add to

the existing area (the effect is cumulative; the more you click, the more you add), subtract from the existing area, or intersect with the existing area.

> **QUICK**TIP
>
> You can also press and hold [Shift] and repeatedly click to add pixels to your selection, or press and hold [Alt] (Win) or [option] (Mac), then click to subtract pixels from your selection.

Using the Eyedropper Tool and the Magic Wand Tool

The Contiguous and Tolerance settings are not the only determinants that establish the pixel area selected by the Magic Wand Tool. The area that the Magic Wand Tool selects also has an intrinsic relationship with the settings for the Eyedropper Tool. The sample size, or number of pixels used by the Eyedropper Tool to determine the color it picks up, affects the area selected by the Magic Wand Tool. To understand this, you need to first examine the Eyedropper Tool settings.

Understanding Sample Size

When the Eyedropper Tool sample size is set to Point Sample, it picks up the one pixel where you click on the image. When the sample size is set to 3 by 3 Average, the Eyedropper Tool picks up the color values of the nine pixels that surround the pixel where you click the image and averages them. The sample area increases exponentially to 25 pixels for the 5 by 5 Average setting. The sample size of the Eyedropper Tool influences the area selected by the Magic Wand Tool. Figure 22 shows how different Eyedropper Tool sample sizes change the Magic Wand Tool selections, even when you sample an image at the same coordinates and use the same tolerance setting. As you become familiar with the Magic Wand Tool, it's a good idea to verify or change the Eyedropper Tool sample size as needed, in addition to changing the tolerance setting.

FIGURE 21
Magic Wand Tool options

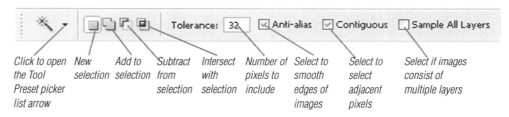

Click to open the Tool Preset picker list arrow | *New selection* | *Add to selection* | *Subtract from selection* | *Intersect with selection* | *Number of pixels to include* | *Select to smooth edges of images* | *Select to select adjacent pixels* | *Select if images consist of multiple layers*

FIGURE 22
Selection affected by Eyedropper Tool sample size

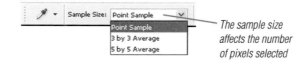

The sample size affects the number of pixels selected

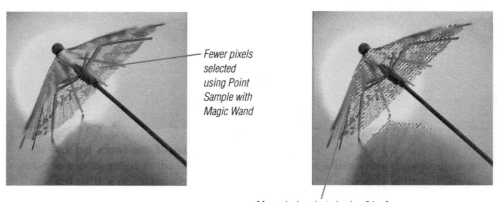

Fewer pixels selected using Point Sample with Magic Wand

More pixels selected using 5 by 5 Average sample with Magic Wand

Select an object using the Magic Wand Tool

1. Verify that the **Fruit and Vegetables layer** is the active layer.

2. Open PS 9-2.psd from the drive and folder where your Data Files are stored, then save it as **Peppermint.psd**.

3. Drag the **Peppermint.psd window** to the right side of the workspace, as shown in Figure 23.

4. Click the **Eyedropper Tool** 🖋 on the tool-box, then set the Sample Size to **5 by 5 Average** on the options bar.

5. Click the **Magic Wand Tool** ⚲ on the toolbox.

6. Type **50** in the Tolerance text box on the options bar, then press **[Enter]** (Win) or **[return]** (Mac).

7. Deselect the **Contiguous check box** (if it is selected).

   TIP   If the Contiguous check box is selected, you'll select only the pixels sharing the same color values that are adjoining each other.

8. In the Peppermint window, click the **bottom-left leaf** at approximately **20 X/175 Y** on the Info palette to select the peppermint plant, as shown in Figure 24.

9. Click the **Move Tool** ⊹ on the toolbox.

10. Position the **Move pointer** ⊹ over the **bottom-left leaf**, drag the plant in front of the lower orange quarter (and in front of the apples) in the Market Fresh image, then compare your image to Figure 25.

You opened a new file, set the Eyedropper Tool sample size to its largest selection setting, used the Magic Wand Tool to select the Peppermint image you opened, then moved the selected image into the Market Fresh image.

FIGURE 23
New image opened and positioned

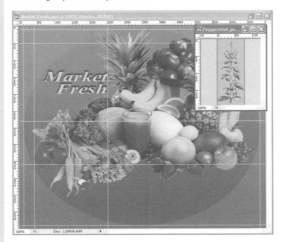

FIGURE 25
Selected object moved to current image

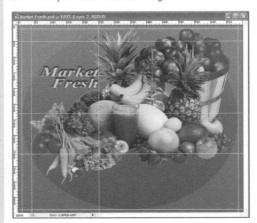

FIGURE 24
Selection indicated by marquee

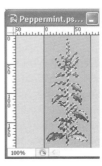

FIGURE 26
Comparison of selections

Selection made
with 5 by 5
Average sample
size captures
more pixels

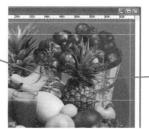

*Selection made with
Point Sample size
captures fewer pixels*

FIGURE 27
Selection positioned in image

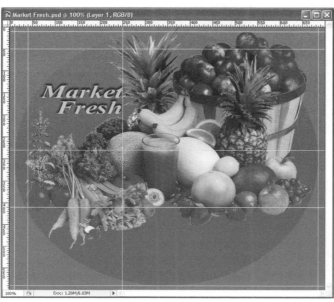

Compare objects selected using different sample sizes

1. Click **Window** on the menu bar, then click **Peppermint.psd**.

2. Click **Select** on the menu bar, then click **Deselect**.

3. Repeat Steps 4 through 10 in the previous steps, but this time, set the sample size for the Eyedropper Tool to **Point Sample** in Step 4 and drag the plant above the green apple in Step 10.

4. Verify that the **Show Transform Controls check box** is selected on the options bar, then compare the two plants in the Market Fresh image, as shown in Figure 26.

    TIP You can see the difference in the plants more easily if you hide and then display the Apples layer. Your results may vary from the sample.

5. Delete **Layer 2** on the Layers palette.

6. Verify that the **Move Tool** is selected and **Layer 1** (with the Peppermint plant) is active, click the top of the peppermint plant with the **Move pointer** ▶⊕, then drag it so it is centered behind the leftmost tomato at approximately **70 X/200 Y**.

7. Hide the rulers, deselect the Transform Controls check box, save your work, then compare your image to Figure 27.

You changed the Eyedropper Tool sample size to its smallest setting, reselected the plant, moved it to the Market Fresh image, deleted one new layer, then repositioned the peppermint plant image.

LEARN HOW TO
CREATE SNAPSHOTS

What You'll Do

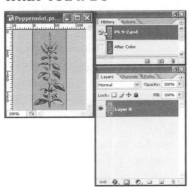

In this lesson, you'll create a snapshot on the History palette, edit an image, then use the snapshot to view the image as it existed prior to making changes.

Understanding Snapshots

As mentioned earlier in this chapter, it is a good work habit to make a copy of an original layer to help you avoid losing any of the original image information. Creating a snapshot is like creating that new copy. The History palette can only record a maximum of 20 tasks, or states, that you perform. When the History palette reaches its limit, it starts deleting the oldest states to make room for new states. You can create a **snapshot**, a temporary copy of your image that contains the history states made to that point. It's a good idea to take a snapshot of the History palette image before you begin an editing session and after you've made crucial changes because you can use snapshots to revert to or review your image from an earlier stage of development. You can create multiple snapshots in an image, and you can switch between snapshots as necessary.

Creating a Snapshot

To create a snapshot, you can click the Create new snapshot button on the History palette, or click the History palette list arrow and then click New Snapshot, as shown in Figure 28. Each new snapshot is numbered consecutively; snapshots appear in order at the top of the History palette. If you create a snapshot by clicking the New Snapshot command, you can name the snapshot in the Name text box in the New Snapshot dialog box. Otherwise, you can rename an existing snapshot in the same way as you rename a layer on the Layers palette: double-click the snapshot, then type the name in the Name text box in the Rename Snapshot dialog box. You can create a snapshot based on the entire image, merged layers, or just the current layer. A snapshot of the entire image includes all layers in the current image. A snapshot of merged layers combines all the layers in the current image on a single layer, and a snapshot of the current layer includes only the layer active at the time you took the snapshot. Figure 29 shows the New Snapshot dialog box.

Changing Snapshot Options

By default, Photoshop automatically creates a snapshot of an image when you open it. To change the default snapshot option, click the History palette list arrow, click History Options, then select one of the check boxes shown in Figure 30. You can open files faster by deselecting the Automatically Create First Snapshot check box.

QUICKTIP

Photoshop does not save snapshots when you close a file.

FIGURE 28

Snapshot commands on the History palette

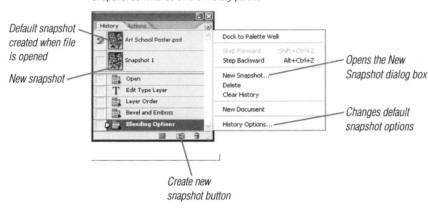

Default snapshot created when file is opened

New snapshot

Opens the New Snapshot dialog box

Changes default snapshot options

Create new snapshot button

FIGURE 29

New Snapshot dialog box

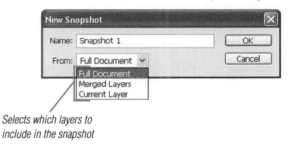

Selects which layers to include in the snapshot

FIGURE 30

History Options dialog box

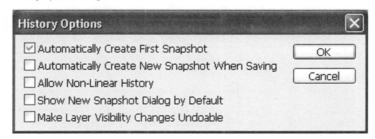

Create a snapshot

1. Deselect any selections in Peppermint.psd.

2. Click **Image** on the menu bar, point to **Adjustments**, then click **Invert**. See Figure 31.

3. Click the **History palette list arrow** 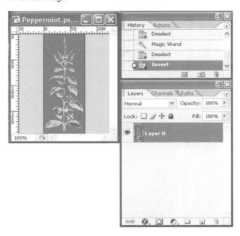, then click **New Snapshot**.

4. Type **After Color** in the Name text box, as shown in Figure 32.

5. Click **OK**.

   The newly named snapshot appears on the History palette beneath the snapshot Photoshop created when you opened the image.

You deselected the selection in the Peppermint image, inverted the color in the image, then created and named a new snapshot.

FIGURE 31
Inverted image

FIGURE 32
New Snapshot dialog box

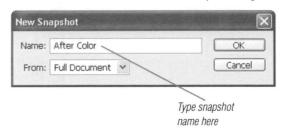

Type snapshot
name here

Use a snapshot

1. Click the **PS 9-2.psd snapshot** on the History palette, then compare your image to Figure 33.

   The image returns to its original color.

2. Click the **After Color snapshot** on the History palette.

3. Close Peppermint.psd, save any changes.

You used the snapshot to view the image as it was before you made changes.

FIGURE 33
Original snapshot view

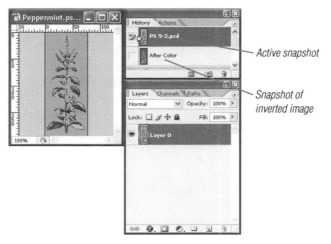

Active snapshot

Snapshot of
inverted image

CREATE MULTIPLE-IMAGE LAYOUTS

What You'll Do

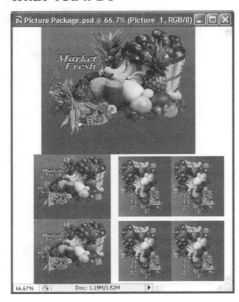

 In this lesson, you'll create a picture package of the current image and then create a folder containing a contact sheet of images.

Understanding a Picture Package

With all the choices available for creating different variations of your images, you might get the idea that keeping track of all these choices is time-consuming or difficult. Not so; to facilitate the task, Photoshop lets you generate several types of multiple-image layouts. Multiple-image layouts are useful when you need to gather one or more Photoshop images in a variety of sizes for a variety of uses. For example, if you create an advertisement, you might want to have multiple image layouts for printing in different publications. Can you imagine what would be involved to create this type of arrangement of images manually? For each duplicate image, you'd have to create a layer, resize it, then position it correctly on the page. A lot of work! You can generate a single layout, known as a **picture package**, which contains multiple sizes of a single image, as shown in Figure 34. The picture package option lets you choose from 20 possible layouts of the same image, and then places them in a single file.

Creating a Web Photo Gallery

You can display your image files on a Web site by creating a Web Photo Gallery. A Web Photo Gallery contains a thumbnail index page of all files you choose. To create a Web Photo Gallery, click File on the menu bar, point to Automate, then click Web Photo Gallery. You can choose which folders to include in the gallery by clicking the Browse button (Win) or Choose button (Mac), choose selective files using the Bridge (Win) or Selected Images from Bridge (Mac), and choose the gallery location by clicking the Destination button. Before you click OK to generate the Web Photo Gallery, you can customize the look of your Web Photo Gallery using the options in the Styles and Options lists.

Assembling a Contact Sheet

Previewing and cataloging several related images could be a time-consuming and difficult chore, but Photoshop makes it easy. It allows you to assemble a maximum of 30 thumbnail images in a specific folder, called a **contact sheet**, as shown in Figure 35. If the folder used to compile the contact sheet contains more than 30 files, Photoshop automatically creates new sheets so that all the images appear.

FIGURE 34
Sample picture package

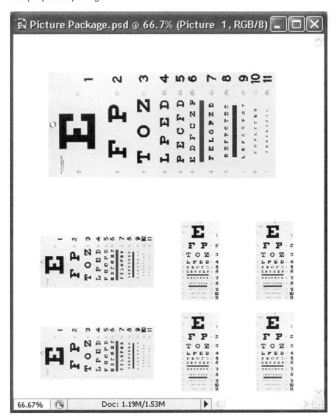

FIGURE 35
Sample contact sheet

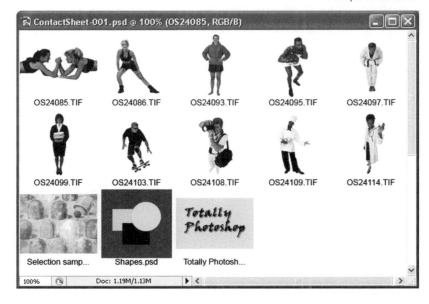

Create a picture package

1. Click **File** on the menu bar, point to **Automate**, then click **Picture Package**.

   The Picture Package dialog box opens.

   TIP   You can use the Browse button (Win) or Choose button (Mac) to select the image you want to package.

2. Verify that **Frontmost Document** appears in the Use text box, click the **Layout list arrow**, click **(1) 5 × 7 (2) 2.5 × 3.5 (4) 2 × 2.5**, then compare your picture package dialog box to Figure 36.

3. Click **OK**.

   TIP   Photoshop creates a temporary storage file (called Market Fresh copy) while it creates the picture package, then deletes the file when it is complete.

4. Save the picture package in the location where your Chapter 9 Data Files are stored, use the default name (**Picture Package.psd**), then close the file.

5. Save your work, then close Market Fresh.psd.

You selected the Picture Package option from the Automate command on the File menu, selected a layout for a picture package, then created a picture package using the Market Fresh image.

Customizing a Picture Package

With so many options available in Picture Package, you might think it would be impossible to customize any further. Well, you'd be wrong. You can adjust the amount of space between images, and even overlap images. If you click the Edit Layout button in the Picture Package dialog box, the Picture Package Edit Layout dialog box opens. See Figure 37. This dialog box lets you add a grid, make more page size changes, and create image zones.

FIGURE 36
Picture Package dialog box

Frontmost Document is pictured by default

3 page sizes are available

16 page layouts are available

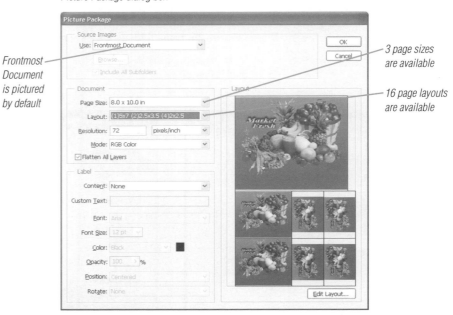

FIGURE 37
Picture Package Edit Layout dialog box

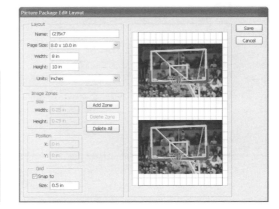

FIGURE 38

Contact Sheet II dialog box

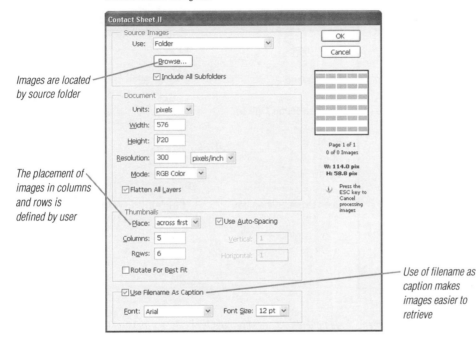

Images are located
by source folder

The placement of
images in columns
and rows is
defined by user

Use of filename as
caption makes
images easier to
retrieve

Create a contact sheet

1. Create a folder on your computer that contains copies of at least three Photoshop images you have created, then name the folder **Contact Sample**.

   TIP   See your instructor if you require assistance. If you do not have three images available, use any three of the Data Files for this or any other chapter.

2. Click **File** on the menu bar, point to **Automate**, click **Contact Sheet II**, then compare your dialog box to Figure 38.

3. Click **Browse** (Win) or **Choose** (Mac), navigate to the **Contact Sample folder**, click **OK** (Win) or **Choose** (Mac), then click **OK** to close the Contact Sheet II dialog box.

   Photoshop opens the files and places them in a new file called **ContactSheet-001.psd**.

   TIP   Photoshop automatically numbers additional contact sheets consecutively.

4. Save ContactSheet-001.psd where your Contact Sample folder is stored, use the default name (**ContactSheet-001.psd**), then close the file and exit Photoshop.

You created a folder and placed images in it, selected the Contact Sheet II option from the Automate command on the File menu, and then created a contact sheet of the images in the folder you created.

Automating Photoshop

Photoshop offers several options for automating the process of creating professional-looking contact sheets. In addition to creating picture packages and contact sheets, you can also use the Automate command (on the File menu) to crop and straighten crooked images, change color modes conditionally, fit an image to a specified size (without distorting the image), and merge multiple images to create panoramas.

Power User Shortcuts

to do this:	use this method:
Clone Stamp Tool	🔧 or S
Create a snapshot	📷
Duplicate selection and move 1 pixel: Left Right Up Down	Press and hold [Ctrl][Alt] (Win) or ⌘ [option] (Mac), then press ← → ↑ ↓
Move selection 10 pixels: Left Right Up Down	⌘ [shift] (Mac), then press ← → ↑ ↓

to do this:	use this method:
Eraser tools	E
Magic Wand	✷ or W
Move selection 1 pixel: Left Right Up Down	▸⊹ ← → ↑ ↓
Open Extract dialog box	[Ctrl][Alt][X] (Win) or ⌘ [option] [X] (Mac)

Key: Menu items are indicated by ➤ between the menu name and its command. Blue bold letters are shortcuts for selecting tools on the toolbox.

The Channels palette, which is located behind the Layers palette, stores the color information about the file. The Channels palette is also used to create and store information about layer masks. Pixels can be isolated by creating a mask, or by using the Extract feature. The Extract feature has its own set of tools and lets you paint around an area that you want on its own layer. There are a variety of eraser tools. The Eraser Tool, for example, deletes pixels it comes in contact with, while the Magic Eraser Tool deletes similarly colored pixels, and the Background Eraser Tool deletes a particular color that falls within the crosshairs of its brush tip. The Clone Stamp Tool does not delete pixels, but makes it easy to move pixels from one area to another.

You can create a snapshot of your image, which lets you return to previous state of the image's appearance with a single mouse click. This is a useful feature that allows you to see what your image looked like at specific phase. You can create arrangements of images. The Picture Package lets you create arrangements of a single image, and the Contact Sheet lets you create an image of up to 30 thumbnails of individual images.

What You Have Learned:

- How to use the Channels palette
- How to create an alpha channel
- How to isolate an object using the Extract feature
- How to delete pixels using eraser tools
- How to repair an image with the Clone Stamp Tool
- How to make selections using the Magic Wand Tool
- How to create and use a snapshot
- How to create a picture package
- How to assemble a contact sheet

Key Terms

Alpha channel   Used to add specific color information by creating and storing masks.

Contact sheet   A document that contains a maximum of 30 thumbnails of images in a specific folder.

Default channels   The color channels that are automatically contained in an image.

Extract feature   Used to isolate a foreground object from its background.

Magic Wand Tool   Lets you choose pixels that are similar to the ones where you first click in an image.

Picture package   A layout of multiple sizes of a single image.

Snapshot   A temporary copy of your image that contains the history states made up to that point.

Spot channel   Contains information about special premixed inks used in CYMK color printing.

Tolerance   The measurement of how close a pixel color must be to another color.

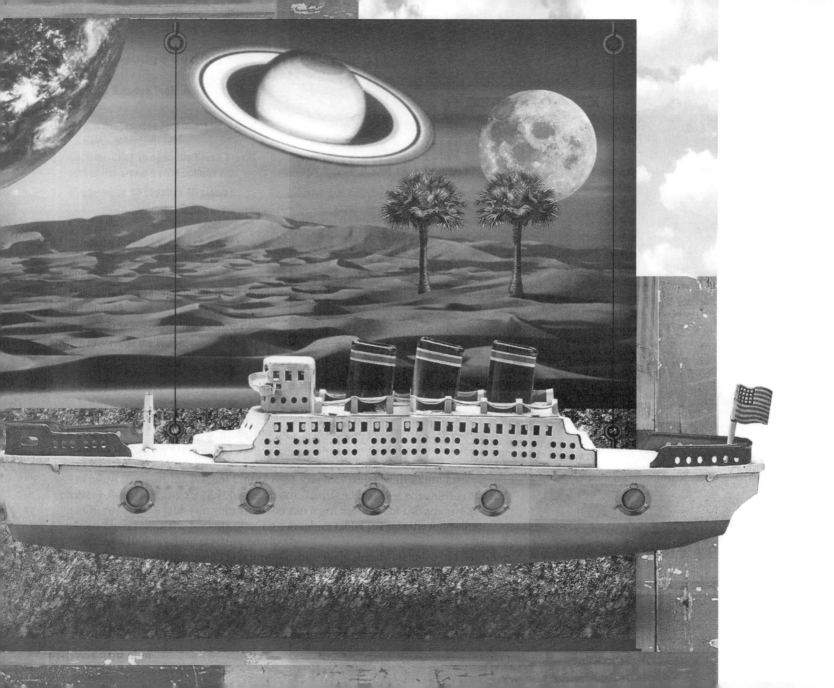

chapter

10

ADJUSTING COLORS

1. Correct and adjust color.

2. Enhance colors by altering saturation.

3. Modify color channels using levels.

4. Create color samplers with the Info palette.

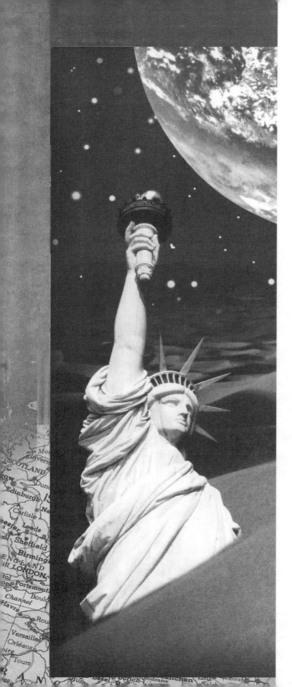

Enhancing Color

Photoshop places several color-enhancing tools at your disposal. These tools make it possible to change the mood or "personality" of a color, by changing its tonal values. **Tonal values**, also called **color levels,** are the numeric values of an individual color and are crucial if you ever need to duplicate a color. For example, when you select a specific shade in a paint store that requires custom mixing, a recipe that contains the tonal values is used to create the color.

Using Tools to Adjust Colors

You can use color adjustment tools to make an image that is flat or dull appear to come to life. You can mute distracting colors to call attention to a central image. You can choose from several adjustment tools to achieve the same results, so the method you use depends on which one you *prefer*, not on which one is *better*.

Reproducing Colors

Accurate color reproduction is an important reason to learn about color measurement and modification. Because colors vary from monitor to monitor, and can be altered during the output process, you can specify exactly the way you want them to look. Professional printers know how to take your Photoshop settings and adapt them to get the colors that match your specifications. Color levels, depicted in a **histogram** (a graph that represents the frequency distribution—for example, the number of times a particular pixel color occurs), can be modified by making adjustments in the input and output levels. Moving the input sliders toward the center increases the tonal range, resulting in increased contrast. Moving the output sliders toward the center decreases the tonal range, resulting in decreased contrast.

QUICKTIP

You can make color adjustments directly on a layer, or by using an adjustment layer. Directly applying a color adjustment affects only the layer to which it is applied. Applying a color adjustment using an adjustment layer affects all visible layers beneath it.

Tools You'll Use

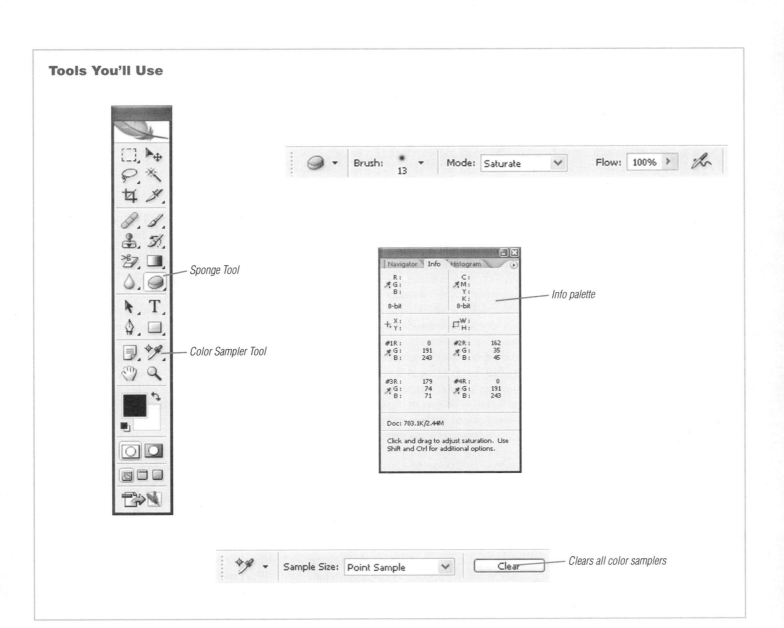

Sponge Tool

Color Sampler Tool

Info palette

Brush: 13   Mode: Saturate   Flow: 100%

Navigator | Info | Histogram

R :   C :
G :   M :
B :   Y :
                   K :
8-bit   8-bit

X :   W :
Y :   H :

#1R :   0   #2R :   162
G :   191   G :   35
B :   243   B :   45

#3R :   179   #4R :   0
G :   74   G :   191
B :   71   B :   243

Doc: 703.1K/2.44M

Click and drag to adjust saturation. Use
Shift and Ctrl for additional options.

Sample Size: Point Sample   Clear   Clears all color samplers

CORRECT AND ADJUST COLOR

What You'll Do

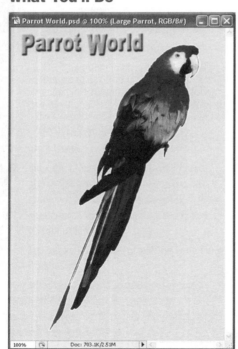

Making Color Corrections

Learning to recognize which colors need correction is one of the hardest skills to develop. Adjusting colors can be very difficult because, although there is a science to color correction, you must also consider the aesthetics of your image. Beauty is in the eye of the beholder, and you must choose how you want your work to look and feel. Add to this the problem of reconciling hardware differences, in which *my* red may look very different from *your* red, and you can see how color management can become a can of worms. A **color management system** reconciles the differences between different devices.

Using a Color Management System

Photoshop has a way to deal with hardware discrepancies: the device profile. A **profile** (also called an ICC profile) can be created for specific devices and embedded in an image, and is used to define how colors are interpreted by a specific device. ICC stands for International Color Consortium. You can create a profile by clicking Edit on the menu

bar, then clicking Color Settings. Use the list arrows in the Working Spaces section. You don't have to use profiles, but you can assign a specific profile by selecting the ICC Profile check box in the Save As dialog box. Doing so embeds the profile in the working space of an image. An image's **working space** tells the color management system how RGB or CMYK values are interpreted. Assigning an ICC profile is different from converting to an ICC profile. Converting occurs during output preparation, when you can select color management options in the Adobe PDF Options dialog box.

Balancing Colors

You can **balance colors** by adding and subtracting tonal values from those already existing in a layer. You do this to correct oversaturated or undersaturated color and to remove color casts from an image. The Color Balance dialog box contains three sliders: one for Cyan-Red, one for Magenta-Blue, and one for Yellow-Green. You can adjust colors by dragging each of these sliders or by typing in values in the Color

Levels text boxes. You can also use the Color Balance dialog box to adjust the color balance of shadows or highlights by clicking the Shadows or Highlights option buttons.

Modifying Curves

Using the Curves dialog box, you can alter the output tonal value of any pixel input. Instead of just being able to make adjustments using three variables (highlights, shadows, and midtones), you can change as many as 16 points along the 0–255 scale in the Curves dialog box. The horizontal axis in the Curves dialog box represents the original intensity values of the pixels (the Input levels), and the vertical axis represents the modified color values (the Output levels). The default curve appears as a diagonal line that shares the same input and output values. Each point on the line represents each pixel. You add curves to the line to adjust the tonal values.

Analyzing Colors

When you look at an image, ask yourself, "What's wrong with this picture?" Does the image need more blue than yellow? Preserve your work by creating an adjustment layer, then try adjusting the color sliders, and see how the image changes. Then try modifying the curves. Much of the color correction process involves experimentation—with you, the artist, learning and applying the subtleties of shading and contrast.

FIGURE 1
Variations dialog box

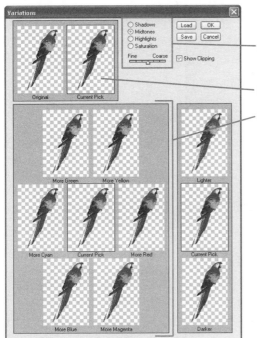

Additional adjustment options

Current selection

Color variations

Using thumbnails to adjust color

You can make color adjustments by viewing thumbnails of variations on your current image. You can see a variety of thumbnails that show you some specific results of color correction. Start by clicking the layer you want to adjust. Click Image on the menu bar, point to Adjustments, then click Variations. The Variations dialog box, as shown in Figure 1, will open, showing your current layer with its settings, and thumbnails of the same layer with lighter, darker, or more of the individual colors from the Color Balance dialog box. This tool lets you see what a layer would look like if it had more of a particular color, *without* making any modifications to the actual image. You can use the Variations dialog box as a tool to help you develop your color correction skills.

Modify color balance settings

1. Start Photoshop, open PS 10-1.psd from the drive and folder where your Data Files are stored, update the text layers if necessary, then save the file as **Parrot World**.

2. Click the **Default Foreground and Background Colors button** 🔳.

3. Click the **Large Parrot layer** on the Layers palette.

4. Click **Image** on the menu bar, point to **Adjustments**, then click **Color Balance**.

5. Drag the sliders so that the settings in the Color Levels text boxes are +**60** for Cyan/Red, –**40** for Magenta/Green, and –**50** for Yellow/Blue, then click **OK**.

6. Compare your image to Figure 2.

You modified the color balance settings by using the sliders. As you drag the sliders, you can see changes in the image on the active layer.

FIGURE 2
Color balanced layer

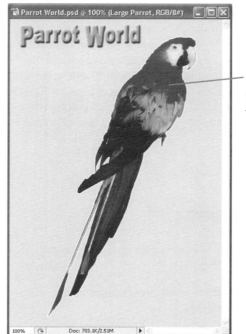

Intensified reds, magentas, and yellows

Using the Auto Adjustments commands

You can make color adjustments using the Auto Adjustments commands on the Image menu. You can use three Auto Commands (Auto Levels, Auto Contrast, and Auto Color) to make color adjustments automatically without any additional input. The Auto Levels command adjusts the intensity levels of shadows and highlights by identifying the lightest and darkest pixel in each color channel and then redistributing the pixel's values across that range. You can use the Auto Contrast command to make simple adjustments to the contrast and mixture of colors in an RGB image; it works by analyzing the distribution of colors in the composite image, not in the individual color channels. The Auto Color command adjusts the contrast and color mixtures using the image itself to make the adjustment, resulting in neutralized midtones.

FIGURE 3
Curves dialog box

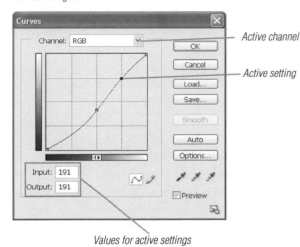

Active channel

Active setting

Values for active settings

FIGURE 4
Image with modified curves

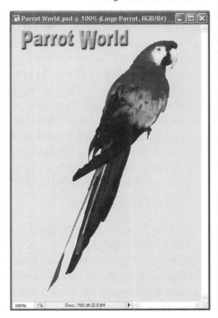

Using the Color Settings dialog box

You can use the Color Settings dialog box to save common color management controls, such as custom color settings. You might want to create a custom color setting, for example, to match a specific proofing setup used by a commercial printer. To open the Color Settings dialog box, click Edit on the menu bar, then click Color Settings.

Modify curves

1. With the Large Parrot layer still active, click **Image** on the menu bar, point to **Adjustments**, then click **Curves**.

2. Click the **center of the graph** at the point on the line where the input and output values both equal **128**.

3. Drag the point down so that the input value equals **128** and the output value equals **104**.

   Did you notice that the image's colors change as you drag the line? You can see the changes if the preview check box is checked.

   TIP Move the dialog box out of the way if it blocks your view.

4. Click the **point where the curve intersects the right vertical gridline** (input value equals approximately 191, and output value equals approximately 178).

   TIP The point that you click in the Curves dialog box is called the **active setting**.

5. Drag the **active setting** up and to the right as needed until the input and output values both equal **191**, as shown in Figure 3.

   TIP After you select the active setting, you can also change its location by changing the values in the Input and Output boxes.

6. Click **OK**.

7. Save your work, then compare your screen to Figure 4.

You modified curves settings by using the Curves dialog box.

ENHANCE COLORS BY
ALTERING SATURATION

What You'll Do

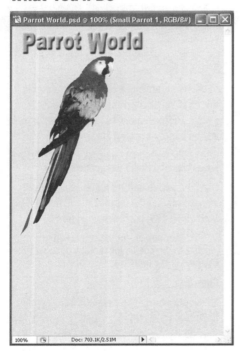

In this lesson, you'll modify the appearance of an image by altering color saturation.

Understanding Saturation

Saturation is the purity of a particular color. A higher saturation level indicates a color that is more intense. To understand saturation, imagine that you are trying to lighten a can of blue paint. For example, if you add some gray paint, you decrease the purity and the intensity of the original color or desaturate it. Photoshop provides two methods of modifying color saturation: the Hue/Saturation dialog box and the Sponge Tool.

Using the Sponge Tool

The Sponge Tool is located on the toolbox, and is used to increase or decrease the color saturation of a specific area within a layer. Settings for the Sponge Tool are located on the options bar and include settings for the brush size, whether you want the sponge to saturate or desaturate, and how quickly you want the color to flow into or from the Sponge Tool.

QUICKTIP

You can reset the active tool to its default settings by right-clicking the tool on the options bar, then clicking Reset Tool.

Using the Hue/Saturation Dialog Box

Hue is the amount of color that is reflected from or transmitted through an object. Hue is assigned a measurement (between 0 and 360 degrees) that is taken from a standard color wheel. In conversation, hue is the name of the color, such as red, blue, or gold and described in terms of its tints or shades, such as yellow-green or blue-green. Adjusting hue and saturation is similar to making modifications to color balance. You can make these adjustments by using the Hue, Saturation, and Lightness sliders, which are located in the Hue/Saturation dialog box. When modifying saturation levels using the Hue/Saturation dialog box, you have the option of adjusting the entire color range, or preset color ranges. The available preset color ranges are shown in Figure 5. To choose any one of these color ranges, click the Edit list arrow in the Hue/Saturation dialog box *before* modifying any of the sliders.

Using Saturation to Convert a Color Layer to Grayscale

Have you ever wondered how an image could contain both a color and a gray-scale object, as shown in Figure 6? You can easily create this effect using the Hue/Saturation dialog box. This image

was created by clicking the layer containing the life buoy, opening the Hue/Saturation dialog box, then changing the Saturation setting to –100.

FIGURE 5
Preset color ranges in the Hue/Saturation dialog box

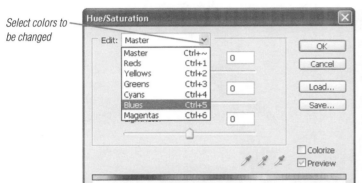

Select colors to be changed

FIGURE 6
Grayscale layer

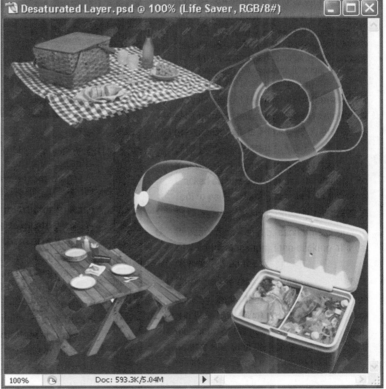

Saturate a color range

1. Click the **Small Parrot 1 layer** on the Layers palette to make it active, then make the layer visible.

2. Click the **Indicates layer visibility button** 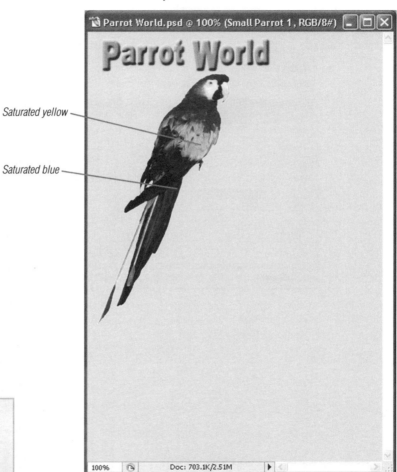 on the Large Parrot layer to hide it.

3. Click **Image** on the menu bar, point to **Adjustments**, then click **Hue/Saturation**.

4. Click the **Edit list arrow**, then click **Blues**.

5. Drag the **Saturation slider** to **+40**.

6. Click the **Edit list arrow**, then click **Yellows**.

7. Drag the **Saturation slider** to **+30**.

   The image's blues and yellows are intensified.

8. Click **OK**, then compare your image to Figure 7.

You changed the saturation of two preset color ranges. As you altered the saturation, the richness of the colors became more defined.

FIGURE 7
Modified blues and yellows

Parrot World.psd @ 100% (Small Parrot 1, RGB/8#)

Parrot World

Saturated yellow

Saturated blue

100%   Doc: 703.1K/2.51M

Getting more color data using HDR images

High Dynamic Range images, which use 32 bits per channel, allow real-world levels of illumination to be represented. The level of detail afforded by using 32 bits per channel means that imagery is more realistic and better able to simulate light conditions and a wider range of color values.

FIGURE 8

Reds saturated with the Sponge Tool

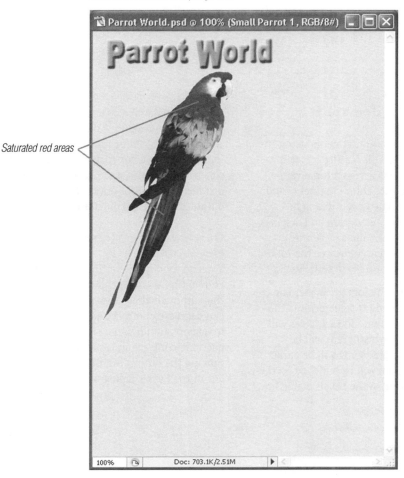

Saturated red areas

Saturate using the Sponge Tool

1. Click the **Sponge Tool** on the toolbox.

   TIP The Sponge Tool might be hidden beneath the Dodge Tool or the Burn Tool on the toolbox.

2. Click the **Click to open the Brush Preset picker list arrow**, then double-click the **Hard Round 13 pixels brush tip**.

3. Click the **Mode list arrow** on the options bar, click **Saturate**, then set the Flow to **100%**.

4. Click and drag the pointer over the **red areas** (head and tail feathers) of the parrot.

   The red color in the saturated area is brighter.

5. Save your work, then compare your screen to Figure 8.

You used the Sponge Tool to saturate specific areas in an image. The Sponge Tool lets you saturate spot areas rather than an entire color on a layer.

Correcting faulty exposures

The Exposure adjustment feature lets you correct for under- or over-exposure in images. By making adjustments to the black points (which can result in an image being too dark) or the white points (which can result in an image appearing too light), you can make corrections that will make an image's exposure settings just right. You can make exposure adjustments by clicking Image on the menu bar, pointing to Adjustments, then clicking Exposure.

MODIFY COLOR CHANNELS
USING LEVELS

What You'll Do

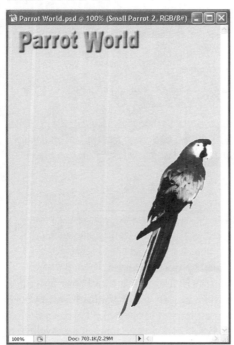

In this lesson, you'll use levels to make color adjustments.

Making Color and Tonal Adjustments

You can make color adjustments using the Levels dialog box. This feature lets you make modifications across a tonal range, using the composite color channel or individual channels. The Levels dialog box takes the form of a histogram and displays light and dark color values on a linear scale. The plotted data indicates the total number of pixels for a given tonal value.

There is no "ideal" histogram shape. The image's character and tone determine the shape of the histogram. Some images will be lighter and their histogram will be bunched on the right; some will be darker and their histogram will be bunched on the left. When working in the Levels dialog box, three triangular sliders appear beneath the histogram representing shadows, midtones, and highlights. Three text boxes appear for input levels (one box each for the input shadows, midtones, and highlights). Two text boxes appear for output levels (one for output shadows and one for highlights).

Correcting Shadows and Highlights

You can modify the settings for shadows and highlights independently. By moving the output shadows slider to the right, you can decrease contrast and *lighten* the image on an individual layer. You can decrease contrast and *darken* an image by moving the output highlights slider to the left in the Levels dialog box.

FIGURE 9
Levels dialog box and Histogram palette

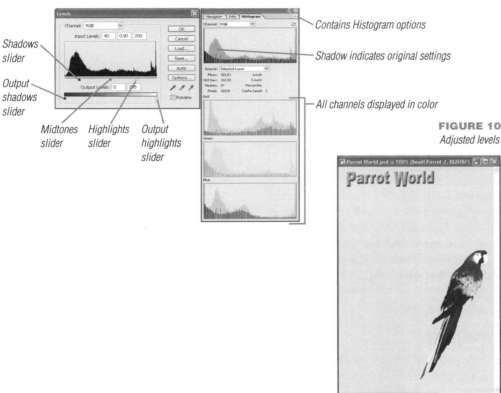

Shadows slider

Output shadows slider

Midtones slider Highlights slider Output highlights slider

Contains Histogram options

Shadow indicates original settings

All channels displayed in color

FIGURE 10
Adjusted levels

Understanding the Histogram palette

Using the Histogram palette, you can watch as you adjust color settings such as levels, curves, color balance, and hue/saturation. When the Histogram palette opens, you'll see the compact view: a single chart containing a composite channel for the image. You can view all the channels in color using the menu options on the list arrow on the palette. As you make color adjustments, the Histogram palette is updated. In addition to the modifications, the original settings are displayed as a light-colored shadow. This makes it easy to see how the settings have changed.

Adjust color using the Levels feature

1. Click the **Small Parrot 2 layer** on the Layers palette to make it active, then make the layer visible.

2. Click the **Indicates layer visibility button** on the Small Parrot 1 layer to hide it.

3. Click the **Histogram palette tab** Histogram.

4. Click the **Histogram palette list arrow**, then click **Expanded View** (if it is not already expanded).

5. Click the **Histogram palette list arrow**, then click **All Channels View**.

6. Click the **Histogram palette list arrow**, then verify that the Show Statistics and Show Channels in Color commands at the bottom of the menu contain check marks.

7. Click **Image** on the menu bar, point to **Adjustments**, then click **Levels**.

8. Drag the **Shadows slider** to **40**, the **Midtones slider** to **0.90**, and the **Highlights slider** to **200**, click the **Source list arrow** on the Histogram palette, then click **Selected Layer**. See Figure 9.

   Did you notice that the levels on the Histogram palette changed as you modified the Levels settings?

9. Click **OK**, then compare your work to Figure 10.

10. Save your work, then reset the palette locations.

You modified levels for shadows, midtones, and highlights. You were also able to see how these changes were visible on the Histogram palette.

CREATE COLOR SAMPLERS
WITH THE INFO PALETTE

What You'll Do

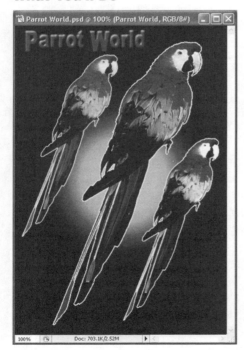

In this lesson, you'll take multiple color samples and use the Info palette to store color information.

Sampling Colors

In the past, you've used the Eyedropper pointer to take a sample of an existing color. By taking the sample, you were able to use the color as a background or a font color. This method is easy and quick, but it limited you to one color sample at a time. Photoshop has an additional feature, the **Color Sampler Tool**, that makes it possible to sample—and store—up to four distinct color samplers.

> QUICKTIP
>
> The color samplers are saved with the image in which they are created.

Using Color Samplers

You can apply each of the four color samplers to an image or use the samplers to make color adjustments. Each time you click the Color Sampler Tool, a color reading is taken and the number 1, 2, 3, or 4 appears on the image, depending on how many samplers you have already taken. See Figure 11. A color sampler includes all visible layers and is dynamic. This means that if you hide a layer from which a sampler was taken, the next visible layer will contain a sampler that has the same coordinates of the hidden layer, but the sampler will have the color reading of the visible layer.

Using the Info Palette

The Info palette is grouped with the Navigator and Histogram palettes. The top-left quadrant displays actual color values for the current color mode. For example, if the current mode is RGB, then RGB values are displayed. The Info palette also displays CMYK values, X and Y coordinates of the current pointer location, and the width and height of a selection (if applicable), as shown in Figure 12. When a color sampler is created, the Info palette expands to show the color measurement information from that sample. Figure 13 shows an Info palette containing four color samplers. After you have established your color samplers but no longer want them to be displayed, click the Info palette list arrow, then deselect Color Samplers. You can display hidden color samplers by clicking the Info palette list arrow, then clicking Color Samplers.

Manipulating Color Samplers

Color samplers, like most Photoshop features, are designed to accommodate change. Each color sampler can be moved by dragging the sampler icon to a new location. After the sampler is moved to its new location, its color value information is updated on the Info palette. You can individually delete any of the samplers by selecting the Color Sampler Tool, holding

[Alt] (Win) or [option] (Mac), then clicking the sampler you want to delete. You can also delete all the samplers by clicking the Clear button on the options bar.

QUICKTIP

Each time a color sampler is deleted, the remaining samplers are automatically renumbered. If you have defined four samplers and you want to add another sampler, you need to first clear an existing sampler.

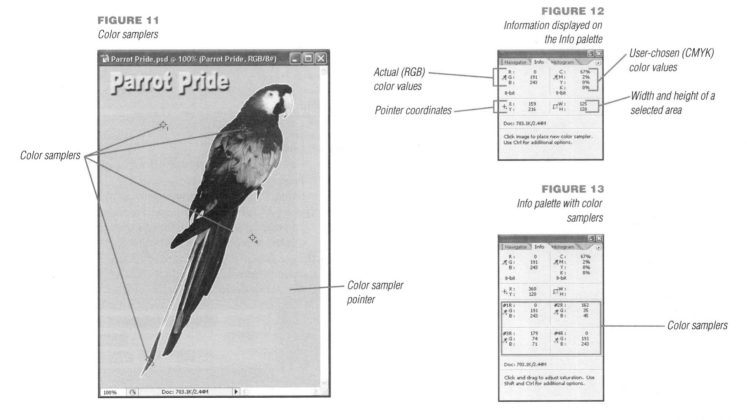

FIGURE 11
Color samplers

Color samplers

Color sampler pointer

FIGURE 12
Information displayed on the Info palette

Actual (RGB) color values

Pointer coordinates

User-chosen (CMYK) color values

Width and height of a selected area

FIGURE 13
Info palette with color samplers

Color samplers

Create color samplers

1. Click the **Indicates layer visibility button** for the Large Parrot and Small Parrot 1 layers on the Layers palette, so that all layers in the image are visible.

2. Display the rulers in pixels (if they are not already displayed).

3. Click **Window** on the menu bar and select **Info** to display the Info palette (if it is not displayed).

4. Click the **Color Sampler Tool** on the toolbox.

   TIP   The Color Sampler Tool is located on the toolbox and may be hidden under the Eyedropper Tool.

5. Using Figure 14 as a guide, click the image in four locations.

6. Click the **Info palette list arrow**, then click **Color Samplers** to hide the color samplers.

7. Repeat Step 6 to display the color samplers.

8. Hide the rulers.

You sampled specific areas in the image, stored that color data on the Info palette, then hid the color samplers.

FIGURE 14
Color samplers in image

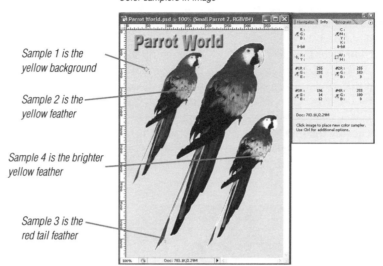

Sample 1 is the yellow background

Sample 2 is the yellow feather

Sample 4 is the brighter yellow feather

Sample 3 is the red tail feather

Creating a spot color channel

Printing a Photoshop image can be a costly process, especially if a spot color is used. A **spot color** is one that can't easily be re-created by a printer, such as a specific color used in a client's logo. By creating a spot color channel, you can make it easier for your printer to create the ink for a difficult color, assure yourself of accurate color reproduction, and save yourself high printing costs. If you use this feature, you won't have to provide your printer with substitution colors: the spot color contains all of the necessary information. You can create a spot color channel by displaying the Channels palette, clicking the Channels palette list arrow, then clicking New Spot Channel. Create a meaningful name for the new spot channel, click the Color box, click the Color Libraries button in the Color Picker dialog box, click the Book list arrow, then click a color-matching system. You can also create a custom color by clicking the Picker button in the Custom Colors dialog box. If you have created a color sampler, you can use this information to create the custom color for the spot color channel. Click OK to close the Custom Color dialog box, then click OK to close the New Spot Channel dialog box.

FIGURE 15
Unsharp Mask dialog box

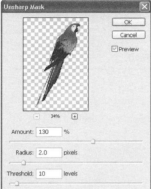

FIGURE 17
Lighting effect applied

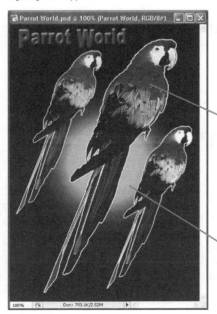

Unsharp Mask changes the
appearance of the Large
Parrot layer

Lighting effect changes
the appearance of the
Backdrop layer

FIGURE 16
Lighting Effects dialog box

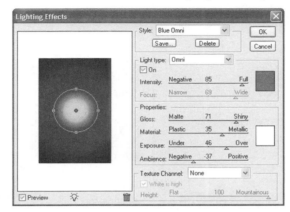

Apply a color sampler and filter and add a lighting effect

1. Make the **Large Parrot layer** active.

2. Click **Filter** on the menu bar, point to **Sharpen**, then click **Unsharp Mask**.

   You are now ready to put the finishing touches on your color-corrected image.

3. Adjust your settings in the Unsharp Mask dialog box as necessary so they match those shown in Figure 15, then click **OK**.

   These settings emphasize the edges and create the illusion of a sharper image.

4. Make the **Backdrop layer** active.

5. Click **Filter** on the menu bar, point to **Render**, then click **Lighting Effects**.

6. Adjust your settings in the Lighting Effects dialog box so they match those shown in Figure 16, then click **OK**.

7. Double-click the **Parrot World layer thumbnail**, then click **Set the text color box** on the options bar.

8. Type the R, G, and B values in sample 3 on the Info palette in the Color Picker dialog box, click **OK**, then click the **Commit any current edits button** ✔ on the options bar.

9. Save your work, hide the color samplers, then compare your screen to Figure 17.

10. Close the Parrot World image, then exit Photoshop.

You added the Unsharp Mask and Lighting Effects filters to make the objects stand out more dramatically against the background. You also changed the type color using the values from a sampled color.

Power User Shortcuts

to do this:	use this method:
Adjust color with thumbnails	Image ➤ Adjustments ➤ Variations
Adjust saturation	Image ➤ Adjustments ➤ Hue/Saturation
Balance colors	Image ➤ Adjustments ➤ Color Balance
Choose color range	Click Edit list arrow in Hue/Saturation dialog box, click color range
Convert color layer to grayscale	Image ➤ Adjustments ➤ Hue/Saturation
Create color sampler	Click ✒, click image using ✒ in image
Create spot color channel	Click Channels, click ▸, New Spot Channel
Delete color sampler	Click ✒, press [Alt] (Win) or option (Mac), click sampler using ✂

to do this:	use this method:
Modify curves	Image ➤ Adjustments ➤ Curves
Modify levels	Image ➤ Adjustments ➤ Levels
Move color sampler	Click sampler with ▸⊕
Open Histogram palette	Histogram
Open Info palette	Info
Saturate with Sponge Tool	⬭ or O
Show/Hide color samplers	Click Info, click ▸ ➤ Color Samplers

Key: Menu items are indicated by ➤ between the menu name and its command. Blue bold letters are shortcuts for selecting tools on the toolbox.

Photoshop offers many settings and tools you can use to affect the colors in layers or select areas of the image. Photoshop tools enable you to tweak colors in a variety of ways including making color adjustments using the Levels dialog box and monitoring the Histogram palette. Everyone wants colors to look nice, but as designers, Photoshop professionals also want their colors to reproduce accurately. If you don't want to work with all the tools and settings, or prefer to let the software determine the colors, there are Auto Adjustments commands that will make adjustments for you.

By modifying color settings and precise measurement, you can ensure that once your color image goes to a commercial printer, the yellows, blues, and reds you see on your monitor are what you'll see on the printed page.

What You Have Learned:

- How to modify color balance settings
- How to modify curves
- How to saturate a color range
- How to use the Sponge Tool
- How to use Levels to adjust color
- How to create color samplers
- How to apply a color sampler

Key Terms

Balance colors   The process of adding and subtracting tonal values from those already existing in a layer.

Color management system (CMS) Method of reconciling differences between different devices so colors can be reproduced accurately.

Color Sampler Tool   Tool that makes it possible to sample—and store—up to four distinct color samplers.

Histogram   A graph that represents the frequency distribution of colors and is used to make adjustments in the input and output levels.

Hue   The name of the color, such as red, blue, or gold. Also, the amount of color that is reflected from or transmitted through an object.

Tonal values   Also called color levels. The numeric values of an individual color, which can be used to duplicate a color.

Spot color   A color that can't easily be re-created by a printer, such as a specific color used in a client's logo.

ICC profile   Created for specific devices and embedded in an image, and is used to define how colors are interpreted by a specific device. ICC stands for International Color Consortium.

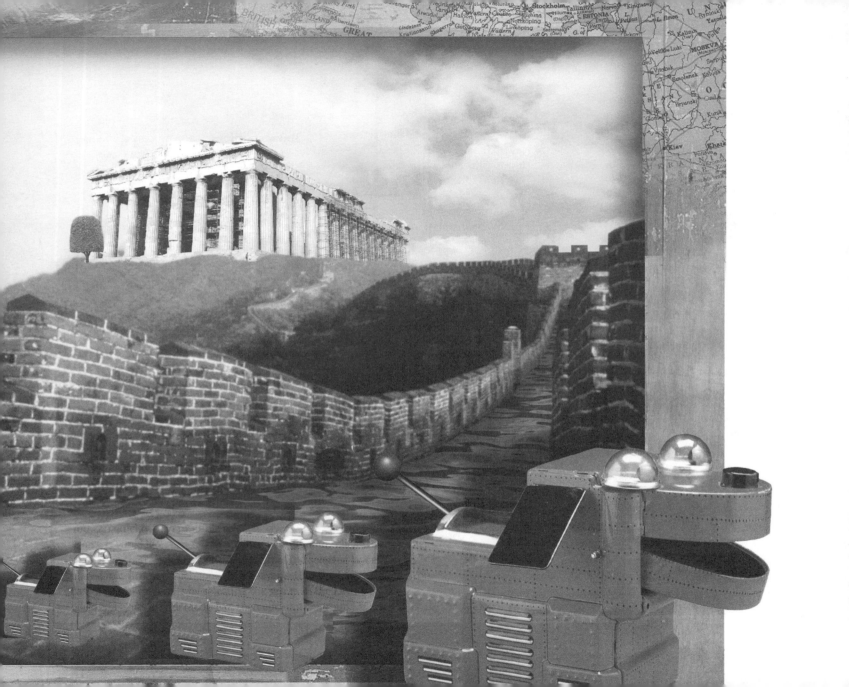

chapter

11

USING CLIPPING MASKS,
PATHS, & SHAPES

1. Use a clipping group as a mask.

2. Use pen tools to create and modify a path.

3. Work with shapes.

4. Convert paths and selections.

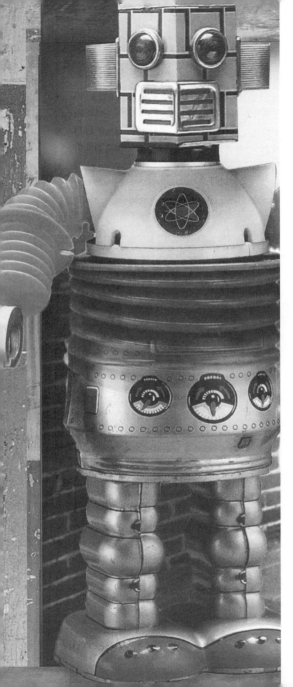

11 USING CLIPPING MASKS,
PATHS, & SHAPES

Working with Shapes

Photoshop provides several tools that help add stylistic elements, such as shapes, to your work. You can add either a shape or a rasterized shape to an image. A **shape** is simply a vector object that keeps its crisp appearance when it is resized, edited, moved, reshaped, or copied. A **rasterized shape** is converted into a bitmapped object that cannot be moved or copied; the advantage is that it occupies a small file size. The disadvantage is that a bitmapped object is resolution dependent. You can add either kind of shape as a predesigned shape, such as an ellipse, circle, or rectangle, or you can create a unique shape using a pen tool.

Defining Clipping Masks and Paths

A **clipping mask** (also called a **clipping group**) creates an effect in which the bottommost layer acts as a mask for all other layers in the group. You can use a **path** to turn an area defined within an object into a separate individual object—like an individual layer. A **path** is defined as one or more straight or curved line segments connected by **anchor points**, small squares similar to fastening points. Paths can be either open or closed. An **open path**, such as a line, has two distinct **endpoints**, anchor points at each end of the open path. A **closed path**, such as a circle, is one continuous path without endpoints. A **path component** consists of one or more anchor points joined by line segments. You can use another type of path called a **clipping path**, to extract a Photoshop object from within a layer, place it in another program (such as QuarkXPress or Adobe Illustrator), and retain its transparent background.

> **QUICK**TIP
>
> A shape and path are basically the same: the shape tools allow you to use an existing path instead of having to create one by hand. A path has a hard edge and is vector-based.

Creating Paths

Using a path, you can manipulate images on a layer. Each path is stored on the **Paths palette**. You can create a path using the Pen Tool or the Freeform Pen

Tool. Each **pen tool** lets you draw a path by placing anchor points along the edge of another image, or wherever you need them, to draw a specific shape. As you place anchor points, line segments automatically fall between them. The **Freeform Pen Tool** acts just like a traditional pen or pencil. Just draw with it, and it automatically places *both* the anchor points and line segments wherever necessary to achieve the shape you want. With these tools, you can create freeform shapes or use existing edges within an image by tracing on top of it. After you create a path, you can use the **Path Selection Tool** to select the entire path, or the **Direct Selection Tool** to select and manipulate individual anchor points and segments to reshape the path. Unlike selections, multiple paths can be saved using the Paths palette. When first created, a path is called a **work path**. The work path is temporary, but becomes a permanent part of your image when you name it. Paths, like layers, can be named, viewed, deleted, and duplicated.

Tools You'll Use

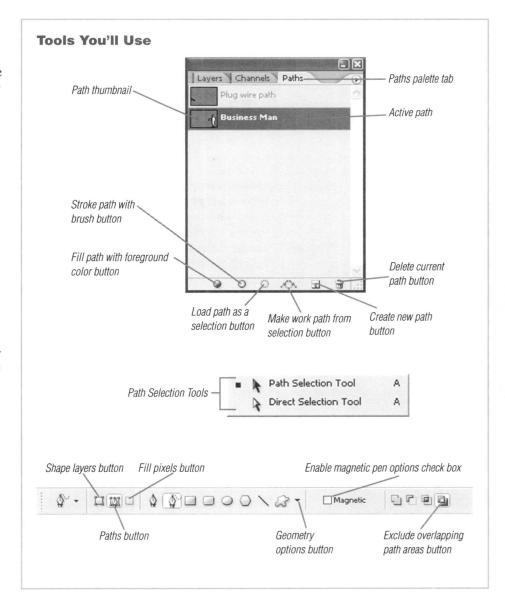

Path thumbnail

Paths palette tab

Active path

Stroke path with brush button

Fill path with foreground color button

Delete current path button

Load path as a selection button

Make work path from selection button

Create new path button

Path Selection Tools

Path Selection Tool — A
Direct Selection Tool — A

Shape layers button   Fill pixels button

Enable magnetic pen options check box

☐ Magnetic

Paths button

Geometry options button

Exclude overlapping path areas button

USE A CLIPPING
GROUP AS A MASK

What You'll Do

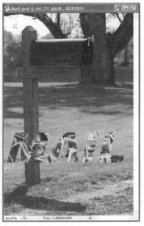

In this lesson, you'll rasterize a type layer, then use a clipping group as a mask for imagery already in an image. You'll also use the Transform command to alter an object's appearance.

Understanding the Clipping Mask Effect

If you want to display type in one layer using an interesting image or pattern in another layer as the fill for the type, then look no further. You can create this effect using a clipping mask (also called a clipping group). With a clipping group, you can isolate an area and make images outside the area transparent. This works very well with type, and can be used with a variety of images. Figure 1 shows an example of this effect in which type acts as a mask for imagery. In this effect, the (rasterized type) layer becomes a mask for the imagery. The image of the roses is *masked* by the text. For this effect to work, the layer that is being masked (the imagery, in this case) *must* be positioned above the mask layer (in this case, the type layer) on the Layers palette.

FIGURE 1
Sample clipping mask effect

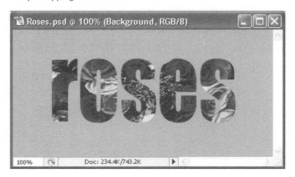

Rasterizing Text and Shape Layers

To use type or a shape in a clipping mask, the type or shape layer must first be rasterized, or changed from vector graphics into a normal object layer. Rasterizing changes the vector graphic into a bitmapped object, one that is made up of a fixed number of colored pixels. **Vector graphics** are made up of lines and curves defined by mathematical objects called vectors. The advantage to using vector graphics for shapes is that they can be resized and moved without losing image quality.

QUICKTIP

Bitmapped images contain a fixed number of pixels; as a consequence, they can appear jagged and lose detail when resized.

Using Transform Commands

Before you create a clipping mask, you might want to use one of the transform commands on the Edit menu to reshape layer contents so the shapes conform to the imagery that will be displayed. The transform commands are described in Table 1. Samples of the transform commands are shown in Figure 2. When a transform command is selected, a **bounding box** is displayed around the object. The bounding box contains **handles** that you can drag to modify the selection. A **reference point** is located in the center of the bounding box. This is the point around which the transform command takes place.

QUICKTIP

You can change the location of the reference point by dragging the point to a new location within the bounding box.

TABLE 1: Transform Commands

command	use
Scale	Changes the image size. Press [Shift] while dragging to scale proportionally. Press [Alt] (Win) or [option] (Mac) to scale from the reference point.
Rotate	Allows rotation of an image 360°. Press [Shift] to rotate in increments of 15°.
Skew	Stretches an image horizontally or vertically, but cannot exceed the image boundary.
Distort	Stretches an image horizontally or vertically, and can exceed the image boundary.
Perspective	Changes opposite sides of an image equally, and can be used to make an oval appear circular, or change a rectangle into a trapezoid.
Rotate 180°	Rotates image 180° clockwise.
Rotate 90° CW	Rotates image 90° clockwise.
Rotate 90° CCW	Rotates image 90° counterclockwise.
Flip Horizontal	Produces a mirror image along the vertical axis.
Flip Vertical	Produces a mirror image along the horizontal axis.

FIGURE 2
Sample transformations

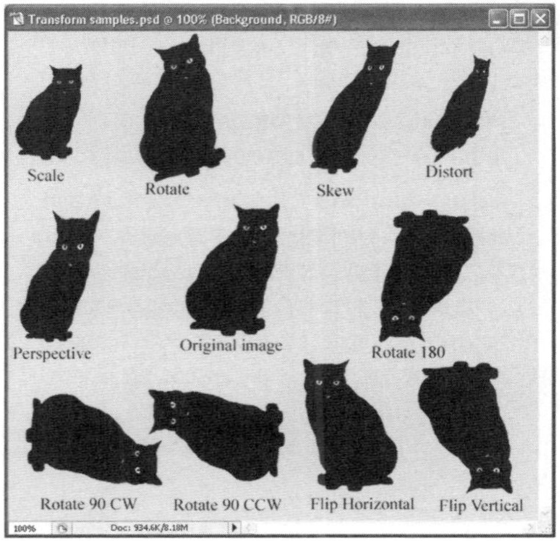

Transform a type layer for use in a clipping mask

1. Open PS 11-1.psd from the drive and folder where your Data Files are stored, update the text layers, then save the file as **Mail**.

   The MAIL type layer is active.

2. Click **Layer** on the menu bar, point to **Rasterize**, then click **Type**.

   The Mail layer is no longer a type layer, as shown in Figure 3.

3. Click the **Move Tool** ⊹ on the toolbox (if necessary).

4. Click **Edit** on the menu bar, point to **Transform**, then click **Skew**.

5. Type -**15** in the Set horizontal skew text box on the options bar so the type is slanted, as shown in Figure 4.

   TIP   You can also drag the handles surrounding the object until the skew effect looks just right.

6. Click the **Commit transform (Return) button** ✔ on the options bar.

7. Turn off the guides if they are displayed, and then compare your image to Figure 5.

You rasterized the existing type layer, then altered its shape using the Skew command and the Set horizontal skew by entering the value in the text box on the options bar. This transformation slanted the image.

FIGURE 3
Rasterized layer

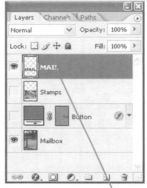

No longer a
type layer

FIGURE 4
Skew options bar

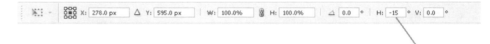

Set horizontal
skew text box

FIGURE 5
Skewed layer

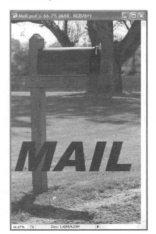

FIGURE 6
Preparing to create the clipping mask

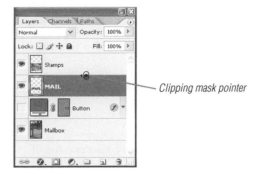

— Clipping mask pointer

FIGURE 8
Layers and History palettes

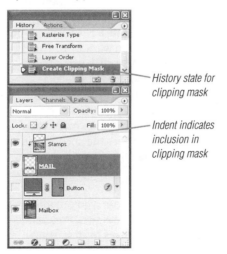

— History state for clipping mask

— Indent indicates inclusion in clipping mask

FIGURE 7
Effect of clipping mask

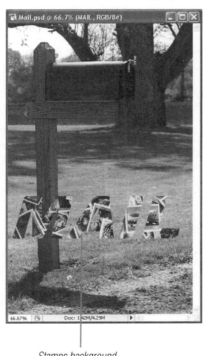

Stamps background visible through text

Create a clipping mask

1. Drag the **MAIL layer** beneath the Stamps layer.

2. Click the **Indicates layer visibility button** on the Stamps layer on the Layers palette.

   The Stamps layer will serve as the fill for the clipping mask.

   > TIP It's a good idea to first position the layer that will act as a mask *above* the layer containing the pattern so that you can adjust its size and shape. After the size and shape are the way you want them, reposition the mask layer *beneath* the pattern layer.

3. Point to the horizontal line between the MAIL and Stamps layers, press and hold **[Alt]** (Win) or **[option]** (Mac), then click, as shown in Figure 6.

4. Release **[Alt]** (Win) or **[option]** (Mac).

   The clipping mask is created. The stamps background becomes visible through the text.

5. Save your work, then compare your image to Figure 7 and the Layers palette to Figure 8.

You created a clipping mask using the Mail and Stamps layers. This effect lets you use the imagery in one layer as the fill for an object in another layer.

USE PEN TOOLS TO CREATE
AND MODIFY A PATH

What You'll Do

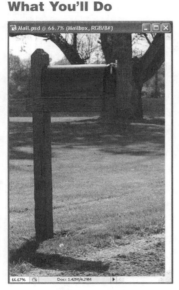

In this lesson, you'll create and name a path, expand the path to give it a wider, more curved appearance, then fill it with the foreground color.

Using Pen and Shape Tools

You have seen how you can use a clipping mask to create a mask effect. You can also create a path to serve as a mask by using any of the shape tools—the Pen Tool, the Freeform Pen Tool, or the Magnetic Pen Tool. You can modify a path using any of the following Pen tools: the Add Anchor Point Tool, Delete Anchor Point Tool, Convert Point Tool, Direct Selection Tool, and the Path Selection Tool. Table 2 describes some of these tools and their functions. When you select a pen tool, you can choose to create a shape layer or a path by choosing the appropriate option on the options bar.

Creating a Path

Unlike temporary selections, paths you create are saved with the image they were created in and stored on the Paths palette. Although you can't print paths unless they are filled or stroked, you can always display a path and make modifications to it. You can create a path based on an existing object, or you can create your own shape with a pen tool. To create a closed path,

you must position the pointer on top of the first anchor point. A small circle appears next to the pointer, indicating that the path will be closed when the pointer is clicked. Figure 9 shows an image of a young woman and the Paths palette containing three paths. The active path (Starfish 1) displays the starfish in the lower-right corner. Like the Layers palette, each path thumbnail displays a representation of its path. You can click a thumbnail on the Paths palette to see a specific path. The way that you create a path depends on the tool you choose to work with. The Pen Tool requires that you click using the pointer each time you want to add a smooth (curved) or corner anchor point, whereas the Freeform Pen Tool only requires you to click once to begin creating the path, and places the anchor points for you as you drag the pointer.

Modifying a Path

After you establish a path, you can modify it and convert it into a selection. For example, you can add more curves to an existing path, widen it, or fill a path with the fore-ground color. Before you can modify an unselected path, you must select it with the Direct Selection Tool. When you do so, you can manipulate its individual anchor points without affecting the entire path. Moving an anchor point automatically forces the two line segments on either side of the anchor point to shrink or grow, depending on which direction you move the anchor point. You can also click individual line segments and move them to new locations. If you are working with a curved path, you can shorten or elongate the direction handles associated with each smooth point to adjust the

amount of curve or length of the correspon-ding line segment.

Other methods for modifying a path include adding anchor points, deleting anchor points, and converting corner anchor points into smooth anchor points, or vice versa. Adding anchor points splits an existing line segment into two, giving you more sides to your object. Deleting an anchor point does the reverse. Deleting anchor points is helpful when you have a bumpy path that is the result of too many anchors. Converting corner points into smooth points can give your drawing a softer appearance; converting smooth

points into corner points can give your drawing a sharper appearance.

QUICKTIP

Each time you click and drag using the Add Anchor pointer, you are adding smooth anchor points. You use two direction handles attached to each anchor point to control the length, shape, and slope of the curved segment.

QUICKTIP

You can press [Alt] (Win) or [option] (Mac) while you click a path thumbnail to view the path and select it at the same time.

FIGURE 9
Multiple paths for the same image

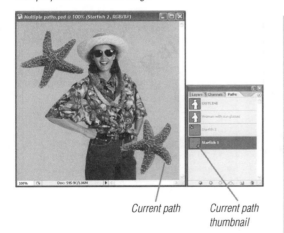

Current path   Current path
                          thumbnail

TABLE 2: Pen Tools

tool	button	use
Pen Tool	◊	Creates curved or straight line segments, connected by anchor points.
Freeform Pen Tool	◊	Creates unique shapes by placing anchor points at each change of direction.
Magnetic Pen Tool	☑ Magnetic	(Activated by clicking the Magnetic check box on the options bar.) Lets the Freeform Pen Tool find an object's edge.
Add Anchor Point Tool	◊+	Adds an anchor point to an existing path or shape.
Delete Anchor Point Tool	◊-	Removes an anchor point from an existing path or shape.
Convert Point Tool	⊾	Converts a smooth point to a corner point and a corner point to a smooth point.

Create a path

1. Click the **Indicates layer visibility button** 👁 on the MAIL layer on the Layers palette so that it is no longer visible.

2. Click the **Mailbox layer** on the Layers palette.

   Hiding layers makes it easier to work on a specific area of the image.

3. Click the **Freeform Pen Tool** ✒ on the toolbox.

4. Click the **Paths button** ▨ on the options bar (if it is not already selected).

5. Click the **Geometry options list arrow** on the options bar, then adjust the settings so that your entire options bar matches Figure 10.

6. Use the **Freeform Pen Tool pointer** ✒ to trace *the vertical and horizontal posts* that hold the mailbox. (Single-click when you reach the starting point and the small 'O' appears in the pointer.)

7. Click the **Paths palette tab** ⌐Paths⌐.

8. Double-click the **Work Path layer** on the Paths palette.

9. Type **Post path** in the Name text box.

10. Click **OK**, then compare your path and Paths palette to Figure 11.

You created and named a path using the Freeform Pen Tool.

FIGURE 10
Freeform Pen Tool settings

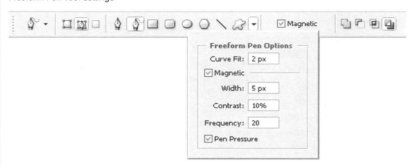

FIGURE 11
Path and Paths palette

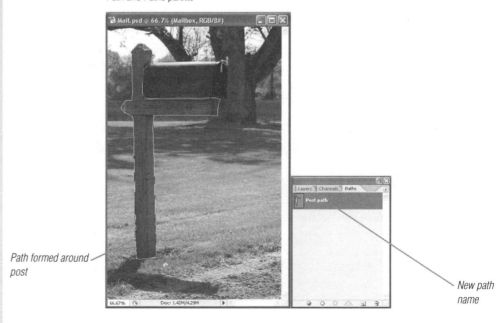

Path formed around post

New path name

FIGURE 12

Using handles to modify a path

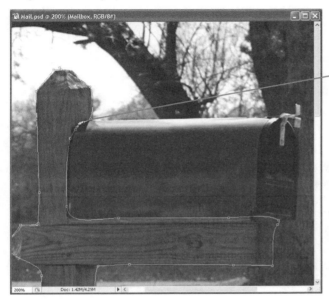

Drag a point to adjust the curve

FIGURE 13

Fill Path dialog box

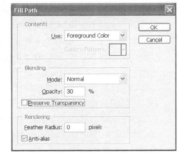

FIGURE 14

Modified path

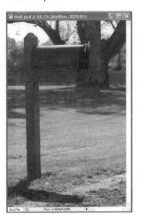

Modify a path

1. Zoom into the mailbox so the zoom factor is **200%**, then click the **Add Anchor Point Tool** ⌖⁺ on the toolbox.

2. Click a point near the curve at the top of the mailbox, then drag a handle so the curve conforms to the left side of the mailbox, using Figure 12 as a guide.

   As you drag the new anchor points, direction handles appear, indicating that you have added smooth points instead of corner points. You can drag any of these points so they conform to the shape you want for the path.

3. Zoom out to the original magnification, then click the **Eyedropper Tool** 🖊, on the toolbox.

4. Click the **mailbox** to sample its color.

5. Click the **Paths list arrow** ⊙ on the Paths palette, click **Fill Path**, modify the settings in the Fill Path dialog box using Figure 13 as a guide, then click **OK**.

6. Deselect the path, by clicking a blank area of the Paths palette.

   TIP The Mailbox layer on the Layers palette must be selected or the Fills path with foreground color button on the Paths palette will not be available.

7. Save your work, then compare your image to Figure 14.

You modified an existing path, then filled it with a color from a color existing in the image.

WORK WITH SHAPES

What You'll Do

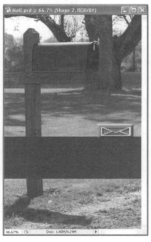

In this lesson, you'll create two shapes, then modify and add a style to a shape layer.

Using Shape Tools

You might find that the imagery you are working with is not enough, and you need to create your own shapes. There are six shape tools on the toolbox for creating shapes. A shape can occupy its own layer, called a **shape layer**. When you select a shape or pen tool, three buttons appear on the options bar to let you specify whether you want your shape to be on a new or existing shape layer, be a new work path, or be rasterized and filled with a color. Shapes and paths contain **vector data**, meaning that they will not lose their crisp appearance if resized or reshaped. You can create a rasterized shape using the Fill pixels button, but you cannot resize or reshape the rasterized shape.

Creating Rasterized Shapes

You cannot create a rasterized shape on a vector-based layer, such as a type or shape layer. So, to create a rasterized shape, you must first select or create a non-vector-based layer, select the shape you desire, then click the Fill pixels button on the options bar. You can change the blending mode to alter how the shape affects existing pixels in the image. You can change the opacity setting to make the shape more transparent or opaque. You can use the anti-aliasing option to blend the pixels on the shape's edge with the surrounding pixels. If you want to make changes to the content of a shape's blending mode, opacity, and anti-aliasing, you must make these changes *before* creating the rasterized shape; since the rasterization process converts the detail of the shape to an object layer. After you rasterize the shape, you can make changes to blending mode and opacity to the *layer* containing the shape.

Creating Shapes

A path and a shape are essentially the same, in that you edit them using the same tools. For example, you can modify a path and a shape using the Direct Selection Tool. When selected, the anchor points are white or hollow, and can then be moved to alter the appearance of the shape or path. When you click a shape or path with the Path Selection Tool, the anchor points become solid. In this case, the entire path is selected, and the individual components cannot be moved: the path or shape is moved as a single unit. A shape can be created on its own layer and can be filled with a color. Multiple shapes can also be added to a single layer, and you can specify how overlapping shapes interact.

(Painting tools are used when individual pixels are edited, such as by changing a pixel's color on a rasterized shape.)

Embellishing Shapes

You can apply other features such as the Drop Shadow and the Bevel and Emboss style, or filters, to shapes. Figure 15 shows the Layers palette of an image containing two layer shapes. The top layer (in Yellow) has the Bevel and Emboss style applied to it.

QUICKTIP

When you first create a shape, it is automatically filled with the current foreground color.

FIGURE 15
Shape layers on the Layers palette

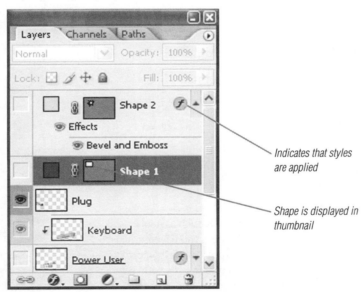

Indicates that styles are applied

Shape is displayed in thumbnail

Create a shape

1. Click the **Rectangle Tool** ▭ on the toolbox.

2. Click the **Shape layers button** 🔲 on the options bar.

3. Make sure the Style picker list arrow displays the Default Style (None) 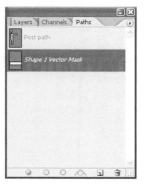.

4. Verify that the **Create new shape layer button** 🔲 on the options bar is selected.

5. Display the rulers in pixels and display the guides.

6. Drag the **Marquee pointer** ✛ from approximately **1 X/510 Y** to **555 X/685 Y** using the guides to draw the rectangle. Compare your Paths palette to Figure 16.

7. Compare your image to Figure 17.

   The shape is added to the image, and the Rectangle Tool is still active.

You created a new shape layer, using the Rectangle Tool. The new shape was created on its own layer.

FIGURE 16
Path created by shape

FIGURE 17
Shape in image

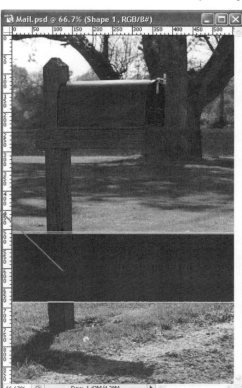

New shape

Export a path into another program

As a designer, you might find yourself working with other programs, such as Adobe Illustrator, Adobe Freehand, or QuarkXPress. Many of the techniques you have learned, such as working with paths, can be used in all these programs. For example, you can create a path in Photoshop, then export it to Illustrator. Before you can export a path, it must be created and named. To export the path, click File on the menu bar, point to Export, then click Paths to Illustrator (Win) or Write to Illustrator (Mac). The Paths list arrow (Win) or Write list arrow (Mac) in the Export Paths dialog box lets you determine which paths are exported. You can export all paths or one specific path. After you choose the path(s) that you want to export, choose a name and location for the path, then click Save.

FIGURE 18
Additional shape in image

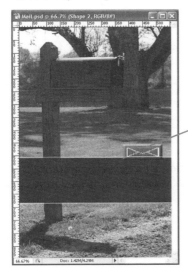

New shape

FIGURE 19
Style added to shape

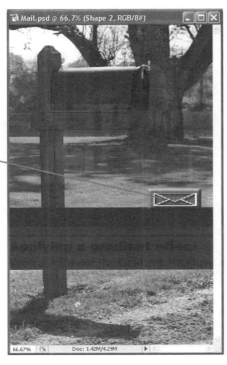

Custom shape
with Drop Shadow
style

Create and Modify a custom shape

1. Click the **Layers palette tab** | Layers ⟩ , then select and display the **Button layer**.

2. Click the **Custom Shape Tool button** 🐾 on the options bar.

3. Click the **Click to open Custom Shape picker list arrow** →▾ , then double-click **Envelope 2** (the first shape from the right in the second row).

4. Drag the **Marquee pointer** ✛ over the flat surface of the button from approximately **390 X/470 Y** to **510 X/505 Y**.

5. Display the **Swatches palette**, click the **color box** on the options bar, click the **seventh swatch** (White) from the left in the first row of the Swatches palette, then click **OK** to close the Color Picker dialog box. Compare your image to Figure 18.

6. Verify that the **Shape 2** mask thumbnail on the Layers palette is selected.

7. Click the **Add a layer style button** 📀 . on the Layers palette.

8. Click the **Drop Shadow**, then click **OK** to accept the current settings.

9. Save your work, turn off the guides and ruler display, then compare your image to Figure 19.

You created an additional shape layer, changed the color of the shape, then applied a style to the shape.

CONVERT PATHS AND
SELECTIONS

What You'll Do

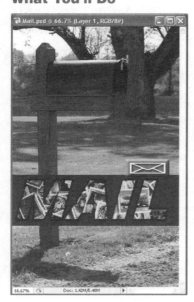

In this lesson, you'll convert a selection into a path, then apply a stroke to the path.

Converting a Selection into a Path

You can convert a selection into a path so that you can take advantage of clipping paths and other path features, using a button on the Paths palette. First, create your selection using any technique you prefer, such as the Magic Wand Tool, lasso tools, or marquee tools. After the marquee surrounds the selection, press and hold

Customizing print options

Because a monitor is an RGB device and a printer uses the CMYK model to print colors even a well-calibrated monitor will never match the colors of your printer. Therefore, professional printers use standardized color systems such as Pantone or Toyo.

In the course of working with an image, you may need to print a hard copy. In order to get the output you want, you can set options in the Page Setup dialog box. To open this dialog box, click File on the menu bar, then click Page Setup. The relationship of the length to the width of the printed page is called **orientation**. A printed page with the dimensions 8½" W × 11" L is called **portrait orientation**. A printed page with dimensions 11" W × 8 ½" L is called **landscape orientation**.

For additional printing options, click File on the menu bar, click Print with Preview, then in the Print dialog box click the More Options button. Here you can gain increased control over the way your image prints. For example, pages printed for commercial uses might often need to be trimmed after they are printed. The trim guidelines are called **crop marks**. These marks can be printed at the corners, center of each edge, or both. After you open the Print dialog box, select Output from the Show More Options list arrow. Then you can select the Corner Crop Marks check box and/or Center Crop Marks check box to print these marks on your image.

[Alt] (Win) or [option] (Mac), then click the Make work path from selection button on the Paths palette, as shown in Figure 20.

Converting a Path into a Selection

You can convert a path into a selection. You can do this by selecting a path on the Paths palette, then clicking the Load path as a selection button on the Paths palette.

Choosing the Right Method

Are you totally confused about which method to use to make selections? You might have felt equally at sea after learning about all your paint tool choices. Well, as with painting, you need to experiment to find the method that works best for you. As you gain experience with Photoshop techniques, your comfort level—and personal confidence—will grow, and you'll learn which methods are *right for you*.

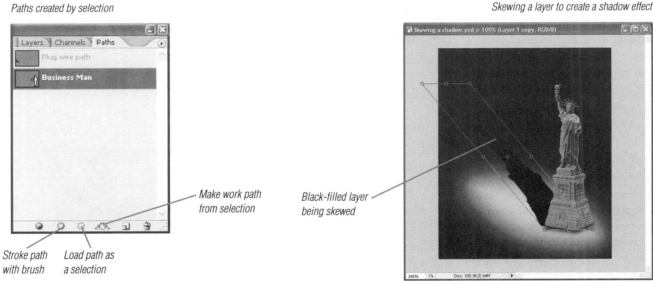

FIGURE 20
Paths created by selection

Make work path from selection

Stroke path with brush   Load path as a selection

FIGURE 21
Skewing a layer to create a shadow effect

Black-filled layer being skewed

Using the Transform command to create a shadow

You've already experienced using the Transform command to change the existing shape of an object or type. You can also use this command to simulate a shadow. To do so, you simply duplicate a layer, then fill the copy of the layer with black by changing the background color to black, then press [Ctrl][Shift][Backspace] (Win) or [Shift] ⌘ [Delete] (Mac). Make the black copy the active layer, then use the Transform command to skew the object. Figure 21 shows an example of this technique.

Convert a selection into a path

1. Display the **MAIL layer** and the **Stamps layer**.
2. Click the **MAIL layer** on the Layers palette.
3. Click the **Magic Wand Tool** on the toolbox.
4. Click anywhere in the burgundy color behind the word MAIL.
5. Click the **Add to selection button** on the options bar, click the open area in the **A**, click **Select** on the menu bar, then click **Inverse**. Compare your image to Figure 22.
6. Click the **Paths palette tab** .
7. Press and hold **[Alt]** (Win) or **[option]** (Mac), click the **Make work path from selection button** on the Paths palette, then release **[Alt]** (Win) or **[option]** (Mac).

   TIP Pressing [Alt] (Win) or [option] (Mac) causes the Make Work Path dialog box to open. You can use this to change the Tolerance setting. If you don't press and hold this key, the current tolerance setting is used.

8. Type **1.0** in the Tolerance text box, then click **OK**.
9. Double-click **Work Path** on the Paths palette.
10. Type **Mail path** in the Name text box of the Save Path dialog box, then click **OK**. Compare your screen to Figure 23.

You created a selection using the Magic Wand Tool, then converted it into a path using the Make work path from selection button on the Paths palette.

FIGURE 22
Selection in image

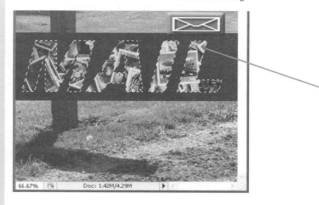

Selected object

FIGURE 23
Selection converted into path

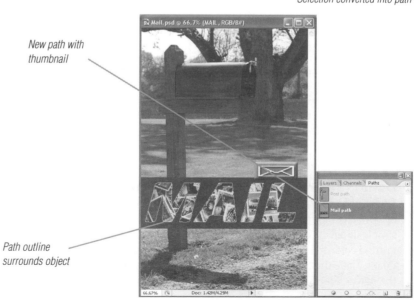

New path with thumbnail

Path outline surrounds object

FIGURE 24
Stroked path

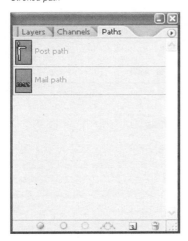

FIGURE 26
Completed image

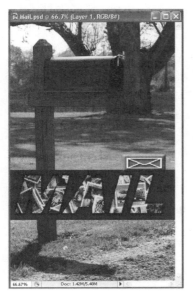

FIGURE 25
Layers palette

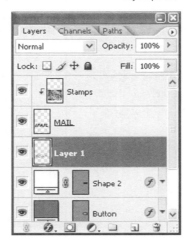

Stroke a path

1. Click the **Eyedropper Tool** on the toolbox.

2. Click the **first swatch** (Black) from the right in the second row of the Swatches palette.

3. Activate the **Shape 2 layer** on the Layers palette, then create a new layer above it.

4. Click the **Mail path** on the Paths palette, then click **Brush Tool** on the toolbox, click the **Click to open the Brush Preset picker**, click the **list arrow**, click **Reset Brushes** to reset the tools, click **OK**, then click **No**.

5. Click the **Paths list arrow** on the Paths palette, click **Stroke Path**, click the **Tool list arrow**, click **Brush**, then click **OK**.

6. Click anywhere on the Paths palette to deselect the path, then compare your palette to Figure 24.

7. Click the **Layers palette tab** `Layers`, then compare your Layers palette to Figure 25.

8. Save your work, then compare your image to Figure 26.

9. Close the file and exit Photoshop.

You stroked a path, using a color from the Swatches palette and a command from the Paths list arrow.

Power User Shortcuts

Key: Menu items are indicated by ➤ between the menu name and its command. Blue bold letters are shortcuts for selecting tools on the toolbox.

to do this:	use this method:
Add an anchor point	✎⁺
Change perspective	Edit ➤Transform ➤Perspective
Convert a selection into a path	⌢⌣
Convert a point	⌐
Create a clipping group	Press and hold [Alt] (Win) or option (Mac), position pointer between layers, then click using ◄▨
Create a custom shape	✿ or Shift U
Create a line	＼ or Shift U
Create a new shape layer	▢
Create a new work path	▨
Create a polygon	⬡ or Shift U
Create a rectangle	▭ or Shift U
Create a rounded rectangle	▢ or Shift U
Create an ellipse	◯ or Shift U
Delete an anchor point	✎⁻

to do this:	use this method:
Deselect a path	Click an empty space on Paths palette
Distort a selection	Edit ➤ Transform ➤Distort
Draw freeform shapes	✎ or Shift P
Draw paths	✎ or Shift P
Draw along the object's edge	☑ Magnetic
Export a path	File ➤ Export ➤ Paths to Illustrator
Fill a layer with background color	[Ctrl][Shift][Backspace] (Win) or [⌘][Delete] (Mac)
Flip a selection	Edit ➤ Transform ➤ Flip Horizontal or Flip Vertical
Load path as a selection	◯
Repeat last transform command	Edit ➤ Transform ➤ Again or [Shift][Ctrl][T] or [Shift][⌘][T] (Mac)
Rotate a selection	Edit ➤Transform ➤ Rotate
Scale a selection	Edit ➤ Transform ➤ Scale
Skew a selection	Edit ➤ Transform ➤ Skew
Stroke a path	◯

Using the bounding box and transform commands, you can change the shape of layer contents. Using clipping groups and masks you can use the contents of one layer to fill the shape of another layer. Shapes can be any combination of ellipses or rectangles, or any of the custom shapes that are provided. Photoshop gives you many ways to make selections, including using pen tools to trace the edges of an object, and then save that selection as a path. A shape can be created on its own layer, then modified, filled, and embellished with layer styles.

What You Have Learned:

- How to fill a shape with a pattern in another layer
- How to reshape the contents of a layer
- How to create and modify a path
- How to create a shape layer
- How to create and embellish a custom shape
- How to convert a path into a selection
- How to convert a selection into a path
- How to add a border to a path

Key Terms

Anchor points   Small squares similar to fastening points that connect as one or more straight or curved line segments to define a path.

Clipping mask   Effect used to display the image or pattern from one layer into the shape of another layer. (Also called a clipping group.)

Path   One or more straight or curved line segments connected by anchor points.

Pen tools   Let you draw a path by placing anchor points along the edge of another image.

Vector data   A shape or path that will not lose its crisp appearance if resized or reshaped.

Work path   A temporary path that has been created but not yet named.

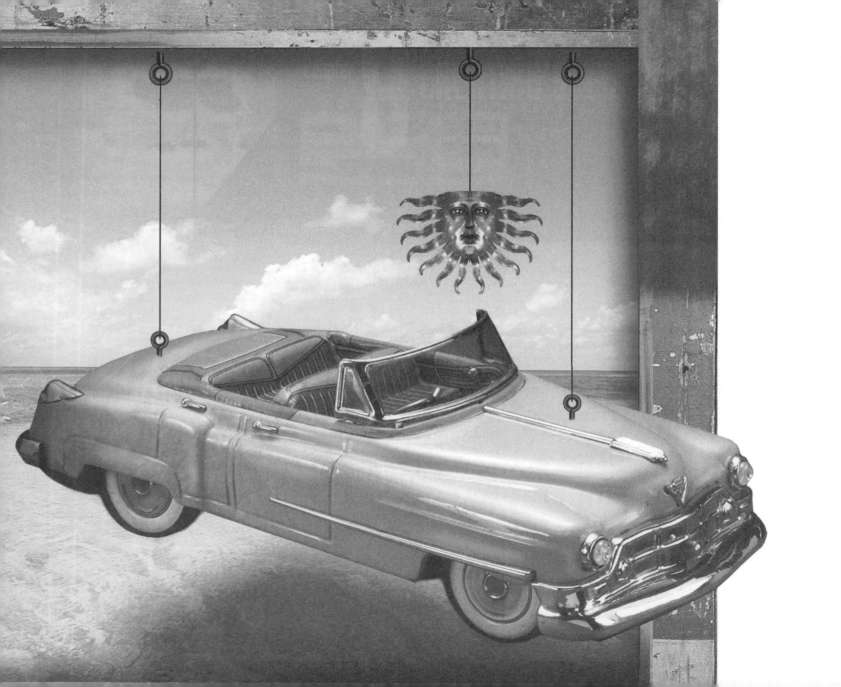

chapter

12

TRANSFORMING
TYPE

1. Modify type using a bounding box.

2. Create warped type with a unique shape.

3. Screen back type with imagery.

4. Create a faded type effect.

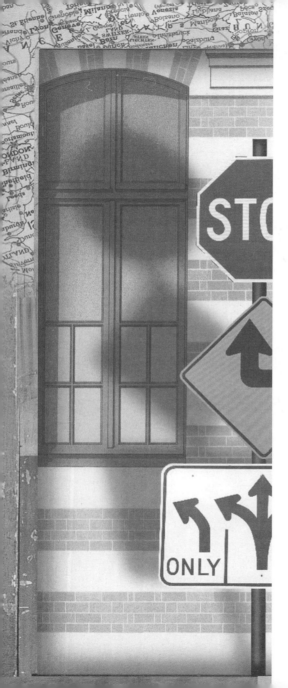

Working with Type

Type is usually not the primary focus of a Photoshop image, but it can be an important element when conveying a message. You have already learned how to create type and to embellish it using styles, such as the Drop Shadow and the Bevel and Emboss styles; and filters, such as the Twirl and Wind filters. You can further enhance type using techniques such as transforming or warping.

Transforming and Warping Type

When you want to modify text in an image, you can simply select the type layer, select the Horizontal Type Tool, then make changes using the options bar. You can also modify type by dragging the handles on the type's bounding box. A **bounding box** (or transform controls box) is a rectangle that surrounds type and contains handles that are used to change the dimensions. Many of the Photoshop

features that can be used to modify images can also be used to modify type layers. For example, type can be modified using all the transform commands on the Edit menu except Perspective and Distort. For more stylized type, you can use the Create warped text button to create exciting shapes by changing the dimensions. **Warping** makes it possible to distort type so that it conforms to a shape. Some of the distortions available through the warp feature are Arc, Arch, Bulge, Flag, Fish, and Twist. You do not need to rasterize type to use the warp text feature, so you can edit the type as necessary after you have warped it.

> **QUICK**TIP
>
> If you want to use the Perspective or Distort commands, or you want to apply a filter to type or create a clipping mask, you must first rasterize the type.

Using Type to Create Special Effects

In addition to adding styles to type, you can also create effects with your type and the imagery within your image. One popular effect is **fading type**, where the type appears to originate in darkness and then gradually gets brighter, or vice versa. You can use the Gradient Tool to fade type. The **screening back** effect displays imagery through the layer that contains type. One way to create the screened back effect is to convert a type layer into a shape layer, add a mask, and then adjust the levels of the shape layer. As with graphic objects, adding special effects to type changes the mood, style, and message of the content. You'll probably want to experiment with all your choices to strike just the right note for a particular project.

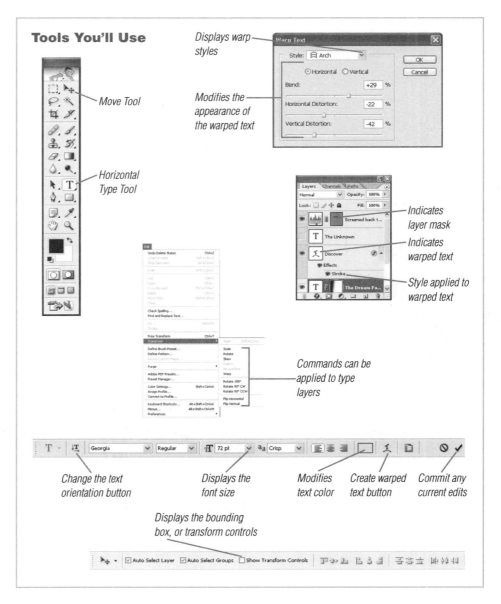

Tools You'll Use

Move Tool

Horizontal Type Tool

Displays warp styles

Modifies the appearance of the warped text

Indicates layer mask

Indicates warped text

Style applied to warped text

Commands can be applied to type layers

Change the text orientation button

Displays the font size

Modifies text color

Create warped text button

Commit any current edits

Displays the bounding box, or transform controls

MODIFY TYPE USING
A BOUNDING BOX

What You'll Do

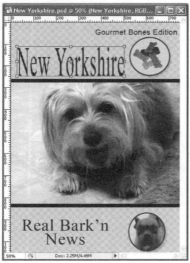

In this lesson, you'll change the dimensions of type using a bounding box.

Selecting the Bounding Box

A bounding box, such as the one shown in Figure 1, is a tool you can use to control the size and proportions of existing type. You can display the bounding box by clicking the Move Tool on the toolbox, then selecting the Show Transform Controls check box on the options bar. After the transform controls (also known as the bounding box) feature is turned on, it will appear around type whenever a type layer is selected. As soon as you

click a handle on the bounding box, the dotted lines of the box become solid, as shown in Figure 2. At the center of the bounding box (by default) is the **reference point**, the location from which distortions and transformations are measured.

QUICKTIP

You can resize the bounding box to visually change type size instead of specifying point sizes on the options bar.

FIGURE 1
Bounding box around type

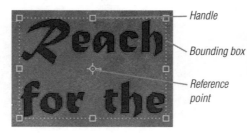

— Handle

— Bounding box

— Reference point

FIGURE 2
Resizing the bounding box

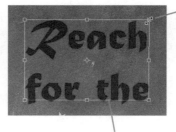

Preparing to resize the bounding box

Outline becomes solid when clicked

Changing the Bounding Box

When the bounding box around type is selected, the options bar displays additional tools for transforming type. Table 1 describes the bounding box options in detail. You can change the size of the bounding box by placing the pointer over a handle. When you do this, the pointer changes to reflect the direction in which you can pull the box. When you resize a bounding box, the type within it reflows to conform to its new shape. As you can see from the table, some of these tools are buttons and some are text boxes.

QUICKTIP
You can use the text boxes to make entries or to visually inspect the results of your changes.

TABLE 1: Transform Control Tools

tool	button	use
Reference point location button	▦	The black dot determines the location of the reference point. Change the reference point by clicking any white dot on the button.
Set horizontal position of reference point text box	X: 772.5 px	Allows you to reassign the horizontal location of the reference point.
Use relative positioning for reference point button	△	Determines the point you want used as a reference.
Set vertical position of reference point text box	Y: 412.0 px	Allows you to reassign the vertical location of the reference point.
Set horizontal scale text box	W: 100.0%	Determines the percentage of left-to-right scaling.
Maintain aspect ratio button	⬙	Keeps the current proportions of the contents within the bounding box.
Set vertical scale text box	H: 100.0%	Determines the percentage of top-to-bottom scaling.
Set rotation text box	∠ 0.0 °	Determines the angle the bounding box will be rotated.
Set horizontal skew text box	H: 0.0 °	Determines the angle of horizontal distortion.
Set vertical skew text box	V: 0.0 °	Determines the angle of vertical distortion.
Switch between transform and warp modes button	⬚	Toggles between manual entry of scaling and warp styles.
Cancel transform (Esc) button	⊘	Returns to the image without carrying out transformations.
Commit transform (Return) button	✓	Returns to the image after carrying out transformations.

Display a bounding box

1. Open PS 12-1.psd from the drive and folder where your Data Files are stored, update the text layers as needed, then save the file as **New Yorkshire**.

   TIP The fonts in this file are various point sizes of Times New Roman and Arial. Please substitute another font if these are not available on your computer.

2. Display the rulers in pixels.

3. Click the **New Yorkshire layer** on the Layers palette.

4. Click the **Move Tool** ⊹ on the toolbox (if it is not already selected).

5. Select the **Show Transform Controls check box** ☐ Show Transform Controls on the options bar. Compare your image to Figure 3.

   Transform control handles surround the bounding box. When you place the pointer on or near a handle, you can transform the shape of a bounding box. Table 2 describes the pointers you can use to transform a bounding box.

You displayed the bounding box of a text selection to make it easier to adjust the size and shape of the layer contents. Resizing a bounding box is the easiest way to change the appearance of an object or type layer.

FIGURE 3
Displayed bounding box

Selected check box indicates that bounding box is displayed

Move Tool selected

Bounding box surrounds active type layer

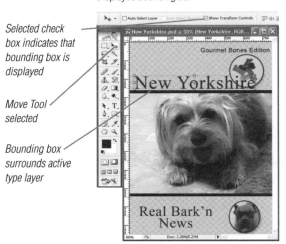

TABLE 2: Transform Pointers

pointer	use to
⤢	Resize bounding box; drag upper-right and lower-left handles.
⤡	Resize bounding box; drag upper-left and lower-right handles.
↔	Resize bounding box; drag middle-left and middle-right handles.
↕	Resize bounding box; drag upper-center and lower-center handles.
↵	Rotate bounding box; appears below the lower-right handle.
↳	Rotate bounding box; appears below the lower-left handle.
↱	Rotate bounding box; appears above the upper-right handle.
↰	Rotate bounding box; appears above the upper-left handle.
↴	Rotate bounding box; appears to the left of the middle-left handle.
↵	Rotate bounding box; appears below the lower-center handle.
▶	Skew type. Press and hold [Ctrl] (Win) or ⌘ (Mac) while dragging a handle.

FIGURE 4
Modified bounding box

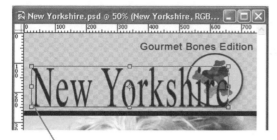

Enlarged type and
bounding box

FIGURE 5
Skewed bounding box

Bounding box and
text it contains takes
up less room

Modify type using a bounding box

1. Drag the **top-center handle** ↕ with the Resizing pointer until you see that the Set vertical position of reference point text box displays approximately **195 px**. Compare your bounding box to Figure 4.

   TIP   When you begin dragging the resizing handles, the option bar changes to display the bounding box transform tools. You can also type values in these text boxes.

2. Drag the **right-center handle** ↔ until the Set horizontal scale text box (W:) displays approximately **75**%.

3. Compare your bounding box to Figure 5 and your options bar to Figure 6. Your settings might differ.

   TIP   A skewed transformation distorts a bounding box using an angle other than 90°.

4. Click the **Commit transform (Return) button** ✔ on the options bar.

5. Save your work.

Using the bounding box, you modified the type by scaling disproportionately.

FIGURE 6
Transform settings

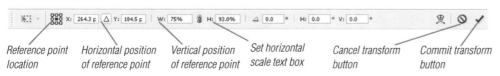

Reference point
location

Horizontal position
of reference point

Vertical position
of reference point

Set horizontal
scale text box

Cancel transform
button

Commit transform
button

CREATE WARPED TYPE
WITH A UNIQUE SHAPE

What You'll Do

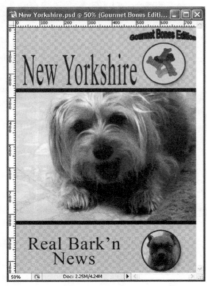

In this lesson, you'll warp text, then enhance the text with color and a layer style.

Warping Type

Have you ever wondered how designers create those ultra-cool wavy lines of text? They're probably using the Create warped text feature, which gives you unlimited freedom to create unique text shapes. You can distort a type layer beyond the limits of stretching a bounding box by using the Create warped text feature. You can choose from 15 warped text styles. These styles are shown in Figure 7. You can warp type horizontally or vertically.

FIGURE 7
Warp text styles

Default setting —

None

Arc
Arc Lower
Arc Upper

Arch
Bulge
Shell Lower
Shell Upper

Flag
Wave
Fish
Rise

Fisheye
Inflate
Squeeze
Twist

Adding Panache to Warped Text

After you select a warp text style, you can further modify the type using the Bend, Horizontal Distortion, and Vertical Distortion sliders in the Warp Text dialog box. These settings and what they do are described in Table 3. A sample of warped text is shown in Figure 8. You adjust the warped style by using the sliders shown in Figure 9.

QUICKTIP

You cannot use the Distort and Perspective transform commands on non-rasterized type; however, you can achieve similar results by warping type.

Combining Your Skills

By this time, you've learned that many Photoshop features can be applied to more than one type of Photoshop object. The same is true for warped text. For example, after you warp text, you can apply a style to it, such as the Bevel and Emboss style, or a filter. You can also use the Stroke style to really make the text pop.

FIGURE 8
Sample of warped text

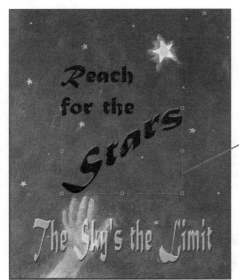

Bounding box surrounds warped text

FIGURE 9
Warp Text dialog box

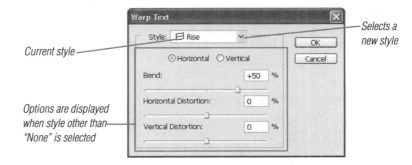

Current style

Selects a new style

Options are displayed when style other than "None" is selected

TABLE 3: Warped Type Settings

setting	use
Horizontal	Determines the left-to-right direction of the warp style.
Vertical	Determines the top-to-bottom direction of the warp style.
Bend	Determines which side of the type will be affected.
Horizontal Distortion	Determines if the left or right side of the type will be warped.
Vertical Distortion	Determines if the top or bottom of the type will be warped.

Create warped text

1. Click the **Gourmet Bones Edition layer** on the Layers palette.

2. Zoom into the image until the magnification factor is 100%.

3. Double-click the **Gourmet Bones Edition layer thumbnail** [T] on the Layers palette.

4. Click the **Set the font size list arrow** on the options bar, then click **12 pt**.

5. Click the **Create warped text button** 𝓣 on the options bar.

6. Click the **Style list arrow** in the Warp Text dialog box, then click **Arc Upper**.

7. Verify that the **Horizontal option button** is selected.

8. Change the settings for the **Bend**, **Horizontal Distortion**, and **Vertical Distortion text boxes** so that they match those shown in Figure 10.

9. Click **OK** to close the Warp Text dialog box, commit any current edits, then compare your type to Figure 11.

10. Use the **Move Tool** ⊹ on the toolbox to drag the type so it is centered over the logo of the bones as shown in Figure 12.

You transformed existing type into a unique shape using the Create warped text button. This feature lets you make type a much more dynamic element in your designs.

FIGURE 10
Warp Text dialog box

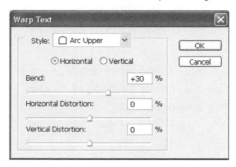

FIGURE 11
Warped text

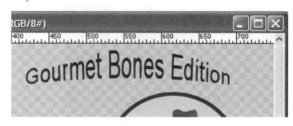

FIGURE 12
Moved type

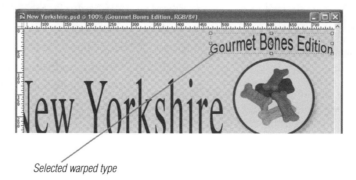

Selected warped type

FIGURE 13
Sampled area

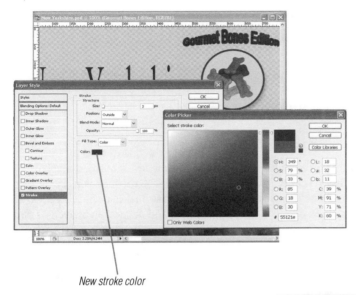

New stroke color

FIGURE 15
Layers palette

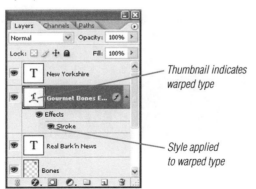

Thumbnail indicates warped type

Style applied to warped type

FIGURE 14
New color applied to warped type

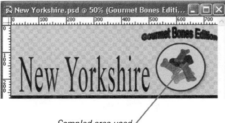

Sampled area used as stroke color

1. Click the **Add a layer style button** 🖉, on the Layers palette.

2. Click **Stroke**.

3. Click the **Set color of stroke button** in the Layer Style dialog box.

4. Verify that the Only Web Colors check box is not selected, then click the image anywhere on the maroon bone (at approximately **650 X/130 Y**), as shown in Figure 13.

5. Click **OK** to close the Color Picker dialog box.

6. In the Layer Style dialog box, make sure the Size is set to **3 px** and the Position is set to **Outside**, then click **OK**.

7. Save your work, zoom out until the magnification level is at **50%**, turn off the bounding box, then compare your image to Figure 14 and the Layers palette to Figure 15.

You added a Stroke style to the warped text and changed the color of the stroke using a color already present in the image.

SCREEN BACK TYPE
WITH IMAGERY

What You'll Do

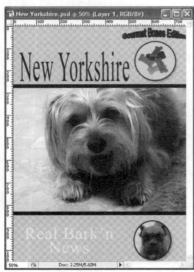

In this lesson, you'll convert type to a shape layer using the Convert to Shape command, then adjust the levels to create a screened back effect.

Screening Type

Using many of the techniques you already know, you can create the illusion that type appears to fade into the imagery below it. This is known as **screening back** or **screening** type. You can create a screened back effect in many ways. One method is to adjust the opacity of a type layer until you can see imagery behind it. Another method is to convert a type layer into a shape layer, which adds a vector mask, then adjust the levels of the shape layer until you achieve the look you desire. A **vector mask** makes a shape's edges appear neat and defined on a layer. As part of this screening back process, the type assumes the shape of its mask. Figure 16 shows a sample of screened back type. Notice that the layer imagery beneath the type layer is visible.

FIGURE 16
Screened back type

Image visible beneath screened back text

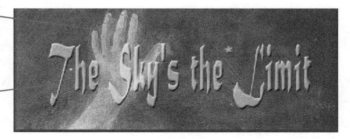

Screened back text

QUICKTIP

You can always adjust a layer's opacity so you can see more underlying imagery.

Creating the Screened Back Effect

Before converting a type layer, it's a good idea to duplicate the layer. That way, if you are not satisfied with the results, you can easily start from scratch with the original type layer. After the duplicate layer is created, you can convert it into a shape layer, using the Layer menu. After the layer is converted, make sure the original layer is hidden. Using the Levels dialog box, you can increase or decrease the midtones and shadows levels, as shown in Figure 17, to create different effects in the screened back type.

QUICKTIP

Whenever you select a shape layer, a path surrounds the shape.

Adding Finishing Touches

Adding effects to a layer can give your screened back type a more textured or three-dimensional look. For example, you can add the Bevel and Emboss style to a screened back shape layer, as shown in Figure 18. Here, the Bevel and Emboss style serves to accentuate the type. You can also add filter effects such as noise or lighting to make the text look more dramatic.

FIGURE 17
Levels dialog box

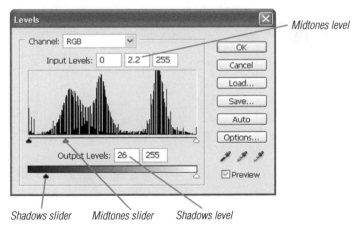

Midtones level — Shadows slider — Midtones slider — Shadows level

FIGURE 18
Screened back type with Bevel and Emboss style

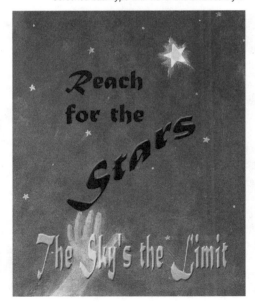

Convert a type layer to a shape layer

1. Click the **Real Bark'n News layer** on the Layers palette.

2. Click the **Layers palette list arrow** ⊙.

3. Click **Duplicate Layer**.

   TIP   When duplicating a layer, you have the option of keeping the duplicate in the current image, placing it in another image that is currently open, or in a new image, by clicking the Document list arrow in the Duplicate Layer dialog box, then clicking another filename or New.

4. Type **Screened back type** in the As text box, then click **OK**.

5. Click the **Indicates layer visibility button** 👁 on the Real Bark'n News layer on the Layers palette, then compare your Layers palette to Figure 19.

6. Click **Layer** on the menu bar, point to **Type**, then click **Convert to Shape**, as shown in Figure 20.

   The type layer is converted to a shape layer. Figure 21 shows the Layers palette (with the converted type layer state and vector mask thumbnail) and the History palette (with the Convert to Shape state).

In preparation for screening back type, you created a duplicate layer, then hid the original from view. You then converted the duplicate layer into a shape layer.

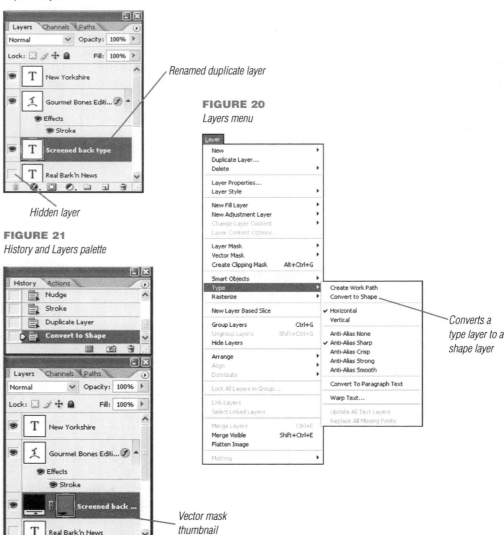

FIGURE 19
Duplicate layer

Renamed duplicate layer

Hidden layer

FIGURE 20
Layers menu

Converts a type layer to a shape layer

FIGURE 21
History and Layers palette

Vector mask thumbnail

FIGURE 22
Levels dialog box

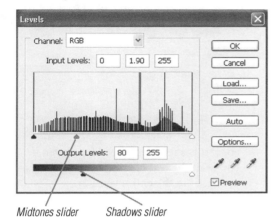

Midtones slider   Shadows slider

Adjust layer content

1. Click **Layer** on the menu bar, point to **Change Layer Content**, then click **Levels**.

   Did you notice that when the Levels dialog box opened, the fill color of the letters became transparent so the letters are formed by outlines?

2. Drag the **Input Levels midtones slider** to the left, until the middle Input Levels text box reads **1.90**.

   The content of the layer is now less transparent.

3. Drag the **Output Levels shadows slider** to the right until the left Output Levels text box reads **80** as shown in Figure 22.

   The content of the layer now looks brighter.

4. Click **OK**.

5. Click **Layer 1** on the Layers palette. The path surrounding the text disappears, making the modifications more visible.

6. Save your work, then compare your image to Figure 23.

You modified the midtones and shadows levels on the shape layer to make the text less transparent. You adjusted the Output Levels shadows slider to make the pixels that make up the text appear brighter.

FIGURE 23
Screened back type

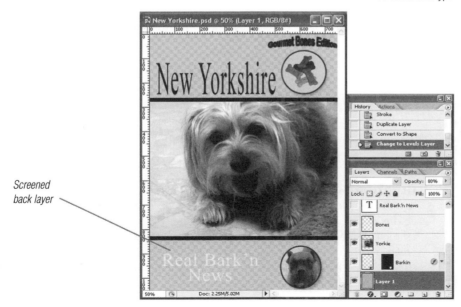

Screened back layer

CREATE A FADED
TYPE EFFECT

What You'll Do

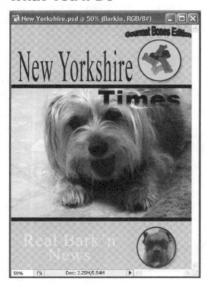

 In this lesson, you'll use the Gradient Tool to make text appear faded in one area and brighter in another. You'll also apply a lighting filter.

Creating a Fade Effect

In addition to being able to change the font, size, color, and shape of your text, you might want to create the illusion that type is fading away in order to add an element of mystery to your masterpiece. You can create this effect using a type layer, a layer mask, and the Gradient Tool. You can apply this effect to part of a type layer, if you want the text to look as if it's fading in or out, or to the entire layer.

QUICKTIP

Type does not have to be rasterized to create the fade effect.

Creating semitransparent type

You can use blending options to create what appears to be semitransparent type. To do this, create a type layer and apply any layer styles you want. The Satin style, for example, can be used to darken the type, and the Pattern Overlay style can be used to create a patterned effect. In the Layer Style dialog box, drag the Set opacity of effect slider to the left and watch the preview until you get the amount of transparency you like. Any background images behind the type will appear as the fill of the type.

Using the Gradient Tool

Before you can apply the fade effect, you need to create a layer mask for the type layer. You create the layer mask by clicking the Add layer mask button on the Layers palette. Then, you click the Gradient Tool on the toolbox. You can experiment with different types of gradient styles, but to create simple fading type, make sure Linear Gradient is selected, click the Click to open Gradient picker list arrow, then click the Black, White button on the Gradient palette.

FIGURE 24
White chrome type effect

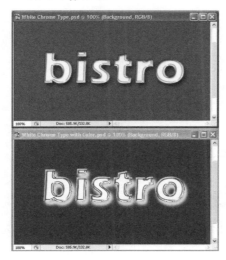

Creating white chrome type

By now, you've come to realize that not only can you create cool type by warping and fading it, you can also apply other techniques to create a variety of unique effects. For instance, you can give type the illusion of white chrome, and even add color to the chrome effect. To create this effect, start with black type in a large point size. Add a drop shadow, switch the foreground color to white, then fill the type with the new foreground color by pressing [Alt][Backspace] (Win) or [option][delete] (Mac). Add an Inner Shadow style, then the Satin style (with a low Distance setting). See the top of Figure 24. To add color to the effect (at the bottom of Figure 24), modify the Hue/Saturation setting and the Curves setting.

Create a fade effect

1. Click the **Yorkie layer** on the Layers palette.

2. Click the **Horizontal Type Tool** T. on the toolbox, click above the dog's left eye at approximately **360 X/360 Y**, set the font to **Arial Black**, the alignment to **Left align text**, the font size to **48 pt**, then type **Times** as shown in Figure 25.

3. Click the **Commit any current edits button** ✔ on the options bar.

4. Click the **Add layer mask button** ◨ on the Layers palette.

5. Click the **Gradient Tool** ◨. on the toolbox.

   | TIP The Gradient Tool might be hidden under the Paint Bucket Tool on the toolbox.

6. Click the **Linear Gradient style** ◨ on the options bar.

7. Click the **Click to open Gradient picker list arrow** on the options bar.

8. Double-click the **Black, White** style (top row, third from left), then compare the settings on your options bar to Figure 26.

9. Verify that the layer mask is selected, press and hold **[Shift]**, drag the **Gradient pointer** ┼ from the bottom of the Times text letter 'm' halfway up in the letter 'm', then release **[Shift]**. Compare your text to Figure 27.

10. Save your work.

You added a layer mask and a gradient to create a faded type effect.

FIGURE 25
New type in image

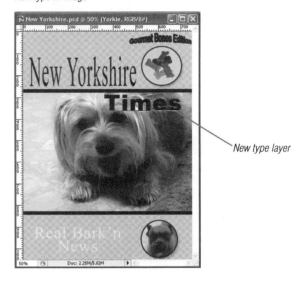

New type layer

FIGURE 26
Options for the Gradient

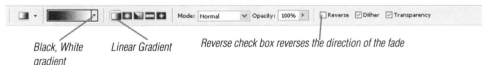

Black, White gradient   Linear Gradient   Reverse check box reverses the direction of the fade

FIGURE 27
Faded text in image

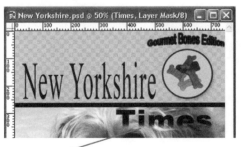

Bottom half of type is faded

Add a lighting effect

1. Click the **Barkin layer** on the Layers palette.

   Make sure the layer mask thumbnail is selected, not the mask thumbnail.

2. Click **Filter** on the menu bar, point to **Render**, then click **Lighting Effects**.

3. Make sure that the **Default style** and **Spotlight Light type** are selected, and that the light source is directed from the lower-right corner, then click **OK**.

4. Hide the rulers, turn off the bounding box, save your work, then compare your image to Figure 28.

5. Close the image, then exit Photoshop.

You added a lighting filter to give the image a more polished appearance.

FIGURE 28
Lighting effect

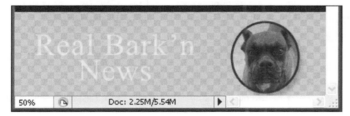

Warping objects

You can warp any rasterized object by clicking Edit on the menu bar, pointing to Transform, then clicking Warp. When you do this, a grid displays around the object. Clicking and dragging any of the points on the grid allows you to transform the shape of the object. Once you have selected this command, the options bar displays the Warp list arrow. You can use a custom shape, in which you drag the handles that surround the object, or you can select a shape from the list to use to warp the object.

Power User Shortcuts

to do this:	use this method:
Adjust color levels	Layer ➢ Change Layer Content ➢ Levels
Change warp type color	Double-click ⊤ , click ■
Commit a transformation	✔
Convert type to a shape	Layer ➢ Type ➢ Convert to Shape
Create faded type	⊡ , ▣ , ▦ , click to open Gradient picker list, then drag pointer over type
Create warped type	Double-click ⊤ , click ⊥
Display a bounding box	⊹ or **V**, select ☐ Show Transform Controls

to do this:	use this method:
Scale a bounding box	Press [Shift] while dragging handle, click ✔
Screen back type	Duplicate layer, hide original layer, convert type to shape, then adjust Levels
Select Gradient Tool	▣ or **Shift G**
Skew a bounding box	Press [Ctrl] (Win) or ⌘ (Mac) while dragging handle, ✔
Stroke a type layer	⊘ , Stroke, Set color of stroke button
Turn off bounding box display	⊹ or **V**, deselect ☑ Show Transform Controls

Key: Menu items are indicated by ➢ between the menu name and its command. Blue bold letters are shortcuts for selecting tools on the toolbox.

The shape of type can be modified by displaying the bounding box and dragging its handles. You can also warp type to create wavy, interesting shapes. And like other layers in Photoshop, you can always apply one or more layer styles to enhance the effect of the shaped or warped type. The screening back effect can be used to make type appear as if it's fading into a background; fading from light to dark, or dark to light.

What You Have Learned:

- How to fill a shape with a pattern in another layer
- How to reshape the contents of a layer
- How to create and modify a path
- How to create a shape layer
- How to create and embellish a custom shape
- How to convert a path into a selection
- How to convert a selection into a path
- How to add a border to a path

Key Terms

Bounding box   A rectangular box that surrounds an object and contains handles that you can drag to modify the object. (Also called a transform control box.)

Fading type   Effect in which type appears to originate in darkness and gradually gets lighter, or vice versa.

Reference point   The location from which distortions and transformations are measured.

Screening back   Effect in which type appears to fade into the imagery beneath it.

Warping   The ability to distort layer contents so that it conforms to a shape.

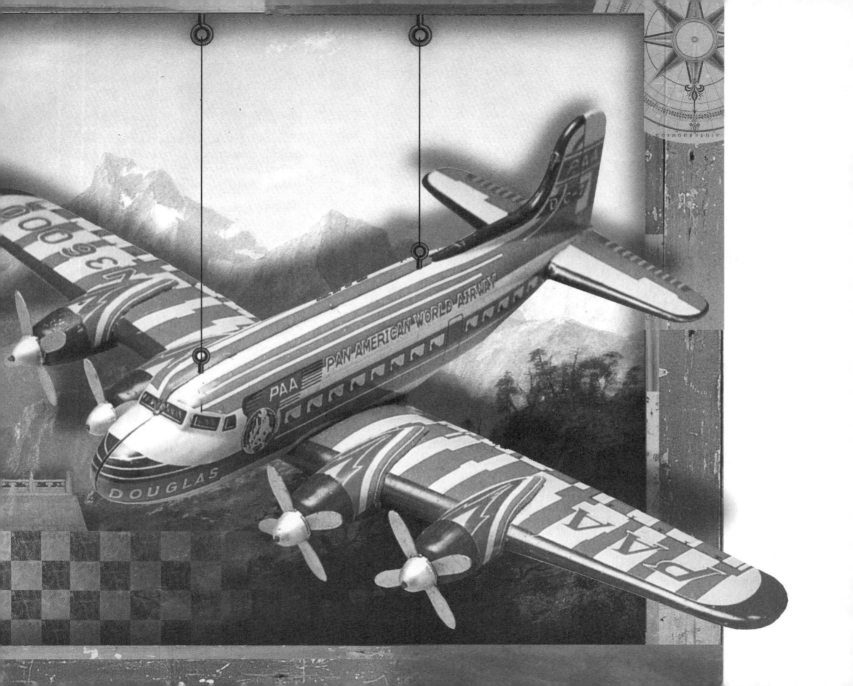

13

LIQUIFYING
AN IMAGE

1. Use the Liquify tools to distort an image.

2. Learn how to freeze and thaw areas.

3. Use the mesh feature as you distort an image.

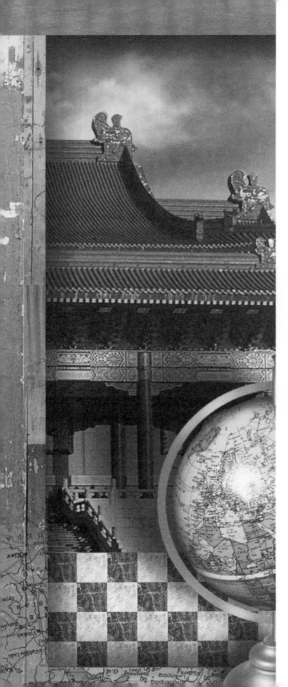

Distorting Images

If you want to have some fun with an image, try your hand at the Liquify feature. Like the Smudge Tool and the distort filters, you can use it to distort an image. But unlike those tools, the Liquify feature gives you much more control over the finished product. This feature contains 12 distinct tools that you can use to create distortion effects.

Using the Liquify Feature

The Liquify feature lets you make an image look as if parts of it have melted. You can apply the eight Liquify distortions with a brush, and like other brush-based Photoshop tools, you can modify both the brush size and pressure to give you just

the effect you want. You can use the two non-distortion Liquify tools to freeze and thaw areas within the image. Freezing protects an area from editing and possible editing errors, whereas thawing a frozen area allows it to be edited. With these two tools, you can protect specific areas from Liquify distortions, and can determine with great accuracy which areas are affected.

Using Common Sense

Because the effects of the Liquify feature are so dramatic, you should take the proper precautions to preserve your original work. You can work on a copy of the original image, or create duplicate layers to ensure that you can always get back to your starting point.

Tools You'll Use

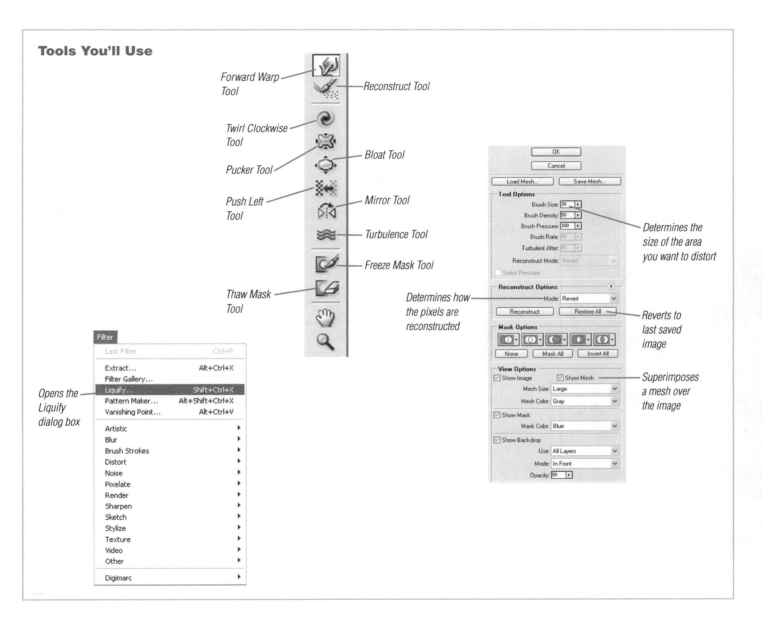

Forward Warp Tool

Reconstruct Tool

Twirl Clockwise Tool

Pucker Tool

Bloat Tool

Push Left Tool

Mirror Tool

Turbulence Tool

Freeze Mask Tool

Thaw Mask Tool

Determines the size of the area you want to distort

Determines how the pixels are reconstructed

Reverts to last saved image

Superimposes a mesh over the image

Opens the Liquify dialog box

USE THE LIQUIFY TOOLS
TO DISTORT AN IMAGE

What You'll Do

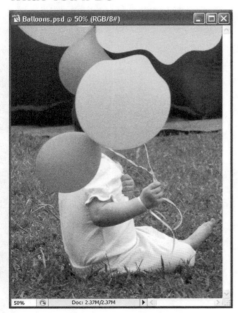

In this lesson, you'll use the Warp Tool in the Liquify dialog box to create distortions.

Using the Liquify Dialog Box

With the **Liquify feature**, you can apply distortions to any rasterized layer. When you use the Liquify command, the contents of the active layer appear in a large preview window in the Liquify dialog box. The distortion tools—used to apply the Liquify effects—are displayed on the left side of the dialog box; the tool settings are displayed on the right side. Unlike other tools that you use in the image window, you can only access the Liquify tools from the Liquify dialog box. (The Liquify feature is similar to the Extract feature in this respect.) In this dialog box, you can create eight different types of distortions.

> QUICKTIP
>
> As you apply distortions, the effects are immediately visible in the preview window of the Liquify dialog box.

Exploring the Possibilities

Compare Figures 1 (the original image) and 2 (the distorted image). As you can see from the altered image, you can use this feature to make drastic changes in an image. The following Liquify tools were used for the distorted image:

- The Twirl Clockwise Tool was used repeatedly on the topmost book.
- The Pucker Tool was used on the third book eight times. (The Pucker Tool pulls the pixels toward the center of the brush tip.)
- The Bloat Tool was used repeatedly on the sixth book. (The Bloat Tool pushes pixels away from the center of the brush tip, which can create a more subtle effect.)

QUICKTIP

You can use distortions to create wild effects or to make subtle mood changes within an image. You can also use the Liquify tools to endow a person with instant weight gain—or weight loss!

Going Wild with Distortions

Of course, you can create wild, crazy distortions using the Liquify feature, and it is a lot of fun. As you can see from Figure 2, you can create some rather bizarre effects using these tools, but you can also use the distortion tools very conservatively to just correct a flaw or tweak an image.

FIGURE 1
Undistorted image in Liquify dialog box

Twirl Clockwise Tool

Pucker Tool

Bloat Tool

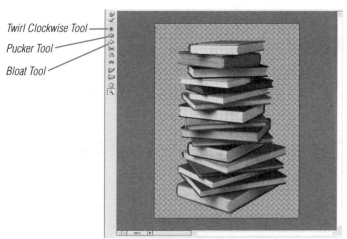

FIGURE 2
Distortion samples

Effect of the Twirl Clockwise Tool

Effect of the Pucker Tool

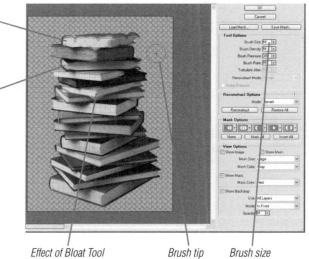

Effect of Bloat Tool   Brush tip   Brush size

Open the Liquify dialog box and modify the brush size

1. Open PS 13-1.psd from the drive and folder where your Data Files are stored, then save the file as **Balloons**.

2. Click **Filter** on the menu bar, then click **Liquify**.

3. Make sure the following check boxes are not selected: Show Mesh, Show Mask, and Show Backdrop.

4. Click the **Forward Warp Tool** 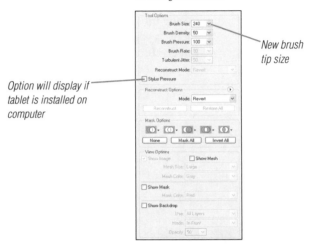 in the Liquify dialog box (if it is not already selected).

   The Liquify tools are described in Table 1.

5. Double-click the **Brush Size text box**, type **240**, then press [**Enter**] (Win) or [**return**] (Mac).

   TIP You can adjust the brush size by typing a value between 1 and 600 in the text box, pressing [[] to decrease by 2 or []] to increase by 2, or by clicking the Brush Size list arrow, then dragging the slider to a new value.

6. Adjust your settings in the Liquify dialog box so that they match those shown in Figure 3.

   TIP The Stylus Pressure check box option will appear dimmed if you do not have a graphics tablet attached to your computer.

You opened the Liquify dialog box, then chose the Forward Warp Tool and a brush size.

FIGURE 3
Choosing a brush size

New brush tip size

Option will display if tablet is installed on computer

TABLE 1: Liquify Tools

tool	button	use
Forward Warp Tool		Pushes pixels forward during dragging.
Reconstruct Tool		Unpaints recently distorted pixels completely or partially.
Twirl Clockwise Tool		Rotates pixels clockwise during dragging.
Pucker Tool		Moves pixels toward the center of the active brush tip.
Bloat Tool		Moves pixels away from the center of the active brush tip.
Push Left Tool		Moves pixels perpendicular to the brush stroke.
Mirror Tool		Copies pixels to the brush area.
Turbulence Tool		Randomly scrambles pixels.
Freeze Mask Tool		Protects an area from distortion.
Thaw Mask Tool		Makes a frozen area available for distortions.

FIGURE 4
Positioned pointer

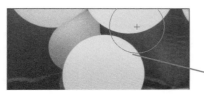

Forward Warp Tool
brush tip pointer

FIGURE 5
Enlarged balloon

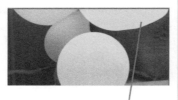

Enlarged yellow
balloon pushes pink
balloon out of view

FIGURE 6
Effect of Forward Warp Tool

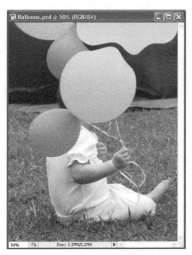

1. Position the **Forward Warp Tool pointer** ⊕ over the bottom-right edge of the yellow balloon, as shown in Figure 4.

2. Drag the **yellow balloon** to the right and down so it pushes the right pink balloon out of the image, as shown in Figure 5.

   TIP   You can return an image to its previous appearance by clicking Restore All in the Reconstruction Options section of the Liquify dialog box. The Reconstruct button undoes each action of the brush, much like the Undo command or History palette.

3. Use the **Forward Warp Tool pointer** ⊕ in different locations of the yellow balloon to create a curved effect around the bottom.

4. Click **OK** to close the Liquify dialog box.

5. Save your work, then compare your image to Figure 6.

You used the Forward Warp Tool to distort the pixels of the balloon in an image. By dragging, you pushed the pixels forward, giving the balloon a larger, distorted appearance.

LEARN HOW TO FREEZE
AND THAW AREAS

What You'll Do

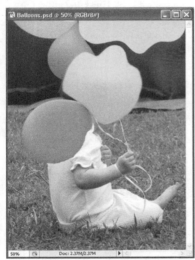

In this lesson, you'll freeze an area of an image, make distortions, then thaw the areas so that they can be edited.

Controlling Distortion Areas

Like storing food in the freezer to protect it from spoiling, you can **freeze** areas within an image so that the Liquify tools leave them unaffected. Using the Liquify dialog box, you can protect areas within an image, then **thaw** them—or return them to a state that can be edited—and make necessary distortions. You control which areas are distorted by using the Freeze Mask and Thaw Mask Tools in the Liquify dialog box.

Freezing Image Areas

You can selectively freeze areas by painting them with a pointer. The View Options section in the Liquify dialog box lets you display frozen areas in the preview window. By default, frozen areas are painted in red, but you can change this color to make it more visible. For example, Figure 7 shows an image that has not yet been distorted. If you froze areas of this image using the default red color, they would not be visible because of the colors in this image.

QUICK TIP

To isolate the exact areas you want to freeze, try painting a larger area, then using the Thaw Mask Tool to eliminate unwanted frozen areas.

Reconstructing Distortions

No matter how careful you are, you will most likely either create a distortion you don't like, or need to do some sort of damage control. Unlike typical Photoshop states, individual distortions you make using the Liquify feature do not appear on the History palette, and therefore cannot be undone. You can, however, use the History palette to delete the effects of an entire **Liquify session**, but only *from the time you open the Liquify dialog box until the time you close it*. How distortions are reconstructed is determined by the mode used. If you want to reconstruct, you can do so by using one of five different reconstruction modes in the Liquify dialog box. Each mode affects the way pixels are reconstructed, relative to frozen areas in the image. This allows you to redo the changes in new and innovative ways.

QUICKTIP
You can use any combination of reconstruction tools and modes to get just the effect you want.

Undergoing Reconstruction

Figure 8 shows several reconstructed areas as well as a frozen area painted in blue.

Using the Reconstruct Tool and the Stiff mode, the tail feathers of the chicken were restored to their original condition. The Rigid mode was used on the feet, and the beak was reconstructed using the Loose mode. You can use several methods to reconstruct an image:

- Click Restore All in the Liquify dialog box.
- Choose the Revert mode, then click Reconstruct in the Liquify dialog box.

- Click the Reconstruct Tool, choose the Revert mode, then drag the brush over distorted areas in the Liquify dialog box.
- Click the Cancel button in the Liquify dialog box.
- Make distortions in the Liquify dialog box, then drag the Liquify state to the Delete current state button on the History palette.

FIGURE 7
Original image

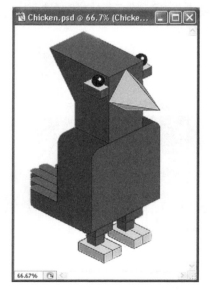

FIGURE 8
Frozen areas and distortions in preview window

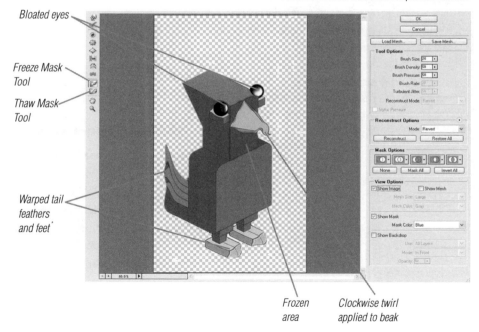

Bloated eyes

Freeze Mask Tool

Thaw Mask Tool

Warped tail feathers and feet

Frozen area

Clockwise twirl applied to beak

Freeze areas in an image

1. Click **Filter** on the menu bar, then click **Liquify**.

2. Click the **Freeze Mask Tool** 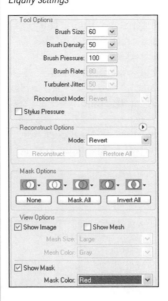 in the Liquify dialog box.

3. Double-click the **Brush Size text box**, type **60**, then press **[Enter]** (Win) or **[return]** (Mac).

4. Click the **Show Mask check box**, click the **Mask Color list arrow**, then click **Red** (if it is not already selected). Compare your Liquify dialog box settings to Figure 9 and make any necessary adjustments.

5. Drag the **Freeze pointer** ⊕ over the shirt (just underneath the lowest orange balloon), using Figure 10 as a guide.

   Table 2 describes the reconstruction modes available in the Liquify dialog box.

You modified Liquify settings, then froze an area within the image by using the Freeze Mask Tool. Freezing the areas protects them from any Liquify effects you apply going forward.

FIGURE 9
Liquify settings

FIGURE 10
Frozen area

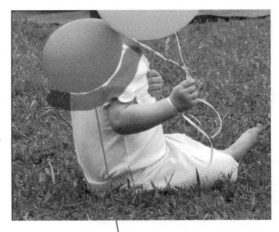

Red area is frozen

TABLE 2: Reconstruction Modes

mode	use
Revert	Changes areas back to their appearance before the dialog box was opened.
Rigid	Maintains right angles in the pixel grid during reconstruction.
Stiff	Provides continuity between frozen and unfrozen areas during reconstruction.
Smooth	Smoothes continuous distortions over frozen areas during reconstruction.
Loose	Smoothes continuous distortions similar to the Smooth mode but provides greater continuity between distortions in frozen and unfrozen areas.

FIGURE 11
Distortions in image

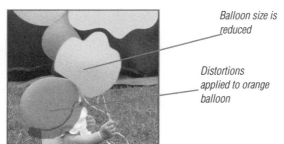

Balloon size is
reduced

Distortions
applied to orange
balloon

FIGURE 12
Distortions applied

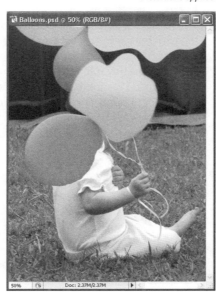

FIGURE 13
History palette

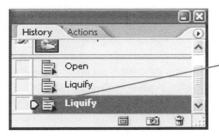

State indicates most
recent distortions

Distort unprotected areas of an image

1. Click the **Pucker Tool** 🎨 in the Liquify dialog box.

2. Change the brush size to **382**.

3. Position the center of the **Pucker pointer** ⊕ over the **turquoise balloon**, then press and hold the mouse button until it is noticeably smaller.

4. Click the **Bloat Tool** ◇ in the Liquify dialog box.

5. Using a brush size of **400**, center the **Bloat pointer** ⊕ over the left side of the lower **orange balloon**, then press and hold the mouse button until the orange balloon increases in size and pushes into the turquoise balloon.

6. Compare your image to Figure 11.

7. Click **None** in the Mask Options section to remove the mask.

8. Click **OK**.

   The distortions are applied to the image.

9. Save your work, then compare your image to Figure 12, and the History palette to Figure 13.

After distorting an area, you thawed a protected frozen area and applied the distortions to the image.

USE THE MESH FEATURE AS
YOU DISTORT AN IMAGE

What You'll Do

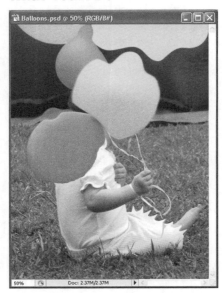

In this lesson, you'll use the mesh feature to assist you when making distortions.

Using the Mesh Feature

The **mesh** is a series of horizontal and vertical gridlines superimposed on the preview window. You can easily see the effects of your distortions while working in an image by turning on the mesh. Although this feature is not necessary to create distortions, it can be helpful for seeing how much distortion you have added. The mesh can be controlled using the View Options section in the Liquify dialog box, shown in Figure 14. A distorted image, with the default medium-size, gray mesh displayed, is shown in Figure 15.

> **QUICK**TIP
>
> Distortions on the gridlines look similar to isobars on a thermal map or elevations on a topographic map.

Changing the Mesh Display

You can modify the appearance of the mesh so that it is displayed in another color or contains larger or smaller grid-

lines. You may want to use large gridlines if your changes are so dramatic that the use of smaller gridlines would be distracting. As shown in Figure 16, you can use the large gridlines to see where the distortions occur. If the mesh color and the colors in the image are similar, you may want to change the mesh color. For example, a yellow mesh displayed on an image with a yellow background would be invisible. A blue mesh against a red background, as shown in Figure 16, is more noticeable.

Visualizing the Distortions

When the mesh feature is on and clearly visible, take a look at the gridlines as you make your distortions. Note where the gridlines have been adjusted and if symmetrical objects have equally symmetrical distortions. For example, distortions of a rectangular skyscraper can be controlled so that they are equivalent on all visible sides. If symmetry is what you want, the mesh feature gives you one method of checking your results.

Getting a Better View of Distortions

The active layer is always shown in the Liquify dialog box, but you might find it helpful to distort imagery with its companion layers visible. You can do this in two ways. One way is by selecting the Show Backdrop check box in the Liquify dialog box, and selecting which layer (or all layers)

you want to be visible with the selected layer. You can then adjust the opacity of the backdrop layer(s) to make the layer(s) more visible. This technique distorts only the layer selected on the Layers palette. The other way is by merging visible layers: Click the highest layer on the Layers palette, click the Layers palette list arrow, then click Merge Visible. When you open the merged layers in the Liquify dialog box, all the imagery will be visible and can be altered by distortions. One way of

ensuring that you can get back to your original layers—in case things don't turn out quite as you planned—is by making copies of the layers you want to combine before you merge the layers.

QUICKTIP
You can always turn off the mesh feature if it is distracting.

FIGURE 14
Mesh display options

FIGURE 16
Distorted image with large blue mesh

FIGURE 15
Distorted image with default size and color mesh

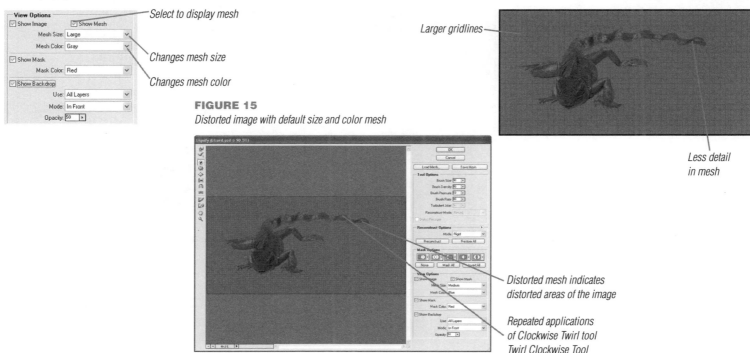

Select to display mesh

Changes mesh size

Changes mesh color

Larger gridlines

Less detail in mesh

Distorted mesh indicates distorted areas of the image

Repeated applications of Clockwise Twirl tool Twirl Clockwise Tool

Turn on the mesh

1. Click **Filter** on the menu bar, then click **Liquify**.

2. Verify that the **Bloat Tool** ✧ is selected in the Liquify dialog box, then change the brush size to **100**.

3. Select the **Show Mesh check box**.

4. Click the **Mesh Color list arrow** Gray ▾, then click **Blue**.

5. Verify that the **Mesh Size list arrow** Medium ▾ is set to **Medium**.
   Compare your image and settings to Figure 17, then make any adjustments necessary so that your settings match those shown in the figure.

You turned on the mesh and changed the mesh color and verified the setting of the mesh size.

FIGURE 17
Medium blue mesh over an image

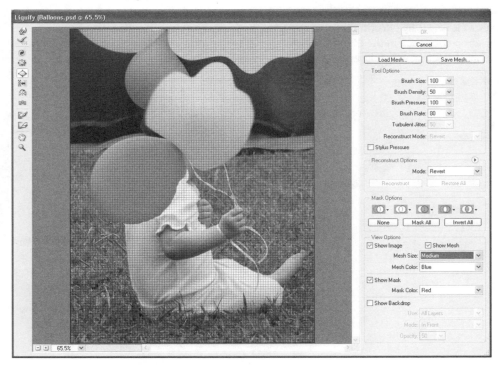

FIGURE 18
Warped sleeve and ribbon

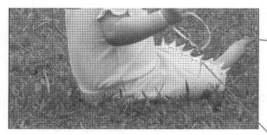

— Distorted mesh

— Waves created with
Warp Tool

FIGURE 19
Distortions applied to image

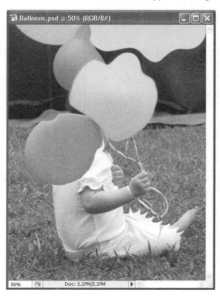

Distort an image with the mesh feature activated

1. Position the **Bloat pointer** ⊕ over the area of the highest orange balloon (between the pink and yellow balloons), press and hold the mouse button until you see the mesh being distorted, then release the mouse button.

2. Repeat Step 1 on the blue area above the lowest orange balloon.

3. Click the **Forward Warp Tool** in the Liquify dialog box, then change the brush size to **25**.

4. Drag the **Forward Warp pointer** ⊕ in the bottom edge of the baby's pink skirt so that it forms spikes, as shown in Figure 18.

5. Click the **Mesh Size list arrow**, then click **Large**.

   The gridlines appear larger.

6. Click the **Show Mesh check box** ☑ Show Mesh to turn off the mesh.

7. Click **OK**.

8. Save your work, then compare your image to Figure 19.

9. Close the image, then exit Photoshop.

You added new distortions to the image and modified the mesh size. After viewing the distortions with the larger mesh, you turned off the mesh and viewed the image.

Power User Shortcuts

to do this:	use this method:
Bloat an area	Filter ≻ Liquify, ⟡ or B
Change freeze color	Filter ≻ Liquify, Mask Color list arrow
Change mesh color	Filter ≻ Liquify, select Show Mesh check box Gray
Change mesh size	Filter ≻ Liquify, select Show Mesh check box, Medium
Change brush size	Filter ≻ Liquify, 100 or [[] or []]
Freeze pixels	Filter ≻ Liquify, ✎ or F
Open Liquify dialog box	Filter ≻ Liquify or [Shift][Ctrl][X] (Win) or ⌘ [shift][X] (Mac)
Pucker an area	Filter ≻ Liquify, ▩ or S
Reconstruct pixels in an area	Filter ≻ Liquify, ✎ or R

to do this:	use this method:
Reflect pixels in an area	Filter ≻ Liquify, ▩ or M
Return image to prewarp state	Click Restore All in Liquify dialog box, click Cancel in Liquify dialog box, or drag state to 🗑 on the History palette
Shift pixels in an area	Filter ≻ Liquify, ⠿ or O
Thaw frozen pixels	Filter ≻ Liquify, ✎ or D
Turn mesh on/off	Filter ≻ Liquify, ☐ Show Mesh
Turn Backdrop on/off	Filter ≻ Liquify, ☐ Show Backdrop
Twirl an area clockwise	Filter ≻ Liquify, ◉ or C
Warp an area	Filter ≻ Liquify, 🖐 or W

Key: Menu items are indicated by ≻ between the menu name and its command. Blue bold letters are shortcuts for selecting tools on the toolbox.

The Photoshop Liquify feature lets you move pixels within an image. Pixels can be pushed, rotated, or dragged towards or away from the center of a brush tip, or perpendicular to a brush stroke. You can use the Liquify feature to copy or randomly scramble parts of images. This feature can be used to create weird and bizarre imagery (such as giving someone a really wild hairdo), or to make subtle changes to imagery (such as removing some unwanted pounds from someone's waistline). Parts of an image can be protected from change by freezing and then thawing selective areas, and modifications made during a Liquify session can be reconstructed using a variety of settings.

What You Have Learned:

- How to distort images with Liquify tools
- How to modify Liquify settings
- How to control the Liquify session by freezing and thawing
- How to reconstruct distortions
- How to visualize distortions using the mesh
- How to change the mesh display

Key Terms

Freeze   The ability to lock areas within an image so they are unaffected by Liquify tools.

Liquify feature   Applies distortions to layers using distinct tools in the Liquify dialog box.

Liquify session   The duration from when you open the Liquify dialog box until it is closed.

Mesh   A series of horizontal and vertical gridlines superimposed on the Liquify preview window.

Thaw   The ability to return areas within an image so they can be affected by Liquify tools.

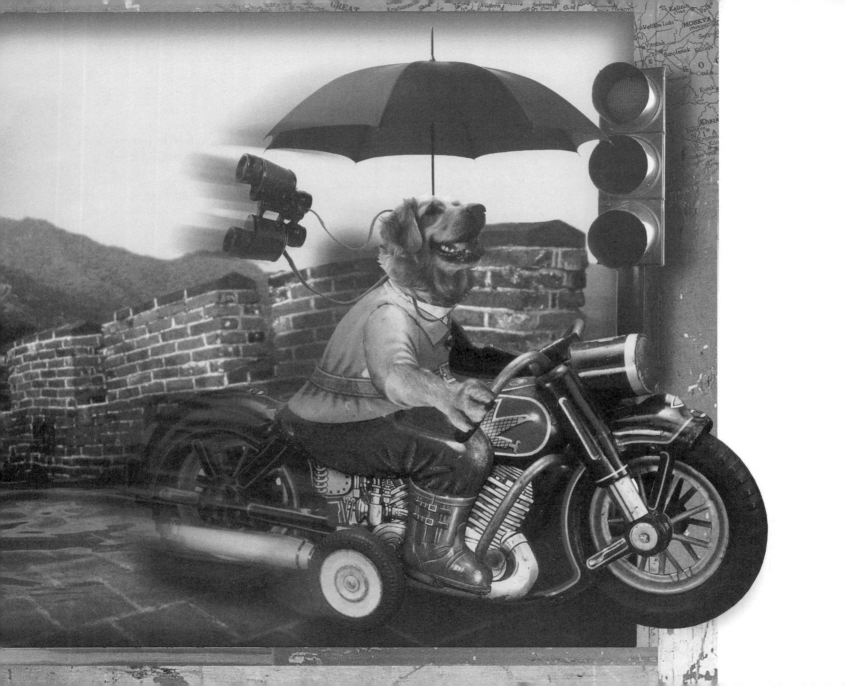

14

PERFORMING IMAGE
SURGERY

1. Delete unnecessary imagery.

2. Correct colors in an image.

3. Tweak an image.

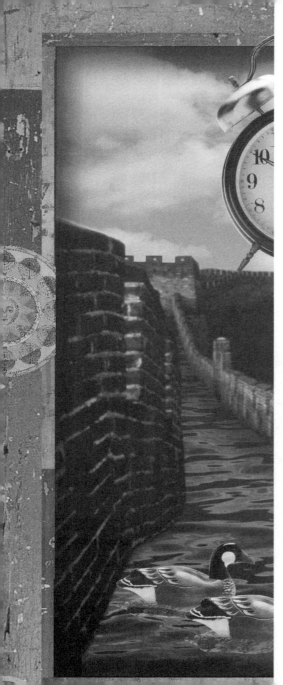

14 PERFORMING IMAGE
SURGERY

Understanding the Realities

By now you've realized that working with Photoshop is not always about creating cool effects and exciting images. Sometimes, your main task is problem-solving. You don't always have access to perfect images. Or if you did, you wouldn't need the arsenal of tools that Photoshop provides. Often, we find ourselves with images that need some "help." Perhaps the colors in an image are washed out, or maybe the image would be perfect except for an element that you don't want or need.

Assessing the Situation

In some situations, there may be many obvious ways to achieve the look you want in an image. A smart Photoshop user knows what tools are available, evaluates an image to see what is needed, then decides which methods are best to fix the problem areas in the image.

Applying Knowledge and Making Decisions

People who can apply their Photoshop knowledge effectively are in demand in today's job market. The ability to assess what tools are needed in the first place is as much a part of Photoshop expertise as knowing how to use the tools. You can approach the same design problem in many ways; that your job is to determine which approach to take to make an image look right. And it is up to you to determine what "right" is. By the time your image is finished, you may feel as if it has undergone major surgery.

> **QUICK**TIP
>
> Image surgery often goes unappreciated. You may spend a lot of time cleaning up edges and eliminating "dirt" and smudges—deffects that often are noticeable in an image only when they've been neglected!

Tools You'll Use

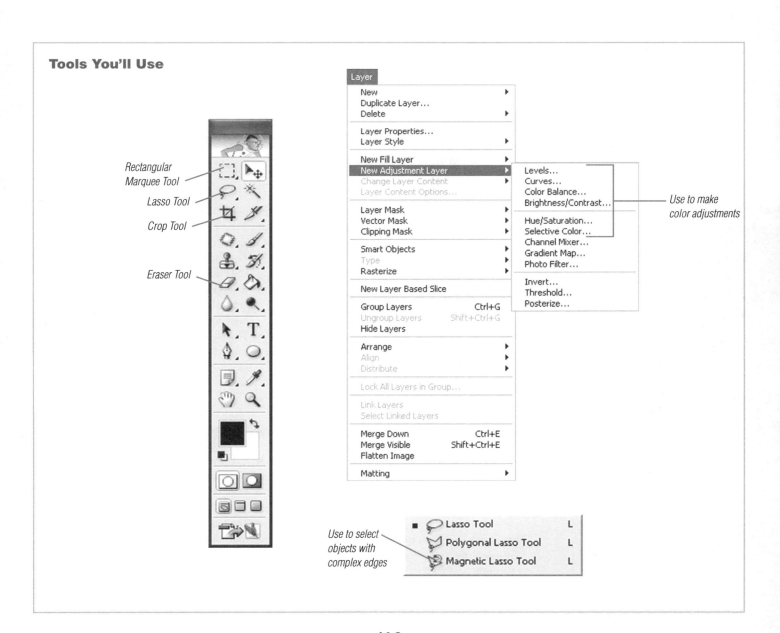

Rectangular Marquee Tool

Lasso Tool

Crop Tool

Eraser Tool

Layer

New ▶
Duplicate Layer...
Delete ▶

Layer Properties...
Layer Style ▶

New Fill Layer ▶
New Adjustment Layer ▶
Change Layer Content ▶
Layer Content Options...

Layer Mask ▶
Vector Mask ▶
Clipping Mask ▶

Smart Objects ▶
Type ▶
Rasterize ▶

New Layer Based Slice

Group Layers   Ctrl+G
Ungroup Layers   Shift+Ctrl+G
Hide Layers

Arrange ▶
Align ▶
Distribute ▶

Lock All Layers in Group...

Link Layers
Select Linked Layers

Merge Down   Ctrl+E
Merge Visible   Shift+Ctrl+E
Flatten Image

Matting ▶

Levels...
Curves...
Color Balance...
Brightness/Contrast...

Hue/Saturation...
Selective Color...
Channel Mixer...
Gradient Map...
Photo Filter...

Invert...
Threshold...
Posterize...

Use to make color adjustments

Lasso Tool   L
Polygonal Lasso Tool   L
Magnetic Lasso Tool   L

Use to select objects with complex edges

DELETE UNNECESSARY
IMAGERY

What You'll Do

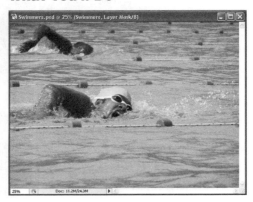

In this lesson, you'll use your skills and a variety of tools to conceal unwanted imagery. You'll also add a new layer from a selection and add a layer mask.

Evaluating the Possibilities

Now that you have some experience creating and editing images, your assessment abilities have probably sharpened. You are more accustomed to deciding what imagery is useful for a particular project. You may also find that you've begun looking at images in terms of their potential usefulness for other projects. You might, for example, see a great element in one image and think, "That object has a crisp edge. I could isolate it using the Magnetic Lasso Tool and use it for this other project."

QUICKTIP

Don't be surprised when a simple touch-up job that you thought would take a few minutes actually takes hours. Sometimes what appears to be a simple effect, is the one that requires the most work.

Performing Surgery

Removing unwanted imagery can be time-consuming and frustrating, but it can also be extremely gratifying (after you're finished). It's detailed, demanding, and sometimes complicated work. For example, Figures 1 and 2 show the same image *before* and *after* it underwent the following alterations:

- The TIFF file was saved as a Photoshop PSD file.
- Selection tools were used to create separate layers for the background, the backdrop, and the candles.
- The candles layer was duplicated, as insurance—just in case it became necessary to start over. See the Layers palette in Figure 3.
- The backdrop color was changed from black to pure blue violet.
- The candles on the left and right sides were eliminated by using eraser tools.
- Extraneous "dirt" and smudges were eliminated by using eraser tools.
- Contrast was added to the candles by using an adjustment layer.
- The Liquify feature was used to extend the individual flames and to smooth out the candle holder at the bottom of the image.
- The Noise filter was applied to the Backdrop layer, to give it more texture and dimension.

QUICKTIP

Developing critical thinking skills allows you to make decisions, such as discarding image information.

Understanding the Alternatives

Could these effects be achieved using other methods? Of course. For example, the bottom of the image was modified using the Forward Warp Tool in the Liquify dialog box, but a similar effect could have been created using a painting tool such as the Smudge Tool. The effect of the Noise filter could also have been created using the Grain filter. How many different ways can you think of to get the imagery from Figure 1 into the

separate layers shown in Figure 2? It's possible that you can create these effects in many ways. For example, you might want to use the Magnetic Lasso Tool to select areas with clearly defined edges, then zoom in and use the Eraser Tool to clean up dirt and smudges. Or you just may decide to keep it simple and use the Rectangular Marquee Tool to copy and paste pixels from one area to another.

Preparing for Surgery

Even if you think you've got it all figured out, sometimes things do not go the way you plan them. Doesn't it make sense to take the time to prepare for a worst-case scenario when using Photoshop? Of

course. You can easily protect yourself against losing hours of work by building in some safety nets as you work. For example, you can duplicate your original image (or images) just in case things go awry. By creating a copy, you'll never have to complain that your original work got clobbered. You can also save interim copies of your image at strategic stages of your work. Above all, make sure you plan your steps. To do this, perform a few trial runs on a practice image before starting on the *real* project. Until you get comfortable reading the states on the History palette, write down what steps you took and what settings you used. Careful planning will pay off.

FIGURE 1
Original TIFF file

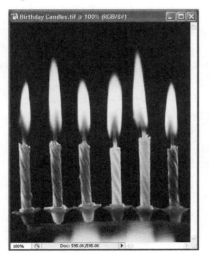

FIGURE 2
Modified image

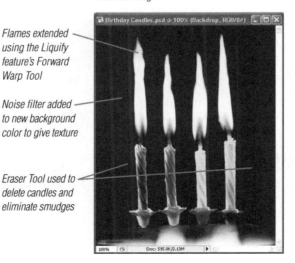

Flames extended using the Liquify feature's Forward Warp Tool

Noise filter added to new background color to give texture

Eraser Tool used to delete candles and eliminate smudges

FIGURE 3
Layers palette of modified image

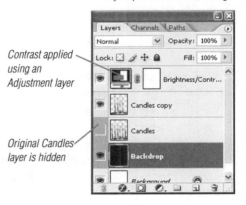

Contrast applied using an Adjustment layer

Original Candles layer is hidden

Prepare the image for surgery

1. Open PS 14-1.jpg from the drive and folder where your Data Files are stored.

2. Use the **Format list arrow** in the Save As dialog box to change the file from a JPG to the Photoshop (*.PSD, *.PDD) format, then save the file as **Swimmers.psd**.

3. Click **Layer** on the menu bar, point to **New**, then click **Layer From Background**.

4. Type **Swimmers** in the Name text box.

5. Click the **Color list arrow** in the Layer Properties dialog box, then click **Violet**.

6. Click **OK**.

7. Drag the **Swimmers layer** on the Layers palette to the **Create a new layer button** .

   A copy of the Swimmers layer (named Swimmers copy) is created. Compare your image and History and Layers palettes to Figure 4.

8. Click the **Swimmers layer** on the Layers palette.

9. Click the **Indicates layer visibility button** on the Swimmers copy layer.

   Table 1 reviews some of the many possible selection methods you can use to remove unwanted imagery.

You saved a JPG file in the Photoshop PSD format, converted a Background layer into an image layer, then made a copy of the image layer.

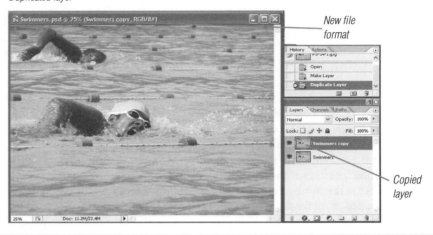

FIGURE 4
Duplicated layer

New file format

Copied layer

TABLE 1: Image Removal Methods

tool	name	method
	Magnetic Lasso Tool	Trace an object along its edge, then click Edit ≻ Clear.
	Magic Wand Tool	Select by color, then click Edit ≻ Clear.
	Clone Stamp Tool	Press and hold [Alt] (Win) or [option] (Mac), click sample area, release [Alt] (Win) or [option] (Mac), then click areas you want to remove.
	Rectangular Marquee Tool	Select area, select Move Tool, press and hold [Alt] (Win) or [option] (Mac), drag selection to new location.
	Elliptical Marquee Tool	Select area, select Move Tool, press and hold [Alt] (Win) or [option] (Mac), drag selection to new location.
	Eraser Tool	Drag over pixels to be removed.
	Patch Tool	Select source/destination, then drag to destination/source.

FIGURE 5
Selection in image

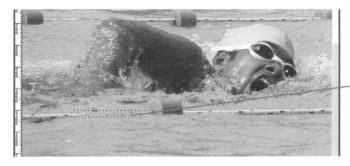

Imagery surrounded
by marquee

FIGURE 6
Cleared selection

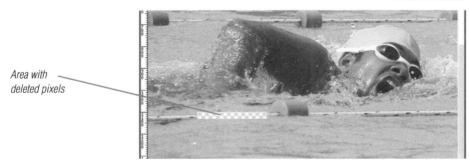

Area with
deleted pixels

Select imagery with the Rectangular Marquee Tool

1. Verify that the rulers are displayed in pixels, then click the **Zoom Tool** 🔍 on the toolbox.

   | TIP   Make sure the Resize Windows To Fit check box on the options bar is selected.

2. Click the **lowest-left piece of yellow rope** until the zoom level is 50%.

3. Click the **Rectangular Marquee Tool** ⬚ on the toolbox, then change the Feather setting to **0**.

4. Drag the **Rectangular Marquee pointer** ╋ around the rectangular section of yellow rope to the left of the orange buoy (from approximately **220 X/1070 Y** to **540 X/1100 Y**).

   Compare your selection to Figure 5.

   | TIP   You can also use the Eraser Tool to delete the rope hidden by the water, although it would be difficult to erase all the nooks and crannies. You can also choose to cover these pixels rather then remove them.

5. Click **Edit** on the menu bar, then click **Clear**.

   | TIP   You can also cut a selection by clicking Edit on the menu bar, then clicking Cut, which allows you to paste the selection elsewhere by clicking Edit on the menu bar, then clicking Paste.

6. Click **Select** on the menu bar, then click **Deselect**.

   Compare your image to Figure 6.

You used the Zoom Tool to get a closer look at an image, then used the Rectangular Marquee Tool to eliminate unwanted imagery.

Duplicate imagery

1. Verify that the **Rectangular Marquee Tool** ⬚ is selected.

2. Select a rectangular area of rope that is clearly above the water from approximately **1000 X/1050 Y** to **1350 X/1100 Y**. Compare your selection to Figure 7.

3. Press and hold **[Ctrl][Alt]** (Win) or ⌘**[option]** (Mac), drag the selection to the deleted object, then release **[Ctrl][Alt]** (Win) or ⌘**[option]** (Mac).

   The selection is duplicated over the deleted pixels.

   TIP Pressing and holding [Ctrl] (Win) or ⌘ (Mac) lets you temporarily convert the current tool to the Move Tool.

4. Click **Select** on the menu bar, then click **Deselect**.

5. Use any Photoshop tools, such as the Clone Stamp Tool, to fill in any missing areas until you are satisfied with the results.

   Compare your screen to Figure 8.

   TIP You can use pixels from anywhere in the image.

You selected areas within the image and then duplicated them to cover deleted imagery and make the image look more natural.

FIGURE 7
Selected area

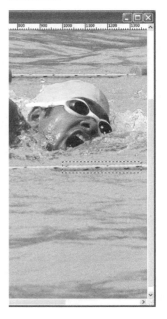

FIGURE 8
Image with duplicated pixels

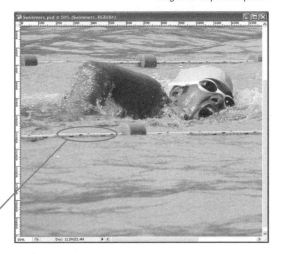

Duplicated
pixels

DESIGNTIP **Fooling the eye**

You can fool the eye when you replace pixels in an image. Even if the replacement pixels are not completely accurate, the eye can be tricked into thinking that the image looks reasonable. For example, you can duplicate ground and sky pixels, and most viewers will accept them as looking "right." However, the reverse is not necessarily true. If you remove something from an image but leave some pixels behind, viewers are likely to think that something is wrong. For example, if you erase the figure of a woman from an image, but you neglect to eliminate all the pixels for the woman's hair, the reader's eye would probably recognize the incongruity. Remnants of dangling hair would almost certainly bring into question the accuracy of the image.

FIGURE 9
Image with new layer and mask

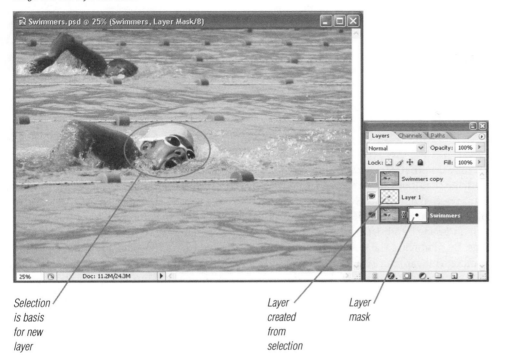

Selection
is basis
for new
layer

Layer
created
from
selection

Layer
mask

Correcting color

You can make color corrections on a layer in a number of ways. One option is to make your corrections directly on the original layer. Another option is to make a copy of the original layer *before* making the corrections on the layer. You can also make your corrections using adjustment layers, and then merge the layers down when you are satisfied with the results. You can add an adjustment layer to the current layer by clicking Layer on the menu bar, pointing to New Adjustment Layer, then clicking the type of adjustment you want to make.

Create a layer from a selection

1. Click the **Elliptical Marquee Tool** ◯ on the toolbox, then verify that the Feather setting is set to **0 px**.
2. Drag the **Marquee pointer** ╋ around the face of the swimmer with the yellow cap from approximately **800 X/660 Y** to **1300 X/1070 Y**.
3. Click **Layer** on the menu bar, point to **New**, then click **Layer via Copy**.

   A new layer containing the selection is created and is the active layer.
4. Click the **Swimmers layer** on the Layers palette.
5. Drag the **Marquee pointer** ╋ around the swimmer with the yellow cap but slightly smaller than the oval used in Step 2 from approximately **830 X/670 Y** to **1260 X/1050 Y**.
6. Click **Layer** on the menu bar, point to **Layer Mask**, then click **Hide Selection**.

   A layer mask is placed over the selection on the Swimmers layer. The mask will be used to conceal pixels while highlighting the image of the swimmer's face.
7. Hide the rulers.
8. Click the **Zoom Tool** 🔍 on the toolbox.
9. Press and hold **[Alt]** (Win) or **[option]** (Mac), click the image until the zoom level is 25%, then release **[Alt]** (Win) or **[option]** (Mac).
10. Save your work, then compare your image to Figure 9.

You created a new layer from a selection, then added a layer mask to a selection.

CORRECT COLORS IN
AN IMAGE

What You'll Do

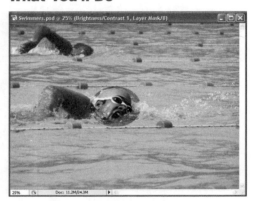

In this lesson, you'll make color adjustments to a specific layer.

Revitalizing an Image

You may find that you are working with an image that looks fine except that it seems washed out or just leaves you in the doldrums. You may be able to spice up such an image by adjusting the color settings. By modifying the color balance, for example, you can increase the red tones while decreasing the green and blue tones to make the image look more realistic and dramatic. After you select the layer that you want to adjust, you can make color-correcting adjustments by clicking Image on the menu bar, pointing to Adjustments, then clicking the type of color adjustment you want to make.

Making Color Adjustments

So, the image you're working with seems to need *something*, but you're not quite sure what. Until you become comfortable making color corrections, do everything in your power to provide yourself with a safety net. Create duplicate layers and use adjustment layers instead of making corrections directly on the original layer. Before you begin, take a long look at the image and ask yourself, "What's lacking?" Is the problem composition, or is it truly a color problem? Do the colors appear washed out rather than vibrant and true to life? Is the color deficiency really a problem, or does the image's appearance support what you're trying to accomplish?

Assessing the Mood

Color can be a big factor in establishing mood in an image. For example, if you are trying to create a sad mood, increasing the blue and green tones may be more effective than modifying specific imagery. If you decide that your image does need color correction, start slowly. Try balancing the color and see if that gives you the effect you want. Keep experimenting with the various color correction options until you find the method that works for you.

FIGURE 10
Hue/Saturation dialog box

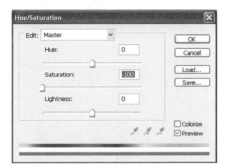

FIGURE 12
Hue/Saturation modified in image

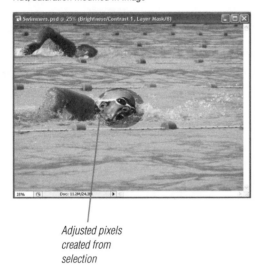

Adjusted pixels
created from
selection

FIGURE 11
Brightness/Contrast dialog box

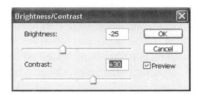

FIGURE 13
Layers palette

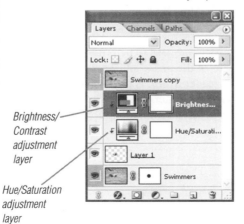

Brightness/
Contrast
adjustment
layer

Hue/Saturation
adjustment
layer

1. Click **Layer 1** on the Layers palette.
2. Click **Layer** on the menu bar, point to **New Adjustment Layer**, then click **Hue/Saturation**.
3. Select the **Use Previous Layer to Create Clipping Mask** check box, then click **OK**.
4. Change the settings in the Hue/Saturation dialog box so that they match those shown in Figure 10, then click **OK**.
5. Click **Layer** on the menu bar, point to **New Adjustment Layer**, then click **Brightness/Contrast**.
6. Select the **Use Previous Layer to Create Clipping Mask** check box, then click **OK**.
7. Change the settings so that they match those shown in Figure 11, then click **OK**.
8. Save your work, then compare your image to Figure 12 and your Layers palette to Figure 13.

You adjusted the hue/saturation and brightness/contrast in the layer created from a selection, making the image of the swimmer's face stand out. You made color adjustments using adjustment layers, which you grouped with the Swimmers layer.

TWEAK AN
IMAGE

What You'll Do

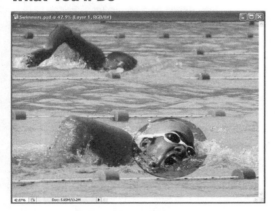

In this lesson, you'll crop out unnecessary imagery. You'll also add a layer style to enhance the image, and draw attention away from the background.

Evaluating What's Next

Every image has its own unique problems, and you'll probably run into a few final challenges when coordinating an image to work with other elements in a final publication or finished product. The last step in preparing an image for production is to decide what final fixes are necessary so that it serves its intended purpose.

Cropping an Image

Sometimes an image contains more content than is necessary. In the image of the swimmers, there's too much water. Of course, *you* have to determine the central focus of the image and what it is you want the reader to see. Is the subject of the image the water, or the swimmers? If your image suffers from too much of the wrong imagery, you can help your reader by getting rid of imagery that is not needed and possibly distracting. This type of deletion not only removes imagery, but changes the size and shape of the image. You can make this type of change using the Crop Tool on the toolbox. When you make a selection within an image, you can use cropped area settings (the Shield check box and the Opacity list arrow) on the options bar to see how the image will appear after it has been cropped.

Adding Layer Styles

Image layers can also benefit from the same layer styles that can be applied to type layers, such as a Drop Shadow.

FIGURE 14
Cropped area in image

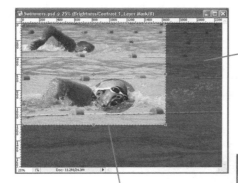

Darker area
will be
deleted
during
cropping

Dotted line
indicates new
boundaries

FIGURE 15
Completed image

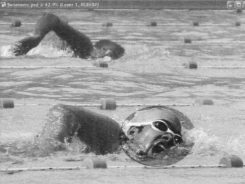

FIGURE 16
Layers palette for completed image

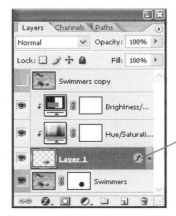

Style applied
to layer

1. Display the rulers in pixels.

2. Click the **Crop Tool** 🔲 on the toolbox.

3. Drag the **Crop Tool pointer** 🔲 in a rectangular area surrounding the two swimmers from approximately **0 X/0 Y** to **1620 X/1200 Y**.

   The area that will be cropped from the image appears darker, as shown in Figure 14.

4. Click the **Commit current crop operation button** ✓ on the options bar.

   The cropped imagery is discarded.

5. Hide the rulers, then resize the image so it fits your screen.

6. Click **Layer 1** on the Layers palette.

7. Click the **Add a layer style button** 🔵. on the Layers palette.

8. Click **Drop Shadow**, accept the existing settings, then click **OK**.

9. Save your work, then compare your image to Figure 15 and your Layers palette to Figure 16.

10. Close the image file and exit Photoshop.

You cropped the image, then applied the Drop Shadow style to the layer created from a selection.

Lesson 3   Tweak an Image

Power User Shortcuts

to do this:	use this method:
Add layer style	🐾, click style(s)
Clear selection	[Delete] (Win) or [delete] (Mac)
Clone an area	📷, or Shift S, press and hold [Alt] (Win) or `option` (Mac), click sample area, release [Alt] (Win) or `option` (Mac), then click areas you want cloned
Create an adjustment layer	Layer ➤ New Adjustment Layer ➤ type of adjustment
Create layer from selection	[Ctrl][J] (Win) or ⌘[J] (Mac)
Crop an image	🔲
Cut selection	Edit ➤ Cut, or [Ctrl][X] (Win) or ⌘[X] (Mac)
Deselect selection	Select ➤ Deselect, or [Ctrl][D] (Win) or ⌘[D] (Mac)

to do this:	use this method:
Duplicate a layer	Drag layer to 🔲
Duplicate a selection and move it to a new location	⬚ or ⭕ or Shift M, create selection, press and hold [Ctrl][Alt] (Win) or ⌘ `option` (Mac), then drag selection to new location
Erase pixels	🧹, or Shift E, drag pointer over pixels to be removed
Magnify an area	🔍 or Z, then click image
Paste selection	Edit ➤ Paste, or [Ctrl][V] (Win) or ⌘[V] (Mac)
Select a complex object	🖋 or Shift L
Select and delete by color	🪄 or W, then click Edit ➤ Clear

Key: Menu items are indicated by ➤ between the menu name and its command. Blue bold letters are shortcuts for selecting tools on the toolbox.

Learning how to best use Photoshop is not an easy task. You may think that the hardest part of learning to use Photoshop is memorizing which tools do what, or what menu contains specific commands that you want to use. While becoming familiar with the commands and menus may be easier said than done, the hardest task can be assessing an image to best understand its redeeming features as well as its flaws. Before you set out to work on an image, you should know what an image needs to accomplish or what message it has to convey. All this, of course, is subjective, but for the project, you are the artist, so these decisions are yours.

Once you've determined what needs to be done, it's up to you to do it. First, you must prepare the image for its transformation. This may mean saving the file in a different format, making copies of layers, and renaming the layers so you can work with them more easily. Remember to build in plenty of safety nets to safeguard your work. You can follow guidelines such as those listed below:

- Make duplicate layers and layers from selections.
- Use adjustment layers rather than adjusting the pixels directly on a layer.
- Don't worry about the ever-growing size of your file, you can always delete layers or flatten the file later.
- Build in enough time in your schedule, it usually takes longer to complete a task than you thought.

What You Have Learned:

- How to assess what an image needs
- How to decide what tools can and should be used
- How to prepare an image for corrections
- How to create a layer from a selection
- How to use color correction to change the mood within an image
- How to call attention to an area by adjusting the hue and saturation
- How to discard unnecessary imagery

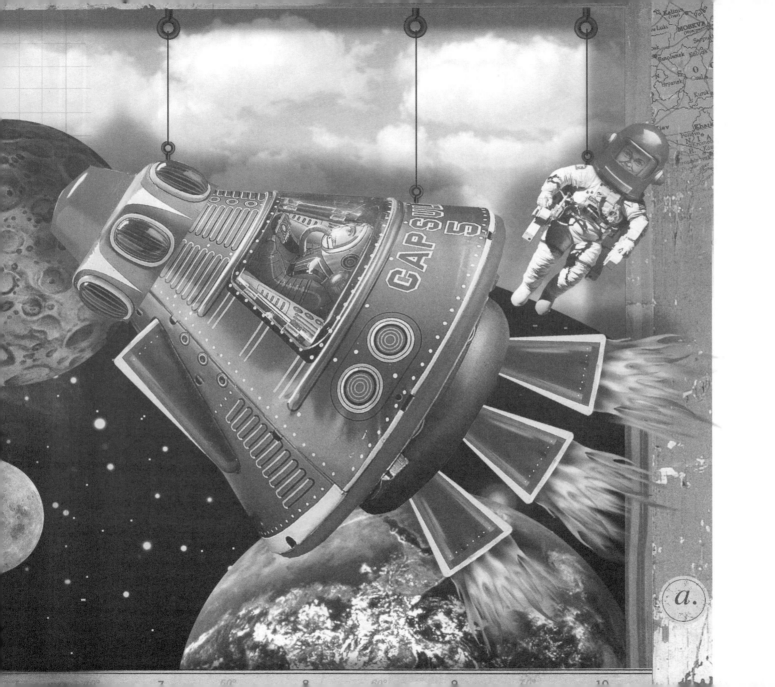

chapter

15

ANNOTATING AND
AUTOMATING AN
IMAGE

. Add annotations to an image.

. Create an action.

. Modify an action.

. Use a default action and create a droplet.

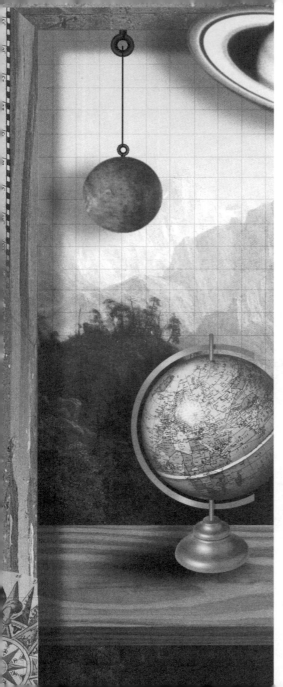

15 ANNOTATING AND
AUTOMATING AN
IMAGE

Creating Annotations

Have you ever wished you could paste a sticky note on an image, to jot down an idea or a message to someone who will be reviewing the design—or better yet, wished you could leave a voice message for them right in the file? Well, in Photoshop you can do both, using visual and audio annotations.

Communicating Directly to Your Audience

By creating written notes and audio **annotations**, you can communicate directly to anyone viewing your image. You can place written comments—like electronic sticky notes—right in the file. If your computer is set up to record sound you can place spoken comments in the image as well. For both types of annotations, anyone opening your image in Photoshop can double-click the text or sound icon, and then read or hear your comments.

Using Automation

Have you ever performed a repetitive task in Photoshop? Suppose you create an image with several type layers containing different fonts, and then you decide that each of those type layers should use the same font family. To make this change, you would have to perform the following steps on each type layer:

- Select the layer.
- Double-click the layer thumbnail.
- Click the Set the font family list arrow.
- Click the font you want.
- Click the Commit any current edits button.

Wouldn't it be nice if there were a way to speed up commonly performed tasks like this one? That's where automation, courtesy of the Actions feature, comes in. Using this feature you can record these five steps as one action. Then, rather than having to repeat each of the steps, you just play the action.

> QUICKTIP
>
> Many programs have a feature that records and then can play back repetitive tasks. Other programs call this feature a macro, script, or behavior.

Tools You'll Use

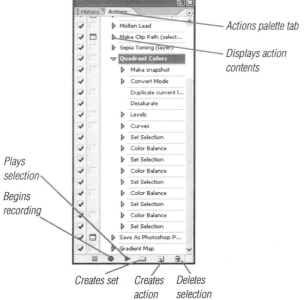

Actions palette tab

Displays action contents

Plays selection

Begins recording

Creates set Creates action Deletes selection

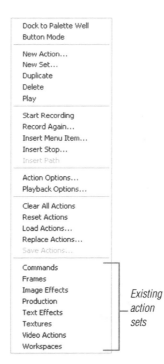

Dock to Palette Well
Button Mode

New Action...
New Set...
Duplicate
Delete
Play

Start Recording
Record Again...
Insert Menu Item...
Insert Stop...
Insert Path

Action Options...
Playback Options...

Clear All Actions
Reset Actions
Load Actions...
Replace Actions...
Save Actions...

Commands
Frames
Image Effects
Production
Text Effects
Textures
Video Actions
Workspaces

Existing action sets

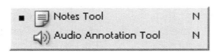

Notes Tool   N
Audio Annotation Tool   N

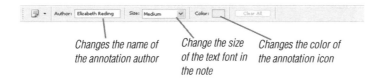

Changes the name of the annotation author

Change the size of the text font in the note

Changes the color of the annotation icon

ADD ANNOTATIONS TO
AN IMAGE

What You'll Do

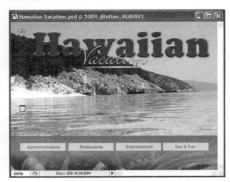

In this lesson, you'll create a text and audio annotation.

Creating a Written Annotation

Written annotations are similar to the yellow sticky notes you might attach to a printout. You can create a written annotation by clicking the Notes Tool on the toolbox, clicking in the image where you want the note to appear, then typing the contents. Each note within a file has an icon that appears on the image in the work area, as shown in Figure 1 (although neither the icon nor the note itself can be printed).

Reading Notes

To open a closed note, you double-click the note icon. You can also right-click (Win) or [control]-click (Mac) the note icon, then click Open Note, as shown in Figure 1. Although you can adjust the size of the note's window, it's not really necessary because scroll bars appear if the amount of text exceeds the window size. You can move the note within the image by dragging the note's title bar or icon.

QUICKTIP

You can delete a selected note by pressing [Delete] or by right-clicking the note (Win) or [control]-clicking the note (Mac), then clicking Delete Note.

Personalizing a Note

By default, the title bar of a note is pale yellow. You can change this color by clicking the Annotation color box on the options bar. When the Color Picker dialog box opens, you can use any method to change the color, such as sampling an area within an existing image. You can also change the type size, and the author of the note by selecting the contents in the Name of author for annotations text box, typing the information you want, then pressing [Enter] (Win) or [return] (Mac).

Creating an Audio Annotation

If you can't be there in person to deliver a live presentation of your image to a client or co-worker, an audio annotation is the next best thing. An **audio annotation** is a sound file that is saved within an image. This feature lets you use your own voice to describe exactly what you want to say. You create an audio annotation by using the Audio Annotation Tool on the toolbox.

When this tool is active, you click the location in the image where you want the annotation, then click the Start button in the Audio Annotation dialog box (Win) shown in Figure 2. Like the note icon, the audio icon can be moved within the image by dragging it. To play the audio annotation, double-click the audio icon, shown in Figure 3 or right-click the icon and click Play in the shortcut menu.

QUICKTIP

The ability to create and hear audio annotations depends on the hardware configuration of your computer. To create an audio annotation, you need a microphone and sound card. To play an existing audio annotation, you need speakers and a sound card.

FIGURE 1
Open note in an image

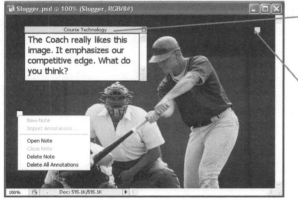

Name of author appears here

Solid color indicates closed note

FIGURE 2
Audio Annotation dialog box

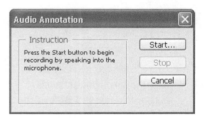

FIGURE 3
Audio annotation

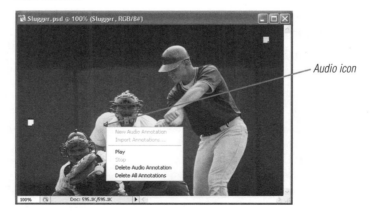

Audio icon

Create a text annotation

1. Open PS 15-1.psd from the drive and folder where your Data Files are stored, update the text layers (if necessary), save the file as **Hawaiian Vacation,** then turn off any displayed guides (if necessary).

2. Click the **Notes Tool** ☐, on the toolbox.

3. If your name does not appear in the Name of author for annotations text box on the options bar, select the contents of the text box, type **Your Name**, then press **[Enter]** (Win) or **[return]** (Mac).

4. Click the **Font size used for notes list arrow** Medium ☐ on the options bar, then click **Medium**.

5. Click the **Swatches palette tab** Swatches . Click the **Annotation color box** ☐ on the options bar, then click **RGB Yellow** (the second swatch from the left in the first row).

6. Click **OK**. Compare your options bar to Figure 4. The Annotation color box is yellow.

7. Display the Rulers in pixels, then click in the water above the left-most button at approximately **30 X/220 Y**.

8. Type the text shown in Figure 5.

9. Click the **Note close button** at the top of the note.

10. Click the **note icon**. Turn off the ruler display, then compare your image to Figure 6.

You used the Notes Tool to create a written annotation within an image. You specified an author and type size for the note, and you changed the color of the note title bar and icon using the Swatches palette. Notes are a great way to transmit information about an image.

FIGURE 4
Options for the Notes Tool

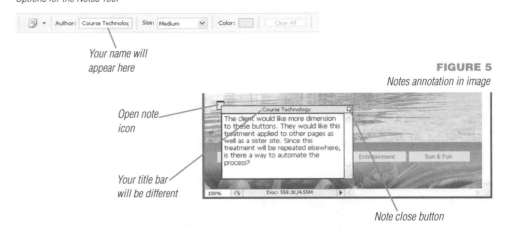

Your name will appear here

FIGURE 5
Notes annotation in image

Open note icon

Your title bar will be different

Note close button

FIGURE 6
Notes annotation icon

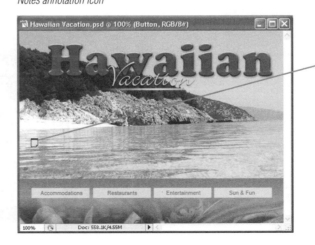

Closed note icon has the same color as the note title bar

FIGURE 7
Audio Annotation Tool options

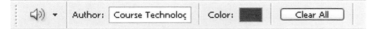

Create an audio annotation

1. Press and hold the left mouse button on the **Notes Tool** 📄. on the toolbox until a list of tools appears.

2. Click the **Audio Annotation Tool** 🔊 on the toolbox.

   TIP In order to complete these steps, you need a sound card and microphone installed on your computer.

3. Click the **Annotation color box** on the options bar, then click anywhere in the word "Hawaiian".

4. Click **OK**. Compare your options bar to Figure 7.

FIGURE 8
Audio annotation in image

5. Click in the upper-left corner of the image.

6. Click **Start** in the Audio Annotation dialog box.

7. Record the following message: **"This project is on a tight budget. Please streamline anywhere possible."**

8. Click **Stop** in the Audio Annotation dialog box.

9. Double-click the **audio icon** to hear the message you just recorded.

10. Save your work, then compare your image to Figure 8.

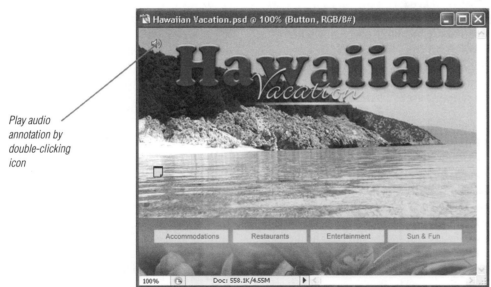

Play audio annotation by double-clicking icon

You used the Audio Annotation Tool to create an embedded sound message. You also changed the color of the audio icon by sampling a color existing in the image.

CREATE AN
ACTION

What You'll Do

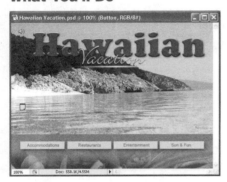

In this lesson, you'll create an action.

Simplifying Common Tasks

Suppose you are responsible for maintaining the ad slicks for all your company's products (and there are a lot of them). What would you do if the company decided to change their image designs so that each existing product advertisement would be shown with Drop Shadow and Inner Shadow styles? (Resigning your position is *not* an option.) Instead, you can create an action to speed up this monumental task.

Understanding Actions

Most tasks that you perform using a button or menu command can be recorded as an action. Each action can contain one or more steps and can also contain a **stop**, which lets you complete a command that can't be recorded (for example, the use of a painting tool). Actions can be stored in sets, which are saved as .atn files and are typically named by the category of actions they contain. For example, you can create

multiple type-related actions, then store them in a set named Type Actions. You access actions from the Actions palette, which is normally grouped with the History palette. You can view actions in list mode or in button mode on the Actions palette. The **list mode**, the default, makes it possible to view the details within each action. The **button mode** displays each action without details.

> **QUICK**TIP
>
> The act of creating an action is not recorded on the History palette; however, the steps you record to define a new action are recorded on the History palette.

Knowing Your Options

You use commonly recognizable VCR-like buttons to operate an action. These buttons are located at the bottom of the Actions palette and let you play, record, stop, as well as move forward and backward in an action.

Recording an Action

When recording is active, the red Recording button on the Actions palette appears. The action set also opens as soon as you begin recording, to show all the individual actions in the set.

QUICKTIP

To test your actions, first you can create a snapshot of your image. Then you work on an action, make any changes, or record new steps. Use the snapshot to restore the image to its original state. After the image is restored, you can play the action to verify that the steps work.

Playing Back Actions

You can modify how actions are played back using the Playback Options dialog box, as shown in Figure 9. The playback options are described in Table 1. You can open the Playback Options dialog box by clicking the Actions palette list arrow, then clicking Playback Options. The Accelerated, Step by Step, and Pause For options control the speed at which the steps are performed.

QUICKTIP

You can reset the actions to their default settings by clicking the Actions palette list arrow, then clicking Reset Actions. Click OK to delete new actions, or Append to add new actions to the set of default actions.

QUICKTIP

You can return the Actions palette, along with all the other palettes, to their original size and location by clicking Window on the menu bar, pointing to Workspace, then clicking Reset Palette Locations.

FIGURE 9
Playback Options dialog box

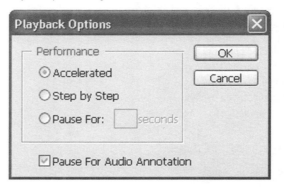

TABLE 1: Action Playback Options

option	description
Accelerated	Plays all steps within an action, then makes all changes.
Step by Step	Completes each step in an action and redraws the image before advancing to the next step.
Pause For	Lets you specify the number of seconds that should occur between steps in an action.
Pause For Audio Annotation	If audio annotations are in use, this option ensures that the annotation is played before the action advances to the next step.

Create an action

1. Click the **Create new snapshot button** 📷 on the History palette.

2. Click the **Actions palette tab** Actions .

   TIP By default, the Actions palette window is small, enlarge it by dragging the bottom edge.

3. Verify that the **triangle** to the left of the Default Actions. Set on the Actions palette is facing to the right and that the set is closed. Compare your palette to Figure 10.

   TIP You can toggle between list and button modes by clicking the list arrow on the Actions palette, then clicking Button Mode.

   You can click the triangle next to a *set* to show or hide the actions in it. You can also click the triangle next to an *action* to show or hide the steps in it.

   TIP When you create an action in the Default Actions. Set or in any set, the action is available in all your Photoshop images.

4. Click the **Create new action button** 🔲 on the Actions palette. The New Action dialog box opens.

5. Type **Button Drop Shadow** in the Name text box.

6. Click the **Color list arrow**, click **Yellow**, then compare your dialog box to Figure 11.

7. Click **Record**. Did you notice that the red Recording button is displayed on the Actions palette and all default actions opened? See Figure 12.

You created a snapshot to make it possible to easily test the new action. You used the Create new action button on the Actions palette to create an action called Button Drop Shadow.

FIGURE 10
Actions palette with detail hidden

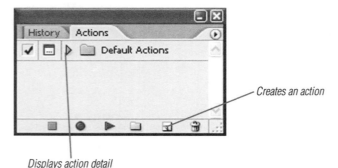

Creates an action

Displays action detail

FIGURE 11
New Action dialog box

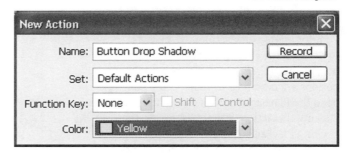

FIGURE 12
New action

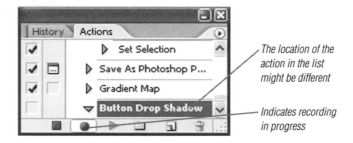

The location of the action in the list might be different

Indicates recording in progress

FIGURE 13
Layer Style dialog box

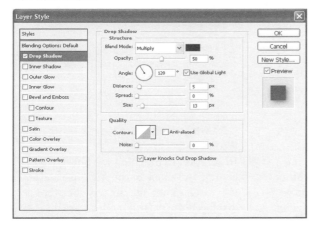

FIGURE 14
Selected action

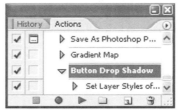

FIGURE 15
Modified image

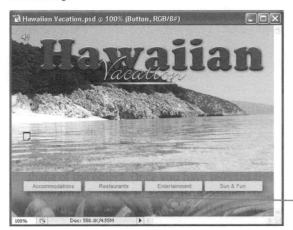

Drop shadow
behind buttons

1. Click the **Button layer** on the Layers palette (if it is not already selected).

2. Click the **Add a layer style button** 🦋 on the Layers palette, click **Drop Shadow**, then change your Layer Style dialog box settings so they match those shown in Figure 13.

3. Click **OK**.

4. Click the **Stop playing/recording button** 🔳 on the Actions palette.

5. Click the **Button Drop Shadow action** on the Actions palette. See Figure 14.

6. Click the **History palette tab** History .

7. Scroll to the top of the History palette (if necessary), then click **Snapshot 1**.

   The Button layer returns to its original appearance.

8. Click the **Actions palette tab** Actions .

9. With the Button Drop Shadow action still selected, click the **Play selection button** ▶ on the Actions palette.

10. Save your work, then compare your screen to Figure 15.

You recorded steps for the Button Drop Shadow action. After the recording was complete, you used a snapshot to restore the image to its original state, then you played the action to test it. Testing is an important step in creating an action.

Lesson 2   Create an Action

MODIFY AN ACTION

What You'll Do

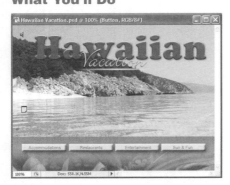

In this lesson, you'll modify the recently created action by adding new steps to it.

Getting It Right
Few of us get everything right the first time you try to do something. After you create an action, you might think of other steps that you want to include, you may want to change the order of some or all of the steps, or you may need to alter an option. The beauty of Photoshop actions is that you can make modifications and additions to them with little effort.

Revising an Action
You can modify an existing action by clicking the step that is after or before the new steps that you are adding. Click the Begin recording button on the Actions palette, record your steps (just as you do when you initially create the action), then click the Stop playing/recording button when you're finished. The new steps are inserted after the existing step.

> **QUICK**TIP
> Because users may not know how to resume playback after encountering a stop, it's a good idea to include a helpful tip that tells them to click the Play selection button after encountering the stop.

Changing the Actions Palette View
In addition to dragging the borders to change the shape of the Actions palette, you can also change the way the steps are displayed. By default, actions are displayed in list mode: the steps appear as a list below each action included in them. Figure 16 shows the actions in the Default Actions set in list mode in which all the detail is accessible but hidden. (Remember that you can display the detail for each action by clicking the triangle next to the action, to expand it.)

Working in Button Mode
In button mode, each of the actions is displayed as a button—without the additional detail found in the list mode. Each button is displayed in the color selected when the action was created and the Play button is not displayed. In button mode, all you need to do to play an action is to click the button. Figure 17 shows the same actions in button mode. You can toggle between these two modes by clicking the Actions palette list arrow, then clicking Button Mode, as shown in Figure 18.

FIGURE 16
Actions displayed in list mode

FIGURE 17
Actions displayed in button mode

FIGURE 18
Actions palette menu

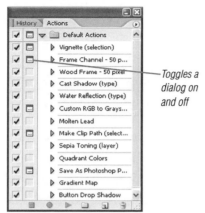

*Toggles a
dialog on
and off*

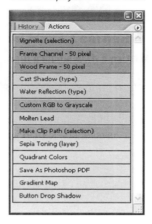

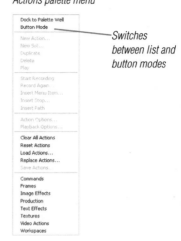

—*Switches
between list and
button modes*

Understanding a stop

In addition to containing any Photoshop task, an action can include a stop, which is a command that interrupts playback to allow you to perform other operations—particularly those that cannot be recorded in an action, or those that might change each time you play the action. You insert a stop by clicking the step *just above* where you want the pause to take place. Click the Actions palette list arrow, then click Insert Stop. The Record Stop dialog box opens, allowing you to enter a text message that appears when the action is stopped, as shown in Figure 19. You select the Allow Continue check box to include a Continue button in the message that appears when the action is stopped. You can resume the action by clicking this button. An action that contains a dialog box—such as an action that contains a stop—displays a toggle dialog on/off icon to the left of the action name on the Actions palette. This icon indicates a **modal control**, which means that dialog boxes are *used* in the action, but are not displayed. When the action is resumed, the tasks begin where they were interrupted. You can resume the action by clicking the Play selection button on the Actions palette.

FIGURE 19
Record Stop dialog box

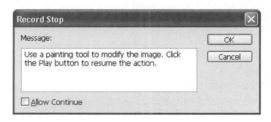

Add steps to an action

1. Verify that the **Button layer** is active.

2. Click the **Set Layer Styles of current layer step** (the first step) in the Button Drop Shadow action on the Actions palette.

3. Click the **Begin recording button** ⬤ on the Actions palette.

4. Click **Image** on the menu bar, point to **Adjustments**, then click **Brightness/Contrast**. Change the settings in your dialog box to match the settings in Figure 20.

5. Click **OK**.

6. Click the **Stop playing/recording button** ⬛ on the Actions palette. Compare your Actions palette to Figure 21.

   The Button Drop Shadow action has a new step added to it.

7. Click the **History palette tab** History , then click **Snapshot 1**.

8. Click the **Actions palette tab** Actions .

9. Click the **Button Drop Shadow action**, then click the **Play selection button** ▶ on the Actions palette. Compare your screen to Figure 22.

You added a new step (which modified the brightness/contrast) to the Button Drop Shadow action. You then tested the modified action by using a snapshot and then playing the action.

FIGURE 20
Brightness/Contrast dialog box

FIGURE 21
New steps added to the Button Drop Shadow action

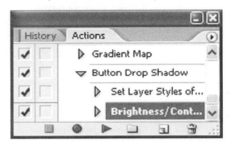

FIGURE 22
Result of modified action

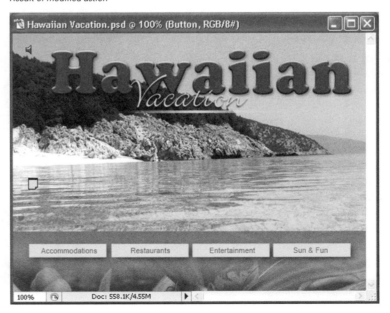

FIGURE 23
Modified image

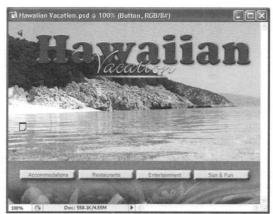

Modify steps in an action

1. Verify that the Brightness/Contrast step on the Actions palette (the second step in the Button Drop Shadow action), is selected.

2. Click the **Begin recording button** ● on the Actions palette.

3. Click the **Add a layer style button** ✱. on the Layers palette.

4. Click **Bevel and Emboss**, then click **OK** to accept the existing settings.

5. Click the **Stop playing/recording button** ■ on the Actions palette.

   The new step is added to the existing action. Table 2 describes other ways to modify actions.

6. Click the **History palette tab** History , then click **Snapshot 1**.

7. Click the **Actions palette tab** Actions .

8. Click the **Button Drop Shadow action**, then click the **Play selection button** ▶ on the Actions palette.

9. Save your work, then compare your image to Figure 23.

You added the Bevel and Emboss style to an action, then you tested the action.

TABLE 2: Methods for Modifying an Action

modification type	method
Rearrange steps	Move an existing step by dragging the step to a new location in the action.
Add new commands	Click the step above or below where you want the new step to appear, then click ▶.
Rerecord existing commands	Click the step you want to duplicate, click ⊙, then click Record Again.
Duplicate existing commands	Click the step you want to duplicate, click ⊙, then click Duplicate.
Delete actions	Click the action you want to delete, then click 🗑.
Delete a step in an action	Click the step you want to delete, then click 🗑.
Change options in an action	Click the step that has options you want to change, click ⊙, then click Action Options or Playback Options.

USE A DEFAULT ACTION
AND CREATE A DROPLET

What You'll Do

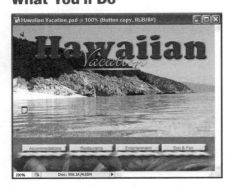

In this lesson, you'll use actions from other sets, and create a droplet.

Taking Advantage of Actions

Photoshop actions can really help your session by automating tedious tasks. You can add a default action to any action you've created. A **default action** is an action that is prerecorded and tested, and comes with Photoshop. You can incorporate some of these nifty actions that come with Photoshop into those you create.

Identifying Default Actions

The default actions that come with Photoshop are Vignette, Frame Channel,

Wood Frame, Cast Shadow, Water Reflection, Custom RGB to Grayscale, Molten Lead, Make Clip Path (selection), Sepia Toning (layer), Quadrant Colors, Save As Photoshop PDF, and Gradient Map. In addition, there are seven action sets that come with Photoshop: Commands, Frames, Image Effects, Production, Text Effects, Textures, and Video Actions. You can load any of these action sets by clicking the Actions palette list arrow, then clicking the name of the set you want to load.

Automating using batches

There may be times when you might need to perform the same action on multiple files. Rather than dragging each image onto a droplet, one at a time, you can combine all of the images into a batch. A **batch** is a group of images designated to have the same action performed on them simultaneously. You can create a batch using all of the files in one specific folder or using all of the Photoshop images that are currently open. When you have opened or organized the files you want to include in a batch, click File on the menu bar, point to Automate, then click Batch. The Batch dialog box opens, offering you options similar to those used for creating droplets. You can also use the File Browser as a source of playing an action by clicking Automate on the File Browser window menu bar.

Understanding a Droplet

A **droplet** is a stand-alone action in the form of an icon. You can drag one or more closed Photoshop files onto a droplet icon to perform the action on the file or files. You can store droplets on your hard drive, place them on your desktop, or distribute them to others. Figure 24 shows an example of a droplet on the desktop. Droplets let you further automate repetitive tasks.

Creating a Droplet

You create a droplet by using the Automate command on the File menu, an existing action, and the Create Droplet dialog box. In the Create Droplet dialog box, you use the Set list arrow to choose the set that contains the action you want to use to create the droplet, then use the Action list arrow to choose the action. Finally, you can choose the location on your computer where you'll store the droplet.

QUICKTIP

When placed on the desktop, a droplet has a unique down-arrow icon filled with the Photoshop logo. The droplet name appears below the icon.

Using Default Actions

You can incorporate any of the default actions that come with Photoshop—or those you get from other sources—into a new action by playing the action in the process of recording a new one. Each time an existing action is played, a new snapshot is created on the History palette, so don't be surprised when you see additional snapshots that you never created. To incorporate an existing action into a new action, first select the step that is *above* where you want the new action to occur. Begin recording your action, then scroll through the Actions palette and play the the action you want to include. When the action has completed all steps, you can continue recording other steps or click the Stop playing/recording button if you are done. That's it: all of the steps in the default action will be performed when you play your new action.

Loading Sets

In addition to the Default Actions, the seven additional sets of actions are listed at the bottom of the Actions palette menu. If you store actions from other sources on your hard drive, you can load those actions by clicking the Actions palette list arrow, clicking Load Actions, then choosing the action you want from the Load dialog box. The default sets that come with Photoshop are stored in the Photoshop Actions folder that is in the Presets folder of the Adobe Photoshop CS2 folder.

QUICKTIP

If you want to save actions to distribute to others, you must first put them in a set. You create a set by clicking the Create new set button on the Actions palette (just like creating a Layer set). Place the action or actions in a set, select the set, click the Actions palette list arrow, then click Save Actions.

FIGURE 24
A droplet on the desktop

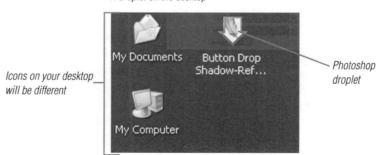

Icons on your desktop
will be different

Photoshop
droplet

Include a default action within an action

1. Verify that the **Set Layer Styles of current layer step** at the bottom of the Actions palette is active (the last step in the Button Drop Shadow action).

   TIP If your Actions palette becomes too messy, you can clear it by clicking the Actions palette list arrow, then clicking Clear All Actions. To restore the Default Actions set, click the Actions palette list arrow, then click Reset Actions.

2. Verify that the **Button layer** is active in the Layers palette.

3. Click the **Begin recording button** ● on the Actions palette.

4. Scroll to the top of the Actions palette, then click the **Water Reflection (type) action**, as shown in Figure 25.

You prepared to insert the Water Reflection default action into the Button Drop Shadow action. If this action had been applied to a type layer, it would have been rasterized before the effect was applied.

FIGURE 25

Action to be added to the Button Drop Shadow action

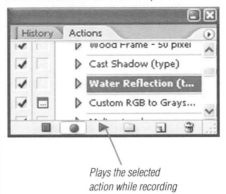

Plays the selected action while recording

FIGURE 26

Example of a Web site that offers Photoshop Actions

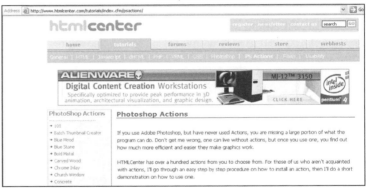

Finding actions on the Web

Actions can be fun to design, and the more practice you get, the more you'll want to make use of them. But no matter how good you are, time is at a premium for most of us. You can find great actions on the Web—and many of them are free! Figure 26 shows one example of a Web site that offers free actions. Just connect to the Web, open your browser and favorite search engine, and search on the text "Photoshop Actions."

FIGURE 27

Water Reflection action in the Button Drop Shadow action

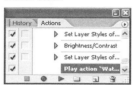

FIGURE 29

Modified Layers palette

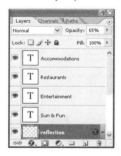

FIGURE 28

Image with replayed action

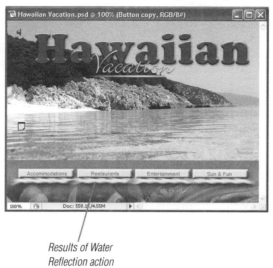

Results of Water Reflection action

Play an existing action in a new action

1. Click the **Play selection button** ▶ on the Actions palette.

2. Click the **Stop playing/recording button** ■ on the Actions palette. A new layer is created. Compare your Actions palette to Figure 27.

3. Click the **History palette tab** History, then click **Snapshot 1**.

    TIP   Some default actions create a snapshot as their initial step. For this reason, you might see multiple snapshots on the History palette.

4. Click the **Actions palette tab** Actions.

5. Click the **Button Drop Shadow action**.

6. Click the **Play selection button** ▶ on the Actions palette.

7. Save your work, then compare your image to Figure 28 and your Layers palette to Figure 29.

    The Water Reflection action added a reflection beneath the buttons.

You included the Water Reflection action in the Button Drop Shadow action. You used the snapshot to revert to the image's original appearance and replayed the action, which modified the image.

Understanding scripts and actions

Like an action, a script is a series of commands that manipulate objects in Photoshop and programs of the Creative Suite. While individual actions are tremendous time savers, you can use Photoshop Scripts to save even more time performing repetitive tasks. A script has the following advantages over an action in that it can:

- contain conditional logic, giving it the ability to make decisions based on content.
- perform actions that involve multiple applications, such as those programs found in the Creative Suite.
- open, save, and rename files.
- be copied from one computer to another. An action would have to be recreated or turned into a droplet.
- use variable file paths to locate and open a file.

You can manage scripts within Photoshop using the Script Events Manager, which is accessed by clicking File on the menu bar, pointing to Scripts, then clicking Script Events Manager.

Create a droplet

1. Click **File** on the menu bar, point to **Automate**, then click **Create Droplet**.

2. Click **Choose** in the Create Droplet dialog box.

   The Save dialog box opens.

3. Type **Button Drop Shadow-Reflection** in the File name text box (Win) or Save as text box (Mac) in the Save dialog box.

4. Click the **Save in list arrow** (Win) or **Where list arrow** (Mac), then click **Desktop**, as shown in Figure 30.

   TIP   You can create a droplet on your hard drive by clicking the Save in list arrow (Win) or Where list arrow (Mac), and clicking the location where you want to store the file.

5. Click **Save**.

6. Click the **Action list arrow** in the Create Droplet dialog box, then click **Button Drop Shadow** (if it is not already selected). Compare your dialog box settings to Figure 31.

7. Click **OK**.

You created a droplet using the Button Drop Shadow action and saved it to the desktop for easy access.

FIGURE 30
Save dialog box

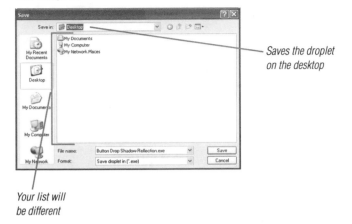

Saves the droplet
on the desktop

Your list will
be different

FIGURE 31
Create Droplet dialog box

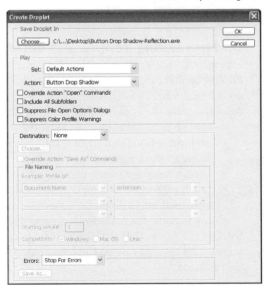

FIGURE 32
Droplet on desktop

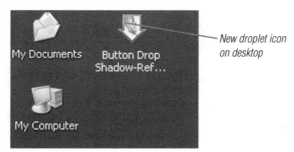

New droplet icon
on desktop

FIGURE 33
Image updated by droplet

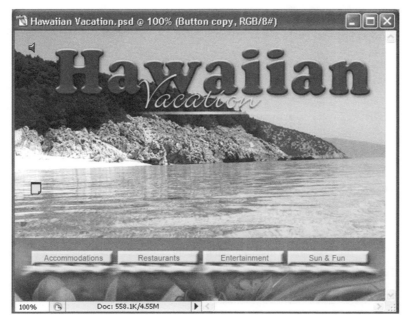

1. Minimize all open windows so the desktop is visible, then compare your desktop to Figure 32.

2. Maximize the Photoshop window.

3. Click the **History palette tab** `History`, then click **Snapshot 1**.

4. Save your work, close the Hawaiian Vacation image, then minimize Photoshop.

   TIP   When Photoshop is *not* running, activating a droplet automatically launches the program.

5. Locate the closed Hawaiian Vacation image on your hard drive, using the file management program of your choice, then adjust the windows so you can see the Hawaiian Vacation file and the droplet icon on the desktop.

6. Drag the **Hawaiian Vacation file** onto the droplet icon (on the desktop).

   The Photoshop window is restored, the Hawaiian Vacation image opens, and the action is replayed.

   TIP   Sometimes a file automatically closes after a droplet has been applied. To see the applied droplet, you must reopen the file.

7. Save your work, then compare your screen to Figure 33.

8. Close the file and exit Photoshop, then drag the **droplet** to the location where your Data Files are stored.

You returned the image to its original appearance by using Snapshot 1 on the History palette, and closed the file. Then you tested the droplet by dropping the Hawaiian Vacation file onto the droplet.

Power User Shortcuts

Key: Menu items are indicated by ➤ between the menu name and its command. Blue bold letters are shortcuts for selecting tools on the toolbox.

to do this:	use this method:
Apply droplet	Drag closed Photoshop file onto droplet
Change audio annotation icon color	🔊 or **Shift N**, click Annotation color color box, choose color, then click OK
Change author display	📝, or **Shift N**, then type name in Name of author for annotations text box
Change Note icon color	📝, or **Shift N**, click Annotation color color box, choose color, then click OK
Close an open note	Click Note close button
Collapse action detail	▼
Create a batch	File ➤ Automate ➤ Batch
Create a droplet	File ➤ Automate ➤ Create Droplet
Create a note	📝, or **Shift N**, then click where you want the note to appear
Create a snapshot	📷 on the History palette
Create an action	🔲 on the Actions palette, select options, then click Record

to do this:	use this method:
Create an audio annotation	🔊 or **Shift N**, click where you want the icon to appear, click Start, record annotation, then click Stop
Delete a note	Select note, press [Delete]
Expand action detail	▶
Open a closed note	Double-click note icon
Play an action	▶
Play audio annotation	Double-click audio icon
Record an action	⚫, then perform tasks
Record an action from another set	⚫, click existing action in another set, click ▶, then click ⬛
Return Actions palette to original size and location	Window ➤ Workspace ➤ Reset Palette Locations
Revert image to original appearance using a snapshot	History, click snapshot
Stop recording	⬛
Toggle Actions palette between list and button modes	⊙, then click Button Mode

So much of our work is collaborative therefore Photoshop includes two annotation tools that make communicating with teammates easy. Within any Photoshop file, you can embed text annotations and you can insert audio annotations (if your computer has the appropriate sound equipment). Text annotations are similar to sticky notes, and audio annotations are sound messages that can be played back through your computer's speakers.

You can speed up repetitive tasks by creating and using actions. You can record your own actions to perform all types of tasks, and you can even incorporate actions supplied with Photoshop into your own actions. Because not everyone gets it right from the start, you can add steps to an action, and modify existing steps. You can even create a stand-alone icon, called a droplet, that others can use to run your actions.

What You Have Learned:

- How to create a written annotation
- How to create an audio annotation
- How to access and display actions
- How to record and playback an action
- How to add steps to an action
- How to modify steps in an action
- How to incorporate default actions within an action
- How to create and run a droplet

Key Terms

Audio Annotation   A sound file that is saved within an image.

Written annotation   Text similar to a sticky note that is attached to a file.

List mode   View that makes it possible to see the details within each action.

Button mode   View that displays the name of each action without the detail, and lets you play the action by clicking a button.

Default action   An action that is prerecorded and tested, and comes with Photoshop.

Droplet   A stand-alone action in the form of an icon.

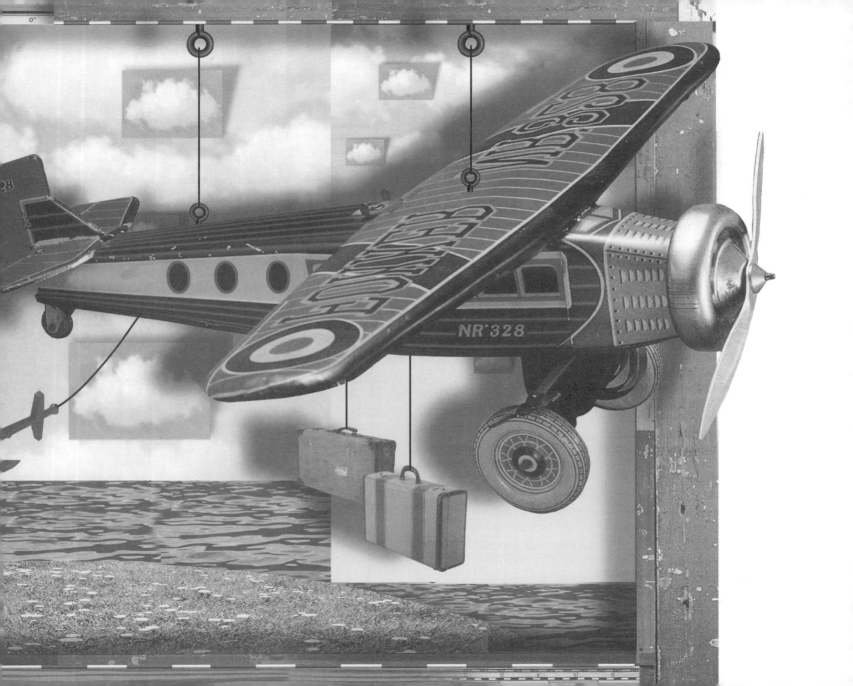

16

CREATING IMAGES FOR
THE WEB

1. Learn about ImageReady.

2. Optimize images for Web use.

3. Create a button for a Web page.

4. Create slices in an image.

5. Create a rollover effect.

6. Create and play basic animation.

7. Add tweening and frame delay.

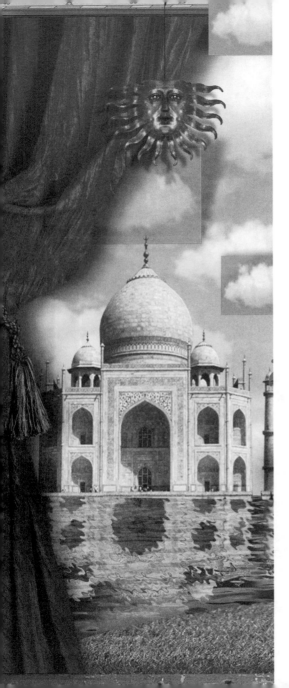

16 CREATING IMAGES FOR
THE WEB

Using Photoshop for the Web

In addition to creating exciting images that can be professionally printed, you can use the tools in Photoshop to create images for use on the Web. Once you have a Photoshop image, you can use Adobe ImageReady CS2 to add the dimension and functionality required by today's Web audience. ImageReady, an additional program in the Creative Suite, is installed by default when you install Photoshop.

Understanding Web Graphics

With ImageReady, you can tailor images and graphics specifically for the Web by creating buttons and other features unique to Web pages. Using both Photoshop and ImageReady, you can combine impressive graphics with interactive functionality to create an outstanding Web site.

QUICKTIP

ImageReady provides the capabilities for dividing one image into smaller, more manageable parts, and for creating more efficient Web-ready files.

Jumping Between Programs

Photoshop and ImageReady are designed to work together, so you can jump between the two programs to make changes in each program. Each program updates changes made in the other. This means you can work in ImageReady, return to Photoshop to tweak an image, then jump back to ImageReady to preview what your work will look like in your Web browser.

Tools You'll Use

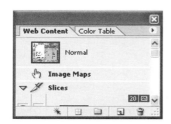

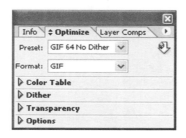

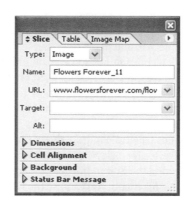

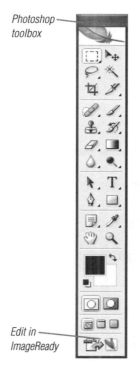

Photoshop toolbox

Edit in ImageReady

ImageReady toolbox

Slice Tool

Rectangle Tool

Toggle Slices Visibility

Preview in Default Browser

Edit in Photoshop

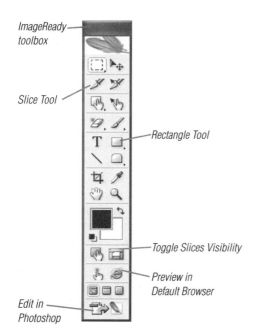

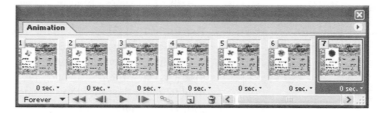

LEARN ABOUT
IMAGEREADY

What You'll Do

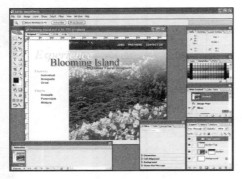

▶ In this lesson, you'll open and rename a file in Photoshop, and then view the image in ImageReady. You'll also change your view of the image, exit ImageReady, then return to Photoshop.

Using Photoshop and ImageReady

Photoshop and ImageReady share similar tools and features, such as the toolbox, the options bar, and many palettes. Most features work identically, but some are found in different locations. For example, in Photoshop, the History palette appears above the Layers palette, but in ImageReady, the History palette is grouped with the Layers and Actions palettes. Figure 1 shows the ImageReady workspace. In addition to selecting the Edit in ImageReady command off the file menu, you can use the Edit in ImageReady button (in Photoshop) or the Edit in Photoshop button (in ImageReady) to switch between the two programs.

Previewing Files for the Web

You can add many sophisticated Web effects to the files you create in ImageReady. To insert and view them in a Web page, you need to follow the procedures dictated by your HTML editor. HTML (Hypertext Markup Language) is the language used for creating Web pages. You can preview most Web effects directly in Photoshop or ImageReady. ImageReady also allows you to preview your files in your Web browser by clicking the Preview in Default Browser button on the toolbox.

> **QUICKTIP**
>
> Because monitor quality, operating systems, and Web browsers will vary from user to user, you should preview your images on as many different systems as possible before you finalize an image for the Web.

Updating Files

Each time you jump between Photoshop and ImageReady, the active program automatically updates the current file. This ensures that you always work with the most current version of the image. To make sure Photoshop is set to update files automatically, click Edit (Win) or Photoshop (Mac) on the menu bar, point to Preferences, click General, select the Auto-Update Open Documents check box, then click OK. To make sure ImageReady is set up to update files automatically, click Edit (Win) or ImageReady (Mac) on the menu bar, point to Preferences, click General, select the Auto-Update Open Documents check box, then click OK.

QUICKTIP

A History state is created whenever Photoshop or ImageReady is automatically updated. This new state lets you know that an update occurred.

Creating Navigational and Interactive Functionality

You can divide an image you create for a Web site into many smaller sections, or slices. You use a **slice** to assign special features, such as rollovers, links, and animation, to specific areas within an image. A **rollover** changes an object's appearance when the pointer passes over (or the user clicks) a specific area of the image. An image sequence, or **animation**, simulates an object moving on a Web page. You can create an animation by making slight changes to several images, and then adjusting the timing between their appearances. When you convert an image to HTML, slices become cells in an HTML table, and rollovers and animations become files in object folders.

Switching Between ImageReady and Other Programs

You can switch from ImageReady to other graphics programs or HTML programs, and then automatically update those files. To set up the programs that you want to switch to, click File on the menu bar, point to Jump To, click Other Graphics Editor or Other HTML Editor, then locate the program you want.

FIGURE 1
ImageReady work area

Similar toolbox

Edit in Photoshop button

Creates the appearance of animation

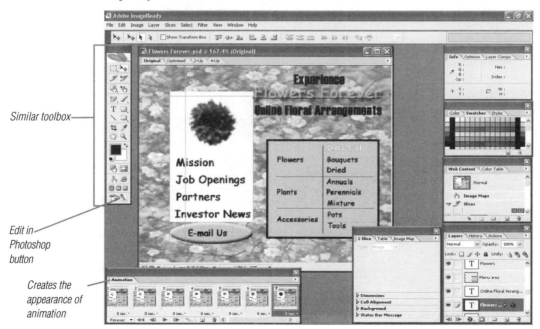

Switch to ImageReady

1. Start Photoshop, open PS 16-1.psd from the drive and folder where your Data Files are stored, then save it as **Blooming Island**.

   TIP Update the text layers if you see a message box stating that some text layers need to be updated before they can be used for vector-based output.

2. Click the **Default Foreground and Background Colors button** ▪️◻ on the toolbox.

3. Verify that the rulers display in pixels.

4. Click the **Edit in ImageReady button** 🔲 on the toolbox.

5. Click the **Toggle Slices Visibility button** 🔲 on the toolbox if the slices are not visible, then display the Animation palette if it is not visible.

   The Blooming Island image opens in ImageReady. Compare your screen to Figure 2.

You opened an image in Photoshop, then jumped to ImageReady.

FIGURE 2
Image in ImageReady

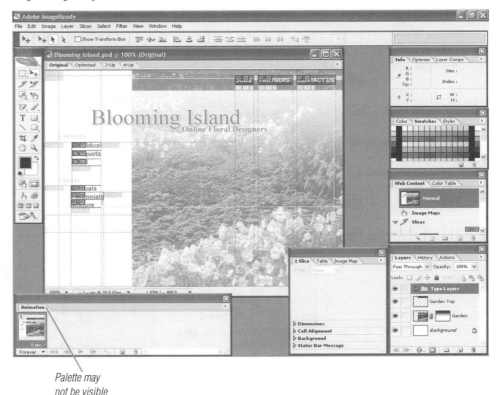

Palette may
not be visible

FIGURE 3

Adjusted image view in ImageReady

Changes
on-screen
view

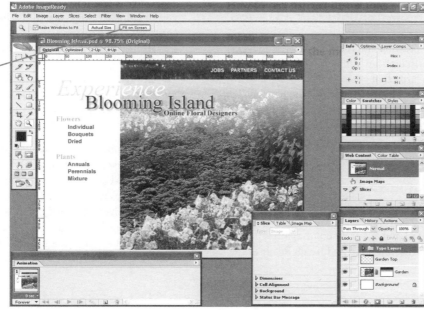

1. Click **View** on the menu bar, then click **Rulers** to display the Rulers.

   > TIP   Many commands, such as displaying rulers, and many shortcut keys are the same in ImageReady and Photoshop.

2. Click **View** on the menu bar, then deselect **Extras** (if necessary).

3. Click the **Zoom Tool** 🔍 on the toolbox.

4. Verify that the **Resize Windows To Fit check box** ☑ Resize Windows To Fit is selected.

5. Click the **Fit on Screen button** on the options bar, then compare your screen to Figure 3.

   The toolbox contains a few tools that help you define areas in a Web image. The History and Actions palette are grouped with the Layers palette. Several new palettes, such as Web Content and Slice, are open by default.

6. Click **View** on the menu bar, point to **Show**, then click **Guides** to display the guides.

7. Click **File** on the menu bar, then click **Exit** (Win) or click **ImageReady** on the menu bar, then click **Quit ImageReady** (Mac).

   ImageReady closes, but Photoshop is still open and available for use.

You adjusted your view of the image, examined the ImageReady program window, and then exited ImageReady.

OPTIMIZE IMAGES
FOR WEB USE

What You'll Do

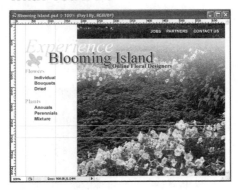

 In this lesson, you'll optimize an image for the Web in both Photoshop and ImageReady. Then you'll modify the optimized image in Photoshop to create a transparent effect.

Understanding Optimization

You can create an awesome image in Photoshop and merge and flatten layers conscientiously, but still end up with a file so large that no one will wait for it to download from the Web. Both ImageReady and Photoshop contain features that let you precisely optimize an image. An **optimized** file is just as beautiful as a non-optimized file; it's just a fraction of its original size.

Optimizing a File

When you optimize a file, you save it in a Web format that balances the need for detail and accurate color against file size. Both Photoshop and ImageReady allow

you to compare an image in the following common Web formats:

- JPEG (Joint Photographic Experts Group)
- GIF (Graphics Interchange Format)
- PNG (Portable Network Graphics)
- WBMP (a Bitmap format used for mobile devices, such as cell phones)

In Photoshop, the Save For Web dialog box has four view tabs: Original, Optimized, 2-Up, and 4-Up. See Figure 4. The Original view displays the graphic without any optimization. The Optimized, 2-Up, and 4-Up views display the image in its original format, as well as other file formats. You can change the file format by clicking one of

Exporting an image

You can export an image with transparency in Photoshop using the Export Transparent Image command on the Help menu. The Export Transparent Image Wizard guides you in selecting the area you want to be transparent. Most commonly, the background becomes transparent instead of white. By default, Photoshop saves the file as an Encapsulated PostScript (EPS) file.

the windows in the dialog box, then clicking the Settings list arrow. In ImageReady, an image opens in the optimization window, where you can change views and formats the same way you do in Photoshop. See Figure 5.

QUICKTIP

You can also use the Photoshop Save As command on the File menu to quickly save a file under a different graphics format by using Photoshop's default settings.

Understanding Compression

GIF, JPEG, and PNG compression create compressed files without losing substantial components. Figuring out when to use which format can be challenging. Often, the decision may rest on whether color or image detail is most important. JPEG files are compressed by discarding image pixels; GIF and PNG files are compressed by limiting colors. GIF is an 8-bit format (the maximum number of colors a GIF file can

contain is 256) that supports one transparent color; JPEG does not support transparent color. Having a transparent color is useful if you want to create a fade-out or superimposed effect. Because the JPEG format discards, or *loses*, data when it compresses a file, it is known as **lossy**. GIF and PNG formats are **lossless**—they compress solid color areas but maintain detail.

FIGURE 4
Optimizing files in Photoshop

Hand Tool

Slice Select Tool

Zoom Tool

Eyedropper Tool

Eyedropper Color

Toggle Slices Visibility Tool

Original image format and size

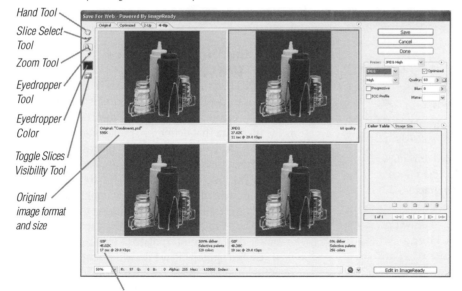

Settings indicate size and download time

FIGURE 5
Optimizing files in ImageReady

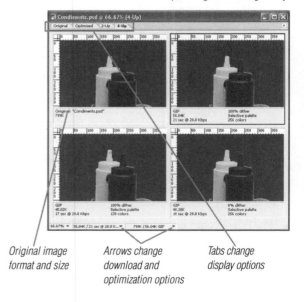

Original image format and size

Arrows change download and optimization options

Tabs change display options

Comparing Image Types

Figure 6 compares optimization of a photograph with a solid color background optimized in both GIF and JPEG formats. If you look closely, you'll see that the GIF colors look streaky and appear to be broken-up, while the JPEG colors appear crisp and seamless. Table 1 lists optimization format considerations. Because you cannot assume that other users will have access to the latest software and hardware, it's a good idea to compare files saved under different formats and optimization settings, and preview them in different browsers and on different computers. Yes, this can be time-consuming, but you'll end up with images that look great in all Web pages.

FIGURE 6
Photograph optimization comparison

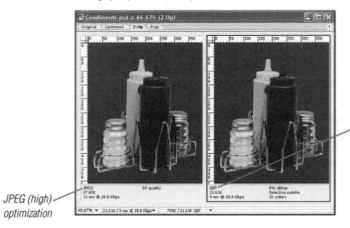

GIF (64 no dither) optimization

JPEG (high) optimization

TABLE 1: Optimization Format Considerations

format	file format	use with
JPEG (very common)	All 24-bit (works best with 16 M colors)	Photographs, solid colors, soft edges
GIF (very common)	8-bit (256 colors)	Detailed drawings, sharp edges (logos, vector graphics), animation
PNG (less common)	24-bit (16 M colors)	Detailed drawings, logos, bitmap graphics
WBMP (less common)	1-bit (2 colors)	Cell phones and other mobile devices

Using the Digital Negative format [DNG]

Adobe DNG (Digital Negative format) is an archival format for camera raw files that contains the raw image data created within a digital camera, as well as the metadata that define what that data means. This format is designed to provide compatibility among the increasing number of Camera Raw file formats. The following Saving options are available:

- Compressed (lossless), which applies a lossless compression to the DNG file.
- Convert to Linear Image, which stores the image data in an interpolated format.
- Embed Original Raw File, which stores the entire original camera raw image data in the DNG file, and JPEG Preview, which specifies whether to embed a JPEG preview in the DNG file.

FIGURE 7
Save For Web dialog box

Outline surrounds selected format

Displayed formats may differ

Magnification level

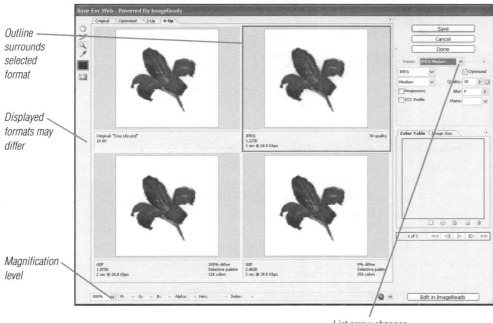

List arrow changes format

Using Transparency and Matte options

When using the Save for Web command in Photoshop, you can determine how the Transparency and Matte options are optimized within an image. Using both of these tools in a variety of combinations, you can blend fully or partially transparent pixels with a color from the Color Picker or Matte menu.

Optimize an image in Photoshop

1. Open PS 16-2.psd from the drive and folder where your Data Files are stored, then save it as **Day Lily** in the folder where your Data Files are stored.

2. Click **File** on the menu bar, then click **Save for Web**.

3. Click the **4-Up tab**.

4. Click the **Zoom Tool** on the left side of the Save For Web dialog box.

5. Click the **top-right image** until all four images are enlarged to **300%**.

   TIP   The zoom level is displayed in the lower-left corner of the Save For Web dialog box. You can also click the Zoom Level list arrow and select a magnification.

6. Click the **Preset list arrow**, click **JPEG Medium**, then compare your dialog box to Figure 7. The Save button saves a file in the selected format, the Cancel button resets the settings and closes the dialog box, and the Done button remembers the current settings and closes the dialog box.

7. Click **Cancel** in the Save For Web dialog box.

   TIP   To complete optimization of the file, you can click the desired format in the dialog box, click Save, enter a new name (if necessary) in the Save Optimized As dialog box, then click Save. You can optimize an image in ImageReady with the same results.

You opened a file, then used the Save for Web command on the File menu to open the Save For Web dialog box. You observed the differences between possible formats, then closed the dialog box without completing optimization.

Optimize an image in ImageReady

1. Click the **Edit in ImageReady button** 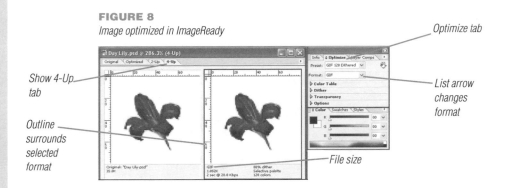 on the toolbox.

   The Day Lily file opens in ImageReady.

2. Click the **Show 4-Up tab** in the ImageReady work area.

   TIP To create a new view of the current image, drag any view tab to a new location in the workspace.

3. Click the **Zoom Tool** 🔍 (if it is not already selected).

4. Click the **Fit on Screen button**
   Fit on Screen on the options bar.

5. Click the **Optimize palette tab**, click the **Preset list arrow**, then click **GIF 128 Dithered**. Compare your image to Figure 8.

6. Click **File** on the menu bar, then click **Save Optimized As**.

7. Navigate to the folder where your Data Files are stored, verify that **Day Lily** is in the File name text box (Win) or the Save As text box (Mac), then click **Save**.

   The optimized file is saved in the designated file and folder. You'll notice that the saved file has hyphens automatically inserted where there were spaces.

8. Click **File** (Win) or **ImageReady** (Mac) on the menu bar, then click **Exit** (Win) or **Quit ImageReady** (Mac) to close ImageReady without saving changes.

   When you exited ImageReady, the file also closed in Photoshop.

You jumped to ImageReady, optimized a file, and then saved the optimized file. After you closed ImageReady, the PSD version of the Day Lily file automatically closed in Photoshop. When you optimize a file, a new copy of the file is saved, and no changes are made to the original.

FIGURE 8
Image optimized in ImageReady

Optimize tab

Show 4-Up tab

List arrow changes format

Outline surrounds selected format

File size

Using raw data from digital cameras

If you're a digital camera photographer, or have access to digital photos, you'll appreciate the ability to use images in the 16-bit Camera Raw format. Sure, the files are twice the size, but the resolution contains 65,000 data points (versus the 256 data points in an 8-bit image). Once an image with raw data is opened, the Camera Raw interface appears. This interface contains magnification and color correction options.

The Camera RAW dialog box shown in the figure contains four buttons in the lower-right corner: Save, Open, Cancel, and Done. The Open button applies changes and opens the image. The Save button converts and saves an image. The Done button applies the changes and closes the dialog box without opening the image. The Cancel button closes the dialog box without accepting any changes. The Camera Raw plug-in is available as a free download from *www.adobe.com* <http://www.adobe.com>. Check this site frequently, as additional camera support is often added to this plug-in.

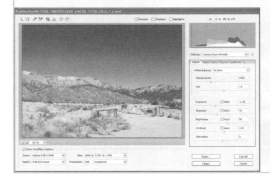

FIGURE 9
Optimized file moved to image

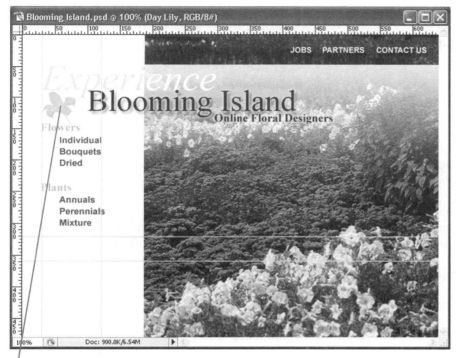

GIF image
in document

Using Camera Raw settings and preferences

The Camera Raw file format is similar to a digital negative. It contains all the information a camera has about a specific image and it is also similar to the TIFF format. It is similar to TIFF in that it does not discard any color information, yet it is smaller than an uncompressed TIFF. Camera Raw settings can be saved (up to 100 settings) and then applied to a specific camera or for specific lighting conditions. The Apply Camera Raw Settings menu allows you to save current settings and add them to the Settings menu, as well as modify settings for Exposure, Shadows, Brightness, Contrast, and Saturation.

Place an optimized image

1. Open the Blooming Island.psd file in Photoshop, display the guides, then select the **Garden Top layer**.

2. Open Day-Lily.gif.

3. Click **Select** on the menu bar, click **Color Range**, then verify that the **Image option button** is selected and that the Fuzziness text box is set to **0**.

4. Click the **white background** of the image in the Color Range dialog box, select the **Invert check box**, then click **OK**.

5. Click the **Move Tool** on the toolbox, verify that the **Show Transform Controls check box** is not selected, then use the **Move pointer** to drag the selection to the Blooming Island image.

6. Drag the day lily so the top-left corner of the image is at **30 X/90 Y** just below the "E" in Experience.

7. Set the Opacity setting to **25%** on the Layers palette.

8. Click the **Layers palette list arrow** , then click **Layer Properties**.

9. Type **Day Lily** in the Name text box, then click **OK**.

10. Click **Window** on the menu bar, click **Day-Lily.gif**, then close the file.

11. Save your work, display the guides, then compare your screen to Figure 9.

You opened an optimized file in Photoshop, dragged it into the Blooming Island image, adjusted the opacity setting, then renamed the layer. The optimized file will be easier for a viewer to load in any Web browser.

CREATE A BUTTON FOR
A WEB PAGE

What You'll Do

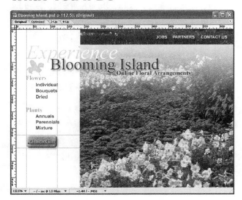

In this lesson, you'll create and name a layer in ImageReady, then create a button to use in a Web page. You'll add type to the button, apply a style, and then link the type and button layers so they can be used as a single object in a Web page.

Learning About Buttons

A **button** is a graphical interface that helps visitors navigate through and interact with a Web site with ease. ImageReady provides several ways for you to create buttons. You can create your own shape, apply a prefor-matted button style, or import a button you've already created. You can assign a variety of actions to a button so that the button completes the required task when clicked or moused-over by someone viewing the site in a Web browser.

Creating a Button

You can create a button by drawing a shape with a shape tool, such as a rectangle, on a layer. After you create the shape, you can stylize it by applying a color or style, and then you can add some text that will explain what will happen when it's clicked.

Saving a file for the Web

Before you can use Photoshop or ImageReady files on the Web, you must first convert them to the HTML format. You can convert all of the slices in ImageReady to HTML by clicking Edit on the menu bar, pointing to Copy HTML Code, and then clicking For All Slices. ImageReady stores the HTML code on the Clipboard so that you can then paste it into your Web page using an HTML editor. Photoshop and ImageReady use default settings when you save optimized images for the Web. You can specify the output settings for HTML format, your HTML editor, and the way image files, background files, and slices are named and saved. To change the output settings in Photoshop, click the Optimize Menu list arrow in the Save For Web dialog box, then click Edit Output Settings. In ImageReady, click an option you want to change from the Output Settings command on the File menu.

QUICKTIP
You can add a link to a button so that when you click it, a new Web page will appear.

Applying a Button Style

You can choose from 65 predesigned ImageReady button styles on the Styles palette, or you can create your own. To apply a style to a button, you must first select a style, then create a button shape.

Before creating the button, double-click one of the button styles on the Styles palette, which appear as thumbnails, or click a style name from the Set style for new layer list arrow on the options bar. Figure 10 shows the button styles on the ImageReady Styles palette. You can also modify a button with a style already applied to it by first clicking one of the shape tools, and then choosing a new style from the Styles palette.

QUICKTIP
Having both Photoshop and ImageReady open will significantly tax your computer's resources. When you're primarily working in ImageReady, it's a good idea to close any unnecessary programs (including Photoshop) and update your files frequently.

FIGURE 10
Button styles in ImageReady

Style thumbnail

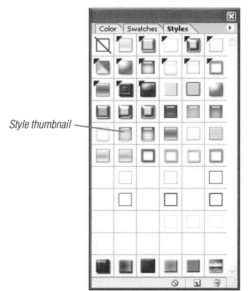

Changing a Web image using Variables

When designing a Web page, you may want to experiment with a variety of text samples (such as text on a button) or different imagery for different occasions. You can do this in ImageReady using Variables. This feature lets you define many data sets, each containing different text or pixel information. You can then insert each data set and easily make changes to your Web page. You define data sets by clicking Image on the menu bar, pointing to Variables, then clicking Define. Each data set is defined for a specific layer, which is selected from the Layer list arrow in the Variables dialog box. You can also view existing data sets for the active file by clicking Next in the Variables dialog box. Once the data sets are defined, you can quickly switch between them by clicking Image on the menu bar, then clicking Apply Data Set. This dialog box lets you apply a specific data set by clicking its name.

Create a button

1. Jump to ImageReady.

2. Click the **Zoom Tool** 🔍 on the toolbox.

3. Click the **Fit on Screen button**
   [Fit on Screen] on the options bar.

4. If necessary, display the rulers in pixels, and view Guides and Extras.

5. Verify that the **Day Lily layer** on the Layers palette is selected.

6. Click the **Create a new layer button** 🔲 on the Layers palette.

   A new layer, Layer 1, appears at the top of the Layers palette, and beneath the Type Layers set.

7. Double-click the name **Layer 1** on the Layers palette, type **QuickGift Button**, then press **[Enter]** (Win) or **[return]** (Mac).

8. Click the **Rounded Rectangle Tool** 🔲 on the toolbox.

   ❙ TIP   The Rounded Rectangle Tool might be hidden beneath the Rectangle Tool.

9. Click the **Set style for new layer list arrow** 🔲⌄ on the options bar, then click **Button-Stone**, as shown in Figure 11.

10. Using the guides as a reference to create a shape beneath the word Mixture in the left column, drag the **Marquee pointer** ✛ from approximately **30 X/320 Y** to **120 X/360 Y**.

    You created the shape that will be used for a button.

You jumped from Photoshop to ImageReady, verified settings, created a new layer, selected the Rounded Rectangle Tool, selected a button style on the options bar, and then created a button.

FIGURE 11
Button style list

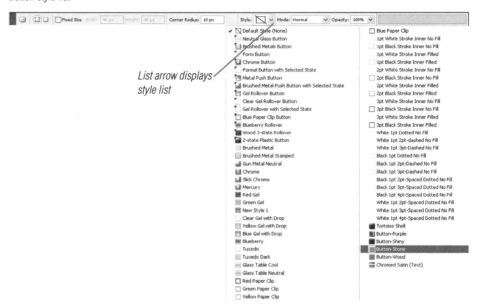

List arrow displays style list

Using Camera Raw adjustment settings

Because the Camera Raw format for each digital camera is different, you can adjust the Camera Raw settings to recreate the colors in a photo more accurately. Using the Calibrate tab, you can choose from the following profiles: ACR 3.0 (which uses the built-in camera profile for Photoshop CS2), Embedded (which uses the profile embedded in the actual Camera Raw file), or ACR 2.4 (which uses the built-in camera profile for Photoshop CS). Use the Hue and Saturation sliders to adjust the red, green, and blue in the image. Camera Raw adjustments made to the original image are always preserved, so you can adjust them repeatedly if necessary. The adjustment settings are stored within the Camera Raw database file or in a sidecar XMP file that accompanies the original Camera Raw image in a location of your choosing.

Add type to a button

1. Click the **Type Tool** T on the toolbox.
2. Click the **button shape** at approximately **40 X/345 Y**.
3. Click the **Set the text color list arrow** on the options bar, click **Other**, change the settings as follows: **R=0, G=255, B=51**, then click **OK**.
4. Click the **Set the font family list arrow** on the options bar, then click **Arial**.
5. Click the **Set the font size list arrow** on the options bar, then click **18 px**.
6. Type **QuickGift**.
7. Click the **Move Tool** ▸⊕ on the toolbox, then center the type on the button.
8. Click the **Add a layer style button** ⦸. on the Layers palette, click **Drop Shadow**, then click **OK** to accept the current settings.
9. Click the **Indicates if layer is linked button** on the QuickGift Button (shape) layer. See Figure 12.

   The type and button shape layers are linked.

10. Save your work.

You added type to a button, applied a style to it, and then linked the QuickGift type layer and the button shape layer.

FIGURE 12
Button created in image

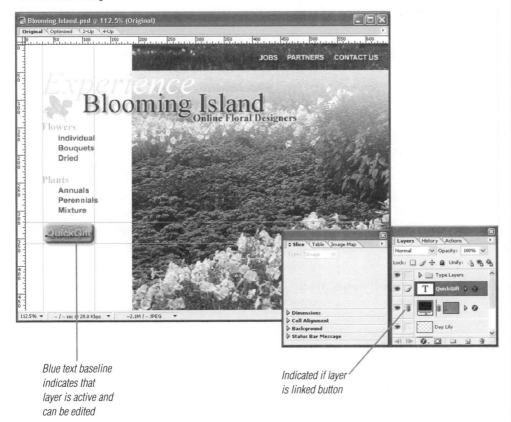

Blue text baseline
indicates that
layer is active and
can be edited

Indicated if layer
is linked button

CREATE SLICES IN
AN IMAGE

What You'll Do

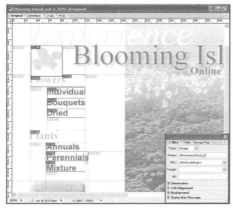

 In this lesson, you'll view the existing slices in the Blooming Island image, create slices around the Flowers and Plants type, resize a slice, and assign a Web address to the slice. You'll also create a new slice from the Day Lily layer on the Layers palette.

Understanding Slices

Using ImageReady, you not only have the ability to work with layers, but you can divide an image into unlimited smaller sections, or slices. ImageReady uses slices to determine the appearance of special effects in a Web page. A **slice** is a rectangular section of an image that you can use to apply features, such as rollovers and links, and can be created automatically or by using any marquee tool or the Slice Tool.

Using Slices

ImageReady uses two kinds of slices: a **user-slice**, which you create, and an **auto-slice**, which ImageReady creates in response to your user-slice. You can use the Slice Tool to create a slice by dragging the pointer around an area. Every time you

QUICKTIP

A slice is always rectangular, even if you create it using an elliptical marquee.

Creating an image map

In addition to assigning a Web address (URL) to a slice, you can select an area in an image and assign it a Web address. This area, known as a **hotspot**, is invisible to the user, just as a slice is. When you click the hotspot, the browser opens a different Web page. The areas that link to different Web pages are known collectively as an **image map**. Unlike a slice, an image map can be a circle, rectangle, or polygon. You can create an image map in ImageReady by selecting the Rectangle Image Map Tool, the Circle Image Map Tool, or the Polygon Image Map Tool from the toolbox. Use any of these tools to create a selection, click the Image Map palette tab, then type a Web address in the URL text box. When you position the mouse over the hotspot in your browser, the Web address appears on the status bar.

create a slice, ImageReady automatically creates at least one auto-slice, which fills in the area around the newly created slice. ImageReady automatically numbers user- and auto-slices and updates the numbering according to the location of the new user-slice. User-slices have a solid line border, auto-slices have a dotted line border, and any selected slices have a yellow border. A selected user-slice contains a bounding box and sizing handles. You can resize a slice by dragging a handle to a new location, just as you do any object.

Learning About Slice Components

By default, a slice consists of the following components:

- A colored line that helps you identify the slice type
- An overlay that dims the appearance of the unselected slices
- A number that helps you identify each individual slice
- A symbol that helps you determine the type of slice

QUICKTIP

When two slices overlap, a subslice is automatically created.

Adjusting Slice Attributes

You can adjust slice attributes by clicking Slices under the Preferences command. Figure 13 shows slice preferences. You can choose whether to display slice lines and numbers and symbols. You can also specify line color and number and symbol opacity. Slice numbering changes as you

FIGURE 13
Preferences dialog box

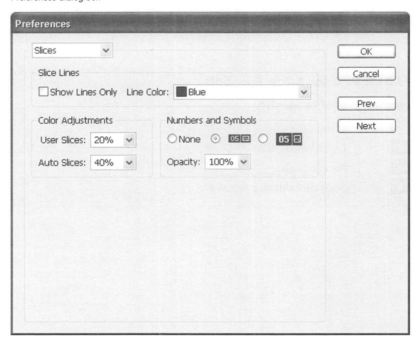

add or delete slices. Each user-slice contains a symbol indicating if it is an image slice or a layer-based slice, if the slice is linked, or if it includes a rollover effect. See Table 2 for a description of the symbols used to identify user slices.

QUICKTIP
It doesn't matter which layer, if any, is active when you create slices using the Slice Tool or any of the Marquee Tools.

Using a Layer-Based Slice

In addition to drawing a slice using the Slice Tool, you can use the New Layer Based Slice command on the Layer menu to create a slice from a layer on the Layers palette. This is an easy way of creating a slice *without* having to draw an outline.

Creating a Layer-Based Slice

Creating a layer-based slice automatically surrounds the image on the layer with a slice, which can be useful if you want to create a slice quickly or if you want a large

slice. ImageReady updates the slice whenever you modify the layer or its content. For example, the slice automatically adjusts if you move its corresponding layer on the Layers palette, or you erase pixels on the layer. In Figure 14, the active slice is an Image slice.

QUICKTIP
To delete a layer-based slice, user-slice, or auto-slice, select the slice, then press [Delete] (Win) or [delete] (Mac) or click Slices on the menu bar, then click Delete Slice.

TABLE 2: User Slice Symbols

symbol	used to identify
⊠	Image slice
◈	Layer-based slice
⊠	No image slice
⊡	Slice containing a rollover

Using the Slice Palette

The Slice palette is grouped with two other Web function palettes in ImageReady. You activate the palettes just as you do in Photoshop, by clicking the tab of the palette you want to use. You use the features on the Slice palette to assign individual settings, features, and effects to the slices you've created in your image. For example, you could set a slice to initiate an action, such as opening another Web page or an e-mail response window when a user clicks the slice on a Web page.

Assigning a Web Address to a Slice

You can assign a Web page to a selected slice by typing its Uniform Resource Locater (URL) in the URL text box. The URL is the Web page's address that appears in the Address (Internet Explorer) or Location (Netscape) text box in your browser. You can designate how that Web page will be displayed in your browser by choosing one of the options on the Target list.

FIGURE 14
Slice palette

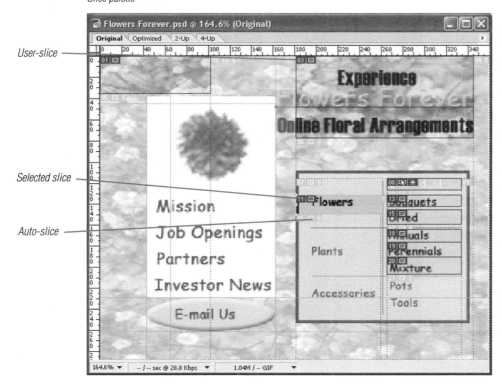

User-slice

Selected slice

Auto-slice

Create a slice using the Slice Tool

1. Click the **Zoom Tool** 🔍 on the toolbox.

2. Click the image at **50 X/200 Y** until the zoom percentage is **200%**.

3. Click the **Slice Tool** ✄ on the toolbox.

   The existing slices in the image are visible, and the colors appear faded.

   TIP You can also create a slice by creating a selection with any marquee tool, clicking Select on the menu bar, then clicking Create Slice from Selection.

4. Drag the **Slice pointer** ✄ around the **Flowers type** (from approximately **30 X/140 Y** to **120 X/160 Y**).

5. Drag the **Slice pointer** ✄ around the **Plants type** (from approximately **30 X/235 Y** to **80 X/255 Y**), then compare your slices to Figure 15.

You viewed the existing slices in the Blooming Island image and created two user-based slices, one for the Flowers text and one for the Plants text.

FIGURE 15
New slices added to image

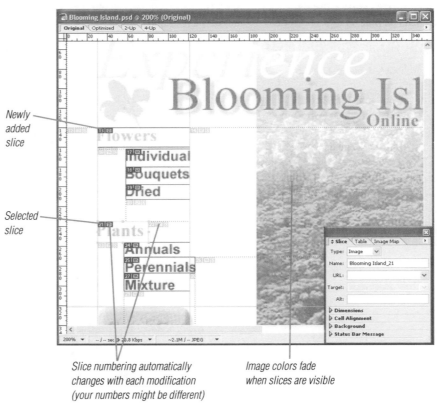

Newly added slice

Selected slice

Slice numbering automatically changes with each modification (your numbers might be different)

Image colors fade when slices are visible

FIGURE 16

New layer-based slice

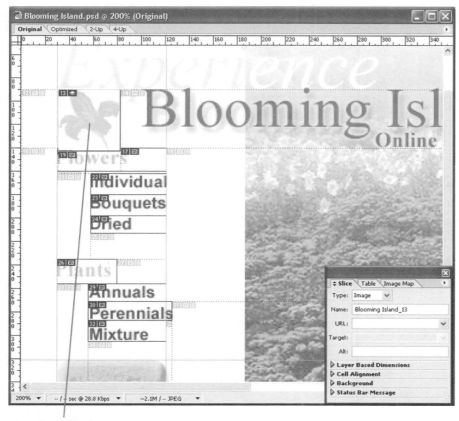

*Layer-based slice does not
display sizing handles*

1. Click the **Day Lily layer** on the Layers palette.

2. Click **Layer** on the menu bar, click **New Layer Based Slice**, then compare your screen to Figure 16.

   A new slice surrounds the Day Lily layer object. Slice numbering automatically changes with each modification so your numbers might be different.

   TIP You can also create a layer-based slice by right-clicking (Win) or [control]-clicking (Mac) the layer, and then clicking New Layer Based Slice.

You made the Day Lily layer active on the Layers palette, then created a slice based on this layer.

Resize a slice

1. Click the **Slice Select Tool** 〰 on the toolbox.

2. Click the **Plants slice**.

3. Drag the **right-middle sizing handle** ←·→ to **120 X**, compare your slice to Figure 17, then release the mouse button.

   TIP Because a layer-based slice is fitted to pixels on the layer, it does not display sizing handles when you select it.

You resized the Plants slice.

FIGURE 17
Resized slice

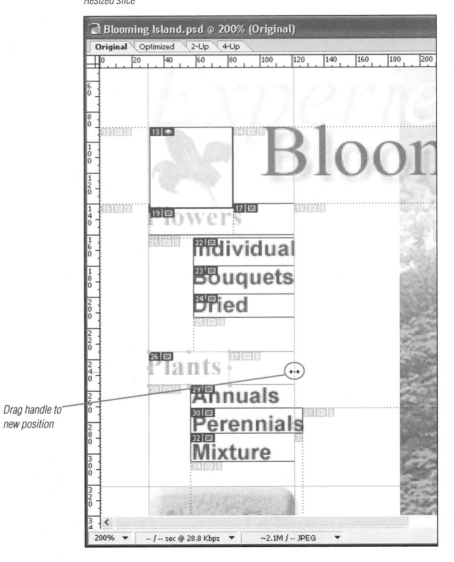

Drag handle to
new position

FIGURE 18
URL assigned to slice

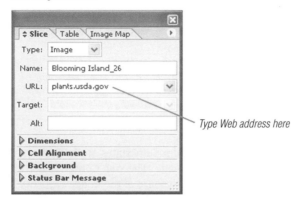

Type Web address here

FIGURE 19
Slice with URL assigned

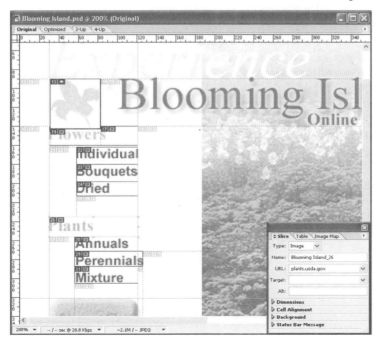

Assign a Web address to a slice

1. Click the **Slice palette tab** ‖ **⇕ Slice** ‖.

    Clicking the up/down arrows on a palette tab causes the palette to expand/contract. Clicking the *palette name* displays the palette.

2. Type **plants.usda.gov** in the URL text box, then compare your Slice palette to Figure 18 and your image to Figure 19.

    | TIP   Your slice numbers might vary.

3. Click **Select** on the menu bar, then click **Deselect Slices** to deselect the Plants slice.

    TIP   To hide slices in your image, click the Toggle Slices Visibility button on the toolbox, or click View on the menu bar, point to Show, then click Slices.

4. Save your work.

You assigned a Web address to a slice using the Slice palette, then deselected the slice.

CREATE A
ROLLOVER EFFECT

What You'll Do

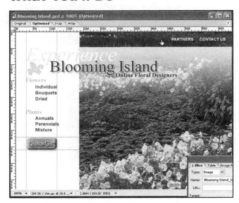

In this lesson, you'll select a slice, make the corresponding type layer active on the Layers palette, view the Web Content palette, and then create a new Over state. You'll also change the font color of the Over state and preview the rollover effect in the image.

Learning About Rollovers

How you introduce and present your content is important to maintaining your visitors' interest, and ultimately, the amount of time they spend viewing your Web site. Web sites that contain interactive features are usually more interesting to users. A rollover is one of the easiest interactive features you can add to a Web page. You can use **rollovers** to respond to a user's action, such as clicking or pointing to (rolling over) an area in your Web page. The change in the Web page can serve as a navigational aid, or it can provide additional choices to the user.

Making Rollovers Happen

The activity of the pointer determines the appearance, or **state**, of the rollover. You can add and modify states on the Web Content palette. The Web Content palette is a live storyboard of the image's journey as you first position the pointer on the image, click it, then leave the image.

Learning About Rollover States

You can add the following states to the Web Content palette: Normal, Over, Down, Click, Out, Up, and None. By default, every slice you create has a Normal state. The Normal state is how an image appears when it is inactive and without any user intervention. Most rollovers have Normal,

Over, and Down states. You can create a rollover out of images of almost any size, and you can control the appearance of each state by using tools and applying styles to its corresponding layer on the Layers palette. After a rollover is created, you can change the type of rollover effect by double-clicking the rollover state on the Web Content palette. When you do this, the Rollover State Options dialog box opens. Choose the type of rollover you want, then close the dialog box. Figure 20 shows an Over state on the Web Content palette as well as the Rollover State Options dialog box.

QUICKTIP

Because layer-based slices are automatically updated when you alter the layer, they offer the most flexibility when you use them to create rollovers.

Previewing Rollover Effects

You can preview the effects of a rollover in ImageReady or in your browser. To obtain immediate feedback on your rollover actions, click the Preview Document button on the toolbox, then move your mouse in the image, and observe the rollover behavior. For a complete review of how the rollover works, you can also click the Preview in Default Browser button on the toolbox. Your Web browser will open the file in an optimized format and display relevant HTML code in a viewing pane below the image. Exit your browser window when you have completed your rollover test. You can test the rollover in Internet Explorer, Safari, Firefox, and Netscape Navigator, assuming you have these programs loaded on your computer.

FIGURE 20
Rollover states

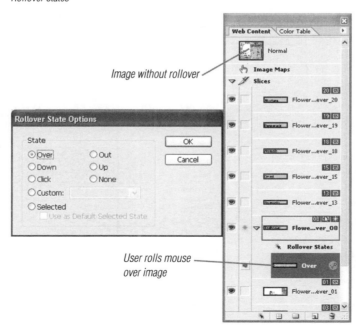

Image without rollover

User rolls mouse over image

Create a rollover state

1. Click the **Hand Tool** ✋ on the toolbox.

2. Drag the image using the **Hand pointer** ✋ down and to the left so that the JOBS type is visible in the top-right corner.

3. Click the **Slice Select Tool** 📐 on the toolbox.

4. Click the **JOBS slice**.

5. Click the **Indicates a layer set arrow** ▷ for the Type Layers layer set on the Layers palette.

6. Click the **JOBS layer** on the Layers palette.

7. Click the **Create rollover state button** 🔲 on the Web Content palette, then compare your Web Content and Layers palettes to Figure 21.

   TIP When you create a rollover, you must first select the layer on the Layers palette where you want the rollover effect to occur.

8. Click **Layer** on the menu bar, point to **Layer Style**, then click **Color Overlay**.

   The type in the Over state and in the image becomes the default color (red), or the last color selected on the Color Overlay palette.

9. Verify that your dialog box settings match those shown in Figure 22, then click **OK**.

You selected the JOBS slice and made the JOBS layer active on the Layers palette. You created a new Over state, and then changed its appearance by applying a new color to it. Animating an image requires you to create multiple Over states, each with a different appearance, to achieve an illusion of motion when the animation occurs.

FIGURE 21
Web Content and Layers palettes

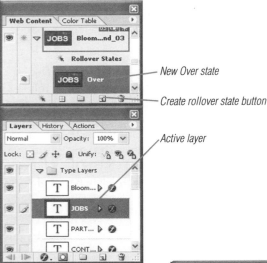

— New Over state

— Create rollover state button

— Active layer

FIGURE 22
Layer Style dialog box

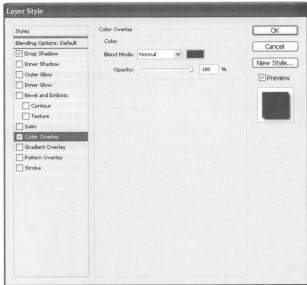

FIGURE 23
Over state appearance changed

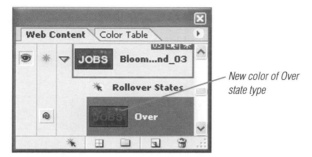

New color of Over
state type

FIGURE 24
Rollover preview in ImageReady

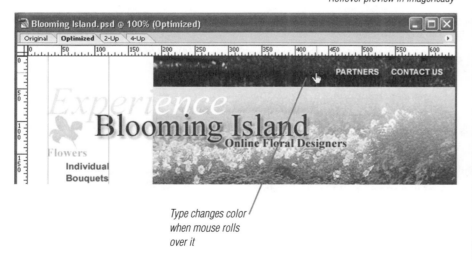

Type changes color
when mouse rolls
over it

Preview a rollover

1. Compare your Web Content palette to Figure 23.

2. Click the **Zoom Tool** 🔍 on the toolbox.

3. Press and hold **[Alt]** (Win) or **[option]** (Mac), then click the image so that the zoom percentage is 100%. 🔍

4. Click the **Toggle Slices Visibility button** 🖼 on the toolbox.

   The individual slices are no longer visible in the image.

   > TIP The Toggle Slices Visibility button remains on until you click it again to turn it off.

5. Click the first **Blooming Island state** above the Over state on the Web Content palette.

6. Click the **Preview Document button** 🖐 on the toolbox.

7. Use the **Preview pointer** 🖐 to roll the mouse over **JOBS** in the image, then compare your screen to Figure 24.

   The JOBS type changes from white to red when the mouse rolls over it.

8. Click the **Cancel Preview (Esc) button** 🚫 on the options bar.

9. Save your work, then close the Blooming Island image, leaving ImageReady open.

You toggled the slices visibility to off so the slices were no longer visible. You used the Preview Document button to preview the rollover effect in the image. Previewing an image encourages you to make sure that all your effects work correctly.

CREATE AND PLAY
BASIC ANIMATION

What You'll Do

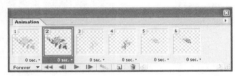

 In this lesson, you'll create basic animation by creating animation frames. For each newly created frame, you'll modify layers by hiding and showing them, and changing their opacity. You'll also play and preview the animation, to test your work.

Understanding Animation

You can use nearly any type of graphics image to create interesting animation effects in ImageReady. You can move objects in your image or overlap them so that they blend into one another. Once you place the images that you want to animate in an image, you can determine when and how you want the animation to play. If you want your users to initiate the animation, you can create different animations for each rollover state that you create on the Web Content palette.

Creating Animation on the Animation Palette

Remember that animation is nothing more than a series of still images displayed rapidly to give the illusion of motion. The Animation palette displays a thumbnail of the animation image in each frame. A **frame** is an individual image that is used in animation. When you create a frame on the Animation palette, you create a duplicate of the current frame, and can then modify it as desired. The layers that

are visible on the Layers palette appear in the selected frame, and thus, in the animation. Here's all that's involved in creating animation:

- Place images on layers in the image.
- Hide all but one layer.
- Duplicate the frame, turn off the displayed layer, then turn on the layer you want to see.

Animating Images

If you look at the Layers palette in Figure 25, you'll see that there are images on two layers. The Animation palette contains two frames: one for each of the layers. When frame 1 is selected, the man appears in the image; when frame 2 is selected, the woman appears. When the animation is played, the images of the man and woman alternate.

Moving and Deleting Frames

To move a frame to a different spot, click the frame on the Animation palette, and drag it to a new location. To select contiguous frames, press and hold [Shift], and then click the frames you want to include. To select noncontiguous frames, press and hold [Ctrl] (Win) or [⌘] (Mac), and then click the frames you want to include. You can delete a frame by clicking it on the Animation palette, then dragging it to the Deletes selected frames button on the Animation palette.

Looping the Animation
You can set the number of times the animation plays by clicking the Selects looping options list arrow on the Animation palette, then clicking Once, Forever, or Other. When you select Other, the Set Loop

Count dialog box opens, where you can enter the loop number you want.

Previewing the Animation
When you're ready to preview an animation, you have a few choices:
- You can use the buttons on the bottom of the Animation palette. When you click the Plays/stops animation button, the animation plays.
- You can also view the animation as it occurs for the user by clicking the Preview Document button on the toolbox and then initiating the animation based on the rollover state you selected.

- You can preview and test the animation in your Web browser by clicking the Preview in Default Browser button on the toolbox. The name of the default browser will display in the button tool tip.

QUICKTIP

You can change the size of the Web Content palette and Animation palette thumbnails by clicking the palette list arrow, clicking Palette Options, clicking a thumbnail size, and then clicking OK. You can select a different-sized thumbnail for each palette.

FIGURE 25
Sample of basic animation

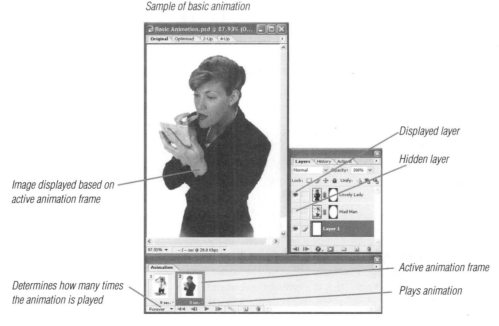

Displayed layer

Hidden layer

Image displayed based on active animation frame

Active animation frame

Determines how many times the animation is played

Plays animation

Create a rollover state

1. Open PS 16-3.psd from the drive and folder where your Data Files are stored in ImageReady, then save it as **Rose Morph**.

2. Click the **Indicates layer visibility button** 👁 on the Stems layer on the Layers palette.

3. Click the **Indicates layer visibility button** 👁 on the Little Rose layer on the Layers palette.

4. Click the **Toggle Slices Visibility button** on the toolbox.

5. Click the **Create rollover state button** 🔲 on the Web Content palette.

   A new Over state is created on the Web Content palette, as shown in Figure 26.

6. Click the **Toggle Slices Visibility button** on the toolbox.

   TIP   You can create different animations for each rollover state.

You created a new Over state on the Web Content palette, and then used the Toggle Slices Visibility button to hide the slice. You'll use this new state to create an animation sequence.

FIGURE 26
New Over state

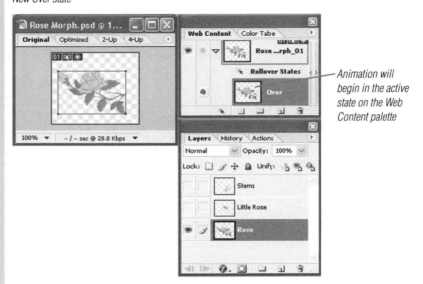

— *Animation will begin in the active state on the Web Content palette*

FIGURE 27
Macromedia Flash Export dialog box

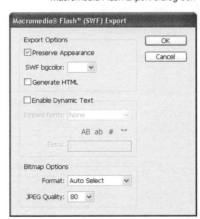

Exporting to Flash

Macromedia Flash is a popular software program for creating animations. Using ImageReady, you can export your work, including animation, directly to the Flash SWF format. To do this, open the image in ImageReady, click File on the menu bar, point to Export, then click Macromedia Flash SWF. Click the options you want in the Macromedia Flash (SWF) Export dialog box (shown in Figure 27), then click OK.

FIGURE 28

Frames created on Animation palette

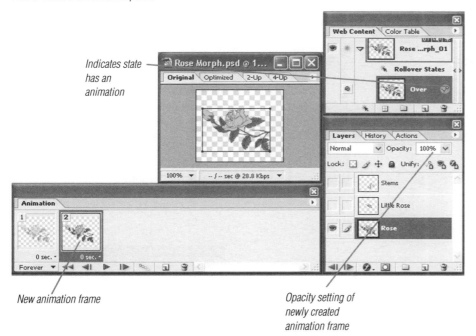

Indicates state has an animation

New animation frame

Opacity setting of newly created animation frame

FIGURE 29

Completed animation frames

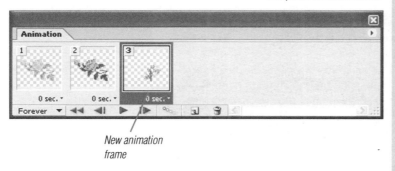

New animation frame

Create and duplicate animation frames

1. Click **Window** on the menu bar, then click **Animation** to open the Animation palette.

2. Adjust the opacity setting of the Rose layer to **50%** on the Layers palette.

3. Click the **Duplicates current frame button** on the Animation palette.

   A new Animation frame is created and is now the active frame.

4. Adjust the opacity setting of the Rose layer to **100%**, then compare your Animation palette to Figure 28.

5. Click the **Duplicates current frame button** on the Animation palette.

6. Click the **Indicates layer visibility button** on the Rose layer on the Layers palette.

7. Click the **Stems layer** to make it active, then click the **Indicates layer visibility button** on the Layers palette for this layer.

   The content from the Stems layer appears in frame 3 of the Animation palette. See Figure 29.

You created an animation frame, duplicated existing frames, and adjusted the opacity of the frames. Duplicating frames with different levels of opacity creates an animated effect when viewed in a browser.

Adjust animation frames

1. Set the opacity setting of the Stems layer to **30%**.

2. Click the **Duplicates current frame button** on the Animation palette, then adjust the opacity setting of the Stems layer to **100%**.

3. Click the **Duplicates current frame button** on the Animation palette. You have now created five frames.

4. Click the **Indicates layer visibility button** on the Stems layer to hide it.

5. Click the **Little Rose layer** on the Layers palette to make it active, then click the **Indicates layer visibility button** [ ] on the Layers palette for this layer.

6. Adjust the opacity setting to **50%**.

7. Click the **Duplicates current frame button** on the Animation palette, then adjust the opacity setting of the Little Rose layer to **100%**. Compare your screen to Figure 30.

You adjusted the opacity of frames using the Layers palette. The adjustment of frame settings lets you simulate movement when the animation is played.

FIGURE 30
Completed animation frames

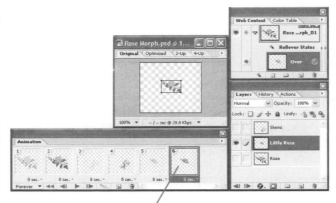

New animation frame

FIGURE 31
Export Animation Frames as Files dialog box

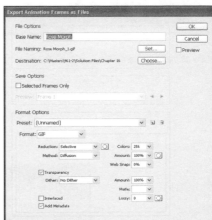

Creating a file from a frame

It's pretty cool that you can turn an image into an animation, right? So, you're probably thinking that it would really be great if you could turn an animation frame into an image. Well, by clicking File on the menu bar, pointing to Export, then clicking Animation Frames as Files, you can do just that. Figure 31 shows the Export Animation Frames as Files dialog box. Use the Choose button to determine where the new file will be saved, and the Format Options section to determine its format.

FIGURE 32
Animation displayed in browser

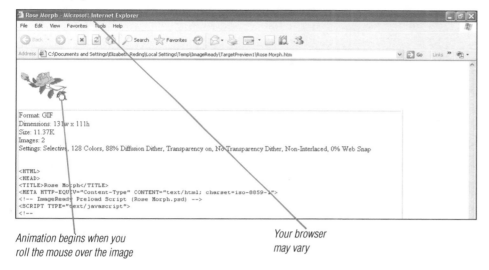

Animation begins when you roll the mouse over the image

Your browser may vary

TABLE 3: Animation Tools

tool	tool name	description
▼	Selects looping options	Determines how many times the animation plays.
◀◀	Selects first frame	Makes the first frame on the palette active.
◀▮	Selects previous frame	Makes the previous frame on the palette active.
▶	Plays/stops animation	Plays the animation.
■	Plays/stops animation	Stops the animation.
▮▶	Selects next frame	Makes the next frame to the right on the palette active.
◦◦◦◦	Tween	Creates frames in slight increments.

Play animation in the image and browser

1. Click the first frame in the animation palette, click the **Plays/stops animation button** ▶ on the Animation palette.

   The Plays/stops animation button changes its appearance depending on the current state of the animation. See Table 3 for a description of the buttons on the Animation palette.

2. Click the **Plays/stops animation button** ■ on the Animation palette.

   The animation stops, displaying the currently active frame.

3. Save your work.

4. Click the **Preview Document button** 🖑 on the toolbox.

5. Move the **Preview pointer** 🖑 over the image, view the animation, then move the pointer off the image.

   The animation begins when you roll the mouse over the image and stops when you roll it off the image.

6. Click the **Preview in Default Browser button** on the toolbox, allow the blocked content if necessary, then compare your preview to Figure 32.

7. Move the **Preview pointer** 🖑 over the image, then move the pointer off the image.

8. Close your browser.

   TIP   The animation might play differently in ImageReady than in your browser, which is why it is important to preview your files on as many different systems as possible.

You played the animation in your image, then viewed it in a browser.

ADD TWEENING AND
FRAME DELAY

What You'll Do

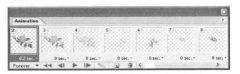

 In this lesson, you'll add tweening to animation and adjust the frame delay for a frame on the Animation palette.

Understanding Tweening

To create animation, you assemble a series of frames, then play them quickly to create the illusion of continuous motion. Each frame represents a major action point. Sometimes the variance between actions creates erratic or rough motion. To blend the motion *in between* the frames, you can tween your animation. **Tweening** adds frames that change the action in slight increments from one frame to the next. The origin of this term predates computer animation, when an artist known as an *inbetweener* hand-drew each frame that linked major action frames (at 24 frames per second!), and thus the term tweening was born.

Using Tweening on the Animation Palette

You can add tweening to a frame by clicking the Tween animation frames button on the Animation palette, and then entering the number of in-between frames you want in the Tween dialog box. You can choose whether you want the tweening to affect all layers or just the selected layer, and if you want the image to change position or opacity. You can also specify the frame on which you want the tweening to start, and specify the number of frames to add in between the frames (you can add up to 100 frames in a single tween). Figure 33 shows a two-frame animation after five tween frames were added. The opacity of the man is 100% in the first frame and 0% in the last frame. Adding five tween frames causes the two images to blend into each other smoothly, or **morph** (metamorphose).

> QUICKTIP
> You can select contiguous frames and apply the same tweening settings to them simultaneously.

Understanding Frame Delays

When you create frames on the Animation palette, ImageReady automatically sets the **frame delay**, the length of time that each frame appears. You can set the delay time in whole or partial seconds by clicking the Selects frame delay time list arrow below each frame. You can set the frame delay you want for each frame, or you can select several frames and apply the same frame delay to them.

Setting Frame Delays

To change the delay for a single frame, click a frame, click the Selects frame delay time list arrow, then click a time. To select contiguous frames, press and hold [Shift], click the frames you want to include, and then click the Selects frame delay time list arrow on *any* of the selected frames. To select noncontiguous frames, press and hold [Ctrl] (Win) or ⌘ (Mac), click the frames you want to include, then click the Selects frame delay time list arrow on any of the selected frames.

FIGURE 33
Animation palette

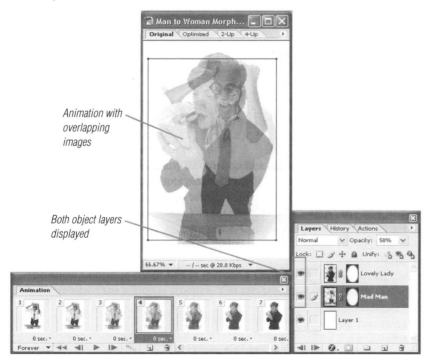

Animation with overlapping images

Both object layers displayed

Correcting pixel aspect ratio in video

This feature automatically corrects the ratio of pixels displayed for the monitor in use. Without this correction, pixels viewed in a 16:9 monitor (such as a widescreen TV) would look squashed in a 4:3 monitor (typical rectangular TV). Use the Pixel Aspect Ratio Correction to turn off the scaling correction and view the image as it looks on a computer (square pixel) monitor. Photoshop automatically converts and scales the image to the pixel aspect ratio of the non-square pixel document. Images brought in from Adobe Illustrator will also be properly scaled. You can assign a pixel aspect ratio to a document by clicking Image on the menu bar, clicking Pixel Aspect Ratio, then selecting a pixel aspect ratio. When you have selected a pixel aspect ratio, the Pixel Aspect Ratio Correction option will be checked on the View menu.

Tween animation frames

1. Click the **Cancel Preview (Esc) button** 🚫 on the options bar.

2. Click the **Over state** on the Web Content palette.

3. Click **frame 3** on the Animation palette.

4. Click the **Tween... button** ⁰ᵒ⁰ᵒ on the Animation palette.

5. Adjust the settings in your Tween dialog box so that they match those shown in Figure 34.

6. Click **OK**.

   Two additional frames are added after frame 2.

7. Click the **Plays/stops animation button** ▶ on the Animation palette, then view the animation.

8. Click the **Plays/stops animation button** ■ on the Animation palette, then compare your palette to Figure 35, which now has 8 frames.

You used the Tween animation frames button on the Animation palette to insert two new frames, then played the animation to view the results. Did you notice that the overall effect is smoother and more fluid motion?

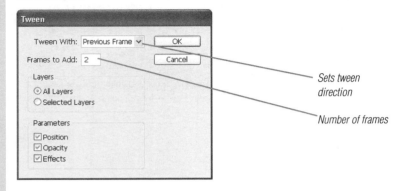

FIGURE 34
Tween dialog box

Sets tween direction

Number of frames

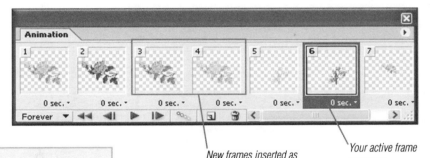

FIGURE 35
Tweening frames inserted

New frames inserted as a result of tweening

Your active frame may vary

Previewing Photoshop documents for video

When you're working on a Photoshop image that you plan to include in a digital video or video presentation, you can use the Video Preview plug-in to see real-time results as you work. Because the images you create in Photoshop are made up of square pixels, and video editing programs usually convert these to non-square pixels for video encoding, distortion can result when you import an image into a video editing program. But with Video Preview, you can check for distortion and make changes before finalizing your image. When the Video Preview plug-in is installed, and your computer is connected to a video monitor via a FireWire, you can access Video Preview by clicking File on the menu bar, pointing to Export, then clicking Video Preview. This command also lets you adjust the aspect ratio as necessary for different viewing systems, such as NTSC, PAL, or HDTV.

FIGURE 36
Frame delay menu

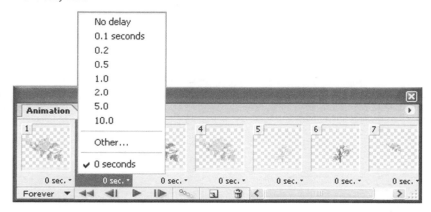

FIGURE 37
Frame delay menu

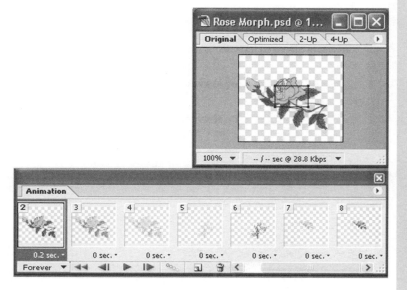

Set frame delay

1. Click **frame 2** on the Animation palette.

2. Click the **Selects frame delay time list arrow** `0 sec.` at the bottom of the selected frame.

3. Compare your frame delay menu to Figure 36, then click **0.2**.

    The frame delay for frame 2 changes to 0.2.

4. Click the **Plays/stops animation button** ▶ on the Animation palette, then view the animation.

5. Click the **Plays/stops animation button** ■ on the Animation palette.

6. Click the **Preview in Default Browser button** 🖥, on the toolbox.

7. Move the **Preview pointer** 🖑 over the image to see the effect of the rollover, then close your browser.

    TIP   Frame delays behave very differently in your browser than in ImageReady—be sure to preview them in your browser to ensure that they play the way you intend them to play.

8. Save your work, then compare your image and Animation palette to Figure 37.

9. Close the Animation palette, close the image, exit ImageReady, then exit Photoshop.

You fine-tuned your animation by changing the frame delay for frame 2, then previewed the animation in ImageReady and in your browser. It's important to preview animations in multiple Web browsers on as many computers as you can manage, so that you can see your work as others will view it.

Power User Shortcuts

to do this:	use this method:
Create a slice	✐
Cycle shape tools	**Shift U**
Cycle through optimize tabs in ImageReady	[Ctrl][Y] (Win) ⌘[Y] (Mac)
Deselect slices	[Ctrl][D] (Win) ⌘[D] (Mac)
Hide/show rulers (ImageReady)	[Ctrl][R] (Win) ⌘[R] (Mac)
Edit in ImageReady	➡▣
Edit in Photoshop	➡▣
Preview Document	✋ or Y
Preview in Browser	🐾 or your Web browser button

to do this:	use this method:
Save Optimized in ImageReady	[Ctrl][Alt][S] (Win) ⌘ option [S] (Mac)
Save Optimized As	[Ctrl][Shift][Alt][S] (Win) ⌘[Shift] option [S] (Mac)
Select all slices in ImageReady	[Ctrl][A] (Win) ⌘[A] (Mac)
Select a slice	✐
Show Animation palette	[F11] (Win)
Start animation playback	▶
Stop animation playback	■
Toggle Slices Visibility in ImageReady	▭ or Q

Key: Menu items are indicated by ➤ between the menu name and its command. Blue bold letters are shortcuts for selecting tools on the toolbox.

Working with large files is a way of life in Photoshop. Unfortunately, large files are not practical on the Web. Photoshop and Adobe ImageReady make it possible to drastically reduce file sizes without sacrificing image quality.

You can use ImageReady to create dynamic, exciting effects in your Web pages by creating interactive buttons. Visitors to your Web pages can use these graphical interfaces to navigate to other pages. You can create rollovers that respond to a user's mouse clicks, as well as complex animations. Animations can be quite sophisticated, providing many frames that move seamlessly from one frame to the next. You can use tweening and frame delays to control the appearance of the animation and how quickly the movement progresses.

What You Have Learned:

- How to jump between Photoshop and ImageReady
- How to reduce file sizes for Web use
- How to place an optimized image on a page
- How to create a stylized button on a page
- How to create and modify slices
- How to assign a Web address to a slice
- How to create and preview a rollover effect
- How to create and preview basic animation
- How to duplicate animation frames
- How to tween frames
- How to add a frame delay

Key Terms

Animation   An image sequence that simulates an object moving on a Web page.

Frame delay   The length of time that each frame appears.

Frame   An individual image within an animation.

Rollover   A feature in which an object's appearance changes when the pointer passes over (or the user clicks) a specific area of an image.

Slice   A specific area within an image to which you can assign special features, such as a rollover, link, or animation.

Tweening   A method of adding frames between two existing frames, that changes the action in slight increments.

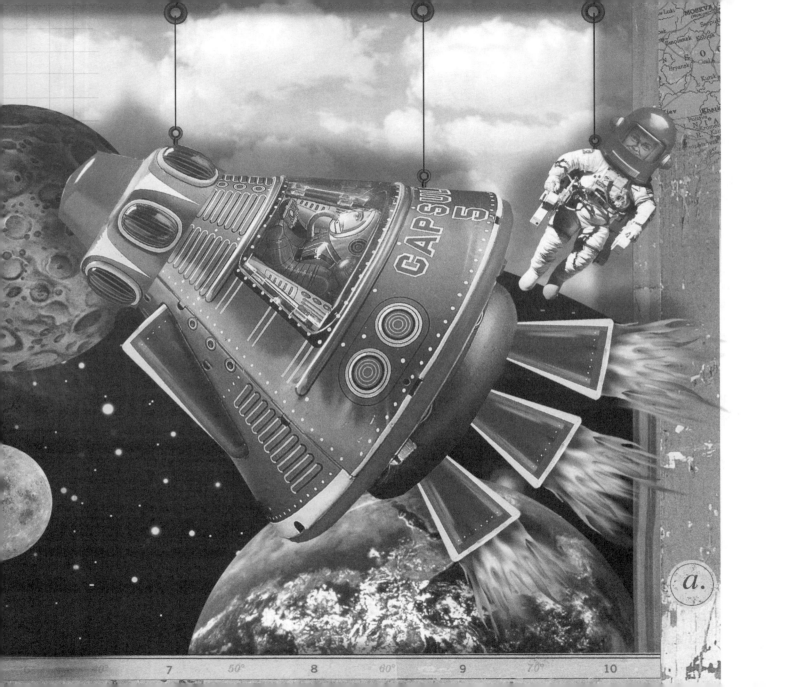

Action
A series of tasks that you record and save to play back later as a single command.

Active layer
The layer highlighted on the Layers palette. The active layer's name appears in parentheses in the image window title bar.

Active setting
In the Curves dialog box, the point that you click and drag to change the input and output values.

Additive colors
A color system in which, when the values of R, G, and B are 0, the result is black; when the values are all 255, the result is white.

Adjustment layer
An additional layer for which you can specify individual color adjustments. The adjustment layer allows you to temporarily alter a layer before making the adjustment permanent.

Adobe Bridge
A stand-alone application that serves as the hub for the Adobe Create Suite.

Adobe ImageReady
A program included with Photoshop that you can use to create buttons, rollovers, and animations.

Alpha channel
Specific color information added to a default channel. Also called a *spot channel*.

Altitude
A Bevel and Emboss setting that affects the amount of visible dimension.

Ambience property
Controls the balance between the light source and the overall light in an image.

Anchor points
Small square handles, similar to fastening points, that connect straight or curved line segments.

Angle
In the Layer Style dialog box, the setting that determines where a drop shadow falls relative to the text.

Animation
The illusion of motion, created by placing a series of images in the same location and adjusting the timing between their appearances.

Annotation
A written and/or auditory note embedded into a Photoshop file.

Anti-aliasing
Partially fills in pixel edges, resulting in smooth-edge type. This feature lets your type maintain its crisp appearance and is especially useful for large type.

Artistic filters
Used to replicate natural or traditional media effects.

Audio annotation
A sound file that is saved within a Photoshop file.

Auto-slice
A slice created by ImageReady. An auto-slice has a dotted-line border.

Background color
Used to make gradient fills and to fill in areas of an image that have been erased. The default background color is white.

Background Eraser Tool
Used to selectively remove pixels from an image, just as you would use a pencil eraser to remove unwanted written marks. The erased areas become transparent.

Balance colors
Process of adding and subtracting colors from those already existing in a layer.

Base color
The original color of an image.

Base layer
The bottom layer in a clipping group, which serves as the group's mask.

Baseline
An invisible line on which type rests.

Baseline shift
The distance type appears from its original position.

Batch
A group of files designated to have the same action performed on them simultaneously.

Bitmap
A geometric arrangement of different color dots on a rectangular grid.

Bitmap mode
Uses black or white color values to represent image pixels; a good choice for images with subtle color gradations, such as photographs or painted images.

Bitmap type
Type that may develop jagged edges when enlarged.

Blend color
The color applied to the base color when a blending mode is applied to a layer.

Blend If color
Determines the color range for the pixels you want to blend.

Blending mode
Affects the layer's underlying pixels or base color. Used to darken or lighten colors, depending on the colors in use.

Blur filters
Used to soften a selection or image.

Bounding box
A rectangle with handles that appears around an object or type and can be used to change dimensions, also called a *transform controls box.*

Bridge
See Adobe Bridge.

Brightness
The measurement of relative lightness or darkness of a color (measured as a percentage from 0% [black] to 100% [white]).

Brush library
Contains a variety of brush tips that you can use, rename, delete, or customize.

Brush Strokes filters
Used to mimic fine arts effects such as a brush and ink stroke.

Button
A graphical interface that helps visitors navigate and interact with a Web site easily.

Button mode
Optional action display in which each action available in Photoshop is displayed as a button—without additional detail.

Camera Raw
Allows you to use digital data directly from a digital camera.

Channels
Used to store information about the color elements contained in each channel.

Channels palette
Lists all channel information. The top channel is a composite channel—a combination of all the default channels. You can hide channels in the same manner that you hide layers: click the Indicates layer visibility button.

Character palette
Helps you control type properties. The Toggle the Character and Paragraph palette button is located on the options bar when you select a Type tool.

Clipboard
Temporary storage area, provided by your operating system, for cut and copied data.

Clipping mask (Clipping group)
A group of two or more contiguous layers linked for the purposes of masking. Effect used to display the image or pattern from one layer into the shape of another layer.

Clipping path
Used when you need to extract a Photoshop object from within a layer, then place it in another program (such as QuarkXPress or Adobe Illustrator), while retaining its transparent background.

Closed path
One continuous path without endpoints, such as a circle.

CMYK image
An image using the CMYK color system, containing at least four channels (one each for cyan, magenta, yellow, and black).

Color channel
An area where color information is stored. Every Photoshop image has at least one channel and can have a maximum of 24 color channels.

Color management system
Keeps colors looking consistent as they move between devices.

Color mode
Used to determine how to display and print an image. Each mode is based on established models used in color reproduction.

Color Picker
A feature that lets you choose a color from a color spectrum.

Color Range command
Used to select a particular color contained in an existing image.

Color Sampler Tool
Feature that samples—and stores—up to four distinct color samplers. This feature is used when you want to save specific color settings for future use.

Color separation
Result of converting an RGB image into a CMYK image; the commercial printing process of separating colors for use with different inks.

Composite channel
The top channel on the Channels palette that is a combination of all the default channels.

Compositing
Combining images from sources such as other Photoshop images, royalty-free images, pictures taken from digital cameras, and scanned artwork.

Contact sheet
Compilation of a maximum of 30 thumbnail images (per sheet) from a specific folder.

Contiguous
Items that are next to one another.

Crisp
Anti-aliasing setting that gives type more definition and makes it appear sharper.

Crop
To exclude part of an image. Cropping hides areas of an image without losing resolution quality.

Crop marks
Page notations that indicate where trimming will occur and can be printed at the corners, center of each edge, or both.

Darken Only option
Replaces light pixels with darker pixels.

Default action
An action that is prerecorded and tested, and comes with Photoshop.

Default channels
The color channels automatically contained in an image.

Defringe command
Replaces fringe pixels with the colors of other nearby pixels.

Deselect
A command that removes the marquee from an area, so it is no longer selected.

Diffuse filter
Used to make layer contents look less focused.

Digimarc filter
Embeds into an image a digital watermark that stores copyright information.

Digital camera
A camera that captures images on electronic media (rather than film). Its images are in a standard digital format and can be downloaded for computer use.

Digital image
A picture in electronic form. It may be referred to as a file, document, picture, or image.

Direct Selection Tool
Used to select and manipulate individual anchor points and segments to reshape a path.

Distance
Determines how far a shadow falls from the text. This setting is used by the Drop Shadow and Bevel and Emboss styles.

Distort filters
Create three-dimensional or other reshaping effects. Some of the types of distortions you can produce include Glass, Pinch, Ripple, Shear, Spherize, Twirl, Wave, and ZigZag.

Dithering
Occurs when a Web browser attempts to display colors that are not included in its native color palette.

Droplet
A stand-alone action in the form of an icon.

Drop Shadow
A style that adds what looks like a colored layer of identical text behind the selected type. The default shadow color is black.

Endpoints

Anchor points at each end of an open path.

Eraser Tool

Has the opposite function of a brush in that it eliminates pixels on a layer.

Exposure property

Lightens or darkens the lighting effects ellipse.

Extract feature

Used to isolate a foreground object from its background.

Extrude filters

Used to convert an image into pyramids or blocks.

Fade options

Brush settings that determine how and when brushes fade toward the end of their strokes.

Fading type

An effect in which the type appears to originate in darkness and then gradually gets brighter, or vice versa.

Fastening point

An anchor within the marquee. When the marquee pointer reaches the initial fastening point, a small circle appears on the pointer, indicating that you have reached the starting point.

Feather

A method used to control the softness of a selection's edges by blurring the area between the selection and the surrounding pixels.

Filter Gallery

A feature that lets you see the effects of each filter before applying it.

Filters

Used to alter the look of an image and give it a special, customized appearance by applying special effects, such as distortions, changes in lighting, and blurring.

Flattening

Merges all visible layers into one layer, named the Background layer, and deletes all hidden layers, greatly reducing file size.

Flow

Brush tip setting that determines how much paint is sprayed while the mouse button is held.

Font

Characters with a similar appearance.

Font family

Represents a complete set of characters, letters, and symbols for a particular typeface. Font families are generally divided into three categories: serif, sans serif, and symbol.

Foreground color

Used to paint, fill, and stroke selections. The default foreground color is black.

Frame

An individual image that is used in animation.

Frame delay

In an animation sequence,the length of time that each frame appears.

Freeform Pen Tool

Acts like a traditional pen or pencil, and automatically places *both* the anchor points and line segments wherever necessary to achieve the shape you want.

Freeze

To protect areas within an image from being affected by Liquify tools.

Fuzziness

Similar to tolerance, in that the lower the value, the closer the color pixels must be to be selected.

Gamut

The range of displayed colors in a color model.

Gloss Contour

A Bevel and Emboss setting that determines the pattern with which light is reflected.

Gloss property

Controls the amount of surface reflectance on the lighted surfaces.

Gradient fill

A type of fill in which colors appear to blend into one another. A gradient's appearance is determined by its beginning and ending points. Photoshop contains five gradient fill styles.

Gradient presets

Predesigned gradient fills that are displayed in the Gradient picker.

Grayscale image
Can contain up to 256 shades of gray. Pixels can have brightness values from 0 (black) to white (255).

Grayscale mode
Uses up to 256 shades of gray, assigning a brightness value from 0 (black) to 255 (white) to each pixel.

Guides
Horizontal and vertical lines that you create to help you align objects. Guides appear as light blue lines.

Handles
Small boxes that appear along the perimeter of a selected object and are used to change the size of an image.

Highlight Mode
A Bevel and Emboss setting that determines how pigments are combined.

Histogram
A graph that displays the frequency distribution of colors and is used to make adjustments in the input and output levels.

History palette
Contains a record of each action performed during a Photoshop session. Up to 20 levels of Undo are available through the History palette.

Hotspot
Area within an object that is assigned a URL. This area can then be clicked to jump to the associated Web address.

Hue
The color reflected from/transmitted through an object and expressed as a degree (between 0° and 360°). Each hue is identified by a color name (such as red or green).

ICC profile
Created for specific devices and embedded in an image, and used to define how colors are interpreted by a specific device. ICC stands for International Color Consortium.

Image-editing program
Used to manipulate graphic images that can be reproduced by professional printers using full-color processes.

Image map
An area composed of multiple hotspots; can be circular, rectangular, or polygonal.

Intellectual property
An image or idea that is owned and retained by legal control.

Jitter
The randomness of dynamic brush tip elements such as size, angle, roundness, hue, saturation, brightness, opacity, and flow.

Kerning
Controlling the amount of space between two characters.

Keyboard shortcuts
Combinations of keys that can be used to work faster and more efficiently.

Landscape orientation
An image with the long edge of the paper at the top and bottom.

Layer
A section within an image on which objects can be stored. The advantage: Individual effects can be isolated and manipulated without affecting the rest of the image. The disadvantage: Layers can increase the size of your file.

Layer comp
A variation on the arrangement and visibility of existing layers within an image; an organizational tool.

Layer group
An organizing tool you use to group layers on the Layers palette.

Layer mask
Can cover an entire layer or specific areas within a layer. When a layer contains a mask, an additional thumbnail appears on the Layers palette.

Layers palette
Displays all the layers within an active image. You can use the Layers palette to create, delete, merge, copy, or reposition layers.

Layer style
An effect that can be applied to a type or image layer.

Layer thumbnail
Contains a miniature picture of the layer's content, and appears to the left of the layer name on the Layers palette.

Leading
The amount of vertical space between lines of type.

Libraries
Storage units for brushes.

Lighten Only option
Replaces dark pixels with light pixels.

Lighting Effects filter
Applies lighting effects to an image.

Liquify feature
Applies distortions to layers using distinct tools in the Liquify dialog box.

Liquify session
The period of time from when you open the Liquify dialog box to when you close it.

List mode
The default display of actions in which all action detail can be viewed.

Logo
A distinctive image used to identify a company, project, or organization. You can create a logo by combining symbols, shapes, colors, and text.

Lossless
A file-compression format in which no data is discarded.

Lossy
A file format that discards data during the compression process.

Luminosity
The remaining light and dark values that result when a color image is converted to grayscale.

Magic Eraser Tool
Used to erase areas in an image that have similar-colored pixels.

Magic Wand Tool
Used to choose pixels that are similar to the ones where you first click in an image.

Marquee
A series of dotted lines indicating a selected area that can be edited or dragged into another image.

Mask
A feature that lets you protect or modify a particular area; created using a marquee.

Match Color command
Allows you to replace one color with another.

Material property
Controls parts of an image that reflect the light source color.

Menu bar
Contains menus from which you can choose Photoshop commands.

Merging layers
Process of combining multiple image layers into one layer.

Mesh
A series of horizontal and vertical grid-lines that are superimposed in the preview window.

Modal control
Dialog boxes that are used in an action, and are indicated by an icon on the Actions palette.

Mode
Represents the amount of color data that can be stored in a given file format, and determines the color model used to display and print an image.

Model
Determines how pigments combine to produce resulting colors; determined by the color mode.

Monitor calibration
A process that displays printed colors accurately on your monitor.

Monotype spacing
Spacing in which each character occupies the same amount of space.

Morph
To blend multiple images in the animation process. Short for *metamorphosis*.

Motion Blur filter

Adjusts the angle of the blur, as well as the distance the blur appears to travel.

Noise filters

Used to add or remove pixels with randomly distributed color levels.

None

Anti-aliasing setting that applies no anti-aliasing, resulting in jagged edges.

Normal blend mode

The default blending mode.

Opacity

Determines the percentage of transparency. Whereas a layer with 100% opacity will obstruct objects in the layers beneath it, a layer with 1% opacity will appear nearly transparent.

Open path

A path that comprises two distinct endpoints, such as an individual line.

Optimized image

An image whose file size has been reduced without sacrificing image quality.

Options bar

Displays the settings for the active tool. The options bar is located directly under the menu bar but can be moved anywhere in the workspace for easier access.

Orientation

Direction an image appears on the page: portrait or landscape.

Other filters

Allow you to create your own filters, modify masks, or make quick color adjustments.

Outline type

Type that is mathematically defined and can be scaled to any size without its edges losing their smooth appearance.

Out-of-gamut indicator

Indicates that the current color falls beyond the accurate print or display range.

Palettes

Floating windows that can be moved and are used to modify objects. Palettes contain named tabs, which can be separated and moved to another group. Each palette contains a menu that can be viewed by clicking the list arrow in its upper-right corner.

Palette well

An area where you can assemble palettes for quick access.

Path

One or more straight or curved line segments connected by anchor points used to turn the area defined within an object into an individual object.

Path component

One or more anchor points joined by line segments.

Path Selection Tool

Used to select an entire path.

Paths Palette

Storage area for paths.

Pen Tool

Used to draw a path by placing anchor points along the edge of another image or wherever you need them to draw a specific shape.

Picture package

Shows multiple copies of a single image in various sizes, similar to a portrait studio sheet of photos; Photoshop contains 20 available picture package layouts in multiple sizes.

Pixel

Each dot in a bitmapped image that represents a color or shade.

Pixelate filters

Used to sharply define a selection.

Plug-ins

Additional programs—created by Adobe and other developers—that expand Photoshop's functionality.

Points

Unit of measurement for font sizes. Traditionally, 1 inch is equivalent to 72.27 points. The default Photoshop type size is 12 points.

Portrait orientation

An image with the short edge of the paper at the top and bottom.

PostScript
A programming language created by Adobe that optimizes printed text and graphics.

Preferences
Used to control the Photoshop environment using your specifications.

Preset Manager
Allows you to manage libraries of preset brushes, swatches, gradients, styles, patterns, contours, and custom shapes.

Profile
Defines and interprets colors for a color management system.

Properties color swatch
Changes the ambient light around the lighting spotlight.

Proportional spacing
The text spacing in which each character takes up a different amount of space, based on its width.

Radial Blur filter
Adjusts the amount of blur and the blur method (Spin or Zoom).

Rasterize
Converts a type layer to an image layer.

Rasterized shape
A shape that is converted into a bitmapped object. It cannot be moved or copied and has a much smaller file size.

Reference point
Center of the object from which distortions and transformations are measured.

Relief
The height of ridges within an object.

Render filters
Transform three-dimensional shapes and simulated light reflections in an image.

Rendering intent
The way in which a color-management system handles color conversion from one color space to another.

Resize Image Wizard
Feature that helps you change an image's size for different output.

Resolution
Number of pixels per inch.

Resulting color
The outcome of the blend color applied to the base color.

RGB image
Image that contains three color channels (one each for red, green, and blue).

Rollover
Changes an object's appearance when the pointer passes over (or the user clicks) a specific area of the image.

Rulers
Onscreen markers that help you precisely measure and position an object. Rulers can be displayed using the View menu.

Sampling
A method of changing foreground and background colors by copying existing colors from an image.

Sans serif fonts
Fonts that do not have tails or strokes at the end of characters; commonly used in headlines.

Saturation
The strength or purity of the color, representing the amount of gray in proportion to hue (measured as a percentage from 0% [gray], to 100% [fully saturated]). Also known as *chroma*.

Save As
A command that lets you create a copy of the open file using a new name.

Scanner
An electronic device that converts print material into an electronic file.

Screening back
An illusory effect in which type appears to fade into the imagery below it. Also known as *screening*.

Selection
An area in an image that is surrounded by a selection marquee.

Serif fonts
Fonts that have a tail, or stroke, at the end of some characters. These tails make it easier for the eye to recognize words; therefore, serif fonts are generally used in text passages.

Shading
Bevel and Emboss setting that determines lighting effects.

Shadow Mode
Bevel and Emboss setting that determines how pigments are combined.

Shape
A vector object that keeps its crisp appearance when it is resized and, like a path, can be edited.

Shape layer
A clipping path or shape that can occupy its own layer.

Sharp
Anti-aliasing setting that displays type with the best possible resolution.

Sharpen More filter
Increases the contrast of adjacent pixels and can focus blurry images.

Size
Determines the clarity of a drop shadow.

Sketch filters
Used to apply a texture or create a hand-drawn effect.

Slice
A specific area within an image to which you can assign special features, such as a rollover, link, or animation in ImageReady.

Smart Blur filter
Adjusts the quality, radius, and threshold of a blur.

Smart Guides
A feature that displays vertical or horizontal guides that appear automatically when you draw a shape or move an object.

Smart Object
A combination of objects that has a visible indicator in the bottom-right corner of the layer thumbnail. Makes it possible to scale, rotate, and wrap layers without losing image quality.

Smooth
Anti-aliasing setting that gives type more rounded edges.

Snapshot
A temporary copy of an image that contains the history states made up to that point. You can create multiple snapshots of an image, and you can switch between snapshots.

Source
The image containing the color that will be matched.

Splash screen
A window that displays information about the software you are using.

Spot color
A method of defining a difficult or unique color that couldn't otherwise be easily re-created by a printer.

Spread
Determines the width of drop shadow text.

State
An entry on the History palette, or the appearance of a rollover on the Rollover palette in ImageReady.

Status bar
The area located at the bottom of the program window (Win) or the image window (Mac) that displays information such as the file size of the active window and a description of the active tool.

Step
Measurement of fade options that can be any value from 1–9999, and equivalent to one mark of the brush tip.

Stop
In an action, a command that interrupts playback or includes an informative text message for the user, so that other operations can be performed.

Stroking the edges
The process of making a selection or layer stand out by formatting it with a border.

Strong
Anti-aliasing setting that makes type appear heavier, much like the bold attribute.

Structure
A Bevel and Emboss setting that determines the size and physical properties of the object.

Style
Eighteen predesigned styles that can be applied to buttons.

Stylize filters
Used to produce a painted or impressionistic effect.

Subtractive colors
A color system in which the full combination of cyan, magenta, and yellow absorb all color and produce black.

Swatches palette
Contains available colors that can be selected for use as a foreground or background color. You can also add your own colors to the Swatches palette.

Symbol fonts
Used to display unique characters (such as $, ÷, or ™).

Target
When sampling a color, the image that will receive the matched color.

Texture filters
Used to give the appearance of depth or substance.

Thaw
To remove protection from a protected area in an image so it can be affected by Liquify tools.

This Layer slider
Used to specify the range of pixels that will be blended on the active layer.

Threshold
The Normal mode when working with bitmapped images. The threshold is the starting point for applying other blending modes.

Thumbnail
Contains a miniature picture of the layer's content, appears to the left of the layer name, and can be turned on or off.

Title bar
Displays the program name and filename of the open image. The title bar also contains

buttons for minimizing, maximizing, and closing the image.

Tolerance
The range of pixels that determines which pixels will be selected. The lower the tolerance, the closer the color is to the selection. The setting can have a value from 0–255.

Tonal values
Numeric values of an individual color that can be used to duplicate a color. Also called *color levels*.

Toolbox
Contains tools for frequently used commands. On the face of a tool is a graphic representation of its function. Place the pointer over each button to display a ScreenTip, which tells you the name or function of that button.

Tracking
The insertion of a uniform amount of space between characters.

Transform
To change the shape, size, perspective, or rotation of an object or objects on a layer.

Transform box
A rectangle that surrounds an image and contains handles that can be used to change dimensions. Also called a *bounding box*.

Tweening
The process of selecting multiple frames, then inserting transitional frames between them. This effect makes frames appear to blend into one another and gives the animation a more fluid appearance.

Twirl filter
Applies a circular effect.

Type
Text, or a layer containing text. Each character is measured in points. In PostScript measurement, 1 inch is equivalent to 72 points. In traditional measurement, 1 inch is equivalent to 72.27 points.

Type spacing
Adjustments you can make to the space between characters and between lines of type.

Underlying Layer slider
Used to specify the range of pixels that will be blended on lower visible layers.

URL
Uniform Resource Locator, a Web address.

User-slice
A slice created by you in ImageReady. A user-slice has a solid-line border.

Vanishing Point filter
Used to maintain perspective as you drag objects around corners, and into the distance.

Vector data
A shape or path that will not lose its crisp appearance if resized or reshaped.

Vector graphics
Images made up of lines and curves defined by mathematical objects.

Vector mask
Makes a shape's edges appear neat and defined on a layer.

Version Cue
A file versioning and management feature of the Adobe Creative Suite.

Video filters
Used to restrict colors to those acceptable for tele- vision reproduction and smooth video images.

Vignette
A feature in which the border of a picture or portrait fades into the surrounding color at its edges.

Vignette effect
A feature that uses feathering to fade a marquee shape.

Warping type
A feature that lets you create distortions that conform to a variety of shapes.

Web Image Gallery
Contains a thumbnail index page of all exported images, the actual JPEG images, and any included links.

Web-safe colors
The 216 colors that can be displayed on the Web without dithering.

Wind filter
Conveys the feeling of direction and motion on the layer to which it is applied.

Work path
A path when it is first created but not yet named.

Working space
Tells the color management system how RGB and CMYK values are interpreted.

Workspace
The entire window, from the menu bar at the top of the window, to the status bar at the bottom border of the program window.

Written annotation
Text similar to a sticky note that is attached to a file.

motion filters, comparing, 8-7
multiple, 5-26
Neon Glow filter, 5-27, 8-10
Noise filters, 8-6, 8-20
Paint Daubs filter, 8-10
Palette Knife filter, 8-10
Pinch filter, 5-24
Pixelate filters, 8-4, 8-6
Plastic Wrap filter, 8-10
Poster Edges filter, 8-11, 8-12, 8-18
Radial Blur filter, 8-7
Render filters, 8-6, 8-24–8-27
reusing, 8-18
Ripple filter, 5-24
Rough Pastels filter, 8-11
Sharpen filters, 8-6
Shear filter, 5-24
Sketch filters, 8-6
Smart Blur filter, 8-7
Smudge Stick filter, 8-11
softening effects, 4-25
Solarize filter, 8-16, 8-19
Spherize filter, 5-24
Sponge filter, 8-11
Stylize filters, 5-25, 8-6, 8-14–8-19
Texture filters, 5-25, 8-6
Twirl filter, 5-24–5-25, 8-20, 8-22
Underpainting filter, 8-11
Unsharp Mask filter, 4-24, 5-27, 10-17
Vanishing Point filter, 8-8
Video filters, 8-6
Watercolor filter, 4-24–4-25, 8-11
Wave filter, 5-24
Wind filter, 5-25, 8-14, 8-17
working with, 4-28
Zigzag filter, 5-24
Filter Gallery, 8-4
applying filters with, 8-12, 8-18
combining effects of multiple filters, 8-18
repeating filter application, 8-19
Filter menu, 2-12
filtering files, 1-10, 1-13
fixing imperfections. See also corrections
analyzing images, 9-17
with Clone Stamp Tool, 9-16–9-19
methods, 9-2
flattening
compared to merging layers, 2-8
layers into one layer, 2-17, 2-21
to reduce file size, 1-4, 2-17
Flip Horizontal command, 11-5
Flip Vertical command, 11-5
flipping selections, 3-20
focus, lighting, 8-24, 8-25
Folders palette in Bridge, 1-11

fonts, 5-2
downloading additional, 5-5
font family, 5-4
number of, in text layer, 5-17
samples of, 5-5
sans serif fonts, 5-4
serif fonts, 5-4
symbol fonts, 5-5
foreground color
changing, 4-6
for layer masks, 7-5
sampling, 4-6
setting default, 4-7
formats, file. See file formats
Forward Warp Tool, 13-6, 13-7, 14-5
frames, 16-30. See also animation
Freeform Pen Tool, 11-8, 11-9
creating paths, 11-2–11-3
freeform selection tools, 3-2
Freeze Mask Tool, 13-6
freezing image areas, 13-2, 13-8, 13-10
frequency setting for Magnetic Lasso Tool, 3-11
Fresco filter, 8-10
Full Screen Mode, 1-20
fuzziness setting, color range, 3-17

gamut, color, 4-4, 4-5, 4-7, 4-12
Gaussian Blur filter, 5-25, 5-27, 8-7
.GIF files, 1-5, 16-9, 16-10
Gloss property, 8-24
gradient(s), 4-16
creating from sample color, 4-18
customizing, 4-17
styles, 4-17
Gradient Editor, 4-17
gradient fills, 4-6, 4-16
applying, 4-19, 4-21, 9-11
Gradient Map feature, 4-21, 9-11
color adjustments, 7-23
Gradient picker, 4-16, 4-17
Gradient Tool
blending colors, 4-16–4-19
faded type effect, 12-17
graphic file formats, supported, 1-5
graphics tablets
benefits of using, 6-16
setting pressure, 9-19
grayscale images, 4-20
changing color mode, 4-22
colorizing, 4-20–4-21, 4-23
converting color images to, 4-23, 10-9
duotones, 4-21
tinting, 6-11

grayscale mode, 4-6
converting, 4-20
Group into New Smart Object command, 7-19
Group Layers command, 7-12
grouping layers. See layer groups
Grow command, 3-12
guides, 2-5, 3-6
using Smart Guides, 3-8

halo, 2-13
Hand Tool, 9-9
handles, selection, 3-17
Hard Light mode, 4-26
hardware requirements
for audio annotations, 15-5
Photoshop installation, 1-6–1-7
Healing Brush Tool, 3-17
fixing imperfections with, 3-17, 3-21, 6-5
Help system, 1-28–1-31
bookmarks, 1-30
Contents tab, 1-29
Help topics, 1-28
How To tips, 1-31
Index tab, 1-30
searching for information, 1-31
hidden tools, 1-17
hiding
layers, 1-25, 1-26, 2-8, 7-11, 8-9
palettes, 1-22
highlights
correcting, 4-27, 7-23
Shadow/Highlight dialog box, 4-27
histograms
for color levels, 10-2, 10-12
Histogram palette, 10-13
History Brush Tool, 6-18, APP-4
History palette, 1-5, 1-25
deleting states on, 1-25, 1-27, 5-19
descriptions of alternate methods, 5-18
Liquify session on, 13-8
mask states, 7-10
memory usage, 8-20–8-21
restoring deleted layers, 2-9
snapshots, compared to, 9-2–9-3, 9-24
Horizontal Distortion setting, 5-22, 12-9
horizontal guides, 3-6, 3-8
Horizontal Type Tool, 5-5, 5-6, 5-18, 5-22, 5-28
hotspots, 16-18
How To tips, creating, 1-31
HSB (Hue, Saturation, Brightness) model, 4-5
HTML (Hypertext Markup Language), 16-4–16-5, 16-14
hue, 4-5, 7-23, 10-8

PHOTOSHOP 17

creating, 2-19, 7-12
expanding, 2-17
moving layers to, 2-19
organizing, 2-16–2-17
layer masks, 7-4–7-13
  black foreground, 6-8
  clipping mask, 7-26–7-29
  correcting and updating, 7-5
  creating, 7-4
  creating, using Layer menu, 7-6
  creating, using Layers palette, 7-7
  described, 7-4
  disabling, 7-18, 7-20
  disposing of, 7-18
  enabling, 7-20
  file size, 7-19
  linking and unlinking to layer, 7-10
  modifying, 7-9
  moving, 7-11
  painting, 7-5, 7-8
  Quick Mask Mode, 7-6
  removing, 7-19, 7-21
  selecting, 7-9
  thumbnail, 7-4, 7-9, 7-10, 7-18
  vignettes, 3-22
  white foreground, 6-8
Layer menu
  adding Bevel and Emboss style
    with, 5-22
  adding layers using, 2-10
  creating adjustment layers, 7-22
  creating layer masks, 7-6
Layer Properties command, 2-9
Layer Style dialog box, 5-12–5-15, 7-14
layer styles, 5-12
  adding, 14-12
  applying, 5-12–5-13
Layer via Copy command, APP-12
Layer via Cut command, APP-12
Layers palette, 1-24–1-25, 2-4
  adding effects, 4-25
  adding layers using, 2-11
  creating layer masks, 7-7
  layer effects icon, 5-12
  moving layers on, 1-27
  selecting multiple layers, 7-10
  transparent areas, 1-26
leading, 5-9
Lens Correction filter, 8-22
levels
  adjusting colors using, 7-23, 10-13
  modifying color channels using,
    10-12–10-13
Levels dialog box, 10-13, 12-13
Lighten mode, 4-26

lighting, 8-24–8-27
  adding texture to, 8-25
  adjusting surrounding conditions,
    8-24–8-25
  Ambience property, 8-25
  applying lighting effects, 8-27, 10-17
  custom effects, 8-27
  Directional lighting, 8-24
  Exposure property, 8-25
  Gloss property, 8-24
  Lighting Effects dialog box, 8-24–8-27
  Lighting Effects filter, 8-24, 10-17
  Material property, 8-24–8-25
  Omni lighting, 8-24
  selecting settings, 8-26
  Spotlight lighting, 8-24
  styles, 8-24, 8-25
line spacing, 5-8–5-11
Linear gradient, 4-17
link icon, 7-10
Link Mask state, 7-10
links and Web page buttons, 16-15
Liquify dialog box, 13-4, 13-6, 13-12
Liquify feature, 13-2, 13-5. *See also*
  distortions
  Bloat Tool, 13-4, 13-6
  brush sizes for, 13-6
  deleting unnecessary imagery,
    14-4, 14-5
  Forward Warp Tool, 13-6, 13-7, 14-5
  Freeze Mask Tool, 13-6
  improving photos, APP-14–APP-15
  Liquify session on History palette, 13-8
  Mirror Tool, 13-6
  Pucker Tool, 13-4, 13-6
  Push Left Tool, 13-6
  Reconstruct Tool, 13-6
  Thaw Mask Tool, 13-6, 13-8
  tools, 13-4, 13-6
  Turbulence Tool, 13-6
  Twirl Clockwise Tool, 13-4, 13-6
list mode and Actions feature, 15-8, 15-12
Load Actions command, 15-17
Load Brushes command, 6-19
loading selections, 3-9
locking transparent pixels, 4-14–4-15,
  9-12
logos, 1-4, 5-24
looping animations, 16-31
Loose reconstruction mode, 13-9, 13-10
lossless compression, 16-9
lossy compression, 16-9
Lucinda Handwriting font, 5-5
luminosity, 4-20
Luminosity mode, 4-26

Macintosh interface
  Photoshop window, 1-16–1-18
  right-clicking, 2-11
Macintosh platform, 1-2
  active layer palette background, 5-7
  hardware requirement, 1-7
  keyboard commands, 1-2
  quitting Photoshop, 1-36–1-37
  starting Photoshop, 1-7
Macromedia Flash, 2-5, 16-32
Magic Eraser Tool, 2-13, 9-13
Magic Wand Tool, 2-13, 9-20
  Anti-Aliased settings, 3-16
  Contiguous settings, 3-16, 9-20
  image removal, 14-6
  Sample All Layers check box, 3-16
  selecting using, 3-19, 3-20,
    3-22, 9-22
  tolerance settings, 3-16, 9-20
  using with Eyedropper Tool,
    9-20–9-21
Magnetic Lasso Tool, 2-13, 3-5,
  3-10–3-11, 14-6
Magnetic Pen Tool, 11-9
magnification, zoom factor, 1-32
marquees, 2-12, 3-4. *See also* selection tools
  blur effect, 3-11, 3-22
  changing size of, 3-12
  enlarging, 3-15
  modifying, 3-12
  moving, 3-13, 3-14
masks, 3-22, 7-4. *See also* clipping masks;
  layer masks
  using clipping group as, 11-4–11-7
  vector masks, 12-12
Match Color color adjustment, 7-23
matching colors, 4-30–4-31, 7-23
Material property, 8-24–8-25
Matte options, 16-11
measurements
  guides, 2-5, 3-6, 3-8
  type size, 5-5
  units of measurement and rulers, 2-6
Memory & Image Cache settings, 8-21
memory usage, 8-20–8-21
  controlling, 8-21
  for filters, 8-2, 8-4
  optimizing in Photoshop, 8-20
menu bar, 1-16
Merge Down command, 2-8
Merge Visible command, 2-8, 13-13
merging layers, 2-8, 7-23, 13-13
mesh feature
  activated, distorting image with, 13-15
  changing mesh display, 13-12